DEVIANCE:

Voices From the Margin

DEVIANCE:
Voices From the Margin

Edited by:

JAMES K. SKIPPER, JR.
Virginia Polytechnic Institute and State University

WILLIAM L. McWHORTER
Virginia Polytechnic Institute and State University

CHARLES H. McCAGHY
Bowling Green State University

MARK LEFTON
Case Western Reserve University

Wadsworth Publishing Company
Belmont, California
A Division of Wadsworth, Inc.

This anthology is dedicated to the scores of individuals with whom we have interacted over the past quarter century who were the products of a soiled social identity and whose voices have contributed so much to our understanding of those who live on the margins of society.

Sociology Editor: Curt Peoples
Production Editor: Carolyn Tanner
Designer: Adriane Bosworth
Copy Editor: Carol Dondrea

Printed in the United States of America

5 6 7 8 9 10——90 89 88 87

Library of Congress Cataloging in Publication Data

Main entry under title:
Deviance.

    First-2nd eds. published as: In their own behalf.
    1. Deviant behavior—Addresses, essays, lectures.
I. Skipper, James K.   II. In their own behalf.
HM291.D4837   1981   302.5   81–4511
ISBN 0–534–01011–3   AACR2

ISBN 0-534-01011-3

CONTENTS

PREFACE

Sociologists have long been critical of conceptualizing deviant behavior exclusively from the point of view of rule makers and rule enforcers, or in terms of individual characteristics, or of social structure and environment. To exclude the viewpoint of the person whose behavior is at issue is to ignore deviance as a process of interaction between individuals and the society of which they are a part. In order to understand this viewpoint, it is necessary to let these persons speak for themselves. That is the purpose of this volume.

The contributors to this volume represent many diverse facets of human behavior. However, they do share a common bond. They are regarded with fear, suspicion, condemnation, bewilderment, hatred, or pity by what sociologists often refer to as conventional society. In sociological terminology the contributors are stigmatized, deviant, or occupy disvalued roles—at this point in time. What types of behavior and what types of individuals conventional society will apply these labels to is not always the same. Many are applied differently over time as society itself changes. Thus the outsiders of one era may not be the soiled identities of another. The evolution of the third edition of this collection is a testimony to this pattern. In a large sense it is a product of the trends of the times.

The first edition of this book was published in 1968 under the title *In Their Own Behalf: Voices from the Margin*. It contained 28 selections arranged in alphabetical order by author. No attempt was made to categorize the material by type of behavior. There were no sections, no section introductions, or general introductory chapter. The anthology was made to have as little structure as possible. This format reflected the mood of the late 1960s, with its student emphasis on independence, individualism, and "telling it like it is." It did not seem appropriate to color, with the biases of sociologists and psychologists, first person accounts of individuals whose behavior stretched traditional norms. Therefore, the material was presented undiluted by social scientific interpretation. This was also a period of student unrest. A sizable portion of the college-age population was caught up in antiwar, antiestablishment, civil rights, and women's movements. The selections in this early edition reflected these trends. Included was material from the flower children of the Haight-Ashbury area of San Francisco, Students for a Democratic Society, conscientious objectors to the draft, and users of L.S.D. Also prominent were statements from Black Muslims, nudists, and women who had experienced illegal abortions.

The second edition was published in 1974. By then much of the turmoil of the late 1960s was settling down. The Vietnam war was over, although feelings of guilt remained. The draft was abolished, and supporters of the civil rights movement were losing their missionary zeal. The flower children were no more, and the height of the drug abuse scare was past. The women's rights movement, however, was still in full swing. The second edition, again reflecting the times, attempted to meet the need for more structure in viewing deviant behavior and to focus on the different types of deviant behavior then receiving public attention. The first person accounts were arranged in sections according to types of behavior, and brief 100-word introductions preceded each section. New material was introduced on the women's movement, on rebellion among youth and on prison rebellion, and on violence such as that involved in the Mylai massacre.

This edition, entitled Deviance: Voices From the Margin, *is geared to meet the changing needs of the 1980s.* Students, as well as society in general, are now more conservative, and yet are more permissive in their view toward deviant behavior. While demanding more structure to their study of the subject, they appreciate the reality of first person accounts and can sort out the possible biases of social scientists in interpreting them. Therefore, in addition to including many new selections appropriate to the 1980s, we have also provided this edition with a great deal more structure.

*First, we have included an introductory chapter that discusses in detail both the various theoretical orientations to deviant behavior, and the diverse methodological procedures used by researchers in collecting and analyzing data. This chapter provides an overall framework for interpreting and understanding the first person accounts.

*Second, the accounts are grouped in sections by types of deviance: "Violent Crime," "Alcohol and Drug Abuse," "Sexual Deviance," and so forth.

*Third, each section has its own introduction linking specific deviant accounts to the general theoretical and methodological framework provided in the first chapter.

*Finally, after each selection, there is a series of discussion questions that will aid and direct the student to the sociological significance of the particular first person account.

To provide continuity, seven selections from the second edition were retained since they are still appropriate for the 1980s. Three of these are actually holdovers from the first edition. Previously, we had difficulty obtaining published first person accounts of certain types of deviants—especially hard-core criminals. For this edition we plugged these gaps by personally conducting interviews with deviants and selecting the best possible material for inclusion. We are particularly proud of the fact that seven such pieces are published in this volume for the first time.

We would like to express our appreciation to the authors and publishers who granted us permission to reprint their work, and to the following reviewers for their many helpful suggestions: Ross Purdy of Corpus Christi State University, Regan G. Smith of Sangamon State University, Joseph Sheley of Tulane University, Peter Conrad of New York University, and Edward Sagarin of City College of the City University of New York. Thanks are also due to Michael Wood for helping locate material, Wayne Lawrence for helping conduct interviews, Gail Earls for typing the manuscript, and our colleagues in deviance—Clifton Bryant, Tim Carter, Don Shoemaker, and David Smith—for their support.

James K. Skipper, Jr.
William L. McWhorter
Charles H. McCaghy
Mark Lefton

DEVIANCE:
Voices From the Margin

Section I   INTRODUCTION: THEORY AND METHOD

In the course of daily living we take much for granted about the ways others will behave. We are usually optimistic: We attend classes assuming that instructors will not be under the influence of mind-bending drugs, we go out on dates assuming that our partners will not assault us, and we eat at home assuming that parents are not slipping arsenic into our Hi-C. But occasionally we assume too much. There *are* "spaced-out" teachers, overly aggressive suitors, and lethal parents. So with a touch of pessimism we ask: Why *don't* people behave the way they should?

On the other hand, it is remarkable that we usually *can* take people's behavior for granted—especially since all of us can certainly think of times when it seemed justified, if not plain fun, to pillage, attack, vandalize, and get high. This leads us to the question, Why *do* people behave the way they should? And further: *How* should people behave? Or, put another way: Why are the assaulters, robbers, and junkies "breaking" rules, while the honest, sober drudges are "following" them?

These sorts of questions have puzzled social scientists (to say nothing of theologians and philosophers) for decades, for it is difficult to explain rule-breaking, -following, and -making all at the same time. This triple problem is generally resolved by ignoring it. Social theorists prefer to concentrate on one of the three issues on the assumption that the other two are either less important or self-explanatory once the issue at hand is resolved.

We have no intention of proposing *the* comprehensive theory of deviance. The principal purpose of this book is relatively modest: to acquaint the reader with the viewpoints of those who are frequently regarded and treated as rule breakers. Although the goal is limited, it is important to the extent that the motivations of actors are crucial to understanding their behaviors. It is tempting to both judge and explain the actions of others without listening to their side. But there is no guarantee of the explanation's validity without at least consideration of the actors' rationales.

This introduction briefly describes a variety of sociological concepts and perspectives that will provide you with a context for better understanding the social forces at work in the situations, life styles, and feelings our authors depict.

RULES: OURS OR THEIRS?

It is axiomatic that groups cannot survive without rules or *norms*. Whether the group is as small as a family or as large as a nation, there are standards of conduct and appearance to designate what constitutes conformity or normality. Norms provide group members with routine and predictability: You know how you should act and look, and you know how others should act and look. Depending on the group, the range of what will be tolerated varies. For example, dress among the Amish is very restricted compared to what one sees in downtown Los Angeles. But even in Los Angeles there are limits.

Therefore, norms provide *order* by telling group members what to do or what not to do. Implicit in the limitations that norms impose on behavior is the notion that something will be done if those limitations are exceeded. A rule will be ineffective unless there are means (or, at least, the threat of means) to enforce it. These means for enforcing norms are usually referred to as *sanctions*, and they obviously vary according to groups, norms violated, and so on. For example, the Amish boy caught wearing plaid trousers is likely to be paddled; the nude person openly parading in downtown Los Angeles may end up in the pokey or a mental institution.

Up to this point things seem rather straightforward: Norms are necessary for order within a group because they set standards of and limitations on behavior, and persons deviating from the norms are brought into line by the sanctions accompanying them. Alas, things are not so simple. One might ask: Are the present norms really necessary to provide order? Is the order the norms supposedly maintain the type of order that people want? Are the sanctions accompanying some norms too harsh? Or too lenient? Where do these norms come from in the first place? And what is so bad about somebody being stark naked in public? The problem boils down to the fact that norms are often not agreed upon, and even when there is some agreement on the norms themselves, there is often disagreement over applying the sanctions for violations.

Marshall B. Clinard and Robert F. Meier illustrate this problem by describing the four ways in which deviance can be defined.[1] First, there is the *absolutist* definition. Absolutists regard some norms as universal and self-evident: There are behaviors "everybody" knows are "wrong" or, at least, are a sign of "maladjustment." The absolutists reason that there are "high" human values emphasizing the need for people to reach their full potential, to be happy, and to be productive. Such behaviors as suicide, the use of mind-altering drugs, withdrawal from the bustle of work, and taking of others' lives and property are not consistent with either what people may or what they *should* do. The behaviors are wrong in themselves.

The absolutist approach is seductive, but it fails to recognize the great differences among cultures that make questionable the existence of any universal norm. Even a behavior so obvious as taking a human life is not universally condemned. The Quakers regard the behavior as unjustified under any circumstances, but most societies regard killing favorably during war and in self-defense, and some preliterate societies approve killing the aged, the infirm, babies of an unwanted sex, or anyone who is simply a "stranger."

The second definition of deviance is *statistical:* "Normal" behavior is the behavior that occurs most frequently. The usefulness of this definition is limited because it implies that any behavior in the minority—from murder by meat cleaver to figure skating—is deviant. To be functional, the concept of deviance must incorporate a rule or norm that is violated. Merely being "different" does not necessarily mean that someone is doing what he or she should not.

The third definition discussed by Clinard and Meier is *labeling.* Like the statistical definition, the labeling definition minimizes the importance of norms. However, with this definition the crucial element is *social reaction.* Howard S. Becker describes the labeling approach as follows:

> *Social groups create deviance by making the rules whose infraction constitutes deviance,* and by applying those rules to particular people, and labeling them as outsiders. From this point of view, deviance is *not* a quality of the act the person commits, but rather a consequence of the application by others of rules and sanctions to an "offender." The deviant is one to whom that label has successfully been applied; deviant behavior is behavior that people so label.[2]

Becker goes on to say that since deviance depends on the response of others, there is no assurance that a norm violation is actually involved. Included in the category of "deviants" will be some who have not broken the rules, and excluded will be some who have. Thus, according to Becker, there is *rule-breaking behavior* and *deviant behavior.*[3] The two overlap, but they are not necessarily similar. Whether a person is labeled deviant may depend more on *who* he or she is, than on *what* he or she has done.

The labeling approach to defining deviance depends primarily on the reaction of an audience. While this reaction is crucial to structuring the world of deviants—and is therefore crucial to forming their perceptions and reactions—the approach's neglect of norms is a problem. Audience response is generally predicated on the assumption that the deviant has broken, or at least will break, the rules. Although the audience may allow others to break the rules with impunity, this does not make the norms any less important in defining deviance.

The fourth definition, the one favored by Clinard and Meier, is a *relative* definition of deviance. This definition recognizes the wide cultural variations in norms, as well as the importance of social reaction. Specifically, Clinard and Meier define deviance as:

> Those deviations from norms which are in a disapproved direction and of sufficient degree to exceed the tolerance limits of a social group such that the deviation elicits, or is likely to elicit if detected, a negative sanction.[4]

Clinard and Meier go on to say that, according to the relative definition of deviance, deviance depends on the group that is the audience. Audiences vary in character from time to time and place to place, and so too does deviance. It may take many forms, ranging from acts regarded as crimes, such as burglary, to conditions such as physical impairment. For example, a cripple is unlikely to be regarded as deviant by other cripples. But among "normals," the cripple may face rejection, ridicule, and often public humiliation. Leonard Kriegel's recollection of his first encounter with the apartment steps ("On Being Crippled," selection 21) captures the essence of this public depreciation:

> I couldn't climb them. I stood there, staring at the stairs, hating them not for having defeated me but for having done it so publicly. Too ashamed to look at anyone, too ashamed even to speak I stood there and stared down at the steps, trying to work up enough anger and hatred so that I could show my shame with tears (Kriegel, p. 155).

Of course, simply saying that deviance is relative tells us little about the causes of rule-breaking. This point is a source of contention among sociologists, and it relates to our earlier point concerning the difficulties of simultaneously explaining rule-breaking, -following, and -making. On the one hand are those sociologists who assert that while deviance is relative, there is still wide agreement on some norms not only within a specific culture but also among various cultures. This viewpoint is generally referred to as the *consensus perspective*. Those who take this perspective argue that acts such as homicide, stealing of personal property, the forcible violation of sexual rights, the use of certain drugs, and certain behaviors described as mental disorders, are more or less generally disapproved by the great majority of Americans. Thus, to this group, the principal issue needing explanation is: Why, despite general social condemnation, do people break the rules?

That question, says another group of sociologists, misses the whole point. They argue that the notion of wide consensus on rules is a myth and a smoke screen. Simply put, their claim is that the really important rules—those whose violation constitutes *crime*—protect primarily those with political power. This is the *conflict perspective;* it sees rules as based not on what is good for the general society but rather on what is good for the groups that have attained power.[5] These groups intend to keep power by imposing regulations on the behavior of groups who threaten the status quo. Thus, while the poor person who burglarizes Sears faces jail, the FBI burglarizes with impunity the offices of political dissidents. While it is illegal for citizens to endanger the lives of others, corporations deliberately market dangerous products or allow dangerous working conditions with little fear of legal reaction.

Sociologists holding a conflict perspective concentrate primarily on rule-making and on how the rules and their enforcement reflect a struggle among society's interest groups. Not all conflict sociologists, however, view this struggle in the same way. Some regard the struggle as mainly one between differing normative orientations. Examples here are the laws enacted to control the use of alcohol and drugs, gambling, prostitution, abortion, and other behaviors whose propriety is a matter of moral definition.

Other conflict sociologists see a far greater struggle. The *radical criminologists* regard both criminal law and criminal behavior as a response to the economic-political system of capitalism. For them, rules and their enforcement are based not merely on differing moral orientations, but on the maintenance of the powerful and the wide division between the haves and have-nots. Criminal behavior, in turn, is a response to the uncertain competitive conditions created by capitalism. According to the radical criminologists, crime in capitalist societies is a means of *survival*. David M. Gordon, an economist, writes:

> Capitalist societies depend . . . on basically competitive forms of social
> and economic interaction. Individuals cannot depend on society for
> economic security; they must fend for themselves, finding the best
> opportunities for providing for themselves and family. At any point in
> time, many of the best opportunities for economic survival open to
> different citizens will violate a historically determined set of statutes and
> laws. Although these activities are therefore technically illegal, they
> nonetheless constitute functionally similar responses to the organization of
> institutions in capitalistic societies; they represent a means of survival in a
> society which does not guarantee survival to its citizens.[6]

Gordon goes on to say that crimes associated with ghetto life, with organized crime, and with corporations are all rational responses to the insecurities and uncertainties created in a society based on economic competition.

Regardless of the specific cause of interest group conflict, there is no question that many behaviors regarded as deviant by one segment of society are seen as necessary and legitimate, if not liberating, by another segment. Moreover, differences in interests are accompanied by differences in power and inclination to suppress and restrict competing interests.

The interview with the bank robber ("Bank Robbery: A Feeling of Real Power," selection 3) illustrates the conflict perspective by focusing on the robber's view of the robbery as a mechanism for redistributing wealth in this country:

> Nobody loses when you rob a bank. All the people who got their money
> in the bank they still got it. They don't lose, neither does the bank
> because they are insured. The insurance company does not lose either
> they just raise their rates a little bit. It's not like sticking up a gas station
> and grabbing the cash right out of the guy's pocket. He's got to pay for
> that. You really stung him. It is like taking the food right off his table.
> You rob a bank you take the money out and spend it. You put it back in
> circulation. That is good for everybody. Instead of stealing from people
> you buy things from them. They make a profit too (Skipper and
> McWhorter, p. 33).

ANOMIE: ADAPTING TO STRUCTURAL STRAIN

Although the conflict perspective clarifies aspects of rule-making and -breaking, most sociological approaches to deviance tend toward the consensus perspective. Consensus theorists assume a general social agreement on the norms; the principal issue, then, is to examine the differences between those who obey and those who disobey the norms.

The most ambitious approach to this issue is to consider the role of society's structure in producing deviance. We have seen that radical criminologists blame society's capitalistic economic system, but consensus theorists see society's role in a different light. This is best exemplified by Robert K. Merton's theory based on *anomie*.[7]

Merton defines anomie as a

> breakdown in the cultural structure, occurring particularly when there is an acute disjunction between cultural norms and goals and the socially structured capacities of members of the group to act in accord with them.[8]

Merton's theory involves the interaction of two social components: cultural *goals* and institutionalized *means*. According to Merton there is an overemphasis in American society on success as a goal. It is the American dream that everyone, regardless of class origin, religion, and ethnic characteristics, can succeed. The realities of American society do not match this egalitarian ideal. Socially acceptable means for achieving success are in short supply, and they are not uniformly available to all groups. Individually, the emphasis on success, or the lack of opportunity to succeed do not create anomie. But when *both* exist in a situation where individuals believe the opportunities are equally available, anomie results.

> It is only when a system of cultural values extols, virtually above all else, certain *common* success-goals for the *population* at *large* while the social structure rigorously restricts or completely closes access to approved modes of reaching these goals *for a considerable part of the same population*, that deviant behavior ensues on a large scale.[9]

The premium placed by society on financial success in the absence of legitimate opportunities creates a "disjunction" between goals and means. The individual feels pressure to be a "winner," yet staying within the bounds of accepted norms may only create frustration. What are the alternatives?

According to Merton, *conformity* is the usual adaptation. Despite the great emphasis on success, most people continue to work toward that goal by legitimate means. However, for a substantial number of people—particularly those in the lower social classes—the pressures for success lead to a decreasing reliance on legitimate means, and greater reliance on illegitimate means to make up for the lack of opportunities. This adaptation to anomie is *innovation*: the acceptance of cultural goals but the rejection of the institutionalized means to those goals. Attempting to succeed through legitimate labor is rejected in favor of involvement in organized crime and a variety of property crimes. In short, the social expectations of success lead to a belief that the ends justify the means.

(Merton acknowledges that innovation exists among the higher as well as the lower social classes. After all, "success" is a relative notion. According to American standards, how much money is "enough"? However, Merton is primarily interested in explaining the official statistics, which usually attribute higher rates of deviance to the lower economic groups. The role of anomie in explaining such behaviors as fraud by physicians and corruption among high-ranking politicians has not been thoroughly explored.)

Innovation is not the only possible deviant adaptation to anomie. Disillusion about the possibility of getting ahead may also result in abandoning the goal of success. *Ritualism* is an adaptation in which one decides that he or she cannot get ahead but faithfully adheres to the institutionalized means anyway. Merton cites as examples persons in factories and other bureaucratic organizations who staunchly perform their duties, but who have neither the intention nor the inclination to advance themselves. They avoid rocking the boat and prefer to play it safe by sticking strictly to the rules. One might argue that ritualism is not deviant in the traditional sense. Yet Merton would respond that in America to lack ambition is to be deviant.

Another adaptation to anomie involves rejection of both the cultural goals of success and the institutionalized means for obtaining those goals. This is *retreatism*, a category that includes—according to Merton—a whole range of individuals who have accepted defeat and have effectively withdrawn from society: "psychotics, autists, pariahs, outcasts, vagrants, tramps, chronic drunkards and drug addicts."[10] As Manny ("A Piece of the Action," selection 12) observed:

> Once you are wired behind scag, it is life, nothing else lives. A lush flops, passes out, quits. But a dope fiend hustles, scores, fixes so he can get down. And he has no regrets. He doesn't care at all. The doper is a true isolationist. He doesn't give a damn for others. Only insofar as they are a means to a score (Rettig, Torres, and Garret, p. 93).

Sections IV and VI contain several selections by persons whom Merton would classify as retreatists. The reader can judge whether the authors appear to have been defeated by the expectations of conventional society or whether they have other reasons for their behavior.

The final adaptation is *rebellion*. In this case individuals not only reject the goals and means provided by society, but also seek openly to substitute a new social structure with its own goals and means. In short, rebels—just as the name implies—want social change. Depending on their methods and the threats they pose to the status quo, these "deviants" may be labeled in a variety of ways: "dissenters," religious or political "kooks," "political criminals," "terrorists."

How useful is Merton's theory in explaining deviance? According to his critics, not very.[11] He is correct in assuming that the pursuit of monetary success is a major force in American society. Indeed, we must have money for survival. But beyond that, the definition of what constitutes success, and the varying intensities and methods of its pursuit, are not satisfactorily explained by the theory. One of the problems is Merton's assumption that the lower class is under greater pressure to succeed and therefore more deviant than other classes. This assumption is highly doubtful in light of what is known about crimes by government and by corporations.

Another major problem with Merton's theory is that he assumes too much influence on individuals by the general society, and not enough influence by the various groups of which individuals are members. Stated another way, the "pressures" that individuals experience are more likely to come from smaller groups than from the larger society. According to Edwin M. Lemert:

> Instead of seeing the individual as a relatively free agent making adaptations pointed toward a consistent value order, it is far more realistic to visualize him as "captured," to a greater or lesser degree, by the claims of various groups to which he has given his allegiance. It is in the fact that these claims are continually being preemptively asserted through group action at the expense of other claims, frequently in direct conflict, that we find the main source of "pressures" on individuals in modern society, rather than in "cultural emphasis on goals."[12]

Most sociologists agree with Lemert to the extent that the key to explaining deviant behavior lies less with general society than with the various groups constituting that society.

LEARNING DEVIANCE

A major implication of Lemert's statement is that the United States is a *pluralistic* society. This is another way of saying that our society is not culturally homogeneous but consists of many groups with varying interests. Because of these differences, group members are differentially exposed to behavioral patterns that may be defined as deviant. In some cases the results of differential exposure are obvious: Longshoremen are more likely to engage in knife fighting than are monks. But describing the processes of cultural support for deviance has been a thorny problem for sociologists, particularly since they must deal with larger groups in society.

An early attempt to explain cultural differences and their relationship to deviance was made by Clifford Shaw in the 1920s. Shaw noted that crime and delinquency were concentrated in city zones immediately adjacent to the central business district. These zones were populated by recent immigrant groups and characterized by poverty, deteriorating buildings, and a highly heterogeneous mixture of the young, the aged, the down-and-outers, professional criminals, prostitutes, and so on. Shaw described these areas as undergoing *social disorganization:* that is, standards of conventional society were weak, there was little sense of community, and resistance to deviance patterns was low. Furthermore, once the patterns of deviance were established, they continued over a long period of time, influencing whomever moved into the areas. Shaw claimed that

> delinquency and criminal patterns arise and are transmitted socially just as any other cultural and social pattern is transmitted. In time these

delinquent patterns become dominant and shape the attitudes and behavior of persons living in the area. Thus the section becomes an area of delinquency.[13]

Shaw later rejected the concept of social disorganization in favor of the notion that high deviance areas contain competing economic value systems. Legitimate business exists alongside the illegitimate: criminal gangs, organized crime, corrupt politics, and so on. Involvement in deviance is a matter of both opportunity and the *transmission of values* supporting deviant behavior.[14]

Shaw's ideas were elaborated by Edwin H. Sutherland. He, too, argued that crime as a tradition emerges from *differential social organization*. The many groups in American society are for and against crime in varying degrees.

> So far as delinquency and crime are concerned, a heterogeneity of norms in a society means that both a delinquent or criminal subculture and an antidelinquent or anticriminal subculture have developed. Society has become organized in such a way that a premium has been placed both on refraining from crime and on perpetrating crime. A person may now be a member of a group organized against crime while, at the same time, he is a member of a group organized for criminal behavior. For example, a person who accumulates large sums of money through white-collar crimes may be an ardent advocate of community recreation facilities which, he believes, will prevent juvenile delinquency.[15]

But Sutherland's more important contribution was his elaboration of how crime as a tradition is transmitted. He formulated a theory he called *differential association*. The principal proposition of the theory is that

> a person becomes delinquent because of an excess of definitions favorable to violation of law over definitions unfavorable to violations of law.[16]

Sutherland argues that most of these definitions are learned within intimate personal groups, not from the mass media. It is important to note that the theory does not rest on mere contacts with criminal persons so much as on learning definitions, norms, or patterns of behavior from persons with whom one is closely involved.

Sutherland's theory of differential association has been much researched and has generally stood up well in most tests. Nevertheless, there have been reformulations of the theory to clarify it and broaden its application. One of the more promising attempts is by Ronald Akers who restates Sutherland's central proposition as follows:

> The probability that a person will commit deviant behavior is increased in the presence of normative statements, definitions, and verbalizations which, in the process of differential reinforcement of such behavior over conforming behavior, have acquired discriminative value.[17]

More simply stated, Akers is arguing in terms of a reinforcement perspective: The probability that a person will commit a deviant act is increased if he or she has learned that committing the act is more rewarding than abstaining from it. Unlike Sutherland's theory, which stresses the specific learning of deviant motives and techniques, Akers's theory emphasizes learning that includes the anticipated satisfactions the behavior will bring. What sorts of satisfactions? Obviously there are many types, but one would certainly be the excitement of danger or element of risk that deviance often provides. Malcolm Braly's recollection of his early days ("A Case of Burglary," selection 8) captures this element quite accurately:

> Burglary is an elemental act and the emotions it generates are profound.
> It's a treasure hunt as well as the Lady and the Tiger, a complete and
> separate experience outside ordinary life you may be pretending to live.
> It's another way of reaching the now (Braly, p. 56).

Another example of the satisfaction the deviant choice may provide is the euphoria of drugs. While not the primary motivation for initial usage, the pleasure derived from drug use may be a reason for its continuation. In Florrie Fisher's account of heroin addiction ("Being Hooked," selection 11), this euphoric experience was highly salient:

> Oh, yes, that was it, that was the feeling. Even before I drew the needle
> out I could feel the world loosening up while my vision seemed sharper
> and sharper. Oh, it was a feeling like never before, so good, so wonderful
> (Fisher, p. 79).

SOCIAL CONTROL PERSPECTIVE

According to Shaw, Sutherland, and Akers, the key to understanding deviance is the process by which persons learn how and why to break norms. As we have indicated, some social theorists disagree with this emphasis. They prefer to look at the reverse side of the coin and examine the process by which persons learn *not* to break norms. If deviance can be so profitable and so much fun, they ask, why doesn't everyone violate the rules with wild abandon? Social control theorists say that the answer lies in the way we are socialized into conforming behavior. We learn to find rewards in rule-following and we thus become attached to socially approved behavior. Social control theorists view deviance in terms of a breakdown in this attachment to conventional norms.

Of particular relevance to this book is the social control concept of *neutralization*. Briefly, neutralization is used to justify rule-breaking without rejecting the rule itself. This may sound contradictory until you realize that almost no rule exists without an exception. We say that homicide is wrong, yet we talk about "justifiable homicide." We say that it is wrong for people to beat up one another—unless, of course, it is in a prizefight ring, on a hockey rink, or whenever somebody "deserves" it.

Gresham M. Sykes and David Matza coined the term *techniques of neutralization* in an attempt to explain the behavior of many juvenile delinquents who later seem genuinely ashamed of what they have done, express admiration for "real honest" people, and have some commitment to conventional society.[18] Sykes and Matza claim that techniques of neutralization are a component of Sutherland's "definitions favorable to the violation of law." But rather than learning attitudes that directly oppose conventional rules, the delinquents have learned justifications for bypassing the rules in certain instances. These neutralization techniques include:

Denial of Responsibility

The individual sees himself or herself as not being in control of the situation. "Bad" family, friends, and neighborhood afford few alternatives for "good" behavior. For adults, a frequent example of this technique involves alcohol. How often have you heard, "I wouldn't have done it if I hadn't been drinking"?

Denial of Injury

In this case, the individuals assert that no harm was really done. Shoplifting occurred in a store that could easily afford it, the stolen car was only "borrowed," and the building set afire was going to be torn down anyway.

Denial of Victim

Some people "deserve" what they get. The gullible are "so dumb" they deserve to lose their money, perverts by definition deserve to get beat up, and crooked store owners deserve to be ripped off.

Condemnation of the Condemners

In this instance the deviant regards his or her actions as of less consequence than the behavior of those passing judgment. Police, judges, teachers, and authorities in general are rejected as being corrupt, stupid, and brutal. In effect, deviants claim there is some question about who is "really" deviant.

Appeal to Higher Loyalties

Conventional social controls can be neutralized by one's ties to family, friends, or a cause. Again, deviance does not result from the rejection of the norm, but from higher allegiance to another group. Is it really deviant to protect or avenge those you respect and love?

Control theorists do not agree among themselves about the importance of neutralization. Travis Hirschi argues that many, if not most, delinquents are not as committed to conventional norms as Sykes and Matza believe.[19] Instead, people vary in the degree to which they believe they should obey the norms. The less they believe in the norms, the more likely they are to ignore them. Hirschi's theory is too complex to elaborate here, but the reader will get a sense of the theory from Michael J. Hindelang's concise description:

> [Hirschi's] control theory postulates that delinquent behavior becomes
> more probable as the individual's bond to society weakens. The bond has
> several components: attachment (caring about others, their opinions, and
> expectations), commitment (time, energy, and self invested in
> conventional behaviors), involvement (engrossment in conventional
> activities), and belief (attribution of moral validity to conventional norms).
> Hirschi views these components as generally positively associated and as
> having some independent effects on the likelihood that an individual will

engage in delinquent behavior. His general argument, then, is that as elements of the bond become weakened, delinquency becomes possible, although not necessary.[20]

The reader has undoubtedly noted that the discussion of control theory deals exclusively with juveniles. The extent to which the same arguments can be applied to adults remains unexplored in the sociological literature. On the basis of the selections in this book the reader may wish to speculate on the extent to which adult deviants, as well as juvenile delinquents, either neutralize their behavior—as described by Sykes and Matza—or are simply free from the norms of conventional society—as theorized by Hirschi.

LABELING AND CAREER DEVIANCE

Earlier we referred to the labeling perspective in the context of defining deviance. Specifically, we found that the perspective distinguishes between rule-breaking and deviance. Whether a behavior is deviant depends on audience reaction. Stated another way, the labeling perspective recognizes that rule-breaking is not invariably followed by a negative social response. This obviously raises important questions about *who* is labeled deviant, and *why* they are so labeled while others are not.

Labeling theorists have pushed their perspective still further, however, by asking: What are the effects of being labeled deviant? In the commonsense world many persons might respond that the labeled individual is punished or shamed into refraining from the behavior in the future. The labeling theorists reply that things are not so simple. They argue that exactly the reverse may occur: Instead of deterring the individual, labeling may set him or her on a *career* path of rule-breaking.

The sociologist who first systematically considered the relationship between labeling and career deviance is Edwin M. Lemert. He introduced a distinction between two types of deviance: *primary* and *secondary*. Primary deviance is rule-breaking stemming from original causes which, according to Lemert, may be social, situational, physiological, or psychological. As an example, he suggests that heavy drinking of alcohol may begin for a variety of reasons: death of a loved one, feelings of failure, and so on. But as long as heavy drinking is tolerated by others and is incorporated by the individual into his or her otherwise nondeviant image, the behavior will remain primary and be of little consequence for either the individual or those viewing the behavior.

However, should the drinking produce adverse reactions from others and the drinking continue anyway, a point may be reached where the drinking no longer stems from the original causes but from the reactions. At this time, according to Lemert, the deviance becomes secondary.

> When a person begins to employ his deviant behavior or role based upon it as a means of defense, attack, or adjustment to the overt and covert problems created by the consequent societal reaction to him, his deviation is secondary.[21]

Lemert goes on to describe the sequence of events leading to secondary deviance. There is an interplay between the individual and others' rejection and resentment until the point is reached at which the individual is formally stigmatized. Eventually the individual may accept his or her deviant status and make efforts to adjust to it.[22] Lemert and other labeling theorists argue that, in the process of being publicly identified as deviant, the individual is not merely being chastised but is, in effect, being given a new identity. This identity, in turn, may serve to limit the individual's contacts with conventional society (who wants to hire a "drunk"?), and may alter his or her self-concept ("I must not be able to control my drinking"). Thus excluded from participating in normal roles, the individual may adopt the deviant role because it is regarded as more appropriate by both the individual and those around him or her.[23]

One of the most thorough attempts to apply the labeling perspective to a specific form of deviance has been made by Thomas J. Scheff.[24] Scheff is concerned with the causes of a "career" of mental disorder. In a series of propositions he argues that once a person is labeled mentally ill, he or she is rewarded for playing the role that normals think the mentally ill ought to play. At the same time, the labeled person is discouraged from attempting to resume normal roles. For example, the individual is encouraged to take some time off from work and enter a mental hospital for his or her "own good." Resistance to this suggestion is met by increasing pressure from friends and relatives, which often ultimately results in an involuntary commitment to an institution. In this crisis of being publicly labeled, the individual experiences confusion, a sense of betrayal by loved ones, and a feeling that something is "wrong" after all. With "normal" behavioral alternatives cut off, the individual finds further resistance futile. According to Scheff, the individual is thus forced into secondary deviance: the role of being mentally ill. Ed captures the labeling perspective perfectly ("The Judged, Not the Judges," selection 22) when he notes:

> When the psychiatrist interviewed me he had my records in front of him—so he already knew I was mentally retarded. It's the same with everyone. If you are considered mentally retarded there is no way you can win. There is no way you can gain a favorable report (Bogdan and Taylor, p. 164).

Scheff's theory has its critics, who claim that public labeling and mental hospitalization are based primarily upon a long history of bizarre behavior by the individual. Friends and relatives do not capriciously insist that the individual undergo treatment. Instead, they usually persist in denying the presence of mental illness until the behavior in question finally becomes intolerable. The critics of Scheff argue that a career of mental illness is based principally on the individual's mental state and resulting behavior, not on the whims of social reaction.[25] This debate over the role of labeling in mental illness (or in any form of deviant behavior) remains unresolved. The true state of affairs probably lies somewhere between the extremes of Scheff's and his critics' claims.

THE INTERRELATIONSHIP BETWEEN DEVIANCE
AND CONFORMITY

The reader can see from this all-too-brief review that sociological theories are diverse and often seemingly contradictory. There are different opinions about the source of norms, the functions norms perform, and consensus on norms. There are also disagreements about the sources of deviance. According to Merton, the source lies in anomie, a condition of strain produced by the general culture's goals and the availability of culturally acceptable means to attain the goals. Other theorists, such as Sutherland, argue that the culture contains many groups with various commitments to both legal and illegal norms; deviance is regarded as a consequence of the individual's learning experiences within particular groups. Still others, such as Hirschi, contend that deviance results from a failure to form strong bonds to society and its conventional norms. Finally, labeling theorists such as Lemert emphasize the role of society in the selection of who is labeled deviant, and the role of social reaction in promoting and stabilizing deviant careers.

The selections in this book will not help the reader resolve the differences among these approaches. More probably, he or she will find support in these pages for each of the approaches. Nevertheless, a common theme links most of the selections: Deviance is interrelated with conventional society. While it is true that the deviant is usually set apart from the rest of society—as he or she would be by definition—it is also true that deviance is often curiously supported by society. For example, "deviant" users of drugs, whether heroin (selection 11) or alcohol (selections 9 and 10), are not greatly different from numerous other Americans who consume enormous amounts of over-the-counter and prescription drugs to find peace, courage, or stimulation. The similarity between "good" and "deviant" drug users becomes even more apparent when one compares the Methadone user (selection 13), the prescription forger (selection 5), or the bookmaker (selection 7) to any other businesspeople who cater to consumer demands. In a society that values sex so highly, why should the existence of swingers (selection 14) be regarded as peculiar? Is it so ironic that the reaction to a crime often depends less on the nature of the crime than on the ethical and political considerations of those entrusted to enforce the norms (selection 6)? Indeed, those trusted enforcers may even invent deviance where none exists (selection 20).

Thus, the reader is advised not only to look for the way in which deviants differ from the so-called normals, but also to search out the similarities. In some instances, the reader may find similarities so great that it is questionable who the real deviant is: the actor or the reactor. In other instances, the reader will see that deviance is often a matter of conformity taken to its logical extreme.

THE VALUE OF PERSONAL ACCOUNTS

All the selections in this book represent first person accounts by individuals who have been labeled deviant. In most cases the selections are from previously published works. A few are based on interviews conducted by the senior editors, James K. Skipper, Jr., and William L. McWhorter. We present these accounts because they provide a dimension too frequently overlooked in the study of deviance: the manner in which the actor interprets his or her own behavior.

We frequently impute motives and ideas to people when we answer the questions: Why did he do that? What does she think when people treat her that way? Being fair and objective, we assume we can come close to answering these questions because we know how we would act or think under similar circumstances. Despite our best intentions, however, we cannot be certain that our definition of the situation is in any way similar to anyone else's. We are not "inside" other people's heads, so we cannot know for certain what they see. And we have not had their experiences, so we cannot know for certain how the situation will be interpreted. While this may seem obvious, the actor's interpretation of the situation is often disregarded by social scientists because it does not seem to be objective. But it is objective to the extent that it is real enough to the actor to influence his or her behavior.

W. I. Thomas, a sociologist active in the 1920s, wrote what is now regarded as an axiom:

If men define situations as real, they are real in their consequences. [26]

Thomas argued that the case study or life record that reveals the expressed attitudes of individuals is important because it contributes to understanding the individual's total situation. Even if the individual's viewpoint is completely at odds with the viewpoint of other observers, its impact on the individual's behavior should not be underestimated.

Michael Parenti describes Thomas's conclusions as follows:

An understanding of the situation, as reached by the disinterested investigator, is therefore never complete until he appreciates the meanings experienced by the participants themselves. The scientific observer certainly should arrive at meanings beyond those held by the participants, but a full comprehension of the action's significance is impossible without an understanding of the "realities" as defined both by and for the actors, for it is these definitions which most often give creation to the action. [27]

The first person account is a valuable tool for understanding behavior, but it is not without problems. As we have already mentioned, most of our selections have been previously published elsewhere. Someone who publishes must be reasonably articulate or at least have the ability to give a ghost writer enough material to work with. Since either of these abilities may make the individual unique within a particular class of deviants, one must ask whether the individual is unique in other respects.

Perhaps more importantly, why have the authors seen fit to tell their story, and how do those motives affect the content of their accounts? If publication is purely a financially motivated venture, or if the author has an ax to grind with society in general or some group in particular, will exaggerations or omissions distort the interpretation? The author may believe himself or herself to be completely honest and still let inaccuracies creep into the account.

Just as a writer's intentions may affect content, the audience also influences what is said. The interviews for this book were conducted by persons with a sociological frame of reference. Consequently, the questions asked more or less reflect a sociological orientation. Suppose the interviews had been conducted by psychologists, psychoanalysts, or members of the clergy? The inquiries undoubtedly would be quite different. Would the answers cast a different light on the actors' interpretations of the situations?

Finally, and probably most obvious, to what extent does the passage of time affect the authors' recall? Have important aspects been forgotten? Do more recent experiences color the recollections of earlier situations?

These are important questions the reader should bear in mind when reading the selections. The first person account is not the final word in the quest for explanations of human behavior. Whatever its flaws, however, it provides an invaluable glimpse into a world that conformists, because they are conformists, are unlikely to see under other circumstances. At least, such accounts should satisfy curiosity about "what it is like." At best, they reveal the dynamic affinities between conformers and deviants that are too frequently overlooked.

Notes

1. This discussion of definitions of deviance is based on Marshall B. Clinard and Robert F. Meier, *Sociology of Deviant Behavior*, 5th ed. (New York: Holt, Rinehart and Winston, 1979), pp. 12–15.

2. Howard S. Becker, *Outsiders: Studies in the Sociology of Deviance* (New York: Free Press, 1963), p. 9.

3. Ibid., p. 14.

4. Clinard and Meier, *Sociology of Deviant Behavior*, p. 14.

5. This description of the conflict perspective—especially the radical position—has been necessarily oversimplified. The reader is encouraged to read the works of conflict theorists in order to understand the variety and complexity of their approaches. The following are good sources with which to begin: George B. Vold, *Theoretical Criminology* (New York: Oxford University Press, 1958); Austin T. Turk, *Criminality and Legal Order* (Chicago: Rand McNally, 1969); William J. Chambliss and Robert B. Seidman, *Law, Order and Power* (Reading, Mass.: Addison-Wesley, 1971); Richard Quinney, *Class, State, and Crime: On the Theory and Practice of Criminal Justice* (New York: David McKay, 1977); and any issue of the journal *Crime and Social Justice*.

6. David M. Gordon, *Problems in Political Economy: An Urban Perspective* (Lexington, Mass.: D. C. Heath, 1971), p. 276.

7. This discussion is based on Robert K. Merton, *Social Theory and Social Structure*, rev. ed. (New York: Free Press, 1957), pp. 131–194.

8. Merton, *Social Theory and Social Structure*, p. 162.

9. Ibid., p. 146.

10. Ibid., p. 153.

11. For a thorough review and critique of Merton's anomie, see Marshall B. Clinard, ed., *Anomie and Deviant Behavior: A Discussion and Critique* (New York: Free Press, 1964).

12. Edwin M. Lemert, "Social Structure, Social Control, and Deviation," in Clinard, *Anomie and Deviant Behavior*, p. 68.

13. Clifford R. Shaw, *Delinquency Areas: A Study of the Geographic Distribution of School Truants, Juvenile Delinquents, and Adult Offenders in Chicago* (Chicago: University of Chicago Press, 1929), pp. 205–206.

14. Clifford R. Shaw and Henry D. McKay, *Juvenile Delinquency in Urban Areas* (Chicago: University of Chicago Press, 1942), pp. 164–170.

15. Edwin H. Sutherland and Donald R. Cressey, *Criminology*, 9th ed. (Philadelphia: J. B. Lippincott, 1974), pp. 95–96.

16. Ibid., p. 76.

17. Ronald L. Akers, *Deviant Behavior: A Social Learning Approach*, 2d ed. (Belmont, Calif.: Wadsworth, 1977), p. 43.

18. Discussion derived from Gresham M. Sykes and David Matza, "Techniques of Neutralization: A Theory of Delinquency," *American Sociological Review* 22 (December 1957): 664–670.

19. Travis Hirschi, *Causes of Delinquency* (Berkeley: University of California Press, 1969).

20. Michael J. Hindelang, "Causes of Delinquency: A Partial Replication and Extension," *Social Problems* 20 (Spring 1973): 473.

21. Edwin M. Lemert, *Social Pathology: A Systematic Approach to the Theory of Sociopathic Behavior* (New York: McGraw-Hill, 1951), p. 76.

22. Ibid., p. 77.

23. This description of the labeling perspective is highly simplified. The reader interested in elaboration is referred to Edwin M. Schur, *Labeling Deviant Behavior: Its Sociological Implications* (New York: Harper & Row, 1971) and Edwin M. Lemert, *Human Deviance, Social Problems, and Social Control*, 2d ed. (Englewood Cliffs, N.J.: Prentice-Hall, 1972), pp. 62–92.

24. Thomas J. Scheff, *Being Mentally Ill: A Sociological Theory* (Chicago: Aldine, 1966).

25. For a broad range of criticism of labeling theory as it applies to a variety of deviant behavior, see Walter R. Gove, ed., *The Labelling of Deviance: Evaluating a Perspective* (New York: Halsted Press, 1975).

26. William I. Thomas and Dorothy Swaine Thomas, *The Child of America: Behavior Problems and Programs* (New York: Alfred A. Knopf, 1928), p. 572.

27. Michael Parenti, "Introduction" to William I. Thomas, *The Unadjusted Girl* (New York: Harper Torchbooks, 1967), p. xii.

Section II   VIOLENT CRIME

Crime continues to be one of the most serious problems facing the American people. For the past several decades, the magnitude of the crime problem has been a salient issue in every major political campaign. Many of these elections have fostered such catchwords as "law and order," "safe streets," "get tough with criminals," and "war on crime." Politicians call, with tiresome regularity, for a renewed war on crime, but the problem remains; indeed, the crime problem appears more serious with each issue of the quarterly *Uniform Crime Report*.

Crime is an American way of life, explained sociologist Daniel Bell over two decades ago (Bell, 1953). Through this cogent essay on organized crime, Bell demonstrates that crime is not just a singular act of misconduct, but rather behavior that is symbiotically intertwined with the social and political fabric of society, and law-abiding citizens, police officers, and "gangsters" are all implicated in it. He also points out that crime can be a route of upward social and economic mobility for certain disadvantaged groups in society. One can appreciate this profound sociological insight into crime, but its value is entirely lost on the assault victim or the person whose home has just been burglarized. Few of us feel like the liberal gentleman in a recent cartoon who had just been assaulted and was explaining to reporters, "How do I feel about being mugged? Well, naturally I didn't enjoy it and I certainly don't condone violence or threats of violence as a means toward social change. However, I can empathize with my assailant and realize that in his terms this is a valid response to the deteriorating socioeconomic situation in which we find ourselves." The cartoon was tongue-in-cheek, but it does have an element of truth; however, it is doubtful that many of us would be as sympathetic as this victim.

In recent years more and more attention has been directed at what may be generically called "street crime" or "hard-core crime." These terms generally refer to a wide variety of offenses in which persons are seriously endangered by violence or the threat of violence. They include the offense categories that make up part of the *Uniform Crime Report* and include homicide, aggravated assault, forcible rape, and armed robbery. In addition, the public generally has an accepted stereotypical image of the criminal in which a wide range of characteristics and causes are imputed as motives for his criminal behavior. These may vary from biological abnormalities to psychological quirks to the disorganizing and dehumanizing conditions of urban life. Rarely, if ever, does the layman consider that the same set of social conditions that breed criminal behavior are responsible for the development of law-abiding conduct.

Of all the myriad forms of social behavior that make up events of everyday life, physical violence remains one of the most persistent and fearful of all human activities. Personal violence, collective violence, and violent predatory crime have become salient features of American society. Homicide, although a low-volume crime in terms of numbers (less than 3 percent of all crimes of violence and less than one-half of 1 percent of all index crimes), is such a serious offense in the United States that a person convicted of it can face the most severe legal penalties the state can impose. Only recently have we witnessed the reimposition of the death penalty, although the statistical evidence still suggests that it has not proven to be a successful deterrent.

Although the general cultural theme of violence is woven into the fabric of American society, it is more problematic for certain segments of our population. Violence, like other forms of social behavior, is patterned. The distribution of violent acts shows significant variation according to age, sex, race, social class, ethnic background, and prior criminal involvement. The intrapersonal nature of violence, the presence of alcohol or drugs, and the role of the victim in the precipitation of the final act are characteristics of violence that have all been reaffirmed by recent studies.

The first selection, "A Case of Murder," is an account of a homicide from the viewpoint of the murderer himself. While sociologists have argued successfully for the "subculture of violence" thesis to account for the high incidence of urban violence, the concept is of limited utility in explaining other forms of violent behavior. The subculture of violence suggests that the grinding poverty, unstable community organization, and disorganized family life among lower-class urban residents encourages the development of values that support the use of violence as the solution to personal disputes.

Students will quickly recognize this subculture of violence thesis as a contemporary formulation of the old social disorganization theory, which was presented in the introductory chapter. According to this theory, high rates of crime and delinquency are considered reflections of a breakdown in society. Advocates of this position can point to many conditions that illustrate this breakdown: poverty, deteriorating inner cities, cultural conflict among arriving immigrants, and the lack of a sense of community. However, although it is true that certain areas of the country have higher rates of violence than others, this may not be a manifestation of a general breakdown but rather of differences in social organization. As Sutherland successfully argues, there are many different groups in American society, all of which have varying attitudes toward crime. In this selection one can begin to see the variation in the conditions, attitudes, and circumstances that encourage the use and acceptance of violence as a legitimate form of social expression.

In this particular case the murder took place in a rural area; thus, many of the elements that make up the subculture of violence were not present. However, the actual act of violence did have striking similarities with its urban counterpart. Among these were: (1) the act was an individual crime involving one victim and one offender who were intimately acquainted. (2) Alcohol or drugs were present and either the offender or victim or both were intoxicated or drinking heavily. Although not a direct cause of violence, alcohol may play a very important indirect role in that it may reduce rationality and internal constraints. (3) Firearms, in this case both pistols and rifles, were available. The possibility that death will occur increases substantially when one is shot (61 percent of deaths are by handguns) compared to when one is cut, stabbed or assaulted with other forms of personal weapons. (4) The victim played a role. In the present case, the murder could be described as a victim-precipitated homicide in which the victim, through a circular and ever-increasing hostile interaction with the offender contributed to his own death.

The term *rape* arouses hostile and aggressive feeling in many societies and is considered so serious an offense that it often carries the same penalties as does criminal homicide. Considering the seriousness of rape as a form of sexual deviance, as well as criminal behavior, it is surprising that relatively little has been written about it until very recently. The feminist movement of the 1970s has begun to sensitize us to the nature, distribution, and seriousness of rape, and to the threat it poses to our society. Forcible rape by legal definition (in most jurisdictions) may be committed only by a male. It may be broadly defined as the "carnal knowledge of a female through the use of force or the threat of force." Rape is thus more an act of violence than an act of sexual deviance in that the consent of the woman is absent.

Rape is one of the most difficult of all human activities to study because of the variations in reporting, definitional ambiguities, and different perceptions of the degree of force involved. Our society has what may be characterized as a "schizophrenic" attitude toward rape—on the one hand, we believe that "nice girls" don't get raped and that those women that do, often provoke the attack. Regardless of one's attitude toward rape, the behavior represents intrapsychic conflict related to psychosexual development and is socially and culturally patterned.

The desires, motivations, drives, and rationalizations of rapists are highly variable, but "the fact is that rape grows out of masculine contempt for women" (Goode, 1978: 420). Thus, rape is not just an act of sexual aggression but an exercise in the domination of power. "Force is used instrumentally to secure a desired goal" (Goode, 1978: 421). In the introductory chapter, we suggested that conflict was one approach often used in the examination of deviant behavior. The unequal distribution of power permits one group to dominate or subjugate another. This perspective is very clear in the writings of contemporary feminists. "A society that discourages or prevents women from seeking their own destiny, from wanting to have some of the power and privileges that men enjoy will be one that will excuse certain forms of rape as justified or provoked by the women" (Goode, 1978: 430); "The propagandists for male supremacy broadcast that it is women who cause rape by being unchaste or in the wrong place at the wrong time—in essence, by behaving as though they were free" (Griffin, 1971: 33).

It is an oversimplification to say that rape is caused by the power differentials between men and women, but it is correct to say that many behaviors regarded as deviant by one group are seen as proper and just by another. The motivations for rape have been shown to be related to problems of status and to situational factors that are found more frequently in certain areas or among certain groups within society. "Many men feel that sexual aggression against certain women is justified because they see them as objects of exploitation. These men do not consider what they do as rape because, for them, the mistreatment of women is routine and deeply ingrained. Rape, then, is characteristically not a solitary act, but an expression that certain groups of men have toward women, toward relations between the sexes, and toward human relations in general" (Goode, 1978: 420, 430).

In the selection, "A Rapist Gets Caught in the Act," the masculine contempt for women that is often exhibited by the rapist is clearly documented. The rapist felt that he was fully justified in doing what he did. To him, "women are objects to be used in pursuit of his own private sexual gratification. The will and desire of the woman is relevant only insofar as she permits him to manipulate her into a situation in which exploitation and abuse is facilitated" (Goode, 1978: 420).

In a materialistic and acquisitive society like the United States, where property and material goods are revered, it is not surprising that a number of criminal statutes have been enacted centering on the violation of property rights. Criminologists have focused attention on the rich variety of property offenders, but perhaps none has captured the public's attention as has the bank robber. Robbery is both a violent crime and a property crime. This criminal category is defined by the F.B.I. as "stealing or taking anything of value from the care, custody or control of a person by force or by violence or threat of violence."

Bank robbers are considered "professional" criminals, and as such have been generally discussed under a single theoretical model. The model of the professional criminal has centered largely on the works of Edwin H. Sutherland (1937). He suggested that there are certain essential characteristics of professional criminals and that their behavior may be accounted for by examining their various associations with other criminals. His is essentially a learning theory in which persons become criminals through association with other criminals. As a class of offenders, professionals are highly competent lawbreakers who make large sums of money from their various activities. Bank robberies are particularly lucrative and involve considerable technical skill, lengthy periods of planning, a high degree of organization, swift and efficient execution, and a fundamental understanding of human nature.

In the selection, "Bank Robbery: A Feeling of Real Power," the robber speaks freely of the organizational structure of the profession, the status hierarchy that exists among criminals, and his gradual transformation from delinquency into more serious forms of criminality. In his popular book, *Where the Money Was*, the bank robber Willie Sutton stated that he never felt so alive as when he was robbing a bank. The present article also illustrates the considerable excitement that accompanies a bank heist.

Much of the theorizing about crime has centered on the social and economic conditions that produce the motivation to engage in criminality. However, many offenders may not be any more motivated to engage in lawbreaking than nonoffenders. Their criminal behavior may arise out of some combination of situational pressures and circumstances, along with opportunities for criminality, which are totally outside the actor. This is not to say that early life experiences play no causal role in criminal behavior; they almost certainly do. In many cases, the crime may be a response to nothing more temporal than the provocations and attractions bound up in the immediate circumstances out of which deviant acts arise. This is often found in cases of family or marital disputes, certain cases of sexual offenses, and "one-time loser" property offenders.

Edwin Lemert, in introducing the concepts of primary and secondary deviance, sought to capture the social, psychological, and situational pressures that may lead to deviant behavior. He suggested that primary deviants are responding, in some cases, to situational pressures, as opposed to having a generalized predisposition to engage in criminal behavior. These situations often carry some degree of risk in which one of the potential outcomes is a deviant form. When approached from this perspective, we are forewarned not to make the automatic assumption that criminal conduct is always "motivated" in the sense of being related to long-standing attitudes and psychological concerns of the individual.

In the selection "A Victim of Circumstance?" the situational aspects of deviant behavior are clearly demonstrated. In this particular case the armed robbery was an impulsive act born out of a perceived desperation or crisis in the life of the offender. This was not the carefully planned heist by a gang of "heavies" who make a career out of strong-arm robbery. While the situational factors are important, of equal importance in the causal explanation are the facts that the girl came from a broken home, did poorly in school and eventually dropped out, engaged in sexual activity that resulted in an early pregnancy, and finally became entangled in a relationship with an unstable, impulsive, and manipulative man. These facts further underscore the necessity of viewing deviant behavior from several different perspectives. There is no single theoretical perspective that will explain all forms of deviant behavior; rather, each contributes a part to the understanding of the whole.

References

Bell, Daniel
1953 "Crime as an American Way of Life." *Antioch Review* 13 (June): 131–154.
Goode, Erich
1978 *Deviant Behavior.* Englewood Cliffs: Prentice-Hall, Inc.
Griffin, Susan
1971 "Rape: The All American Crime." *Ramparts* 10 (September): 26–35.
Lemert, Edwin M.
1953 "An Isolation and Closure Theory of Naive Check Forgery." *Journal of Criminal Law, Criminology and Police Science* 44 (September–October): 296–307.
Sutherland, Edwin H.
1940 "White Collar Criminality." *American Sociological Review* 5 (February): 1–12.
1937 *The Professional Thief.* Chicago: University of Chicago Press.

A CASE OF MURDER As told to William L. McWhorter and James K. Skipper, Jr.

Interviewer: Now, what I want to do is to find out a little bit about why you're in here and your prison experiences. So first, I want you to tell me something about why you're here, your present offense.

Respondent: Well, the way I got involved with this man, I was a foreman at the time during when I went to work as a foreman in Martinsville because the guy sent for me, he needed me and I didn't have much work. He wanted me to be a foreman and build a paint crew. So I hired men and fired, and built a paint crew, and this is where I met this man, Jimmy. Somebody told me he needed a job, and I called him on the phone, and he said he was a mediocre painter. So I said, "OK, come on up. I need some help." So the guy, when he was sober, he was all right. You'd think he was the nicest guy you ever met. And he worked hard and he worked diligent. You could trust him when you turned your back, and actually he was not a first-class painter, but he put so much work on, I put a first-class painter with him. So I get to know the guy, I actually liked the guy, somewhat, you know, because he did a honest day's work, and did his best, and that's how I met him, but when he'd get to drinking, sometimes in the evening maybe after work, he'd have a few beers, and it'd seem like his mind started to wander, he'd make strange remarks. First he told me, "I killed this officer in Vietnam." And I think he was grieving about it, I think it's on his conscience. I said, "Well, Jimmy, I was in the war, too, and I saw a lot of strange things happen, guys cracked up and this and that. And they did things that actually they were not responsible for, under normal conditions. And if something like that happened to you, don't grieve about it, it just something that happened in the war, and forget about it, and don't drink too much and think about it." You know what I mean? But this is like, when this fellow gets to drinking, he gets mean. And he stayed at my house a week before they come

around and need some help, asking me to help him, so I get him a house to paint, give him the equipment, give him a place to stay . . .

Interviewer: He was staying with you?

Respondent: Yeah, I let him stay at my house, because he didn't have transportation back to town. But he would drink at night so much, and I didn't know he was going to do that. And he'd have his girlfriends running up and around, late as two o'clock at night laying around with a girl, and the next day he couldn't work. So I was trying to get rid of the guy.

Interviewer: OK, so you were trying to get rid of him after finding out what type of individual he was?

Respondent: Yeah, he was unable to do his work, and it was my daughter's mother-in-law's house he was painting, and I'd go down and inspect his work and I'd have to help him with it. Then he tries to paint the roof, and I said, "Don't worry about it, Jimmy, I'll help you finish the job," so he'd get it done. Now my daughter comes home from work and my son-in-law, and I'd tell them, I said, "I'm helping Jimmy to finish this job, so I can get him back to Martinsville out of my house, I don't want to be associated with him. I'm going to give all his money he's got coming. I just want to get this job done and get him out of here, 'cause you know how he's doing." So that was the idea, and I was doing . . . and we had about one more day to go but it rained on Friday, so he wants to go to town. So I go along with him, whatever he wants to do, I go along with him. So he said, "What do you think about Dale?" I said, "Well, seems to be all right." "Why don't you ask her to come up this evening? We'll mess around, cook up a little something." So I said, "OK." Anything to pacify him, now. One more day and he'll be gone. So, I don't know whether it was all planned or not. We go into town, and I went and got him sixty dollars advance on his salary, and he goes down and meets this girl, she comes to the restaurant,

This interview is contributed by William L. McWhorter and James K. Skipper, Jr.

and he buys a couple of fifths of whiskey, and I asked her, or he asked her, "Why don't you come up this evening, and we'll mess around, and cook up a little something?" She said, "All right, come back and pick me up at four o'clock." So, I went back and got her, and he stayed at home, and he's got this whiskey and beer, and the mixed whiskey, and we come back. In the meantime, for several days, seemed like he'd sit silently and brood. You know, instead of us having a conversation, there was something there, and he was acting strange, and that's why I wanted to get away from him. So anyway, that night, I go bring the girl back, and we went looking for some turtles to cook up. And I finally found some, and everywhere I'd go she'd go. She seemed to be enjoying herself. And I didn't mess around with girls much at that time. Last few years, I hardly ever had anything to do with them. But she seemed different. Other girls come there, and I wouldn't pay no attention. But this one's different, she's just like a fuzzy puppy that you want, she's friendly. So she come in that afternoon, she mentioned this pistol. She said, "Lucille is afraid of guns." I said, "Well, are you?" She said, "No." I said, "Well, do you want to go out in the back and shoot some?" "All right." So we take the two pistols and the rifle out to the backyard and I'd teach her to shoot, and the girl can shoot. I was an army instructor, and I'd instruct her, and she could shoot. I said, "Well, you shot pistols before." She said, "I just do what you tell me to." But anyway, whenever she went, and we seemed to be getting along fine. She was about thirty, twenty, thirty years old. And we come back and Jimmy's carrying the turtle, we ate the turtle, and she cleaned up the kitchen. He borrowed the car and went to make a telephone call. So I see her clean up the kitchen, I says, "I could use somebody like you around here. There's an old song, something about a boll weevil looking for a home. If you're ever looking for a home, why, look me up." You know, just joking, he was joking, nothing serious, no advances. Anyway, he fried the turtle, we all eat. She goes in the front room and sits down, she was watching the TV, then I go in and sit down, and I put my arm around her, cause she's sitting in the middle of the sofa. We was sitting there, watching TV, talking, pick up a book off the coffee table, it was anthropology,

ape-men, all that, and we laughed about that. So, I said, "You sure are a sweet thing." I had my arm around her anyway, so I just pulled her over and kissed her on the cheek. It was just an emotional impulse, you might call it an impulse. Well, she got up, and she went into the kitchen. I thought maybe she was going to get another drink, or something. First thing I know, Jimmy hollered in there, said, "Ray, come in here." I go in there, and he says, "You scared that girl." I said, "Man, I didn't do nothing but kiss her on the cheek. We been friendly, rattling around, I didn't think nothing of it." He says, "Well, she's gone." I said, "Well, out in the dark?" "Yeah." "Well, I don't want that girl out in the dark. I'll go find her and we'll take her home, if she's afraid. She's acting strange to something." Anyway, she's gone out the back, so I . . . he said, "Well, get the hell out of here and find her." He's talking real rough to me. I run and get into the car, and I think I can catch her on the road before she gets to the neighbor's house, but I don't see her anywhere. I go down the road a mile, and I don't see her. I come back up the road a mile. I stopped in a place up there, nobody's seen her. And I come back and he starts cussing at me. I still hadn't seen her, and he's *cussing* me. He's got his hands under the table, by both knees. But that was nothing, it was his idea that I date the girl. She's putting out, she was his brother's former wife, he forced their separation. The lawyer says, "Oh, now, tell the truth about it, you all was up there to make out." I said, "Man, we'd a-made out if the girls wanted to. But it was their perogative. You know, we wasn't gonna force them to. We was just messing around and take them back home. They've been there before. We didn't have to shack up." Anyway, it seemed like that's when, he's cussing, that's when I go to the bedroom to see if my pistols is in there, what's he got in his hands? He wants me to come in the kitchen. He's cussing, I don't want to come to the kitchen, I just come to the hall door. That's when I go back and discover my pistols are missing, but the rifle was still in the closet. The rifle was not supposed to be fully loaded. We shot three times, it only had eight in the beginning, long rifle, supposed to be five in the rifle. I don't remember reloading and putting those other five—four rounds in there, but you have nine rounds, got to have one in the chamber, in the cylinder, see? So, I go in and get the rifle, and I come back and I was getting mad too. I don't get mad too easy, but I get mad, now, I don't deny that, especially in my house. I think I can run this guy out. His girlfriend supposed to come up in a few minutes and pick him up, anyway. He's sitting there. "You can't cuss me in my own house. You get your ass up and get it out of here, so I'll put some lead in it." "I ain't going no goddamn where and you ain't got guts enough to do nothing about it." That's how sarcastic, overbearing that SOB was, he was to sit there in my own house and tell me I ain't got guts enough to do nothing about it. He done took over my house. After me helping him, feeding him, and doing everything for him, a man treating me like that, he's a dog. Naturally, that makes me mad, then, it's my house, too. Now whether he made this hand . . . he done changed position when I come back with the rifle. He turned sideways at the table, but this hand is still setting down under the table. Then he's facing me, though before, he had both hands. I don't know exactly now, after it's all happened, when he said them words, whether he moved his hand or whether I just shot him. Anyway, I shot him twice, through the chest, he fell out on the floor, and I walked around the table, expecting my pistols to be laying there beside of him. But there's no pistol there! Sheez, what've I done now? I go sit down on the bed, and I think it over. I want to shoot myself, but I ain't got no pistol. I think of all that mess. So the law come out there, they asked me . . .

Interviewer: Did you call the law yourself?

Respondent: Yeah. After I think it over, I went to see my brother down the road about two miles, and I told him so he could get a bondsman, and I came back and told my friend to call the law. And I waited, and they come in and asked me a few questions, and I was supposed to answer questions, but some questions you can't answer. That's what confused all of this mess, and this cop asked me, "How many times did you shoot him, Ray?" I said, "twice." So we walk in there, and I said, "He's probably laying on both of my pistols, both of my pistols is missing out of the bedroom. When you get a chance to turn him over, and see if my pistols is under him, cause they're missing." So when the coroner

came and the cop come in and said, "You shot him twice, Ray. Once in the chest and once in the shoulder." But I couldn't figure out how I shot him in the shoulder because I was a crack shot in the army. But he said twice. When it come up to the preliminary hearing, here come the prosecuting attorney with a finger, roaring out, "Nine bullets in that man!" And I tried to tell the lawyer, said, "Didn't shoot him but twice." Now whether that girl was still on the back porch or not with them pistols in her handbag. Now the girl could've hated this boy, cause he broke up her marriage, and then he didn't want to go with her. He'd have to date another girl, but she'd follow him around, see. Now that girl could've planned and could've set him up, and she could've come in and picked that rifle up cause I'd left that rifle setting in the bedroom when I went to call the law. Well, when me and the law come back, the rifle was setting in the hallway wall. He said, "Is that the rifle?" I said, "Yeah, but I thought it was in the bedroom." How come there was nine bullets in it, cause I didn't reload that rifle. And I tried to find out which pistol, there's a .22 pistol in this deal, which was missing, shot the same bullet. I said, "Where did all the bullets . . . did some of the bullets come out of the pistol?" I think to myself, that girl could've come off the back porch, come down, and said, "You son of a bitch, I set you up!" And blasted him some more. You don't know what a woman will do, once they scorn. But I couldn't figure it, and I tell these people, "I do *not* remember shooting him over twice. There wasn't supposed to be but five rounds in the gun." Tried to tell the lawyer, lawyer won't believe nothing I say. Still, if you asked me a thousand times, I say, "I thought I shot him *twice,* and that's all."

QUESTIONS FOR DISCUSSION

1. What is the reason physically violent acts such as murder have become so accepted in the United States and in other countries? Do you anticipate changes in societal attitudes in the future? Why or why not?

2. How do different segments of the population and different social classes cope with physical violence? Do you think these meth-

ods of coping are basically similar or dissimilar?

3. How closely do you feel the victim-precipitated theory or model fits this particular murder? What other sociological theories might be used to explain an incident such as this?

4. Why do you think the accused called the law himself? Do you think you would have reacted in the same way?

A RAPIST GETS CAUGHT IN THE ACT As told to James K. Skipper, Jr. and William L. McWhorter

Interviewer: Can you tell me something about yourself?

Respondent: Sure, why not. I am 32 years old. I am 5 feet 7 inches tall and I weigh 165 pounds. I drive a truck for a living and make pretty good money. I got an old lady and two nice kids. One is 12 a nice girl and a boy almost 9 now. What else is there to say? Oh, yes, I am not dumb. I got a high school diploma. I never got arrested for nothing before, not even a parking violation. What else do you want to know? Yes, I love my wife and I loved my father and mother. Isn't that what you are supposed to say? Well, in my case it is true except for my father. I did not know him very well because he left my mother when I was about four and we never saw him again. I don't think she cared whether she saw him again or not. She never went looking. I guess she figured he didn't have anything she wanted anyway. She never wanted to talk about him much and there wasn't anything for me to talk about. I didn't know enough about him to miss him.

Interviewer: Do you remember anything else about your father?

Respondent: Not really. I guess he had a lot of odd jobs like store clerk, repair man. I think he worked in a mail room once, but was not what you would call a mailman. I mean he did not deliver mail. Mom said he liked to collect coins. That's all I can remember. Like I said he left when I was about 4 maybe it was 5. It does not matter. Anyway I never hated the guy if that's what you are trying to get at. How can you hate someone you don't even remember? You can't blame him for what I did.

Interviewer: What was your relationship with your mother?

Respondent: What do you mean what was my relationship with my mother? I never screwed her if that's what you mean. For Christ sake what type of guy do you think I am? Sure I fucked some women in my time whether they liked it or not, but your own mother that is disgusting. My God man, what do you take me for?

Interviewer: I am sorry, you misunderstood me. I meant how did you get along with your mother. Did you have a happy family life?

Respondent: Oh, I see what you mean. Well it is like this. I loved my mother a lot I really did. She was always good to me and gave me all the things she could afford. She was a waitress at a fancy type restaurant. You know the type where you got to have money and class or you don't get in the door. She worked at night and did not get in until late. I was always asleep when she got home. That's after I was in school. I don't remember before that. She used to get up early and see me off to school and then give me an early dinner before she went to work. I was on my own most of the time since I was about 7. But I didn't mind. I could find things to do for myself. We didn't live in a real bad neighborhood and besides she used to give me money. I always had more money than the other kids to do things. We always used to spend Sundays together and do things like going to movies, out to dinner. Things like that. I always liked to have Sundays with her until I was about 15. Then I didn't like to do it anymore. I had better things to do by then. You know what I mean? Now I kind of miss them. She died in a car crash about a year after I got married. It really came as a shock. I had not seen her much after I got married. Then I got this phone call at work that she had been killed in a head-on collision. It was right here in town. The police said the cars couldn't been going more than 35, but it was enough to kill both drivers. I really felt bad about it. After all she had done for me, she deserved something better. Anyway, you can't blame her either for what I have done. It couldn't be her. It was all just me.

This interview is contributed by James K. Skipper, Jr. and William L. McWhorter.

Interviewer: What do you think was the cause of your conduct?

Respondent: Well if you mean my wife you are crazy. I have had a normal sexual life with my wife. We have two kids don't we? I am normal in every respect. I have never beat my wife or my kids. I have fooled around a little in my day but nothing serious. You get me? I take my women one at a time. That way nothing gets serious. It does not interfere with your life. At least not until now it has not. My wife never knew nothing.

Interviewer: You mean your wife was not aware of your affairs with other women?

Respondent: Now there you go again. I didn't say I had affairs with other women did I? That's not right. What I meant was sometimes you just have the urge to go out and fuck the living shit out of some broad. You don't have to like them. You don't have to want to ever see them again. You just get the urge to go out and fuck one of them. It does not matter who they are or what they look like. You just want to do it. It has nothing to do with loving your wife. Once it is over it is over. Anyway I suppose it is normal for a guy to want to do that once or twice a year. I think most women expect it.

Interviewer: You mean women would not consider it a case of rape?

Respondent: Hell no, Hell no. I mean most women like to get their box battered as much as a man likes to get his balls off. They want to be grabbed and taken hard. It makes them feel like a woman. I know that to be a fact. And what's more you feel more like a man when you do it that way. This time I just got unlucky and got a cold hearted bitch. That's the only difference.

Interviewer: Could you describe the circumstances of your present offense?

Respondent: OK I guess so. There really is not much to tell though. I got up one morning. It was a hot day in August. I had not got much sleep the night before. I felt kind of mean and ugly. My wife was nagging again. The kids were getting on my nerves even before I got out of the house. I had trouble starting the truck and I was late to work. The boss did not like that much, I could tell he didn't. But he did not yell at me or nothing. He just told me to get going and make up the time as best I could. I tried but

I got stuck in traffic and it got later and later. By lunch time I was so far behind I was not going to make all my deliveries by 5:00 no matter what I did. I stopped at this little diner and had a few beers. I did not feel like eating at all. Then I thought by God what you need is a good piece. That ought to fix you up good. Just go out and grab yourself a broad. Hell I was not going to make my deliveries anyway. It was after 2:00 by then. So I got me back in the truck and started cruising around looking. About an hour went by and nothing. I thought oh God don't let this be my unlucky day. Then I saw this woman standing alone at a bus stop. She was not much to look at. Skinny as a rail, about 40 years old I would say. I pulled up and asked her if she could give me directions to County Line Road. She told me the way right off. But I pretended not to understand. After she told me again and I said I still did not get it, I asked her if she would like to get in the truck and show me. I knew she must be going in that general direction because that is the way the bus was going. She hesitated for a moment and looked to see if the bus was coming. It was not. She said, "Well I suppose it would be OK. You look like a nice enough kid, but I am not going quite that far." Right then I figured I had her. So I says, "Hop in." She does and we are on our way. I know a good place just outside of town down a side road where there is an old abandoned barn. It is not far from the road, but you can't see it from the road and sound does not carry from it very well. I have been there before. I figure it is safe. We get to talking real nice. I start thinking about how I am going to grab her. We miss her stop and she doesn't even seem to know. Finally she realizes it and says, "You missed my stop! You missed my stop! You even missed County Line Road." I apologized and play dumb and say I didn't know we had passed them. I stop the truck and start to turn around and then I say, "Wait a minute. We are just a couple of miles from another of my deliveries. Would you mind if we just drove a little farther down this road?" She agrees if it will not take long. I assure her it won't and we are on our way again. Before you know it we are at my safe place. I grab a couple of packages out of the back and start toward the trees to the barn. I stop and say, "Hey I hate to leave you alone in the car. Why don't you walk with me to the house? It is just through the trees." She thinks that is a good idea and we start out. We get about 200 feet from the barn through the trees and she sees it is no farm house and says, "I am going back." I grab her by the arm and she starts fighting and screaming. I figure I got a real loony this time I am never going to make it to the barn. It might as well be right here on the ground. I tell her to be quiet and quit fighting. She won't stop so I slug her one and that takes most of the steam out of her and she falls down and starts groaning. I figure let her groan. Nobody is going to hear that. I plop down on her and start to get her dress off and in the meantime I get my cock out. I may have got my cock close to her, but I sure never got it in let alone come. The last thing I remember is a big crash on my head. It felt like the whole world came down on my head. I remember waking up and thinking lord my God that must have been the biggest come I ever had. I remember them picking me up and taking me to a police car. I can't move my hands they are cuffed. I don't know what the hell happened to me. It was not until much later until I figure it out. You know what happened?

Interviewer: No I do not. Please tell me what happened.

Respondent: Well it was like this. There was some Goddamn 19 year old kid fucking his broad in the barn. They hear the goings on outside and instead of getting scared and running away the cocksucker sneaks up behind me and crowns me on the head with a quart beer bottle. No wonder I went out like a light. The son of a bitch never gave me a chance to explain. And he had been doing the same thing! If I had caught him in the barn I sure as hell would not have tried to break his head. I would let him alone. Anyway he called the police on his C.B. I never

did find out where he had his car hid. I sure never saw it. Well I did not have a leg to stand on. The woman was half naked and had a cut lip and black eye. My cock was out, and there were two witnesses. She claimed rape and I swear I never got in her. But all the evidence looked against me. This is the first time for me. I have pushed a few women around before when I got the urge and fucked them. But I never hurt them and they never said nothing about it. I don't think this woman would have either if that prick had not hit me over the head. What right did he have to do that? I never did nothing to him. I never saw him before. I guess I just got unlucky.

QUESTIONS FOR DISCUSSION

1. How do you think the continuing feminist movement will affect the attitudes our society has toward rape? Do you foresee the definition of rape changing as society changes?

2. Men rationalize rape because "they see them [women] as objects of exploitation." How should we go about destroying this attitude? How has the role of women contributed to the acceptance of this rationalization?

3. Since rape is viewed as an expression of attitude rather than as a single act, how must society initiate action to prevent rape?

4. How did the attitudes the rapist had toward women, sex, and relationships in general contribute to his actions?

5. What are some similarities and differences between sexual offenses and nonsexual physical offenses such as murder? Could the same sociological theories and causal patterns account for both?

BANK ROBBERY: A FEELING OF REAL POWER *As told to James K. Skipper, Jr. and William L. McWhorter*

Interviewer: When did you first get involved in crime?

Respondent: My mother and father were separated when I was a little kid. I was put in a foster home when I was four. I don't remember how many different homes I was in about 9 or 10 I would guess. I didn't like school and stayed away whenever I could get away with it. I didn't get along with the teachers and I was always getting in trouble. The teachers thought for a while I was retarded and put me in a class for retarded children. That didn't help much and when I was 12 I got sent to reform school. I had not committed any crime although by that time I was hanging around with some guys who had.

Interviewer: What was the reason you were sent to reform school?

Respondent: I think it was because I was too much of a problem for the teacher and the school. They wanted to get rid of me. They were pretty sure I was smoking pot which I was, but they never caught me, not even selling it. They sent me to reform school for smoking, ordinary smoking in school. I used to light up in the class when I felt like it. I did it so many times they finally got fed up and got rid of me. I think the official reason was they called me a fire menace and a bad influence on the other kids.

Interviewer: Were you selling pot at this time?

Respondent: Yes, but only on a small scale. I was pretty young at the time. I got the stuff from some of the older guys who were really into it. I didn't make much money. There is a limit to how much of that stuff you can peddle around a grade school. The authorities would like you to believe it is a big problem. First they don't have any money. You never get any repeat customers. Most of them get sick as a dog when they try it. I ended up using half the stuff myself. But I suppose you can say that was my start in

a career of crime, if you consider that a crime. I have always thought of it as providing a service.

Interviewer: What was it like being in reform school?

Respondent: Well, I was there for 4 years until I was 16 and they had to let me go. I hated it the whole time. It is not as bad as prison, but damn close. I didn't learn a thing in the school. I hated the whole bit. I just decided there was nothing they could teach me so I just made myself not listen to them and I refused to do the work. I think they thought I was retarded too. I was a little guy and a loner. I used to get the hell beat out of me by the other boys until I started to grow. Then I learned to defend myself and they left me alone after that. I would say the only thing reform school did for me was make me be tough and determined that I was going to get back at people when I got out. When I got out I started working for the guys in the dope rackets. I worked hard, they liked me and I started making good money for a kid. I really felt like I was somebody. I was showing people this was no dumb retarded kid. Once I almost got busted. I got scared, I sure didn't want to go to prison. I thought, well, I have some money saved up, maybe I will go straight. So I got a job as a car salesman. I found out right away they are the biggest crooks in the world. They lie all the time and cheat every customer they can. That's the only way they can make money. It is not so bad with new cars. At least people get new cars even though they get overcharged. Used cars is a different story. The dealers only fix up those things which the customer can see. They really don't try to make them safe and in good running order. Why I have seen cars sold where they knew the brakes wouldn't last 1,000 miles and they never told the customer. I couldn't do that, I just couldn't. I have done a lot of illegal things in my life, but I never did them with the idea in mind

This interview is contributed by James K. Skipper, Jr. and William L. McWhorter.

I was going to hurt someone. Sometimes it happens, but it was a mistake. It was not planned that way it just happens. There is also a lot of cheating going on in servicing of cars. Sometimes people pay for servicing that was never done, or things were not checked out. Other times, they charge for new parts when used parts were put in. The profit is fantastic. The owners never know the difference. I think the car business is the biggest rip off of all time. They really get away with murder. I mean that. Did you ever hear of a car dealer getting charged with a crime? Of course not, they have been getting away with it for years and I suppose they will continue to. Well that kind of business is just not for me.

Interviewer: What did you do after that?

Respondent: I kicked around for awhile, a few odd jobs like that. Really not very much, I just enjoyed life for awhile. Course I did peddle a little pot on the side just for the hell of it. Then I just ran out of money and got in the drug racket full time for about 2 years before I got busted. They gave me three years. I had a pretty hard time in prison. I don't like rules. I did not follow them on the outside. I figured why the hell should I follow them on the inside. Again I was a loner. I didn't make any friends at first. I just fought everyone, other prisoners, guards, the warden, everyone. So I did a lot of "hole time" that's solitary. You know there is not a lot of love in prison it is all hate. You get to hate everyone and everything at first. Then you begin to figure out if you are going to survive you got to have something to hold on to. The ones that don't, don't survive.

Interviewer: What was it you held on to?

Respondent: What was it that I held on to? Well, it was like this. I held on to the belief that I was going to get out someday even if I didn't get paroled which I had no chance for since I screwed up so much. When I got out I was never going to get caught again. I was going to smart up and do some big things. That is what kept me going. I decided I was going to get into something where I was more on my own and I could feel like I was somebody. Dope peddlers really are not thought of much by other cons. Besides if you are not in at the top, you never get the big money and when the squeeze is on you always take the rap. The guys in the organization make all the money and you get the peanuts until the heat's on and then you get the shit and they just get another sucker to push for them.

Interviewer: You said you wanted to get into something with more status. Don't dope peddlers have very high status?

Respondent: They think they do when they are outside and in the business, but you find out you don't when you are in prison and are with all types of cons. You see, when you are outside you only know the guys in your line of action. You don't get to meet all types, in prison you do. In prison, there is a kind of an up and down ladder by which you judge guys. It goes like this: At the very bottom you got the stoolies. It does not matter what type their action was outside. If they squeal or rat on a con they are a stoolie. Next you have child molesters. Everybody hates their guts because nobody understands why they did what they did. Not much above them are the guys who are in for rape. You see with both the child molester and rapists there is no profit in it. If you get caught you got a lot of years, but if you do not get caught, you got nothing going for you. You got no profit. Then come petty thieves, the pickpocket, shoplifter, guys who tried to knock off a gas station or a grocery store. It is all small time stuff. You take a big risk for not getting much. There is not much percentage in it. Next come the drug pushers. They are about average on the ladder. They might be higher, but many of them are addicts too. I was not until I got in prison. That's when I got started. But then I figure you got a good reason for taking drugs. Next up are the con men, the fast talkers. I don't know why they are up so high. I never liked any of them much. Safe crackers are high. They really have a skilled trade. They are admired. They got a chance to make it big. Usually they are not bad guys to know. Very high are the bank robbers. You have to have skill for that too. Besides it takes real guts to do jobs like that. Not only do you get rich quick you get fame out of it. What you did gets written up in the papers. Word gets around that you were one of the guys in on the job. Of course you have got to deny it you don't want nobody to rat on you, but people usually know. At the top are the big men in the syndicate. They are the ones with the big bucks and do the planning.

Everybody treats them with respect, and you better if you know what is good for you.

Interviewer: Was it the status that made you want to become a bank robber?

Respondent: Well yes, but not altogether. Everybody likes to be admired, but that was only part of it. I thought the payoff was greater for less risk than pushing dope. Hell, there is a Goddamn crusade against pushers. They are really out to get you. It is almost like a religion with the police. It was like they are thinking they are saving the community or something everytime they catch a pusher. It is not that way with a bank robbery. Sure, they try to find out who did it. And if they do fine, but if they don't they don't sweat it. I guess they figure the bank was insured anyway so what the hell. That is if no one got hurt. If you shoot someone that's different and if you kill someone they are likely to really be on your tail. And, whatever you do, don't shoot a policeman. That's murder. I mean it. Then they never are going to let you alone. Besides what appealed to me about robbing banks is that you are more or less on your own. You call the shots. You decide when you are going to do it and how. You don't spend half your life taking orders. And hell you are not hurting anybody. Nobody loses when you rob a bank. All the people who got their money in the bank they still got it. They don't lose, neither does the bank because they are insured. The insurance company does not lose either they just raise their rates a little bit. It's not like sticking up a gas station and grabbing the cash right out of the guy's pocket. He's got to pay for that. You really stung him. It is like taking the food right off his table. You rob a bank you take the money out and spend it. You put it back in circulation. That is good for everybody. Instead of stealing from people you buy things from them. They make a profit too.

Interviewer: How does one learn how to become a bank robber?

Respondent: I don't know how other people do it. What I did once I decided that is what I wanted to do, was to get to know the bank robbers in prison. I tried to learn everything I could from them. There is not much to do in prison and if you put your mind to it you can learn a lot from the other cons. Once you get to know them they don't mind telling you about their capers. What is really important is to learn how they were caught and what mistakes they made. That way you figure you won't make the same mistakes and won't get caught. I also learned some contacts to use on the outside but they never helped me much.

Interviewer: Is it safe to say that prison was not helpful in reforming you?

Respondent: Of course prison did not reform me. Confinement is useless in changing anyone's behavior as far as going straight is concerned. Prison teaches you to be tough, to be smart, smart enough not to get caught again. If a guy is going to go straight he decides that when he gets caught and they send him to prison. He decides before they ever take him in. Being in prison does not do that. The decision is made before that. Although I seen some guys who come in with the attitude that they are not going to do things the same. They are going to change their ways. Then after they are in for awhile they change and say what the hell once a con, always a con. They start making plans for doing the same thing when they get out. Prison has a negative effect. It never does anybody any good.

Interviewer: After you did your time how did you get started on your new career?

Respondent: Well, I didn't right away. Even though I thought I learned a lot in prison, and I was confident, you don't do things alone. I was young and the only guys I could get to work with me were other young kids all inexperienced. I really didn't trust them. So I waited and let it be known that I was interested. In the meantime I held up a liquor store. I did it more to show people I was ready and had the guts than for the money. Shortly after that I got some offers to knock off some liquor stores, but I said no I didn't want to get in the habit. I was looking for banks. Finally, I got my chance. Three guys asked me if I would drive the getaway car for them when they hit a bank. I figured this was it, I was on my way. I was not in on the planning. They told me to lay low and they would get in touch with me when I was needed. Hell, I was not told when or where. I just waited for two weeks then it happened. I got the word just about an hour before we left. One of the guys was with me the whole time after I knew where and when we were going. They were taking the necessary precautions with a new guy. The robbery went off OK and I was where I was supposed to be at the right time with the car. I got $1,000 for that and a promise of more the next time. I drove 4 maybe 5 times for those guys. Last time out I got a little over $2,000 for about 30 minutes work. You see you got to work your way up in the business. The lowest spot is the guy who drives the car. The next step is to be one of the guys who goes into the bank. The highest man on the ladder is the guy who gets the money from the teller. The person who is really Mr. Big is the guy who does the planning. Sometimes he comes on the caper and sometimes he does not. If he is really big, he is nowhere close to the bank when you hit it. He has got an alibi all set up. We were not that big.

Interviewer: How did you feel the first time you went on a job?

Respondent: I was scared the first time I drove the car. My hands were shaking on the wheel while I was waiting for them to come out. It seemed like it took them an hour in there. I kept thinking this is it, this is it, this what you been waiting for, don't blow it, don't blow it. Before I knew it, they were out, in the car, changing clothes and we were home free. I really didn't get excited until it was all over. Then it was difficult waiting for the next time.

Interviewer: Did you ever plan the jobs yourself?

Respondent: Yes and no, I never planned them all by myself. After I had been at it for about a year I got in with another gang. By that time I had worked my way up. I was no longer the driver. Then I was in on the set up from the start. We had a scheme going following armored cars. We figured out when banks had a lot of cash on hand and hit them at that time. Gosh, I remember the first time I went into a bank with a gun in my hand. It was a thrill. Let me tell you what a thrill. All those people standing around shaking in their boots not knowing what you are going to do. And then all that money coming out. The feeling of real power. I mean really having power over both people and money. It was the ultimate high. Just standing there holding that gun and watching what was happening. There was something sexual about it. I got an erection right there in the bank. I came close to coming right there in my pants. The guys kidded me about it afterwards. They

said they didn't know which gun I was going to shoot!

Interviewer: Did you have a sexual reaction every time you robbed a bank?

Respondent: No, just that first time. But I always got a hard on the night before a job just thinking about what it was going to be like. I always needed a woman as soon as I could get one after the job was over. I can't explain to you what a high it is when you hit a bank. It sure beats any type of drug you can think of.

Interviewer: Did you ever run into any difficulty in any of the banks?

Respondent: Just once. You see if you got the job planned right and everyone cooperates nothing is going to go wrong. You don't want any trouble if you can help it. What you do first is scare the hell out of everybody right away and wave your guns around. Then when you got them in a state of shock, you have got to make sure they understand that you don't want to hurt them. All you want is the money. If they cooperate, they won't get hurt. Most of the time it works if you know what you are doing and don't run into any hero types. Once just as we were about to leave the bank a woman screamed and would not stop. I tried to shut her up by hitting her across the side of the head with my pistol. It went off and hit some guy in the arm on the other side of the bank. I did not mean to do that. It was an accident. It would not have happened if the woman hadn't screamed. In 34 robberies that is the only time I ever hurt someone.

Interviewer: Under what circumstances did you finally get caught and arrested?

Respondent: Well, there really were no circumstances at all. We didn't make any mistakes and we really didn't get caught. What happened was it was like this. It was real simple and real stupid. One of the 4 guys I was working with was living with this chick and one night he got drunk and slapped her around quite a bit. She got pissed and went straight to the cops. She was so mad she spilled everything about everybody. Why she did that I don't know. She did not stand to gain anything, but we sure stood to lose a lot. As for me, they came to my apartment one afternoon with a warrant. It was almost two months since the robbery. I thought it had long been forgotten. They found over $15,000 in cash in my dresser and from then on it was downhill.

They got one of the guys to confess and that was that. I got 6 years.

Interviewer: Did you serve the full 6 years?

Respondent: No I got out on parole after 4 years. I decided to just do my time. I was kind of depressed. It was hard for me to believe I was back in the jug again. I kept thinking I did not do anything wrong to get caught. It was not my fault, but hell you have got to work with other people and you got to trust someone otherwise you can't pull it off. But when you trust them you lose control. That's what happened to me. So I decided when they put me in that time I will try to go straight for awhile. I got going to the prison school and found I kind of liked it. It beat working. I earned a high school diploma. Would you believe that? Now I am out on parole and am taking college courses. I kind of like it. I may be able to make it going straight. You know I really don't have much to show for those years in jail. Sure I robbed a lot of banks but the money was not all that good. I didn't save a penny. You got to start thinking about the rest of your life. If I get caught again, God only knows how many years they will send you up for. That is nothing to look forward to and something always to be afraid of. I hope to go straight but I can't guarantee it. We will just have to wait and see.

QUESTIONS FOR DISCUSSION

1. What circumstances give rise to crime career patterns in youth? How are these patterns continued into adulthood?

2. Compare the organizational structure of bank robbery to that of a socially accepted profession.

3. How are the types of criminal acts and the skills involved related to the status hierarchy of the criminal world? Is it a linear relationship?

4. What reflection does the statement "once a con, always a con" have on our current prison system? What might be a more successful way of dealing with criminal offenders?

5. What role does trust, or lack of it, play in the criminal's mind and subculture?

A VICTIM OF CIRCUMSTANCE? As told to James K. Skipper, Jr. and William L. McWhorter

Interviewer: Could you tell me a little about yourself—how old you are, where you are from, and about your family?

Respondent: There isn't much to tell. I am 20 years old. I come from Norfolk, Virginia. I went to junior high school before I quit. My parents separated when I was young and my grandmother raised me in Norfolk, Virginia. I got six sisters and one brother. I don't remember much about my parents. I did not see them much. Like I said my grandmother raised me. I think my father was a longshoreman or something like that.

Interviewer: Why did you quit school?

Respondent: Oh it was not that bad, but I preferred to work. Besides I got pregnant in high school and dropped out. Later after I had the baby I got married to a hospital aide. But it did not work out. We separated and I started working as an aide in a hospital. Then I started working as a cashier.

Interviewer: Why are you in prison?

Respondent: I committed a crime. It was armed robbery. You see I was doing OK in my job, but then I went to the doctor once and found out that I might have cancer of the brain and that sort of upset me and I quit my job and wanted to go to California to meet my brother. Then there was this guy who was in the Navy who I cared for a lot. He wanted to go with me. My brother had sent me money. But this guy's car had complications and had to be fixed. So we had to wait, and it was too late at night to start out. I had given up my apartment. So he says let's go to a motel for the night. So we go to a Sheraton. We don't have any intentions of robbing it. But as we walk in he says, "Why don't we just rob this hotel?" I looked at him and said, "Is this for real?" I thought we were just going to spend the night.

Interviewer: You mean you had no intentions of robbery before you entered the motel?

Respondent: That's right it was just an impulse thing. We just walked up to the cash register and he pulled out a weapon and asked for the money. We had never talked about it before that. It just happened like that. We asked for all their money and they opened the cash register and gave it to us and we put it in an overnight case. Nobody tried to stop us. Nobody said anything. There were just two people behind the desk. There was nobody else around. I think they were scared. We just walked out and got in the car.

Interviewer: How did you feel about it? Were you scared?

Respondent: No I wasn't scared. I was nervous and kind of excited. I had never done anything like that before. I was excited about it.

Interviewer: What did you do when you got back in the car?

Respondent: We lit out for the Hampton tunnel, but before we could get more than about a mile the police were after us. We could see them in the distance and hear their siren. I told him to stop and give up, cause I didn't want to go to jail. I figured we might have a chance if we just gave up right then. I had never been to jail before and sure didn't want to go. But he would not stop. He tried to make a U turn and the car hit a pole and came to a stop. We got out and started to run. In the panic and rush I left my purse in the car, but we had the overnight case with the money. We came to this tall fence and it was hard to climb. In going over I fell and messed up my face. I got some pretty bad scars from it. We ran and ran until we came to this apartment building. We ran up to an apartment and R——— knocked on the door. When no one came right away he just kicked the door open. A man and his wife were standing there. The man says, "What the hell do you want?" R——— says, "Someone is after us and we need a car bad." The man says he does not have one. We

---

This interview is contributed by James K. Skipper, Jr. and William L. McWhorter.

should go to apartment A. So we race down to apartment A. R——— knocks on the door. No one comes right away, so he kicks that door open. So there is this girl, a white girl and she is pregnant. I didn't know it then but she was in her ninth month. She looked very frightened. We told her that we were not going to harm her, but we needed a place to stay for a while because people were after us. She must have had a lot of faith in God because she helped us. She helped me clean my face up. Then she gave us some old clothes to put on. So we asked her if she had a car because we needed transportation bad. She said she didn't have a car but the man downstairs had one. She took us down there and as it turns out R——— knows the guy. They were in the Navy together, R——— tells him what's happening and about the police and everything. So T——— says I will help you get out of town. He hid us in the back of his van and put some blankets over us. By then it was 4:00 a.m. but the police were still out on the streets looking for us. T——— told us to stay down while we're riding past them. We rode until we got to Military Highway and the policeman stopped the van and asked T——— if he had seen anybody trying to get away. T——— told him no and he was getting ready to let him go on but then one policeman wanted to check the back of the van. I knew it was all over then. The police opened the door, saw us and said, "Get the fuck out. We got you, you damn bastards." I nearly shit I was so scared. I thought they were going to shoot. But they didn't treat me brutal or nothing. They just slapped me around a bit. They put us in the police car and took us down to the station.

Interviewer: What happened when you got to the police station?

Respondent: They questioned me. I did not know quite what to say. R——— had told me to tell them he made me do it. So I did and they made me sign this statement that I would cooperate with them.

Interviewer: You admitted that you had committed the robbery?

Respondent: I guess so, but I really did not think of it that way at the time. I was plenty scared. I didn't know what was going to happen. I just said he made me do it.

Interviewer: Did you have a trial?

Respondent: Yes, there were two trials. One was for armed robbery and the other was for breaking and entering. R——— was tried separate from me. The first trial was for the robbery. There was no jury or anything just this white judge. My lawyer had me plead not guilty. But the judge found me guilty and gave me 16 years with 10 suspended.

Interviewer: Did you think the judge was fair with you?

Respondent: Definitely not. He was prejudice cause I was black and poor. I didn't have any record before and we didn't hurt anybody. How could he give me 16 years? They got all the money back didn't they? It was not fair at all. And my lawyer said the judge had considered giving me 25. He thought he was being easy on me. Can you believe that? I became very bitter about everything after that. I mean I might as well have planned the robbery in the first place. I couldn't have got worse.

Interviewer: Were you put in jail after the trial?

Respondent: Yes, I was in jail for about 5 months until my trial for breaking and entering came up. I was pretty hardened up by then and I knew what to expect. They were not going to listen to me. They were just going to stick it to me.

Interviewer: Did they?

Respondent: They sure did. No jury again, there was just this white judge. I plead not guilty. After all I did not knock the door down. The judge he don't listen. He just gives me 5 more years with two suspended. Then they sent me to this prison.

Interviewer: Have you been in this prison ever since?

Respondent: No. After about a year I got out on a work release program. But I got charged with possession of marijuana. It was not fair. I was in this girl's apartment with some friends and the police came in and found some pot on the floor. It was not mine, but the others said I was the one that brought it in so they charged me with possession. I had never seen it before. But I had the record so they got me for it. When we went before the judge there was no proof so he dismissed the charges.

Interviewer: Did you feel this was a fair judge?

Respondent: Not really, he just figured I was going back to prison anyway and he might as well get somebody else.

Interviewer: Do you think you will be able to get a parole?

Respondent: No I don't get along very well in this place. It is too routine. There are no changes. There is nothing to do. Besides I don't get along with most of the other girls. I have gotten into a couple of scrapes when they have tried to "make" me. I don't go for that crap. I have just protected myself. But it does not give me a very good record. I would rather not go into it anymore.

Interviewer: When all is said and done, how do you account for your present circumstances?

Respondent: Well I got a raw deal. I was a victim of circumstances. I am no criminal. I had never done anything wrong before the robbery. It was all chance done on the spur of the moment. I just went along with things. We did not plan no robbery it just happened. I didn't even do anything. R——— did it all. I just happened to be with him. We did not hurt anybody and the money was returned. So what's so wrong? I made a mistake, sure, but to go to prison? That's injustice. To suffer through all this. They were all prejudice against me. I am very bitter about what happened. That is all I have to say.

Interviewer: Just one last question. If you had gotten away with the robbery, what would you have done then?

Respondent: I don't know. I had better not say anymore.

QUESTIONS FOR DISCUSSION

1. What role did the situation have in this particular case? What other causal factors may be pinpointed, and what is their role compared to the situational characteristics?

2. Do you think she was unfairly sentenced? Why or why not? How might her sex and race have affected the judge's decision?

3. What actions might the girl have taken to prevent her participation in these illegal acts, which would have consequently kept her out of prison?

4. What type of future exists for a girl who has been through experiences such as this? How have they shaped the attitudes and biases she now possesses?

5. Do you think that this girl's delinquency may be attributed to the widespread causal explanation of the "malignant home situation"? Explain why or why not.

Section III   **NONVIOLENT CRIME**

In the preceding section we considered three types of lawbreaking that the person on the street thinks of as "crime." Although crimes of violence are the ones of concern to most people, they actually contribute little to the overall criminality in our society. The great bulk of the crime problem in this country consists of various forms of property offenses. The old notion that crime does not pay simply is not true. If we examine criminal statistics we find that Americans are committing millions of property crimes and gaining very handsomely from them.

In a society where material goods and property are highly prized it is not surprising that a number of criminal statutes centering on their violation have been enacted. In this section we examine two of the more traditional forms of property crimes, forgery and burglary. In addition to these, two other more subtle and invidious forms of nonviolent crimes, bookmaking and bribery, are also presented.

One of the most prominent developments in criminology in the past several decades has centered about the concept of "white collar crime," Edwin H. Sutherland's term for violation of the laws designed to regulate business affairs. More recently, the term has been extended and expanded to include "respectable" persons who violate the law. *Respectable* is used in the sense that these people are often able to escape the stigmas associated with criminals, may evade public censure, and most likely can continue to be "respectable." The number of women committing white collar offenses appears to be gaining parity with men although women are not equally involved when all forms of crime are considered. This growing involvement in white collar crime may well be a reflection of the increasing social equality of females resulting from the women's movement of the past decade.

The section "Forging Drug Prescriptions: A White Collar Crime" is an excellent view not only of white collar criminality but of a specific form of nonviolent criminal behavior—forgery. In accounting for the forgery behavior, one may refer to the work of Edwin Lemert for explanations. His work on forgers suggests that forgery "arises at a critical point in a process of social isolation, out of certain types of social situations, and is made possible by the closure or constriction of behavior alternatives subjectively held as available to the forgery" (Lemert, 1953: 296). Marital disruption appears to play a particularly critical role as an isolating experience, for about 40 percent of the forgers were divorced or separated. This selection is an excellent example of Lemert's "situational deviance," in that the behavior may be accounted for in terms of processes operating at or near the moment of criminality rather than as a historical development of earlier events. Although earlier experiences may obviously contribute to the forgery behavior, such behavior cannot be separated from the problems of the immediate situation that confronts the person.

If we were to construct a status hierarchy of criminal offenders, the professional criminal would certainly be placed among those in the top echelons. The success of the professional criminal depends largely on extraordinary skill, specialization, planning, and highly structured group activity. In order to be successful, the criminal not only has to be surrounded by a supportive group structure but also must acquire a "criminal philosophy" through which he or she can rationalize behavior.

As Bell (1953) so ably pointed out, crime is a group activity in which a number of actors are symbiotically intertwined. Thus, the role of the professional thief is inexorably bound up with the world of fences, fixes, bail bondsmen, corrupt judges, and police on the take. Of these, the fix appears to be of singular importance to the success of the professional criminal.

In the selection "The Thief and the Law," the crucial role of the fix is clearly highlighted. In some cases, the fix is nothing more than a bribe to forestall police interference, but more often it is used after the thief has been apprehended. Here the fix takes on a decidedly different role in that the major purpose is to obtain a reduction of charges or a lighter sentence. As the article points out, there are a number of variables over which the thief has no control that will determine the success of the fix. Thus, the selection once again reaffirms that attorneys, bondsmen, police, judges, politicians, and other ostensibly legitimate persons, in their role as fixers, give color and texture to the portrait of professional criminality in our society.

One of the most persistent features of American society is the moral ambivalence we feel regarding our view of ourselves as both a frontier community where "everything goes" and, at the same time, a small town where blue laws are created and enforced. Nowhere has this paradox been more evident than in our approach to gambling. Americans may gamble illegally (except in a few states), but they do not, in their hearts, believe it to be evil or wicked. Although one may debate the pros and cons of gambling (some $20 billion per year are illegally wagered), it is the backbone of organized crime and as such provides seed money for loan sharking, hijacking, labor racketeering, and narcotics.

In the selection "Bookmaking," the dynamics of this most popular form of gambling are examined. The bookie is simply a businessperson responding to the normal market forces of supply and demand. Because the bookie operates in an illegal atmosphere, he is much more vulnerable in that normal avenues of credit and protection are closed off. In this article several prominent themes are developed that help us understand "making book." Among these are: (1) the tremendous advantage the bookie has over on-track betting; (2) the financial skill and acumen that are needed to survive, including such techniques as extension of credit and lay-off betting; (3) the organizational and interpersonal skills necessary to set up shop and attract and retain clients; and (4) an understanding and appreciation of the symbiotic relationship that develops between the bookie and the police, his clients, his runners, and in some cases organized crime.

Armed robbery accounts for the largest volume of property crimes, but burglaries are the second greatest contributors to the crime index in the United States. This offense is defined by the FBI as "burglary, house breaking, safecracking, or any breaking or unlawful entry of a structure with the intent to commit a felony or a theft." Like other property offenses, burglaries are committed by professionals and amateurs alike. There is a great possibility that those engaging in this type of crime will escape, since in most cases no contact is made with victims who could identify the offender. Three-fourths of the burglaries in 1978 involved forcible entry; of this total, residential burglaries accounted for almost two-thirds.

In the selection "A Case of Burglary," some of the characteristics of the burglar are presented. Among the most obvious is the fact that the overwhelming majority of burglaries are committed by young (85 percent are under 25) males (94 percent). There is considerable literature on the professional burglar, focusing on techniques, acquired skills, habits, and the social structure of the "fence," "fix," "tipster," "good people," and "solid dudes." With few exceptions, the amateur burglar is a neglected area of study.

The present selection gives some insight into the emerging career of an amateur burglar. Perhaps the most prominent theme is the rational and utilitarian aspects of the thefts. He stole in order to become a more effective competitor in the youth culture, that is, to have spending money, to buy sharp clothes, to play pool, to date, or simply to drink chocolate cokes at the local drugstore. The jaundiced view of the adult world, in which everybody is either a crook or a sucker or out to make a buck, was reinforced when he discovered the exaggerated insurance claims made by his victim and the gullibility of the police who actually believed his smooth, well-practiced lies.

References

Bell, Daniel
  1953 "Crime as an American Way of Life." *Antioch Review* 13 (June): 131–154.
Lemert, Edwin M.
  1953 "An Isolation and Closure Theory of Naive Check Forgery." *Journal of Criminal Law, Criminology and Police Science* 44 (September–October): 296–307.
Sutherland, Edwin H.
  1940 "White Collar Criminality." *American Sociological Review* 5 (February): 1–12.
  1937 *The Professional Thief*. Chicago: University of Chicago Press.

FORGING DRUG PRESCRIPTIONS: A WHITE COLLAR CRIME As told to
James K. Skipper, Jr. and William L. McWhorter

Interviewer: I understand you are a registered nurse.

Respondent: Yes, that is correct.

Interviewer: Well, then you understand what I mean when I say we would like to have you give us your background history.

Respondent: Yes I do. You stop me if I get too detailed. I was born and went to school, I mean through high school in West Virginia. I came from a small family just my brother and me. Sometimes we lived with my parents and sometimes when my father was away, he was a coal miner, we lived with my grandparents. My childhood was a happy one. (I suppose you are interested in that.) I went to the University of Virginia School of Nursing for 4 years and got married in school. Afterwards I worked for an ophthalmologist in Charlottesville and had a baby. We lived in Richmond for a while, I had another baby, and then we went to Rhode Island. I worked as a nurse and my husband was an accountant. After I divorced my first husband I lived in West Virginia for a while. I was Director of Nurses at a hospital at Logan. I moved to Massachusetts and was an Assistant Director of Nursing at a hospital near Boston. I got married again to a psychiatrist who was from Turkey. We had some problems adjusting because of the differences in cultural backgrounds. We got divorced. I came back and worked as Director of Nursing at a hospital in Lebanon, Virginia. Then I went back to school in Richmond to get a degree in hospital administration. I got married again to a man with a doctor's degree in education. I started working at the teaching hospital in Richmond in the Quality Assurance Program. That is about all I guess.

Interviewer: With your education and background how is it that you are in prison for narcotics violations?

Respondent: Just stupidity.

Interviewer: Can you describe the events that occurred?

Respondent: Well, it really had to do with my third husband. It is very painful to talk about. Before we got married my third husband was living in West Virginia. He was the owner of a drugstore and his second wife was a pharmacist. She took an overdose of drugs and alcohol and died. He sold the store and moved to Virginia and we got married. I did not know he was an alcoholic and the first year we'd been married he didn't work at all, he just stayed home and I worked. I would come home and find him very, very intoxicated. And the children locked outside the apartment. The children had been beaten, it was just hell. I never knew what to expect. I would go to the hospital and he would be drunk and he'd call the hospital and say he was going to kill himself, I had to come right home. I was really in a very bad mood. I would try to go to work and school three nights a week, and take care of the house. My son was 8 and was doing very badly in school and his father in Alabama wanted him to come live with him so I decided to let him go and he went for about three months but he was very homesick and he wanted to come back. When my husband found out about it he just went berserk! He got drunk for seven or eight days and he just went on a real rampage and he would beat us up, lock us out of the house and everything. Shortly after that time, one day I went shopping and I met this friend who I used to know from my first husband and he asked me to go to lunch with him. I went to lunch with him and he told me he was having a bad love affair and I said I would give him some nerve pills if he wanted me to. And I gave him some medicine I had at home which my husband had brought from his drugstore.

Interviewer: Do you know what they were?

Respondent: Yea, they were valium. Very

This interview is contributed by James K. Skipper, Jr. and William L. McWhorter.

mild valium. We had a whole batch of stuff we brought a whole suitcase of stuff, controlled drugs. About a week after that this man came to the hospital and asked me to go to lunch with him again but instead of going to lunch he took me to his apartment and he made some threats on my life and my children's lives if I didn't give 'em a whole lot of drugs. I told him I would give him some dexedrine, we had some dexedrine at home. He said no, I don't want that, I want praline and if you don't have it I know that you know how to write prescriptions. If you write me some prescriptions and get me that drug, I won't kill your kids. The frame my mind I was in was such that I was not thinking logically and this really just terrified me. I forged some prescriptions and gave him the drugs and I was arrested by the vice squad and I found out that he was working undercover for the vice squad. I was arrested and they told me that if I would cooperate with them and tell them about a drug ring at the hospital they would not prosecute. I didn't know anything about a drug ring so I was prosecuted. I ended up getting sentenced to 20 years with eight years suspended.

Interviewer: What were your feelings at this time?

Respondent: After I was arrested, I was in complete shock. I had never been arrested in my life, I never had even a misdemeanor charge and I was taken to the Richmond city jail and I was shocked with the questions they were throwing at me in front of all these people. Members of the vice squad kept saying, well we have you now, there's no use in denying it. You might as well tell us what we want. I kept asking for an attorney and they kept saying, you gonna sign these papers for us. I never got an attorney, finally they let me call my husband who by then was working for about three months. He came to the jail and they told him I was conspiring to murder him and that his wife was dangerous and he better go home and forget her. So he went home and got drunk, while they kept questioning me about the drug ring at the hospital. If there was a drug ring at the hospital I sure didn't know about it. But they would not believe me.

Interviewer: Did you ever get a lawyer?

Respondent: I got a lawyer several days later. The attorney I happened to get had just graduated from law school and this was his first case. He made a lot of fantastic promises which he could not come through with. I paid him $4500. I had written 13 prescriptions and I was up on 13 separate charges. Ten were misdemeanor charges and 3 were felony charges. I went to court first on the misdemeanor charges and got sentenced to 46 months. The attorney did not do a thing for me. He just took my money. I just really flipped out. I thought my God if I got this on misdemeanor charges what are they going to do to me on the felony charges? So I got rid of that attorney and got another one. He charged me another $4500 and told me the other lawyer screwed things up so badly that if I didn't plea bargain they were going to get me for 30 years. The bargain was that if I pleaded guilty to the lesser two felony charges they would drop the third charge which could have resulted in the most years.

Interviewer: What did you do?

Respondent: Well, I did not know what to do. I was on nerve medication and had been admitted to a psychiatric hospital. I stayed there six weeks. During that time my husband showed up drunk a couple of times and told me he had a gun and was going to blow his brains out and all kinds of ridiculous things. I was really very upset at this point. Finally I went to court and pleaded guilty to the two felony charges. But the judge did not sentence me until two months later. In the end I got 12 years. But between my two times before the judge they put me in the city jail. It was like a zoo.

Interviewer: Could you tell me what it was like?

Respondent: It was horrible. I had never been exposed to the dereliction I saw there. There were just three cells with about 15 women in each cell. At night I was terrified. I slept with my back to the wall because I was afraid somebody was going to come up behind me and choke me to death. There was no privacy. I cried the whole time.

Interviewer: Were you sexually assaulted when you were in jail?

Respondent: No, but I was propositioned. I didn't even know what they were talking about half the time. Some girl came up to me and said "I am a stud want to make it?" I said "That's nice want to make what?" I didn't know what stud meant. The first time I saw a couple of women hugging and kissing and making each other I couldn't believe it. My mouth just fell open. I had not even thought about things like that before. There was always a lot of fighting going on also. I never saw women act like that before.

Interviewer: How were you treated by the staff?

Respondent: Well, they treated me like dirt, but I was not physically mistreated. And I have not been physically mistreated since I have been in prison. Here they treat you like you are just about the worst thing on earth. You lose your sense of identity, but they don't beat you.

Interviewer: Do you find much homosexuality going on in the prison?

Respondent: Not as much as in the city jail, but I would say 85% of this prison population has had homosexual experiences while they are here. I try to stay away from it as much as I can.

Interviewer: How about the use of drugs within the prison?

Respondent: I don't know much about it. Those in the drug culture don't advertise it to those who are not involved. I am sure there are drugs around, but I prefer not to know where they are or who is involved. It is better that way. I am not a drug user. If I had been, I don't think I would have gotten as stiff a sentence. I was in the city jail with a woman who had forged hundreds of prescriptions all over the state of Virginia and they only gave her a one year sentence. I think it was because she used the drugs herself. I think I got a stiff sentence because they convinced the judge I was part of a ring and I would not cooperate with the police. As I said before, I was not part of any ring, and I did not know of any. There was nothing I could tell them, but they did not believe me. I am a coward, I would have told them if I had known anything.

Interviewer: How did you justify writing out the prescriptions in the first place?

Respondent: I rationalized it on the basis that I was protecting myself and my children. It never occurred to me that I would be put in jail. It never occurred to me that I was breaking a big law. I did it because I just wanted this man to leave me alone. I have never, ever, done any-

thing like that before. I have had easy access to drugs in the hospitals I have worked at for years. I never did anything illegal. What hurts more than being in prison is that I lost my nursing license. I worked hard for it. I did not want to lose it.

Interviewer: When this friend of your former husband who turned out to be an informer threatened you, why didn't you call the police?

Respondent: I was scared. It sounds ridiculous, but I was frightened. Every morning I hated to get in my car thinking it was going to blow up or something. I just thought something bad was going to happen. I was not thinking rationally during this period. I was very upset with my whole family situation. I would never allow myself to get in that position again. If it happened again I would react quite differently. I would call the police. I would also react differently to my husband's problem. I would get him professional help rather than let him suffer and hurt others.

Interviewer: Did you feel you were mistreated by the police, courts, or judge?

Respondent: I don't really feel I was mistreated in the sense that I did forge the prescriptions. I feel that I do have a debt to pay to society. But I think spending a year here is enough. I should be allowed out on parole and pay the rest of my debt to society by working for the community in some capacity. In here I am useless to society. I am deeply concerned about the number of people in prison with long sentences. The public does not really know what prisons are like. I never gave a second thought to people in prisons. I figured if you are there you deserve to be there. Now I know there are many legitimate complaints by inmates. There is no rehabilitation in prison. There are too many opportunities to be exposed to things that reinforce previous behavior. We need to find alternatives for treating persons who commit crimes. We should not keep building more and more prisons because there can be no rehabilitation in prison.

Interviewer: Do you feel the courts took into consideration the particular facts of your case?

Respondent: I don't think they considered the circumstances of my case at all. It was very situational. I was having real problems with my husband being drunk and all, and the threats to my life. I was in bad condition and not thinking rationally. I had no previous record. I had been around drugs in my work for sixteen years and not done anything like that before. Why all of a sudden should I have done it? They never seemed to think of that. When I went to court the second time I was heavily medicated. In fact I was just stoned. I don't think that helped much. Besides they thought I was part of a drug ring.

Interviewer: What do you think will be the hardest type of adjustment you will have to make when you leave prison?

Respondent: I think the hardest thing for me to do will be to face people and tell them where I have been. It is very hard for me to say I have been in prison, but it is something I will have to do. It is the only way I can survive reality. When I first came here, I had to get up every morning for 2 weeks and say to myself you are in prison. That was such a shock. Some people go through the whole time and never really admit where they are. I won't go around saying I have been in prison and make an announcement to everybody, but it is a thing that I can't keep hidden. My mother in West Virginia does not tell people where I am. She says that is because of the children and she does not want them to be mistreated. My family and everybody in Richmond knows, even the neighbors. My daughter hurt me very much. She is in the 10th grade. She was telling me about her boyfriends. And she says I can't tell them anything about you. I just can't tell them my mom is in prison. It is things like that that hurt the most along with losing my license to nurse.

QUESTIONS FOR DISCUSSION

1.   How did the husband's alcoholism contribute to the nurse's problem?

2.   How do you think this woman could have better handled her marital and family problems?

3.   What attitudes did the nurse have about the prison subculture? Do you think in time her attitudes will change and her involvement increase?

4.   Compare and constrast the nurse's attitudes toward prison and society to the stereotypic attitudes most people have.

5.   What sociological theory comes closest to explaining criminality of this nature? The nurse claims the circumstances were very situational. How much weight should be placed on the situational aspects of this case?

THE THIEF AND THE LAW *Harry King*

Frankly, after sitting down and analyzing it I come to the conclusion that the only people that really profit from theft is the fix, the judge, and the district attorney. They're the guys who make the money, not the guy who stole it. The guy who stole it is always getting pinched, and they're shaking him down for what he's got. I've had 'em flat pinch me on the street and shake me right down, take me in the car and shake me down and take every penny I had on me. Tell me to get out of the car. I've had that happen, and I didn't say nothing; I had no recourse.

In the old days we used to take and make a deal with the police. We knew we were going to make a deal, or the dicks knew we were going to, and they would have a lot of unsolved crimes. So, to make it easier for everybody we'd just what we called "clean the slate" for them. They'd say, "I got fifteen capers here we haven't been able to solve, will you clean them up for us?" That's all. We'd just sign a confession, I mean it wasn't really a confession. We didn't even know where these capers were. But they never used them against us or anything. It was just to clean the slate for the police department. Our attorney had probably come down and talked to us and asked us if we could do it because he wanted a favor from a policeman, or something like that. You scratch my back, I'll scratch yours. So we would go ahead and do it, knowing that they wouldn't do nothin'.

There was more principles between the thieves and the police department in those days. Now they tell me that a policeman will say yes and turn right around and do no.

When I was rooting we were very close to some policemen. In Portland we used to have to pay off 20 percent to the chief of dicks and a lot of times the guy we beat would holler for five times as much as we got and we would have to give the chief 20 percent of what they hollered for although he knew it was wrong. You see the

criminals haven't got all the rackets; the worst ones are the upright members of society.

Every town has a criminal attorney who is the fix. The jailer would tell you who the fix in town was, or the bull that pinched you because he'd get a commission from the attorney, you know, for it. Everybody wants to tell you. Especially a box man, he's usually got money so they all wanna get cut in on the action. Then they got ten percent of what the attorney gets as his fee, so you have no trouble findin' out.

The attorney will come to see you and talk to you. He asks you where you're from and usually trys to check and see if you're gonna run or not. After he talks to you a little bit why you usually know somebody that he knows, another box man around the country or something, and he'll get you out on bail, get the bail cut down, and get you out on it or take you right out that night on bail. Then you go down and see him the next day and ask him what the score is and he'll tell you it'll cost you so much to get this cut down to a petty larceny beef and that's all there is to it. It's just that simple if the town's not hot.

If the town's hot, and somebody's gotta go to the joint, if you're an outsider you're probably the one to go. But if he can beat it he flat tells you how much it'll be. He has to give the district attorney so much, and possibly the judge, not necessarily the district attorney, might be an assistant in the office that he deals with. Sometimes you can square the beef in the city court and get it dropped. And the dick, if they've got the handout why they get a piece of the action too. Everybody's got their hand out, haven't they?

You won't take off when you're out on bond because that bondsman, you see, it's like the last time, my bond was $100,000 and you didn't customarily put a thief on a $100,000 bond, but my word's good so the bondsman signed for it. You can't just take off when a guy's a right guy you

From Box Man—A Professional Thief's Journal *by Harry King as told to Bill Chambliss. Copyright 1972 by Harper and Row, Publishers. Reprinted by permission.*

just can't take and dump him by runnin' off; that would be foolish to do, because the next time you needed a bond, you wouldn't get the bond, because they're just like safemen, I mean, word gets around. Well, now I can go to New York City and tell them to call Portland and the bondsman there will tell you I'm all right. So even in New York they'll sign a bond and they'll let me out on the cuff because they know I'll go right out and go to work and get it.

Sometimes you're forced into a trial, but not usually. Only about one quarter the time. You wouldn't plead not guilty because a box man, if you're caught, you're right on the caper. They don't pick you up after. The [criminal] lawyer usually couldn't plead before a jury—I got a lawyer in Portland: I listened to him plead a case in the jury room one day and he almost hung this guy. And I told him afterwards, "If I ever have to go to a jury, don't you ever plead for me."

But if he's a fix, that's his field, you see, that's all he understands is connections. I've never found a fix that's a good trial lawyer. A fix has got it all fixed before you go to court and then the district attorney will get up and recommend this way or that way if it goes that far and you'll be granted probation, parole, or whatever they're gonna grant or ask for dismissal if you got enough money, which is a little raw so they don't very often do that. But it's all cut and dried. You know what you're gonna get before you go down to court. I've been to court hundreds of times but I've only been to prison five times.

They can't dismiss the case as a rule. It's pretty raw to do that. They suspend the sentence. They just forget about it. If you're on parole you don't necessarily stay there, it's not a good idea to stay where you were sentenced. The safe squad is usually pretty unhappy about you getting a parole and all they want to do is lock you up. Like Edgar Hoover, he says, "Commit the crime, lock him up, that's the easiest way to take care of him." And they'll roust you and give you a bad time if you've got a suspended sentence or parole, so you usually try and transfer someplace else. Of course, they don't want you there, either, as soon as they find out who you are.

Sometimes you can't get the fix. You run into places, if it is real hot. I've gone into towns and looked the town over and you don't know anybody, you don't contact anybody, and some towns never publish the crime news, outside of murder or something like that, but stickups, box jobs, they don't publish them. So you go in and you don't know whether this town is red hot and you go out and root and you get snatched. You get down there, they're looking for somebody like you and nothing in the world will save you, I don't care what kind of a connection you got. People want a clean town, so they grab the first guy that they can hang on, make a big issue out of it and send him to the joint. Everybody settles down, and "see what a pure town we got." The thieves that was really making the money, they just go on about their business.

The last time I was rootin' I used a policeman for a point man and we built such a fire in Portland, on ourselves that when they did catch us they threw everything but the book at us. You know, and the fix was absolutely useless. I hired a fix but only to cut it down. To throw some of those beefs off me. I will show ya. My bondsman down there put up a $25,000 bond for me. I was being held in the county jail. They'd caught us cold-turkey, right out on this job by accident. A paper boy got a squint at us and my partner just as we walked across in the doorway and he called the bulls and they came out and we were completely surrounded, you know, when we came out of the joint. Half of the money disappeared, in transit, but they just left us alone, you know, and let us go ahead and finish it and then come out.

Well, my lawyer came down to see me right away and he said, "I'll have Joe bail you out." Well, then, Joe was on his way up to the jail to do it when this dick that I knew came up to see me. And he told me, "They got fifty beefs down there they're going to put on you." And I said, "Man, they can't prove them beefs, none of 'em, some of them are mine and some ain't, but they can't prove them." And he said, "No, but Oregon as you know, indicts guys and lets the judge decide whether they're guilty or not." So he said, "All they've got to do is throw them down in front of the grand jury and the grand jury'll indict you." I said, "Oh, I don't think they'll do that." And Joe comes up and put his $25,000 down and before I could get out and be released, they had me on another beef at $100,000. So I bowed my neck and sent for Joe and told him, "Well, I want out." My word was good enough for him for that and he said, "All right, I'll go get the bonds and get you out." And he went down to get 'em and while he was gone, they come up and stood right there with papers for another indictment. Waiting for me to get out.

So sometimes, you got to be thrown to the lions. The district attorney will resort to that, the district attorney has to have so many convictions a year. If you created a big furor in the town. My picture was in the papers for three weeks after we got pinched. And we were Number One news. That's when they can't fix it. All you can do then is try to get all the beefs throwed off except one and go to the pen for that one. That's how come you do actually go in spite of the fix. They all are in business and they have to show some results.

And with the publicity I had, well, in fact when I beat five years off the sentence and got out on probation, there was an awful storm. Why I can't even go to Portland now. You know, without them causing trouble over it. If I was still stealing I'd tear that town apart because I know I can beat 'em for a long time, I know that. But if I was going to do that, I would go from here to down there and have guys case off those joints for me and go from here down to Portland and knock 'em off and come back here and laugh at 'em. And let 'em blow their cork. But, you can't fix some of those, you just can't. And I don't mean by that that you can't fix a murder beef because you can. You know, but sometimes the heat's on too much and you just got to go ahead and go, that's all.

There's a lot of guys that do time who get real good connections and a normal beef they can fix. Two or three box men that I know in Portland, went down the same way but they were small-time box men. When they finally really got nailed, was when they knocked off a canteen—that has all this candy business—they got quite a large sum off that. And the canteen had a lot of strength, you know, they raised so much hell about it day after day. Where the average Hoosier—he believes the police department. He goes down there and says, "Well, I was robbed last night." And he goes home and says they'll catch the thief next week. The bulls know who it was so they go out and shake the

guy down and get some dough off him or pinch him and the lawyer gets some dough, and that's all there is to it. There is no publicity. But if it's a big beef, then everybody gets interested in it because they don't like that heat on. I've seen beefs where all the thieves get mad over it because they all got to leave town over it. And they'd all be mad at the guys that done it.

I went to prison five times and each time it was the same thing, approximately. You know, too much heat. See, when I work, I work real hard. I just believe in it. I mean, it's silly to make $1,000 and go out and spend it, you're broke again. That's perpetual motion. So I don't believe that way. I say, "Well, if we're going to work, we get in a mood for everything and it is let's just keep on plowing, you know, just keep going right on down the line till we got a chunk of money, then lay off."

If you get picked up in a small town, you can deal with the D.A. personally, you know, he gets so few chances to take any dough, that when a thief comes into town, you know, why, he comes out in person and talks with him. He cuts out the attorney and everything else. I've had that happen several times, when I'd get pinched, like that. But little towns are so hard to work in because you can't case the joint off, you know. The Hoosiers know one another real well. And the bull on the beat knows everybody in town— knows where he's supposed to be and what time he's supposed to be home and what he's doing in that neck of the woods and everything else. When he sees a stranger, a couple times in a evening, why right away he begins to think. And some of those little town-clowns are pretty sharp, they've been there for a long time, they get pretty sharp. They wouldn't compete with one in the city, but they're very clever in their own districts.

To give you an illustration of the fix. Recently Danny was released from Montana on parole. He came to Seattle. A short time later he was arrested for possession of narcotics. He had a real sharp lawyer who could do business with the D.A. He went up and got the D.A. straightened around. After getting the case squared around they went to court. The judge was told that in as much as Danny was going to be violated and taken back to the joint they thought they should save time and money and drop the charge. The judge did this. Then the attorney for Danny flew over to Montana. He told the parole board that Danny was being held and tried for possession of narcotics in Seattle and that he thought they should continue Danny's parole. The parole board went along with the idea, not knowing that Danny had the charges dropped here. So consequently Danny remains on parole to this day, no charges against him or anything.

The fix does business with the district attorney and very seldom does he talk to the judge directly. Then when they go to court the judge usually goes along with the district attorney. Quite often the money that's given to the D.A. is split with the judge.

I automatically come in contact with corruption everywhere. But there is a great many people, judges, attorneys, policemen who are honest, extremely so, and I come in contact with the other kind; it is essential that I do. Any attorney I have is automatically a fix. Which 90 percent of the criminal attorneys are, nothing but fixes. They can't take a case before a jury and win. And the policemen that I know are the policemen that will take money. The judges I know, district attorneys I know are all corrupt but I don't say they are all that way. I will say a hell of a good percent of them are. But the point is you can get a fix anywhere; Salt Lake City, Los Angeles, Las Vegas, any of them. Just find a connection that's all.

To fix the average beef costs around four to five thousand dollars. It would be less for petty larceny; they're not much trouble unless they have been in the bulls' hair a lot. And if they have, they want to put him away. They won't listen, you know—nobody can fix it.

In a lot of places if two men are arrested they will come up and tell you that one is going to the joint and one is going to spring. And one of the guys is going and they have to decide who it will be. Is that justice? No, that's what is got me so mixed up. That blindfold should be really permanently tied on there.

There is no such thing as justice in criminal courts. If you've got the money you get the fix. If you haven't got the money, you don't get it. It's just that plain and that simple. A woman set fire to her home in Portland and her father's extremely wealthy. Murder is not a bailable of-fense. While this woman was in jail they passed a law allowing murder to be bailed out. She was immediately bailed out and was turned loose by the jury. She deliberately set fire to her home and burned up two or three of her children. She admitted it. It was a premeditated crime, incidentally. But she was turned loose. How can you expect these guys and kids to believe that there is justice? You can't convince these kids of that when they go up there in these detention homes five or six times. Those things have to be changed.

I'll tell you a little story that I have just seen. I'm down talking to a parole officer one day pertaining to a stabbing. He said he had to take care of it right away. He was supposed to make a presentence of this guy. He sits there and reads what little information has been given to him. He determines what recommendation he is going to make to the judge. He was supposed to have personally investigated this man. I don't condemn him because he is so crowded. But the point is that he sat right there and recommended that the man be placed on probation from what he had. That's not right. That's not the answer to it.

When I was younger and the bulls would take you in you knew right then that you were gonna get a dumping [a beating]. But that didn't do no good either. But right here in this police department they still give you a thumping. I know a friend of mine was killed for shooting at a policeman. They beat him so badly that when they sent him to Walla Walla he died. It was from that beating.

But as a whole there is police violence in Seattle only in a minor way, Portland in a minor way, San Francisco in a major way, L.A. in a major way only they take you to the outlying jails to accomplish it now where there is no danger of the newspapers getting a hold of it. But they will use the brutal methods. I've been through both sides of it; where they treat you with kid gloves and where they are brutal.

When I was a kid in the penitentiary they were very brutal. They threw you in a black hole and they left you there. If you made any noise three or four of them would come in and beat you up. It was very simple. There was just as much crime then as there is today.

The FBI doesn't break heads anymore at all.

It's an illusion that they didn't at one time. They were just as vicious as anybody was. We go through an era, you know. Edgar Hoover is a very dedicated man. He has only one thing in this world that he wants to accomplish and that's to solve the crime and put the person in jail. That's all. He doesn't believe in paroles or anything. At one time, when he first started out, he got a hold of the whip and as the boss he was a pretty vicious man. You probably don't recall, but they shot their own man one time, they were so anxious. Edgar Hoover shot at his own man one time trying to make a name for himself. They have got out of that. They have got to the point where they have become so successful that they don't need to use those methods anymore.

The only way you can beat the law is by moving all the time. The law is easy to beat as long as you keep moving all the time. But you have to continuously move. We've proved that stealing can be very profitable by moving around all the time. I'm a great one for testing out systems and we went from right here in Seattle to Miami one time and stole ourselves silly. We made a terrific amount of money but we never was pinched once because we kept right on moving. And the FBI will tell you that as long as you keep moving, it's awfully hard for them to get you. You'll notice that they never catch any of these most wanted men till they sit down someplace. As long as those guys keep moving, they can't catch them. There's nothing for you to take a hold of, you know, to get the guy. See, you got to commit crimes and keep moving and they won't get you, unless it's just an accident. But the minute you sit down they'll get you because it's the bull's job to know all the thieves in that town. That's what makes them smart dicks.

They call these guys "camera-eye dicks." Well, that's guys that look at mug-shots all the time; men wanted here and there all around the country and they look at them mug-shots and they walk out on the street and start lookin' around. That's why I never go down to skid road or nothing when I'm stealing. I never go but to the best places. 'Cause the bulls never go there. And I can go in town and stay there as long as I want—within reason—and then I'll never be bothered. Never.

I don't dress like a thief, or pimp or anything. After I grew up and began to look around,

found out that I could spot these thieves, you know, a block away the way they dressed and stuff in the old days, I quit dressing like them. I didn't think that it was so smart, anymore. I was raised in what they called the "hoodlums" in San Francisco out of 16th and Mission. It was just a collection of kids—tough kids—out there. I was the only one that wasn't tough I guess, in the whole district. But they all dressed the same. And they thought it was smart. That's when I learned not to. The bulls would come down and roust us and we didn't know how they could spot us. 'Cause we all wore the same caps and shirts. That's when I changed my style of dressing.

In the East, they stay right in one area most of the time. They stay right in New York City, it's so big. You know, they stay there. You give them a year's operation and every bull in New York will know about them, if it's in their field. But then they have the syndicate to fix it if they get busted. Out here they move around from Seattle to Portland, San Francisco to Los Angeles, Salt Lake-Phoenix, like that and it's hard for them bulls to keep up. Today they've got this teletype and stuff where they trade information and the minute they see any inkling of a guy leaving one town and going to another, they teletype it. They put that information together.

The FBI has the money to build it up and they have developed the best techniques that there are and they draw the greatest men in that field to solve a crime. They really don't have to worry anymore. Each one of their agents now is a general agent who can be turned loose on any type of crime. I wouldn't say the FBI are particularly better people. An illustration is that one of their agents in the East tried to sell some evidence that they had to some criminals. And one held up a bank in California, an ex-agent. So they are not better, but they are better with techniques. They are getting things more their way like in the fingerprint system. They are getting more laws passed that are to their benefit. This makes it easier for them to overcome laws.

If you were to read all the laws that have been sneaked in by Hoover and passed, you wouldn't believe it. You actually haven't any rights. You have violated the federal laws so many times it's pathetic. Everyone has. But in your case he doesn't want you. He wants me, the criminal. But it helps him to catch me. You would be surprised at the people who commit crimes today, businessmen who are really con men, and there is nothing they can do. Not a thing can they do to prosecute them. I'm very much against that type of crime.

The FBI has got beyond a brutal stage. They are cold-blooded, when they pull out that pistol they are going to kill you. They don't shoot at your legs or arms to cripple you. They shoot to kill. They carry that .357 magnum and no man carries a gun that big unless he intends to kill someone. That's a brutality in a sense, I guess. I don't really know if it is necessary to carry a gun. I would say off hand that it is like carrying a shotgun; but a shotgun is inconvenient and that's the only reason they don't carry one of them.

The FBI has sent policemen to schools. They have made the FBI school available. I think the school is in Washington, D.C. They have what they call a coordinator. The FBI has a man here who just hangs around the police station. All he does is coordinate between the FBI and the police.

The police department has all the reason in the world to be afraid of the FBI. They [the police] are shaking down guys all the time; prostitutes, criminals, bootleggers. So they are very much afraid of the FBI. The FBI is aware of that. It shows they overlook that. Because the policemen is there. He is there to stay. They don't dare start prosecuting the whole police department or they will get no cooperation. And no police department can get along without the stool-pigeon. The city police has more access to stool-pigeons than the FBI does. So the FBI, being smarter, they cooperate with the city police.

No police department, FBI or otherwise can get along without the stool-pigeon. I would say that 50 percent of their crimes are solved by stool-pigeons. Without them they can't get along. The FBI does not trust the city police in any manner, shape or form. I know two or three agents here real well. I've known them for years. One of them, in fact, was assigned to me at one time and tailed me around. I got tired of it and stepped in a doorway and he lost me for a minute. When he went by I told him that I was going to get a cup of coffee and why didn't we go together. That shook him up. He reminds me of it every once in awhile. Now we are pretty good friends. I also remind him once in awhile that there is a phrase in the Bible that says, "Thou Shalt Not Kill." Usually it perturbs him a great deal when I tell him that. He has no answer to it. I just do it for meanness for I know that he has to carry a gun. But that's defeat in my mind. I never carried a gun because I knew that someday I would have to kill somebody. That's what you carry a gun for. So I never carried one. Because I don't believe it's man's prerogative to take a life.

QUESTIONS FOR DISCUSSION

1. What societal factors have given rise to the role of the "fix"?

2. Where would the fix rank in the criminal status hierarchy?

3. Evaluate the box man from the point of view of a career deviant.

4. What is the relationship, according to this article, between the city police departments and the FBI?

5. "There is no such thing as justice in criminal courts." Do you agree or disagree, and why? How does a quotation such as this influence your attitude toward the criminal justice system in the United States?

BOOKMAKING *Robert C. Prus and C. R. D. Sharper*

A bookmaker is a private citizen who takes bets on events. These events may be of any nature, but the bookmaker is best known in the area of horce racing, where he is typically involved in illegal off-track betting. Paying track odds or less, over the long run, a bookie can expect to make a percentage take as good as or better than the track. Although bookies generally pay less than track odds, they offer clients other advantages, namely: providing action on several tracks, dispensing with the inconvenience and expense of going to the track, and extending credit to regular customers. . . . Clients are informed of relative payoffs and the relationship is a straight exchange proposition:

If you get into bookmaking, you want volume, because the more bets you have coming in, the more likely those odds will be working for you, to where the bets are balancing one another out and you're skimming the cream off the top. This is where it's better to book off the track, then you can book out of four or five tracks. If you're booking one track there's only eight or ten races or whatever and that's all the action you are going to get, so it's rough, because the more bets you have the better your position in the bookmaking business. Now, these hundred dollar or five hundred dollar bets sound good, but you are better off to have all five and ten dollar bets if the big betting is erratic. You have to keep everything in perspective. You don't match up a big bettor with a little one, because that could really hurt you, like especially if you're just starting out. So you have to be careful; if there's too much riding on one horse, you lay some of the action off to other bookmakers in the town. . . .

The daily racing form and the scratch sheet, well if you're booking, that racing form is like your Bible and you have to be on top of it, so that you know what you're getting into with these guys. And that scratch sheet will save a lot of time, because you know which horses won't be running. . . . Now, the worst thing you can do as a bookmaker is to start handicapping those horses yourself, because you will go broke. But if you stick to booking and you're into several tracks with a good volume of even bets, say two- and five-dollar bets, then you can grind out a good wage. . . . You should make between 17 and 25 percent on the total in the long run. You see most tracks go at about 15 to 20 percent, so putting limits on your bets, you should do a little better than the track. Like what I did was give a maximum of fifteen to one. In other words, for a $2 bet, the maximum win was $32; maximum place was $16; and maximum show win was $8. I don't care if the track paid $80 to win for a $2 ticket, all I would give my customer is $32, and I would give 50 to 1 on daily doubles. What the hell, some daily doubles pay $400, so a guy bets $2 and you have to pay off $400, that's a lot of money! So you impose a limit to hold down any losses you might have. Also with these small bettors, if they got lucky, it would take you too long to get your money back. . . .

Now, of course, if you're into bookmaking, you have to have enough money to cover your losses and some bad streaks. Like when I started out, I had two thousand dollars, and I had a partner with a couple thousand. Four thousand, that's all you needed, for two- and five-dollar action. Later we got into some bigger action when we got together a ten-thousand-dollar bankroll. If you're into bigger action, you have to have big money, because they're going to want that money when they win. If you are in this two-five-ten-dollar action and say you are working with runners or you're on the phone,

Reprinted by permission of the publisher, from Robert C. Prus and C. R. D. Sharper, Road Hustler: The Contingencies of Professional Card and Dice Hustlers *(Lexington, Mass.: Lexington Books, D. C. Heath and Company, Copyright 1977, D. C. Heath and Company).*

it's not like the guy is coming up to you and saying, "Here's ten to win on this horse" and waits for the results. You don't have to pay him until the next day. So you get your books together the next morning or that evening and you see who won, who lost. You total up the wins and losses and usually there are more losses than wins, so that by the end of the week, you have a pretty good buck. That's why you impose that limit. Then, if a guy bets twenty dollars, what's the most you can lose—$320 less his twenty is three hundred. You can't lose that much. Horse races—I don't care how they read that racing program—it's tough to win! I don't know anyone that's won betting the horses over the long haul. Booking is a good business and if you have the volume, that's where you make the bread.

Operating on less formal grounds than the track, the bookmaker both gains and loses from his extension of credit to his clientele:

A big thing in bookmaking is that bettors can establish credit with you, which they can't do at the race track. At the race track you bring so much money; if you blow it, you can't go to the window and say, "Hey I want to bet this horse on credit." But as a bookmaker, you may have a client that bets till the end of the week, then he will settle up. Now, if you look at a bookmaker's books, you'll often see that during the beginning of the week, the guy will bet two dollars, then four dollars, then ten, and at the end of the week he might be betting twenty and thirty dollars with you. They're always trying to get even and they are more willing to bet bigger money because it's on credit. It's a little easier to say, "I'll bet twenty," without handing over the cold hard cash. So the credit thing is a big edge to a bookmaker. . . . And, you always pay when they win. It's never "I'll see you when. . . ."

You might go week by week with a guy, where if they win, you pay them off, but if they owe you money, you just take it off, that's the beauty of it. Say a guy owes you forty dollars, and he has a win of say thirty-six dollars or something, so he still owes you four dollars, right. Now, you don't have to go to him; you tell him the next day, you won so much, now you only owe us four dollars. But if he has money coming,

you always pay him right away. That's his reward, and it entices him to bet with you. You keep your customers that way. If you're slow in paying, you'll get a bad reputation in the area and you're pretty well through as a bookmaker. . . .

Now you may have a little trouble getting your money from your clients when they lose, but you can't afford to welch on bets yourself. Like sometimes a guy may get in over his head, say where it's not impossible, but you don't want to pressure him too much because you might lose him as a customer. Sometimes you will go to the man and say, "Okay, everything's erased, you're clean. Start over again." You tell them, "Now don't do this again!", and you get hot at them. Then you may say that instead of a two hundred dollar credit you are only going to extend him a hundred dollar credit. Now he might get a little hot, but he's happier because at least that hundred and eighty, or whatever, is cleared. If he's a good customer and he bets with you almost every day, you are better off to just forget about the money he owes and start over again. You try to get what you can, maybe half or twenty-five percent of the money, and if he's a good customer, you tell him forget about the balance and start fresh. After that you keep a little closer tabs on him, but you try to let the guy run for as much as you think he can handle, because you don't want to lose his action. There is more than one bookmaking establishment in town, so if he's good frequent action and he owes you a hundred, so what, you can wait a while.

In addition to the problems associated with collections, bookies can also run into financial difficulties when they take on larger bets than they can handle or when they have been "past posted":

Another advantage of dealing with a bookie is that betting the book does not affect track odds. Now say a guy puts five hundred in the mutuals. Right away, the odds are going to come down on that horse because more money has been bet on him to win. So naturally, he would love to have a bookmaker where he can bet into him and not affect the odds. Like sometimes you will get this dynamite action where someone wants to put five hundred or a thousand on a horse. You know, like maybe he is connected with an owner or he has some inside information. Now he doesn't want to go to the fifty-dollar window and have some other guys getting ideas from him, to where the odds are down to nothing, so he goes to a bookie.

Now you have to watch the odds when you're taking these big bets. So you figure what you can handle and then lay off the rest to another bookie. You get to know the other bookies and try to develop a good relationship with them, because if you are paying your bettors off, you need a man that you can depend on too. You see, if you want to keep these customers, you should be the only bookie they need, right. So instead of them getting into other books, you try to absorb all their action. If it's too much, you get on that phone and lay it off. . . . Now, on any big bet the first thing you do is to make sure you check for past posting, because this can really hurt you. This is where someone places a bet after the race has already been run. So you have to watch the time and your track times, because some guy might slip it past you or someone you might have working on the phone. Also, you have to watch these small tracks because they're not as precise or security minded as the bigger tracks. Where there's a lot of security, they are actually not only protecting the public, but the bookmakers as well.

SETTING UP SHOP

Although some bookmakers may have more elaborate setups, anyone might become involved in booking by simply not placing that bet for a friend and paying track odds if the friend wins or pocketing the money if he loses. But to move from this sort of "opportunistic booking" (Hindelang, 1971) to a full-time booking enterprise requires not only some knowledge of the basics of booking but also the development of a relatively stable social network:

In this way, booking is like card and crap hustling. You just can't say, "Okay, I'm a bookie," and have the people running up to you. You have to be relating to them, letting them know that you're thinking of getting into action and you've got the money to back it up. So you may have a good idea how things are run, but you have to get them to have confidence in you. You have to be constantly conning people around, letting them see that you have money. Like one of the things I did when I started was to get several guys together and we'd go to the track in maybe two cars. I'd say, "Anyone who wants to bet with me, I'll pay track odds." So one guy might become lucky and win a few dollars, big deal. I didn't cover any daily double bets; if they wanted to bet daily double or anything too big I would go get it at the window. So, you can start off slow like that. Then when the area track closes up, you tell them, "I'm opening up a shop. Do you want to bet into me?" Because they'll follow those horses, so they will bet on them with you, through the newspaper or whatever. You keep creating action like that and soon it snowballs and you build up a reputation. But it's not instantaneous, you just don't get into it and say, "I'm open for business!" It doesn't happen that way. . . .

If you have the money you might have a front, like a cigar store or a greasy spoon, some sort of confectionary, or whatever. I never had anything like that; I didn't have the capital to go and get a store. I was only twenty-two or twenty-three and I felt confident enough that I just opened up in my own home. Some bookies have these fronts. Like this one guy who had a store, a beautiful place, he booked out of there, and he was one of the biggest bookmakers in the area. Later when I got into it, I would lay off a lot of my big action to him. Actually, I started out with this guy as a runner and I learned through him. Like I learned to be careful from him, say about who you take your bets from, or how to avoid getting past posted and to keep your customers from getting too careless in handing you their slips. You see a lot of guys are reckless. You may be in the shop or a pool room, and there will be all kinds of suckers or strangers around, and they will just come up and hand you the slip with their bet. Like they'll have ten to one and place on some horse in this or that race, but they'll hand it to you in front of who knows who. This man was the type that if any of his customers did that, he would give them shit, so he had them all trained. So I learned from him. . . .

Another problem comes when you have somebody working for you. Once in a while you may have a big bet to pay out and you don't know whether the client beat the race or he past posted your guy or whether your man cheated you. You just don't know. So you have to be careful who you hire to get on that phone. A guy on the phone could steal a hundred dollars a day from you, day in and day out, if it was good action, without you knowing about it. You can't keep tabs on him constantly, and the client that he's conspiring with wouldn't have to bet much any given day, and it would add up. So you always have to be on guard because you're in money all the time and people see that, and they want to get a little bit of the action. . . . If you have runners, you would usually pay ten percent of the total gross to them. So, if the man hands you two hundred dollars a day out of his hotel, you would give him twenty bucks. Regardless of whether the horses win or lose, he gets his ten percent. But here again, you have to be careful who you have working for you and when he gets those bets in.

PITFALLS

. . . The bookie has to maintain a relatively fixed location in order to service his clientele. While this stable location brings the business to him, it also makes him more vulnerable to police pressures:

In this area, there was no graft that I could see. Like this one detective was connected with a couple of us, but he was probably more trouble than he was worth. He seemed to be trying to help, so he'd con around and get a little money that way. But actual protection, I'd be very surprised if anyone had it. Okay, so this detective would more or less say, "Be careful this week." Big deal, we were careful every week, it didn't matter whether he told us or not. . . . It's a help, but you still have to work. You can't quit as soon as someone says there's a little heat. If you pack

it in, you're not going to make any money, so you're more alert and take a few more precautions. Now, you may put two bolts on the door instead of one, so it takes them a little longer to break the door down. . . . They have to find something to incriminate you and the only way they can do that is to get in that building, so they break the door down. They'll come with an axe and sledge hammer. They did that with me three times. The third time, I was so aware of what was going on, like I could see them coming, six of them, that as this one guy was raising the sledge hammer, I opened the door, "Hold it, come on in. Don't break the door this time." So they came in and searched the place. Sure, they have a search warrant but they don't show you it before they come in. They just bang the door in and then show you the warrant, when they are in the building looking already. . . . But this last time they came so damn close to finding the record book and I knew they wanted me badly. That scared me and my wife was pregnant at the time, so there was a lot of pressure to quit.

QUESTIONS FOR DISCUSSION

1. In what ways may the bookmaker be considered as residing on the margin of criminality?

2. What are the advantages and disadvantages of going to a bookmaker?

3. What types of problems might disrupt the stability of the social network of a booking agency?

4. Do you consider bookmaking a formal or an informal organizational process? Does it operate on the same principles as all social organizations? Explain your answer.

5. What sociological theory supports the existence of bookmaking?

A CASE OF BURGLARY *Malcolm Braly*

Burglary is an elemental act and the emotions it generates are profound. It's a treasure hunt as well as The Lady or the Tiger, a complete and separate experience outside whatever ordinary life you may be pretending to live. It's another way to reach the *now*.

When I stood on the rooftops, the secret spectator, looking over the scattered lights of Redding, the town lost its capacity to change or diminish me. Here I came to power. This I, here on this dangerous height, hugging himself with excitement, was not the same adolescent who walked these streets in the daylight. He was, I knew, both more and less.

I had marked a large laundry and cleaners on a dark and quiet side street, and circled it looking for a possible entry, very like a mouse looking to chew its way into a pantry. The back door and windows were bolted and barred and I had gained the roof by climbing a drainpipe. The skylight stood like a small triangular house on the graveled tarpaper, and the glass windows were open, raised like wings. They were open because the work below was often hot, and unbarred because Redding was a small quiet town and this business hadn't yet been hit so often that the investment in stronger security seemed worth the money.

I stretched out on the tarpaper to peer into the laundry below. The rising air was warm, heavy with soap and cleaning fluid, and the tarpaper still retained some of the sun's heat. The building was the equivalent of a two-story structure and I was looking down at a drop of approximately twenty feet. Below on the floor I could make out some hampers that appeared to be full, and if I could hit one it would break my fall, but the risk seemed too great. I slid back down the drainpipe and took a clothesline from a nearby backyard. As a rope it was weathered and frayed, but I planned to double it.

I climbed back to the roof and fastened the rope to a ventilation pipe. There's an odd moment when you first lower yourself. You are leading with your most tender parts and several large questions are not yet answered. Will the rope hold? Is there anyone below? Someone who has been asleep, but is now awake and aiming up at you? Your legs tingle, your stomach is hollow, and the emptiness draws at you.

I remember slipping down, tightening and relaxing my grip to slow my descent without burning my palms. I landed in a large hamper, full of damp sheets, and lay still a moment listening intently. It's never completely quiet. All around the concrete, the metal, the wood *tings* and *clicks* as the building slowly cools. It's possible to hear the electricity humming in the wires, and gross machines, thermostatically controlled, *whir* suddenly to life.

As soon as I climbed out of the hamper, even before I was certain no one was in here with me, I had to take a crap. My bowels were electric with it. I rushed to the back door to unbar it so I would have some way out, and then found the toilet, a windowless box, and shit with great excitement. I closed the door and turned on the light. My hands were black from the tarpaper and still red from rope burn. I felt secure here.

When I was finished, I looked the place over carefully to make sure I was alone. Then I went and opened the cash register. There was nothing there but the "bank" left to make change the next morning, between fifteen and twenty dollars, but to me this was a lot of money, and, more, the racks were loaded with clothes. It's impossible to pick clothes in the dark, but if something seemed to fit, I took it back into the toilet where I could use the light. Most things turned out to be the kind of suits sixty-year-old men were then wearing to church, but I found a few things, including a nice gabardine topcoat which fit me perfectly.

My life has handed me a number of ironies

and I have collected them for the instruction they contain. From time to time I intend to pass them on to you, and here is the first.

A regular part of my job at the newspaper was to stop by the police station and the sheriff's office to collect the crime news, and I was routinely given the details of my own burglaries, which I subsequently wrote up for the paper. At first it puzzled me to find my victims exaggerated the amounts I had stolen, but I soon came to realize these false claims were made with an eye to the insurance settlement. They, too, made money on the burglaries.

I bought the saddle shoes, which I found impossible to keep clean, and began to appear at school dances wearing a suit and tie. I asked a popular girl out and, amazing, she accepted, and after the dance I tried to screw her on her parents' front lawn. Kissing was okay, but when I made the critical move to her tit, she pushed me away easily (too easily, I decided in my many recapitulations) and asked, "What if I have a baby?" I knew some of the answers to this familiar question, but none seemed adequate. I walked her to the door and just before she went in, she kissed me hard, then drew back to ask, "Would you really have gone the whole hog?" Her expression held the kind of eagerness I have learned to associate with the exchange of particularly succulent gossip. I nodded and drew her close so she could feel exactly how ready I was. We kissed deeply and I thought: *this is it*. And wondered what I would do now that I was finally here. But it was too much for both of us, and again she slipped from my arms, which opened automatically to release her, and paused a moment in the door to blow me a kiss from the tips of her fingers. How often I replayed this to all the endings implicit, and how seldom I remembered, as now, how it really happened.

These were sweet days and I can, sometimes for long moments, sense my other and distant self just as if I were still there. I can feel myself standing on the stage of the high school auditorium, saying, with what I imagine to be an English accent, "You rang, sir?" We are practicing the Junior Play. Naturally, my emergent ego urged me to hope for the lead, but a lively and outgoing friend has won this prize. Our vehicle is *Charley's Aunt*, and I've been pieced off with the part of Brassett, the butler, who neither "swells a scene" nor "mounts a progress," and is the perfect vice for my vanity because playing Brassett proves I will do anything to be on this magic stage. I clown a lot, tease the girls and miss my cues.

Or I am walking with my English teacher, a tall, pale man with a blue chin, who is married to an unsuccessful writer of children's books. We are walking down Eureka Street into the center of town, across the bridge that spans the Sacramento River. He is reading a poem I have written for the girl who refused me on the lawn, trying not to laugh at my near-comic misspellings. He explains why I must learn to spell. It's hard to read my work for sense because the misspelled words are like tiny rocks in a bowl of mush, distracting to the pleasure of the reader. I listen. This is an adult talking.

The river below the bridge is a deep warm tan. Sometimes I cut school with one friend or another to swim along its banks. I remember a day spent there with Yardstick Rhodes just before he enlisted. Yardstick was named for the size of his tool and he liked to organize circle jerks so he could display this prize. My own tool was not far in his shadow and a third friend said between us we could measure more cock than the entire football team. Yardstick carried his burden with aggressive pride, but my own made me uneasy. I tried to imagine putting it into a girl without splitting her wide open, and it was in wild variance with my image of myself as the new Shelley, the reincarnate Keats, as was my avid interest in the small books Yardstick passed around, where Popeye is hosing Olive Oil (Slurp! Slurp!) with a priapismic majesty which makes even Yardstick look as if he's hung like Cupid, and Wimpey, in nothing but polka-dot shorts and the eternal derby, waits his turn.

Across the bridge I part from my English teacher, he to his home where his heavyset wife is writing sonnets on the redemptive quality of Jesus' love, and I walk on into the center of town to the newspaper office. The editor, his assistant and I make the entire staff. Both men wear green Celluloid visors and the assistant editor shelters a bad eye behind a tinted lens. They are both typing as I enter and the AP wire hammers in a corner, while out in the composing room the linos click and pound and the old web press cranks out the evening paper. My desk is stacked with things I am supposed to file, and my clerical neglect is beginning to spill onto the floor. I'm not unaware that the editor is beginning to give me a few long looks. I'm not the find I appeared to be. But I still can't cope with the filing. All this will come back to me. The time will come when just such dull clerical chores will be the precise labor by which I might win my freedom.

But today I sit hunting and pecking a poem I have written during study hour, and the two editors, who sit facing each other, begin to discuss *Time* magazine, criticizing its snotty tone and strained neologisms. On the AP wire the war is coming to us from all over the world.

Some nights I spend playing pool at the Pastime Pool Hall. I have a wobbly bridge and a slow eye. And other nights I sit with my high school clique in Eaton's Pharmacy drinking chocolate cokes. And walking home I sometimes slip out of this life to pull another burglary. I am content. But I also know this cannot go on.

I was failing in school. My job was almost lost. And once or twice a month I was placing myself in great danger. I didn't think—I was counting the number of times my picture would appear in the yearbook—but I was nevertheless hearing a definite, if wordless, warning. The solution I hit on was not so dumb. I decided to join the Navy.

I was seventeen. No one any longer expected the war to end quickly and at eighteen I was not only eligible for the draft, but would lose the option of choosing the branch of the service in which I wished to fight. No one wanted to be a dogface. The uniforms looked shitty and nice girls didn't want to go out with soldiers. The Navy seemed like a safe, clean place to wait until I grew older and could handle myself.

I announced my decision to my favorite teacher, the one who was directing us in *Charlie's Aunt*, and she looked at me in consternation. "But why go before you have to?"

"I'm not getting anyplace. You see how I do in school."

She replied firmly, "I know what you could do."

"But I don't. I need to be somewhere where I am made to do things."

She looked at me oddly. "What a strange thing for a boy your age to say."

This comment registered only in my vanity.

I quit the newspaper moments before I was due to be fired. When the editor called me aside, I sensed what was coming and immediately told him I had decided to join the Navy. He looked at me with what I recognize now as a decent, but distant pity. "You won't find the Navy very flexible. You can't act there as you have here."

I nodded brightly. "I know. I want that."

He didn't comment on my maturity.

A lot of us were going into the service and my enlistment caused no particular stir. It was expected we would enlist. It was our duty. And when a dance was organized in our honor I was quick enough to pretend it was duty that had called me. The art class drew pleasant caricatures of all of us who were leaving, and we were framed in paper laurels and posted around the gym walls. The dance was attended by Twenty-sweaters, already home on leave, and I recall the figure he cut with his high-laced paratrooper's boots and his overseas cap neatly folded under the shoulder strap of his uniform shirt. When I danced, finally a little bolder, I held the girls tightly, feeling their young tits against my chest, and because they could imagine I was going away to die, they too were touched with a bittersweet urgency, and I received several lingering and frankly sexual kisses.

I traveled with two other recruits on the night train to San Francisco for induction. I read all night in the dimly lighted coach and when my eyes were examined the next morning my usual 20-20 had dropped to 20-40 in one eye and 20-60 in the other. This wasn't quite enough to disqualify me, but when the Navy doctors looked in my mouth my military career was finished. I had a malocclusion so severe they feared the shock of Naval bombardment might cause me to bite the roof of my mouth.

When I returned to Redding it was as an apparition. I had marched off to war and there was no way to return three days later as the same person who had left. Edna Saygrover put me up in a downtown hotel and supplied me with meal tickets, but while she didn't say so, I knew this couldn't last. I thought of going to work as a logger, a romantic notion even then, but I made no move toward this employment.

I went back to school, but the emblematic photos in the yearbook were sharply diminished. My job was finished and the social invitations dried up. I had vacated my presidency of the art league and with it my seat on the student council. I even tried to reclaim my role as Brassett, which now seemed valuable, but the teacher-director told me tactfully, but with honest point, this wouldn't be fair to the boy who had stepped into the part, who was, anyway, doing a better job. I waited for something to happen.

It was raining the night it ended and I walked the two blocks from my hotel to the pool hall wearing the gabardine topcoat I had stolen on my first burglary. When it was my turn to play, I dumped the coat on a bench where it was discovered by the boy who owned it. He was also a student, a remote senior, a gifted athlete, and a natural antagonist to the crowd I usually ran with. He held up the coat to ask the room at large who had left it there.

My opponent said casually, "Isn't that yours?"

The senior turned to stare at me and I was immediately aware of his distaste. For a moment I wondered if I could deny the coat, but in my confusion it didn't seem possible. From this moment on I had no confidence in my ability to change what was obviously happening.

"It's mine," I said, and sealed it.

He showed me a cigarette burn on the hem I had never noticed, to prove the coat was his, and told everyone who was listening the coat had been lost in a burglary of the Nelson Cleaners.

I invented a lie. I had bought the coat from a man in the lobby of the hotel where I was staying, but if it was his, and the burn proved it, then he should have it back and I would take the loss.

But this wasn't enough. He followed the rules and he insisted we report this to the police. Four or five boys had gathered to listen and there seemed no way out of it. The station was two blocks away and we ran there through the rain. I entered not expecting to come out again.

The night officer took my statement and appeared to believe what I told him. I didn't invent anyone, but described a real character I had talked to in the lobby a few nights before. He'd been drunk, so drunk he would have talked to anyone, and when he found I was going to high school, he dredged up a few tatters of his own education to try to impress me with his knowledge of Latin. I described this in minute detail, inventing only the sale of the coat which I claimed I had paid five dollars for.

The night officer dismissed us and the senior said Good Night coldly and went home wearing his own coat. I went back to the hotel. My suitcases were full of stolen clothes, some still in the laundry wrappers. I considered getting rid of them. I considered leaving town, heading north into the woods and the logging camps. Right then. Instead I went to sleep.

QUESTIONS FOR DISCUSSION

1. What do you perceive as the major reasons this boy engages in acts of burglary?

2. What do you think this boy hoped to accomplish by joining the Navy? What does this reveal about his self-image?

3. Why do you think the emotional impact of burglary is so strong?

4. Carefully evaluate the statement, "My life has handed me a number of ironies and I have collected them for the instruction they contain." What far-reaching implications does it have?

Section IV   ALCOHOL AND DRUG ABUSE

Currently, large segments of American society are expressing much concern over the use and abuse of addictive drugs and the prevalence of excessive drinking and alcoholism. These types of deviance are considered to be major social problems for the 1980s. While the so-called hard addictive drugs have received the greatest amount of publicity from the mass media, alcohol is by far the most widely used mood-altering drug in the United States.

The excessive use of alcohol is a problem dating back to pre-biblical times. The number of Americans who drink alcoholic beverages is increasing. Today close to four-fifths of all males and two-fifths of all females drink. The rate of increase is much greater for women than men. Excessive drinking varies by ethnic group. For example, it is more common among native Americans and individuals of Polish and Irish descent than those of Italian, Greek, and Jewish descent. It is more prevalent among men than women and is usually concentrated in the 30–35-year-old age group. Incidence appears to be greater in metropolitan areas, especially the inner city, than in rural areas. It is estimated that 7 to 10 percent of Americans are alcoholics.

An alcoholic may be defined as an individual: (1) whose use of alcohol deviates from the drinking norms of his salient social groups; (2) whose drinking results in an inability to perform normal social roles; (3) whose drinking results in emotional and physical damage; (4) who feels a compulsion to continue drinking once he or she has started even though the individual is aware that it impairs his or her life. Contrary to popular belief, only a minority of alcoholics are of the skid row type. Alcoholics come from all social classes and are found in all occupations. In fact, physicians are reported to have a higher rate of alcoholism than the general population. The story told to Henry Beetle Hough in "Becoming an Alcoholic" is a good illustration of a well-educated, middle-class business excecutive who becomes an alcoholic and finds that he is unable to control his drinking even though he is perfectly aware of how it is adversely affecting his life.

The consequences of alcoholism to society are great. It is the third major cause of death and disability. Thirty-seven percent of all police arrests are individuals who are at least legally intoxicated. The use of alcohol is involved in most homicides and aggravated assaults and in almost half the forcible rape cases. In "A Female Alcoholic," a middle-aged woman gives an account of her family life and drinking patterns. She describes the social environment and conditions that led to her excessive drinking and also the repetitive periods of abstinence that are so characteristic of one stage of alcoholism. It is significant that she had been drinking heavily before she killed her husband.

There are a number of biochemical, nutritional, and behavioral theories of alcoholism, but no single cause has been established. From a sociological standpoint, alcoholism seems to be related to the type of groups one associates with and to their belief about where, when, and how much one ought to drink. The rate of alcoholism is much greater in groups that use alcohol for hedonistic and utilitarian purposes, than in groups where its use is primarily ritualistic and ceremonial.

Jellinek (1960) has presented the view that alcoholism is a disease progressing through a number of different stages. Although not all alcoholics fit his sequential model, the model does provide a useful analytic tool for examining the process of alcoholism. He describes the following four broad phases:

1. Prealcoholic phase—In this phase an individual begins drinking socially and discovers that the consumption of alcohol helps relieve tensions. Over a period of time (six months to two years) the person's tolerance for tension decreases, so that more alcohol is needed to bring about the same degree of relief.

2. Prodromal phase—This phase begins with the onset of blackouts about events that occurred while the person was drinking. The individual becomes preoccupied with alcohol and whether he or she is going to have a great enough supply in various situations. A sense of guilt about drinking begins to develop.

3. Crucial phase—The individual loses control. Once the person starts drinking, he or she has no ability to stop until the supply is exhausted or until the person is so intoxicated that he or she cannot continue. Behavior becomes alcohol-centered. The person becomes more concerned with how various daily activities may interfere with drinking rather than with how drinking may interfere with the activities. The drinker begins to neglect diet, hide the supply of liquor, sneak drinks, and acquire rationalizations and alibis for drinking. The loss of friends and job are common characteristics in this phase.

4. Chronic phase—Binge drinking occurs where the individual engages in prolonged periods of drinking that may last for days at a time. The individual's thinking is impaired and ethical deterioration is likely. The person develops indefinable fears, tremors, and almost total loss of alcohol tolerance.

While Jellinek's model may not fit the patterns of all alcoholics, it is interesting how many of the characteristics he presents are described in the accounts of the two alcoholics included in this section.

A drug may be defined as a substance that is not a food, which by its chemical properties affects the structure and/or function of the living organism (McCaghy, 1976). The most common drugs used in the United States for nonmedical purposes are: barbiturates (downers), amphetamines (uppers), marijuana, L.S.D. (lysergic acid diethylamide), and heroin. Of these, heroin addiction is considered to be the most serious drug problem in the United States. In fact, of all Western countries the United States has the highest rate of addiction. Of all the psychoactive drugs heroin has the highest potential for creating dependence. Moreover, no effective means of terminating dependence has yet been discovered. Ironically, prolonged use of heroin does not result in any disease or damage to body cells or organs. The excessive use of alcohol can be very dangerous to health and can even induce death. But this is not true of heroin except in the case of an overdose.

Heroin is a highly potent derivative of morphine. Its usual form is a white, odorless crystalline powder. It is bitter to the taste. It produces an extreme state of euphoria or "high" in which the individual attains a sense of well-being and a loss of anxiety. Feelings of pain, fear, hunger, and remorse lose their salience. Addiction is the compulsive craving for the drug, accompanied by increased tolerance and physical and psychological dependence. The dependence is created not so much by the craving for the high as by fear of the withdrawal symptoms; these may be very severe—fever, chills, vomiting, shaking, runny nose, and so on. In her graphic account "Being Hooked," Florrie Fisher exhibits many of the classic characteristics of both the drug euphoria and the withdrawal symptoms. Notice how her husband's reaction to the introduction to heroin is much different from hers.

Because the use of drugs for nonmedical purposes is illegal, it is difficult to discover how many addicts there are in the United States. The number of addicts increased rapidly during the 1960s, but the rate seemed to level off during the late 1970s. Estimates for the 1970s run from 400,000 to 600,000. Male addicts outnumber female addicts about 4 to 1. The 21–30-year-old age group contains over half the known addicts. Close to 60 percent of addicts are Black, while another 15 percent–20 percent are Spanish-speaking. The slum areas of large metropolitan areas, especially New York City, appear to be the largest breeding grounds for drug addicts. Yet, clerical and sales personnel also have a high rate of heroin addiction, as do members of the medical profession. In fact, the rate of opiate addiction among physicians is about 20 times that of the general population (Anslinger, 1957).

The selection "A Piece of the Action" is an excellent portrayal of a young lower-class urban male's rise in the world of organized crime and his subsequent fall into the "retreatist" subculture of the drug addict. The initial novelty, kick, and excitement of smoking pot, snorting cocaine, and mainlining heroin are vividly described. As Manny acquires an expensive heroin habit, his world begins to collapse around him. He loses his job in the rackets, his credibility, and finally his respectability. The pains of drug withdrawal guide his entire life. Like many drug addicts he must steal constantly to maintain his habit.

Several different theories introduced in the first section of this volume have been used to explain drug addiction. Some believe an important condition necessary for addiction is an individual's feeling of inadequacy and despair. Drug addiction is seen as a means of coping with life. It offers an escape from society and from life's problems. Anomie theory holds that people who are unable to achieve success by legitimate means, and are unwilling to use illegitimate means to achieve goals, may adapt by attempting to retreat or escape. One way of doing this is through drug addiction. The individual rejects conventional values in favor of the highs produced by drugs. Thus, one is able to escape from life's frustrating problems and a disappointing socioeconomic position.

A view common among the police is called the "stepping stone" theory of drug addiction. It holds that heroin addiction stems from the use of other illegal drugs such as cocaine and marijuana. Once an individual has tried these drugs, his appetite is supposedly whetted for the greater highs promised from heroin use. Another theory is based on the availability of drugs and is closely related to the labeling perspective. It holds that as society places restrictions and imposes penalties on the nonmedical use of drugs, they become differentially available to the various strata of society. For example, lower-class urban Black males have greater access to the deviant drug culture than do middle-class suburban whites who shun the stigma involved with participation in the illegality of the operation.

Association theory contends that heroin addiction is learned through association with individuals who are addicts, in much the same fashion as other cultural patterns are transmitted. As individuals begin to associate with other addicts and the drug subculture and find themselves dependent on drugs to relieve the distress of withdrawal symptoms, they begin to alter their self-image to that of an addict and play the role of the addict (Lindesmith, 1968).

Methadone is a potent synthetic narcotic analgesic similar in chemical structure to heroin and morphine. It has been used for some years to treat heroin addicts. One dose taken orally lasts for up to a day. Although it produces little euphoria, it does replace heroin in the system and reduces or stops withdrawal symptoms. It is the only maintenance treatment program that has received widespread acceptance. However, the body does acquire a tolerance for methadone, and it may be physically and psychologically addictive. The big difference between heroin and methadone is that methadone is legal and therefore inexpensive. Addicts do not have to have large financial reserves to support their habit.

In the final selection in this section, "The Methadone Blues," Bill Bathurst tells what he thinks about Methadone Maintenance Programs. His general alienation from mainstream society is so great that one doubts that any type of program of this nature will have much effect on the causes of whatever made him become an addict in the first place. As he admits, however, it is a lot easier receiving methadone than cruising the streets looking for illegal ways to support the addiction.

References

Anslinger, Harry
1957 "Interview with Hon. Harry J. Anslinger," *Modern Medicine* 25:170–191.
Jellinek, E. M.
1960 *The Disease Concept of Alcoholism.* New Haven, Conn.: Hillhouse Press.
Lindesmith, Alfred
1968 *Addiction and Opiates.* Chicago: Aldine Publishing Company.
McCaghy, Charles
1976 *Deviant Behavior.* New York: Macmillan.

BECOMING AN ALCOHOLIC *As told to Henry Beetle Hough*

The way to alcoholism is not across a bridge or through a portal marked with warning signs and illuminated with floodlights; it lies across a shadow line that is crossed in heavy darkness, at night, and in obscure cloud and haze.

I know now that my pleasantly controlled social drinking developed into alcoholism as subtly and unnoticeably as some case of diabetes creeps into the life of a victim of this disease.

But certainly there must be signs? Yes, there are signs, but usually they are not of a spectacular sort. They are slight changes of viewpoint and of behavior that the drinker can explain away and usually conceal from those around him. Some of these had already become part of my experience, and it is time to tell about them.

SNEAKED DRINKS

I don't remember the first time. I cannot even guess when the first time was. But I do recall that when I was mixing silver fizzes or highballs or gimlets in the kitchen, a period came when I would sneak one or two in order to be that much ahead of the crowd, or even ahead of Alice, if we were alone.

It was a simple transition from merely tasting a drink to be sure it would greet the palate well, to tossing off one or two for my own hasty indulgence. If I didn't have a head start, my feeling was that I would be laboring under a handicap. Or perhaps I didn't have any feeling as definite as that—perhaps it was that I just wanted the liquor, and there it was.

Once having had the experience of this head start, I wanted it whenever opportunity offered. There was no thought of turning back. I had made a permanent departure so far as drinking was concerned.

The really significant aspect of what may seem trivial was that to sneak drinks ahead of time was not like me. I was not selfish about things, and it was always instinctive and natural for me to follow the practices of courtesy. Here, then, was an instance, even if a slight one, in which alcohol was causing a deviation from my normal behavior.

And I was already committed to concealment that would naturally lead to lying.

LYING ABOUT THE NUMBER

All these things started innocently.

"Look at Gus," somebody said. "He's on his fourth."

"I should say not," said Gus. "You're counting the one I brought in for Elsie."

"What difference does it make? It's a poor night when you don't have a fourth."

"That's so," Gus replied, "and I want it understood that the fourth is still ahead of me, see?"

Persiflage about the number of drinks ran like that, and somebody looked at me and said, "How many has old Pete had?"

And I, embarrassed under Alice's eyes, held up two fingers and said, "Only two." I laughed as I said it, and this wasn't a lie. It was part of the conventional discourse of drinking.

But pretty soon the jocose evasion, or the pretended forgetfulness, or the mock protestations were all turning into deliberate deceit. At first I would usually admit to Alice the next morning just what the extent of my drinking had been. Sometimes her comments were caustic, but it was a long time before we had real quarrels about liquor. I believe one reason real quarrels were postponed was because I stopped being frank.

In the background of my mind I classed this sort of lying along with the social deceits and so-called white lies that are familiar to all the human race, but I was utterly wrong in so doing. Alcoholic lying belongs in a category of its own.

I had not gone far as yet, and I can still believe that my earlier lies were fairly innocent—but they were tainted with alcohol. They did not begin and end in themselves, for they were the first expressions of alcoholic thinking and the alcoholic turn of mind. Honestly confronted and described, they were symptoms.

HAIR OF THE DOG

Long, long before Alice became troubled and critical, I had discovered the value of the classic "hair of the dog that bit you." The drink in the morning that restored, the drink in the morning that was necessary to minister to a bad feeling—here was a formula of renewal.

Hangovers became, though still regrettable, a necessary part of a drinking man's experience. Something had to be done about them. The drink in the morning was the best answer.

Many people who are not alcoholics take drinks in the morning—sometimes—but nevertheless drinking in the morning is one of the primary badges of alcoholism. Here is a danger signal glowing bright red and visible from afar, by night or by day. If a man drinks in the morning as a means of recovery from his drinking the night before, it is possible to make a prediction concerning him that will not be far wrong.

BUT I CAN QUIT WHEN I LIKE

Evasion and vacillation are conspicuous in all human behavior and it is hard to recognize them as especially important in relation to drinking. The woman who departs from her diet is not much different from the man who yields to the temptation of one more highball. We are all human.

The first time doesn't count. It isn't as bad as it seems. I'll pull myself up a bit. If I want to, I can quit right now.

It is in respect to this last that the drinker and the incipient alcoholic have their strongest

argument, for when they say they can quit, the chances are that they are telling the literal truth.

It's easy to stop a man's drinking. You can stop it by locking him up. He can stop it, and generally does, for a week or a month or even longer. All alcoholics stop drinking—most of them stop repeatedly. The stopping is as common a symptom as the drinking. The problem is to remain stopped.

I remember how I used to quit drinking. Alice was pleased with me and I was pleased with myself. I could stop when I wanted to—therefore I had proposed a test and met it satisfactorily—everything was under control. So I thought, but as a matter of cold fact, I had met no test at all and had no reliable inkling whatever as to the extent of my control. Because, having stopped for a while, I invariably began again.

Alice knew even less than I about the danger signals and about my relationship to alcohol, for the reason that I, like most drinkers, kept my experience as completely as possible secret to myself. If a suspicion arose that liquor might be playing too large a part in my life, I had only myself to satisfy, and I was easily convinced by rationalizations and evasions that would not have gone over with Alice if she had been possessed of full information. I let her into my problem—and I denied then that it was a problem—only when there was some outward slip—such as having to be put to bed, or missing time at the office or an engagement with a client.

The awkwardness of the overt occasion was that it had to be explained to someone else, and with reasoning of a sounder sort than I used on myself. But even here the rationalization was usually successful in the end. I was plausible and my stories were plausible, because alcoholism was still a mere hazy ghost of a threat, nothing that was likely to happen to *me*; and because I was bright enough and resourceful enough to tell plausible stories. The alcoholic is likely to be an intellectually able and articulate person. Even if he is not possessed of a formal education, he has a native dynamism that spills over.

All this I put down here, *before any of the major developments of my alcoholism*, because it is precisely at this phase, in advance of serious trouble, that danger signals may be of use; and because it is significant that early changes in habit and viewpoint may find an ultimate development and explanation in terms of alcoholism. The fact that, at the moment, there need be no such inevitable chain of cause and effect, of beginning and end, is far less important than the fact that there very well may be. In my own case, as I shall proceed to show, there was what now appears an inevitable sequence. But I was not looking for danger signals, and if anyone had called them to my attention I would not have observed them.

One reason for this, of course, was that I refused utterly to recognize anything in common between myself, who had been drunk many times, and other men whom I had seen drunk. Even at the stage of which I am now writing, I might well have remembered the drunks I had seen as a boy, and compared my situation to theirs. The young man wearing pointed shoes in the park, who so frightened the tailor's wife—surely I might have felt now some stirring of an alcoholic bond between him and me. But no, not at this time or later, not until much, much later when all had been painfully laid bare, did I discover any relationship running from me to the alcoholic kinship of the world at large.

If I had been able to suspect such a kinship through some secret process of intuition, I would have denied it and refused to acknowledge it to myself. For I was different.

I might get drunk at times, but still I was different.

My own case was distinct and special.

The drinker never sees himself as others see him, and the deliberate mental twist or evasion that enables himself to preserve his confidence in his own difference, and his own independence of general weaknesses and defeats, is capable of being enlarged and distorted as alcoholic thinking replaces the normal processes of which he was once capable. Once you surrender realistic thinking, it is hard to get back. . . .

GUILT

The stranger in my house was not the substance known as alcohol but a fantasy that I myself brought into existence chiefly through a sense of guilt. Guilt led to deceit, but Alice could be deceived only part of the time and ultimately not at all.

The sense of guilt did not make its appearance abruptly on a particular day that can be identified and recalled but, like so many other elements in the pattern of alcoholism, subtly and by almost indistinguishable degrees.

I don't remember that Alice ever demanded, as the wives of drinkers are supposed to do, "Where were you last night?" Or: "Drunk again today, weren't you?" Or: "Where did you go after you left the office?" She did say sometimes: "Say, how many drinks have you had, anyway?" I began lying to her when a tugging sensation of guilt made me ashamed to tell the truth.

But the questioning was most often in her eyes, and this was how it happened more and more. She was not looking for an answer from me. She was seeking the answer for herself. She could tell what shape I was in. She could estimate pretty closely the extent of my drinking, though not so closely as she thought. I contrived ways of preventing her from knowing.

One Washington's Birthday I crawled out of bed with all the grumbling misery of a hangover. The night before, in anticipation of a day of idleness and no responsibilities, I had stayed up late drinking B. & B., benedictine and brandy, with a group of our friends. Nothing was easier for me to drink through a sociable evening but the after-effect was bad. Morning brought the need for a good stiff whisky as soon as possible, and I slipped downstairs and got one, or two, and experienced the anticipated revival—as if disintegration had been avoided by a narrow margin.

I covered my tracks well and was sure that Alice knew nothing about the morning drinks; but later in the day she called to me, "Pete, what happened to that bottle of rye in the cupboard?"

"How should I know?" I snapped back.

"Now if you don't, who does?"

"So you're checking up on me," I said with a good deal of resentment.

"I am not," said Alice, without losing her good nature. She could be exasperatingly patient. "I had to get the cooking sherry, which meant moving the bottle of rye, and how could I help noticing that something had happened to it since yesterday? Why the mystery? If you gave somebody a drink or if you had a drink or two yourself, why not say so?"

But she wasn't being frank, for she knew

why I didn't want to say so. I didn't want to admit sneaking the drinks that morning, along with the disclosure that was necessarily involved. Alice knew what it meant when I needed this quick prescription for a hangover. I was guilty and therefore guiltily anxious to cover up.

After that I made it a matter of custom to keep an extra bottle or two in the cellar, the attic, or the garage—any place where Alice would not come across them. I varied the repository because this seemed the smart thing to do. I couldn't be cornered again. I wouldn't be answerable to Alice for every drink I took, or in a situation which gave her a chance to cross-question me.

The unseen stranger was by no means a constant presence in our household, for some years at least, because alcohol, though I no longer controlled my drinking, was still subordinate. There were long periods when I drank little or not at all. We had our first baby. My older son may now consider himself an eyewitness, though not for a long time aware of the one special difference between his home surrounding and another's. We pursued our life together, and it seemed a natural, settled sort of thing that would grow and develop as year succeeded year. Alice and I talked of plans for the future and looked ahead to a promise that, though obscure, seemed full of pleasant possibilities and sure to be faithfully performed.

We thought of ourselves as normal. We lived in a state of order in a civilized time, with the evidences of a vigorous, healthy, successful American way of life around us. We were part of a wonderful system, as one branch of mathematics is part of a complete and ordered whole; but, since our plane was organic, the branches of our system were more vitally and usefully related. We would naturally share in the happiness and success of the whole.

In some such way as this, I think, any family looks at others, at the segment of society round about, and gains the same assurance that one may gain from looking at a reflection in a mirror. But each outlooking family selects the most desirable aspects it can see and, from these, forms a rationalized and idealized image that it chooses to accept as its own. So easily an assurance is accepted that may be cruelly false and, where alcoholism is concerned, is sure to be false. . . .

I QUIT DRINKING AGAIN

"I can stop drinking any time I want to."

Who is this speaking? It is I. Perhaps it is some man from next door, or a stranger met on the train, saying my words. It is almost any alcoholic, or any person in danger of alcoholism. Famous, famous words. Let my sons learn now how old and worn they are, how often hollow.

As I have said before, they express a genuine truth. But one trouble is that to speak them is not much different from saying, "I can't stop drinking unless I want to."

Do I want to? Do you want to, my chance acquaintance, or my friend? Will my sons want to, at some future time? It may be helpful to consider the question even now. Does any drinker who enjoys alcoholic liquor want to stop enjoying it? Of course not!

"Wanting to" is the catch.

I wanted to stop drinking. I wanted to stay sober and make a good husband and father. I wanted to be clear-headed and to do the best work of which I was capable.

All this, in general terms, was vivid and unqualified. But it did not prevent me, at some given moment, from needing a drink.

I want to stay sober but I need a drink.

That contradiction that appears in these twin statements is one that requires thought. So long as I have the craving, the feeling of need, I do not really want to stop drinking—not at the given moment. What I need, I want, for wanting is surely inseparable from needing. I want a drink now, because I need it.

At the same time I still want to stop drinking, but this is a more general and remoter aim with a little less urgency in the "wanting."

The stopping can always wait a while longer. It is an ideal, long range program. The need is immediate, a thing of the moment, NOW, as jangling nerves and sick cells of my body insist.

I have always planned to call upon my willpower. I have thought of the will as a kind of bulldozer to be brought in when I really make up my mind to overcome all obstacles. *When I really make up my mind*—when will that time come? Long before then I am discovering that willpower is much more effective for accomplishing what I want than for accomplishing what I do not want.

The will helps, obviously, to subordinate various lesser desires and to push through the attainment of a greater gain in the long run. But can it ever help us to do the thing, socially permissible, which we just plainly and in all honesty do not want to do?

In terms of alcoholism, at least, there is only one answer.

Yet, once again, I stopped drinking—for a while. This act of decision and of abnegation somewhat restored my self-esteem and brought an appearance of happiness to my home, but this time did not deceive Alice nor exorcise her haunting insecurity. She must have known by now that she was married to an alcoholic husband, though I doubt if her loyalty would have allowed her to admit it in plain terms. A woman married to an alcoholic husband never knows what will happen.

In reflecting upon my circumstances, it seemed to me that I had let alcohol get the best of me, and that I should knock off entirely until I could be sure of handling it better. I must have a holiday of a sort and after a while I could make a fresh, intelligently considered thing of normal drinking. I would be like other men who drank and got by, apparently with ease.

I was aware, you see, of a physical craving for alcohol. I had trained the cells of my body to expect it, I had accustomed them to make the most of a larger and larger quantity, without many interruptions in the supply. If alcohol was habit-forming—and the smoking of cigarettes, the eating of candy, even taking a nap at noon are also habit-forming—then I had slipped into the groove too far and would have to declare some revision.

I was aware of this, for even my ingenuities of self-deceit could not disguise a conclusion so obvious to Alice and everyone else who knew me well. I could hardly be the one person to ignore what others showed me they recognized clearly.

I was not aware, however, that my bodily craving for alcohol was less important in the long run than another reliance I had come to place in it. I wasn't the fellow I wanted to be unless I could make myself so with timely doses of liquor. I had used alcohol to build up a relationship with the life of which I wanted to be a part. Physical gratification was nothing as compared to the use of alcohol for this self-administered act of creation.

It was as simple as that, though I did not know it then or for a long time. When I reassured myself that I had no concealed drive for revenge upon either of my parents, or for escape from any fantasy of long ago, or any of the other psychic forces of the underground that I had heard about second or third hand, my reassurance was complete—but wholly groundless. For me to be an alcoholic by psychic conditioning, it was not necessary to find any such dramatic mutilation from long ago.

It was necessary only for me to have placed reliance upon alcohol for adjustment to and in the competition of the world.

Liquor helped establish me with the people I must know. It protected me from unpleasant reminders. It softened anxieties. It helped me to a better opinion of myself. It seemed to give me the ability to work more effectively and longer. It was the difference between a well-rounded life and the narrow, specialized life of tensions and pressure to which otherwise I was committed.

Without liquor I was like a tightly coiled spring from which any impact or even any stir of air could evoke shrill twanging sounds.

With the mysterious power of alcohol I had tried and was still trying to make myself a man of charm, wit, and urbanity, a man of prowess in professional life, a man not troubled by nerves, a man who would never be tempted to look back over his shoulder.

So when I stopped drinking and admitted that I missed the physical gratification, I was also experiencing this other deprivation. I was prevented from being the man I had made of myself, the man I thought I wanted to be.

It was inevitable that I should soon start drinking again, for a little while without alcohol has a wonderful way of wiping out apprehension. Liquor may have the best of other men, but I see perfectly how I can and will control it. The new page has been turned.

But I did not begin this time with Alice's consent. For a while I drank only when she was not around and when I thought she would not know. I drank moderately and decently and assured myself there was every reason to expect no more trouble. I had learned my lesson and, as an intelligent man, applied its obvious conclusions.

When Alice did find out, she made no scene; she had suspected for some time what was going on.

"If you are going to take a drink," she said, "you don't have to hide it from me. You don't, do you? I don't want you to."

"I've just been proving to myself that I can handle it," I said. "I know now that I've got it licked. I'll never go off the deep end again."

She accepted my confidence at its face value, for how could she doubt when I so obviously believed? Perhaps she too believed for a while.

But within a month I had bottles concealed in the cellar, the attic, the car, the garage—one or all at different times—and within two months came a Monday morning when I was not fit to go to the office. I was without a drink that Monday morning, for Alice was watching me and I could not get to my liquor supply.

"How long are you going to go on like this?" she asked.

I swore. I threw myself into a tantrum. What sort of perfection did she think she had married? What was she accusing me of? Should I feel like a sinner because I had accumulated a little hangover? How would she feel if I had kept watching her like a plainclothesman, begrudging her every drink and making her feel that liquor should be measured by the drop? On I went, yackety-yacketing, almost convincing myself that it was Alice's fault my mouth tasted so badly, my head ached, and I could not remember what I had done the night before.

That Monday passed, but by now the relationship between Alice and me had changed completely and permanently. Even when our lives seemed normal, there was the stranger in our house, the unspoken awareness between us. She knew there would be a next time. She knew she must have a reserve of independence and leadership. She knew she must prepare to be responsible for the boys if need be.

To the extent that I recognized her attitude, I resented it. She had no right to be superior. Something about her seemed pushing me all the time. Pushing, watching, suspecting. When I wasn't guilty, she would make me feel guilty, and at such times I was sorry for myself.

We exposed our raw nerves to each other. We quarreled more and more. I knew that liquor was at the bottom of everything that didn't go well, but I had no intention of cutting it out again. Why should I? I was handling it all right.

When my sons suspected the truth, when they began to compare the life of their home with others, when they not only suspected but *knew*, they alone can say. I shall not ask them now. But as they read these words, they will piece together meanings that first were vague shadows long ago. They knew something for a long time, then they knew all. . . .

SMALL VOICE

One summer evening, not early, not late, but when the dusk was beginning to gather, I walked toward my house in the New Jersey suburb with considerable uneasiness. I had made several stops on my way from the office and I knew I was not in good shape. For this I suffered a sense of guilt, yet I had stopped short of drunkenness and considerably short of starting off on a spree, and for this I suffered a sense of dissatisfaction and persecution. I was irritable. I was mean.

If good luck held, Alice wouldn't be at home. This was her day for a meeting and tea of some kind, and those things broke up late. Sometimes she fixed supper for the boys ahead of time and left something for me, and didn't get back until almost bedtime.

At first I thought I would take my chances and walk right up to the front door—but Alice might be home and I didn't relish the idea of confronting her. Maybe it would be better to skirmish around back and ease into the house. At least I could see how things were, fix myself up a little, and maybe contrive to face Alice on ground of my own choosing.

"I didn't hear you come in," she might say, without even looking at me carefully. "How were things in the city?"

And I would say, "Not bad, not bad at all. What's for a guy who's hungry?"

The light touch often worked. So I walked in by the side of the hedge that separated our yard from the next. I covered the most exposed area and was soon under the shelter of deep shadow; but in this darkness my foot struck against a child's wagon or some other object, and I tripped over into the hedge, sprawling. If I had been really steady, I probably wouldn't have tripped. As I remained for a measurable span of time, entrapped in privet, I made out two small boys crouching a short distance away. They were playing in their own yard and I had probably scared them.

But the fright was soon over. One of the kids said to the other, "It's only Gussie's old man."

Gussie is reading these words now. He is my youngest son. Perhaps he has not come across the old nickname for a long time—at one period of his life he was called this after a character in a comic strip.

I extricated myself from the hedge and went into the house by the back door. No one was home. It turned out later that Alice had skipped the meeting and tea and had taken the boys to the early show of some educational movie.

Alone in the hollow shell of a house I gave way to bitter emotion. Tears ran down my cheeks. "It's only Gussie's old man." What would those kids say to Gussie tomorrow? What would he say to them? Was I so much of an unreliable character that anything could be expected of me? Other fathers remained upright, but I stumbled into hedges. Why not face it—I arrived home half slewed over and staggering. Why wouldn't children notice it even more readily than anyone else?

I know now that my tears were alcoholic. It was thoroughly in alcoholic character to go through all this emotion without any idea of doing anything to remedy the original situation. . . .

I did not drink for a considerable time. I forgot or suppressed the revelation that I might be (after all, it was never certain in my own mind) what is known as a periodic, a drinker who goes back to the bottle as certainly as a homing pigeon to its loft. I began to feel well, at least physically.

You don't keep pushing against something when there is really nothing there to push. You don't put forth effort when obviously no effort is required. So it was with my dramatic resolution to exert my willpower: at first I derived some satisfaction from rolling the bulldozer along the ramparts and observing that all was clear. But I

wasn't even tempted to drink, and the parade of needless force seemed foolish. After a while I forgot about it.

I assumed that a drinkless state was going to be natural to me, for a long, long time, if not forever. I had learned my lesson.

But the time came, and I now have no distinct recollection of just when it was, that I craved a drink. The physical sickness and misery were long gone. At first I wanted a drink without really being aware of the craving. I wanted to be let off the hard driver's seat of my job. I wasn't sleeping well. I was restless.

"How did things go at the office?" Alice asked.

"It's a rat race," I said.

She looked at me with that secret, observing quality in her gaze. She looked at me often that way.

"A rat race," I said. "But don't worry. I'm not going out and get pickled."

"I didn't think you were."

"You looked at me that way," I told her.

Alice didn't understand—so I had often told myself. She had her feminine intuition about many things, but she couldn't know what went on inside a man. I resented the responsibility and authority that had, through the years, passed from me to her because of alcohol. I couldn't be whittled down any more. Just because of what was past, she had no right to expect that the future was going to be the same. . . .

"Don't worry," I said. "I'll be home early."

I was home early.

Alice watched me and I knew she was watching me. Certainly she was justified, and I couldn't deny that, but a man doesn't want to be watched all the time. And when I had said the job was a rat race, I had meant just that.

There were words that you used, and everyone knew what they meant. A lot of city people never had seen the wire spring from a bale of hay when it was cut, but they said themselves that things had "gone haywire" and the expression was commoner than most phrases deriving from their own experience. A "rat race" was not a competition between rats in a cage, but it was the way we lived and worked and tore ourselves to pieces with haste, anxiety, frustration, and uncompleted tasks or effort that fell short always and had to be renewed. Our personal affairs and our civilization were a rat race, and every day things went haywire.

I wanted a drink but I did not take one. There were plenty of chances but I just didn't. I wouldn't.

When I wanted to and didn't, I felt unsatisfied but reassured. The old willpower was working. Yet why should I keep myself forever away from the satisfaction of a single drink? It wasn't the use of alcohol that was bad, it was the abuse. I had abused it and had suffered and had come out a wiser man.

But one drink—why wasn't I entitled to it after so long? As a boy and as a younger man I had begun drinking at will and stopped at will, and wasn't that the real function of willpower?

Still I didn't take the drink.

Not for a day after that thought crossed my mind, or two days, or three days. But the next week I did. Then it seemed that I had been anticipating that drink for a long time, as if it were a Miltonian "far off divine event" toward which my destiny moved. Not consciously but deep inside I had waited and looked forward and shaped the expectancy of all my body cells for the alcohol that was coming.

The drink was like arriving home after a long and difficult journey at sea or in desert country. It was like the completion of a rhyme. It was like an appointment kept suddenly after the opening of sealed orders. Alice had known about the orders but I had kept them sealed from myself.

The first drink, however, was incomplete as it always has been and always will be for an alcoholic.

When you start something, it isn't always desire that is the important factor. You can get along, and often do, with too little sleep and partial satisfaction of hunger. You break off a pleasant social talk in order to get to work on time. But the first drink is a process begun and not finished. It lacks the completion that is somehow as inevitable as the progression of a chemical reaction in nature.

I took that first drink after leaving the office half an hour early in the afternoon. Without explaining the matter to myself, I had even allowed in advance for the extra time.

At nine o'clock, in a high state of intoxica-tion, I engaged a room in a small hotel because it wasn't possible to go home that night. I tried to get Alice by telephone but she didn't answer. She didn't need to hear from me—she already knew. She had called my office to find out when I left, and the rest was perfectly clear. She had stayed alone often enough because of my drunkenness, but this time she hadn't wanted to, so she had taken the boys and gone to a friend's house for the night. What had she told the boys? They may remember, as they read these lines. I guess she hadn't had to explain much. They knew as well as she.

I did not go home until the third day.

It wasn't the same story. It never was quite the same, for although the basic circumstances were present—the sickness of body and spirit, the unbearable racking and torment of nerves, the self-reproach—there was always something new. This time the new and bitter element was the realization—why had I not grasped it before?—that Alice would never again place real confidence or dependence in or upon me.

I was marked. I had marked myself. Now she could not even pretend convincingly to believe my protestations.

"I know you mean what you say," she told me after the crisis was over, "but you can't help yourself."

"I can't help myself?"

"No."

Implausible as this may seem, the idea was a new one to me. I was hurt and disturbed that Alice should believe it. The fact that she did believe it made it something to be reckoned with, almost as if it were true. But it couldn't be true . . . and then I ran through the old familiar routine. I am, after all, an intelligent man. I am perfectly capable of regulating my own conduct.

Alice might have said, though she didn't, *"Intelligence has nothing to do with it."*

Willpower has nothing to do with it.

To come to this conclusion earlier is one of the important challenges for those around an alcoholic as for an alcoholic himself. The act of drinking, which seems voluntary and for so many men and women is voluntary, becomes quite otherwise for the alcoholic. It is compulsive. One might well say, "The poor guy can't help it."

Drinking originates in forces as beyond conscious control, though different in kind, as the symptoms of scarlet fever.

It is a gift of the human mind to be able to learn by experience; but there are hidden drives behind many actions, and these hidden drives are not taught by experience or anything else. In one sense the alcoholic is aware of the lessons to be drawn from his life, but at the same time there are strange and sometimes fantastic forces that bid him ignore or deny what should be obvious. He is under this inner compulsion to go on repeating a cycle he can change only if he himself is changed.

Ben Jonson wrote of "the wild anarchy of drink," and so far as the human will and intelligence are concerned it is, for the alcoholic, the wildest of anarchies. Yet beyond his will it follows a familiar routine like the typical fever chart of an illness.

Thus come about the almost endless repetitions in an ever-descending course. Thus I found the repetitions in my own alcoholic life, and that is why I make record of them here.

Repetition is the essence of alcoholism. The expectation of reform or improvement, in the absence of some major change in the alcoholic's personality, is unlikely. Ordinary rules don't apply. The matter is almost always beyond reasoning.

It happens. It will happen again.

Over and over, under circumstances essentially the same though outwardly different, I made my protestations, denials, and assurances to Alice. At the times I made them, they were true. My penitence, self-accusation, and firm determination to free myself from alcohol were all real. Yet often I did have some reservations or at least awareness of extenuating circumstances that I knew it would be impossible to communicate to any other person, even to Alice. No one, outside this identical experience, can understand the quality and nature of the ordeal an alcoholic undergoes.

Alice was sympathetic. She wanted to understand. But words do not communicate the nature of a man's maladjustment and need when the very routine of life and work has become a discipline, the nerves jangle and shriek, the flesh and blood rebel. There is no adequate analogy. And to understand how these frictions, tensions, and clashes prevail over the rational behavior so natural to other human beings is harder when the break to alcohol seems to occur sometimes so suddenly, without resistance or warning. The pattern is not plain under observation, or it has twists and deviations.

QUESTIONS FOR DISCUSSION

1. In terms of Jellinek's phases of alcoholism, which phase best characterizes the experiences of this man?

2. To what degree does the excitement of drinking and being deviant contribute to the man's alcoholism?

3. What part do periods of abstinence play in the developing alcoholic?

4. What do you believe were the underlying causes of this man's excessive drinking? How might they have been treated?

5. Do you believe that the attitude and behavior of the man's wife was a contributing factor to his alcoholism? How might she have altered her behavior?

A FEMALE ALCOHOLIC As told to William L. McWhorter and James K. Skipper, Jr.

Interviewer: I guess the first and most obvious question to ask is are you an alcoholic?

Respondent: Well now that's a good question. I reckon I am, least ways that's what them psychologist, or whatever you call them, told me. I spent 6 weeks in the alcohol ward in Northcentral Mental Hospital and onced I was released stayed off the bottle for near bout 6 months. Course that's not the only time I had been in the hospital. I had been there lots of time and always would stay straight for about 6 or 7 months after I was let out. But always, my husband would start drinking and I would get nervous and so, would start hitting the bottle again.

Interviewer: Did your husband also have a drinking problem?

Respondent: Oh yea! In fact he was the cause, most of the time, for my drinking. He was also committed to the hopsital but when he got released he went straight to the liquor store and got a couple of fifths and we would start fighting and fussing and drinking together. He was always bad to drink and would like to argue about the littlest old thing. I think just to get me riled up so I would start drinking.

Interviewer: Have you drank most of your life?

Respondent: I guess so, at least since I was fourteen. You see we always had liquor around the house—you know, what they call homebrew or mountain wine and of course white lightning or moonshine. I saw my mother take a drink now and again but never seen her drunk. My daddy drank liquor too but I only saw him drunk one time. All my brothers and sisters, there were 7 of us, they all drank too. Not much when we was young but that where I got started. It made you feel good and I got to where I liked the taste.

Interviewer: Tell me something about your early life and how you became involved in excessive drinking?

Respondent: Well, I guess you could say I growed up fast. I got married when I was fourteen and didn't have much of what you call a childhood. My husband was 12 years older than me and was my first cousin's nephew, so we had knew one another for awhile. Anyway we was both working, he was at the hospital, janitorial work and I was at the blanket factory. We was married 6 years before our daughter was born. Those were pretty good years, we were boarding near where we worked and was doing all right. We was drinking but I wasn't drinking too much but he was getting drunk pretty regular. He was terrible jealous and would accuse me of running around and seeing other men. This always led to big fights so finally I quit and just stayed home. After that I figured he would leave me alone. I took in sewing and made money that way. I also could drink on the job cause I always had a bottle beside the sewing machine and I would nip all day long. Just sorta stay high. My customers began to recognize this and some came by and drank with me and others would bring a bottle at Christmas time or on my birthday.

Interviewer: It sounds like your marriage was not very pleasant.

Respondent: It wasn't but with time you remember only the good times and not the bad. After our daughter was born I stayed home and did not go back to work. I thought this would be the best since my husband couldn't accuse me of seeing other men. Course that didn't happen. He still said I was seeing them during the day when he wasn't there. I led what you might call a sheltered life after that. He believed in women staying home and not going out. My neighbors hardly ever saw me because I stayed in all the time. When we would go to town and a man would ask me a question or hold a door open for me he would go crazy—accusing me of all sorts of things. So it was just easier to stay home. I

This interview is contributed by William L. McWhorter and James K. Skipper, Jr.

won't blame it all on him. I accused him of seeing other women and flirting. When we did go to a party and did social drinking I'd get mad if he talked to other women and he'd get mad if I talked to other men so we stopped going out. I can say one thing for him, he was a worker. He always worked, even though he might be hung over he always worked.

Interviewer: Where is your husband now?

Respondent: Oh, didn't they tell you? You really don't know. Well, the law says I strangled him to death. I don't deny that I was choking him but I really don't believe I killed him. What happened was this: after our son left to go back to his foster home we got to drinking. We did stay sober the whole time he was home but when he left we got to drinking and pretty well got lit. I went into the dining room where I had an old sofa and laid down to go to sleep. My husband went into the back of the house to the bedroom to sleep. I remember him getting up and going out and bringing back more liquor and some groceries. After he had put them away he went back in the bedroom. In a little while I saw, and the doctors say I was hallucinating, but I don't think I was. Anyway I see this girl pass by the hall and go out the back door. I laid there a minute and then I seen my husband pass by the hall too. I knowed what he was up to because, well I don't know how to put it, it's well, you know sorta embarrassing, but well *anyway* his penis was erect and sticking through his shorts. He only had on his shorts and a towel around his neck. I remember the towel because he said he was going to put it on the pillar so he wouldn't get it dirty. Well when I saw him I got up and went back there and grab the towel around his neck and twisted it. They say a drunk don't know their own strength so maybe I did twist it pretty good. He did not struggle so I must not have been choking him because if you are being choked you gonna fight. He slipped down on the floor and me on top of him, still holding the towel. Well I am afraid to let him up cause of what he might do to me, so I drag him down the hall, through the dining room and to the living room where I call the rescue squad and the police. He was still alive because I listen to his heart and he was still straight up, if you know what I mean. A little foam was coming out of his mouth but he was still breathing. Well just as the rescue men come

up the walk I knew he was dead cause that's when he went down—you can always tell by that. Anyway they come in and said he was dead, didn't give him oxygen or nothing. The police came and took me down to jail and asked me a lot of questions. I knew all of the police because I had spent a lot of time in jail for public drunkenness and disturbing the peace. So they knew both me and my husband real well.

Interviewer: What happened after your arrest?

Respondent: I was charged with murder. The police and the papers, it was all written up in the papers, made it sound like a soap opera. They said things I never told them. I got what you call your public defender and he said to plead guilty and maybe they would reduce the charge. That's what I done and the judge gave me 4 years for voluntary manslaughter. Those police sure did hate to see me go. I stayed in jail 4 months and kept that place spic and span. They said it had never been cleaner and wanted me to stay.

Interviewer: A moment ago you spoke of your daughter. Do you have other children and if so how did they react to your drinking?

Respondent: This is the roughest thing to take. It brings tears to my eyes. My daughter got married at 16 to a boy who is exactly like her father. I knowed she married just to get out of the house and this makes me sad. No children should have to leave their homes because the parents are fighting. She is married and has a little baby. Her husband is a spoiled mama's boy who works when he wants to. His mother has taken care of them and that is not right. But I don't say nothing and stay out of their business. My daughter will drink socially but not much but her husband is always drinking beer and whiskey. I had 2 boys after my daughter, all the kids was 6 years apart. My oldest son started getting into trouble real early but nothing real bad. Just hung out with a bad crowd. Finally we had to go to court and they took him away from us and put in a foster home. He did not like it there and ran away all the time. Finally the court sent him to live in Mountain Gap and he board there and went to high school. He finished up there and we all went to his graduation. I was so proud of him and he is now in junior college. He wrote me the nicest letter the other day and told me he did not blame me for what all had happened and he understood. He has turned out real well and I am awful proud of him especially seeing what kind of home situation he grew up in. The youngest boy is fourteen and in a foster home that he likes and is doing fine. I see him when he comes up here to visit. He is going to be all right because he was not exposed to all the bad things that the other children were. He was taken away from us when he was real little.

Interviewer: Looking back on your life can you now understand how you became an alcoholic?

Respondent: I think so, although so much has happened and so much could have been different. I believe when I get out of here I won't drink anymore but I am afraid. Who is going to hire me? I am old and don't have any skills. This worries on my mind. What happened to my husband was for the best. He was in poor health and could have suffered for a long time. I don't hold anything against him—it takes two to fight. Although we fought, he hit me and I'd hit him, we'd choke one another I did not mean to kill him. I am real sad about our family and what has happened to our children. Drink is a strange thing—you know you become somebody else—like me—I was always quiet and sheltered but seems like drinking frees you. Course a person

should be free to begin with and not have to drink. See those spots on my face, my husband use to make fun of me and tease me. I went to the doctor and he said I was all right but these spots were still there. When I drank they seem to go away and I did not eat as much. I am fat now but when I was drinking I was skinny. Life can be awful rough but you just got to do the best you can with what you got. I hope I can get out of here and get back to what's left of my family.

QUESTIONS FOR DISCUSSION

1.   Is there anything in this woman's family history that would lead one to believe she was a potential alcoholic?

2.   Do you believe this woman would have killed her husband if she had not been drinking?

3.   Does the woman fit into any of Jellinek's phases of alcoholism?

4.   In what respects does this woman fit the pattern of the "typical" alcoholic?

5.   Did the drinking of the woman's husband play any part in his death? Was the husband a victim or a participant in his own demise?

BEING HOOKED *Florrie Fisher*

I don't know just when I really got hooked on heroin. I never stopped long enough to find out after that first shot at the party, I just kept popping every day.

Up to this point Davy and I had only been smoking pot. David was getting it; I don't know anything about how to get it. I knew people used to meet the sellers on the corner and you could buy five sticks of pot for a dollar apiece, but I never knew any of the connections that sold loose pot.

One night, only a few months after we were married, we went to an after-hours club on Fifty-seventh or Fifty-eighth Street, off Broadway, for a party. A lot of the big-name jazz boys had gathered and the jamming was going full steam by the time we got there; it was the kind of music you can't pay to get during the regular club hours.

Some of the call girls I knew were right there on the dance floor rubbing elbows with the Park Avenue debutantes. Gene Krupa was there, and when he took off on a drum solo everyone crowded around the bandstand.

After Gene's solo some of the Negroes moved in with their gut-level New Orleans jazz. God, how I wanted to get out there and dance, but this was one of the few things Davy had never learned to do.

Suddenly Jerry Klein, one of his musician buddies, was beckoning us into a dark corner, near the dimly lit lounge entrances. Jerry was young, no older than Davy, but taller. He had long blond hair which he kept tossing back out of his eyes by jerking his head backward. His eyes were watery blue and darted from spot to spot. He never looked directly at us.

"Want to step the evening up? I got something here," he half-whispered.

I was already having a ball, but was game for anything. Davy knew what he meant, even if I didn't. "Got some good stuff?"

"Right from the horse," Jerry chuckled.

I was first. He bent over me and I felt a quick, stinging jab in my leg, which startled me. I hadn't expected him to move so fast. That was it. My introduction to heroin, to "horse," to "schmeck" had taken only that instant.

Davy had walked away to talk to another musician, but I couldn't care less where he was. I stood there for a minute waiting for something to happen, but right then nothing did. I didn't know then that a skin pop took longer to work than a mainline shot. But by the time Davy drifted back to my side I was turned on like an electric current had suddenly flashed through my belly; it was a terrific sensation which seemed to lift me out of the room, yet brought everything into sharper focus.

It didn't lay me low at all. In fact, as I walked back to our table I was terrifically elated. The excitement I'd felt when Jerry had held out the needle was nothing to the excitement which gripped me now as I swayed with the dancers or tapped the table with the rhythm of the music.

"How is it, is it good?" Davy asked.

"Daddy, it's the greatest . . . where's it been all my life? Find that guy, get some, quick, you'll love it!"

Davy left me and I just sat there. There could be no worries, no problems in this beautiful world. It was even more tremendous than the way I'd felt when Davy started me on pot, before I'd become so accustomed to pot that the highs weren't so good anymore. Oh, it was wonderful, wonderful.

But Davy's shot was too strong. He was deathly ill within about ten minutes after he had it, so some friends shoved us both into a cab and sent us home.

Who wanted to go home? I looked at Davy without a shred of concern or compassion, but helped him up the stairs as he retched over and over again.

He stretched out on our bed, still heaving, then lay back without breathing.

I thought he was dead, and at that moment the only thought I had was, "Now I can get back to the party." But the real love I had for him was strong enough to cut through the haze, and I held a mirror to his mouth to see if there was any breath left in him.

The mirror frosted slightly, so I rolled him over and started artificial respiration until he came to. The minute he was asleep normally, I was out of the apartment, out of the building and in a cab back to the club.

Oh, it was my world, my oyster. I felt wonderful, there were no problems, it was inconceivable that there could be anything wrong. And if anything did go wrong, well, what the hell, no sweat. With this great feeling I never doubted that I could handle anything and handle it easily.

After an hour or so I felt the effect beginning to wear off.

Oh, no, no . . . I couldn't let it get away from me, this great feeling. I hunted for Jerry. He was on the bandstand backing up a hot saxophonist who was taking off on "Deep Purple."

Instead of enjoying the music as I had before, my only thought now was for the break when I could get hold of another shot from Davy's friend, regain that rapturous, shining feeling.

Coming off the stand, he spotted me and laughed. "It didn't take you as long to get back as I expected. How's Davy?"

"Fine, just fine. Hey, how about another shot of that stuff?"

"Anything to oblige."

This time he gave me the needle, and I stared at it, hypnotized. I wanted to use that needle, it was so beautiful. I wanted nothing more than to plunge it into my vein. Even more than the feeling from the heroin, I wanted to feel that needle as I stabbed it into my trembling arm.

Oh, yes, that was it, that was the feeling. Even before I drew the needle out I could feel the world loosening up while my vision seemed sharper and sharper. Oh, it was a feeling like never before, so good, so wonderful.

Somehow I got home a few hours later. David was still sleeping between spells of vomiting, but even as I brought him hot soup and slapped a cold, wet cloth on his forehead, I could think only of getting another shot, reaching Jerry and that magic.

But I didn't have to find him, he found me, about mid-afternoon.

"Thought you might want me to drop by to see how Davy is doing," he drawled, leaning carelessly against the doorjamb.

"Hey, yes, that's nice of you. Say, that was great stuff. How about another shot?" I asked eagerly.

"Sure, it's great, I get only the best quality. But you know, baby, it costs me a lot. I can't give out charity."

Hell, I had money. . . . I had over five hundred dollars I'd put away from hustling over the past few days.

"Well, how much are you charging for charity?"

"For a friend like you I'll make it five dollars a cap. Anyone else, it would be ten."

I quickly bought ten caps. He offered to show me how to get it ready, but I'd seen some of the girls shooting and didn't want to be delayed with pointless instruction, so I hurried him out.

Heating a spoon over the burner on the gas stove, I melted down half a capful, as I'd seen the others do. Then I carefully drew it into a hypodermic needle a girl friend had left with us when she thought the cops were tailing her.

That was it, that was the way! Within seconds after I'd plunged the needle into my vein, I knew I'd already mastered the technique.

"What the hell you doing?" asked Davy, stumbling out of the bedroom.

"Shooting, like last night," I said. "Here, I've got enough for us both, maybe this time it won't make you sick . . . try it, it's really great."

"Where'd you get it?" he persisted.

"From your friend, Jerry Klein, he was just here."

"Some friend," muttered Davy, pouring himself some stale coffee.

He glared at me, then said, "Listen, kid, once at a party for a kick, that's all right, but another shot today, that could be bad."

But his words drifted over me without effect. Who needed his sermon? Nothing could ever happen I couldn't handle.

He talked on for a while, then realizing his words weren't reaching me, shook his head and got up. "I'll be back when you get off the nod," I remembered him saying, and he went to bed.

That was how the pattern began. I'd wake up with a shot, go to sleep with a shot. I'd have a shot before going to a trick.

I even convinced myself that it helped business, for I would be so dreamy, so detached that what I did really didn't matter. There were a lot of things I wouldn't do to please a trick when I started, but when I was high nothing made very much difference. "This is great," I'd tell myself. "With a shot the whole thing is just great."

Nothing mattered, nothing was sordid, depraved, there were no decisions to make, no worries so long as I had that all-important, all-necessary shot. And just that easily, just that simply, I slid into the habit, became an addict, a junkie, hooked on a life that left my twenties and thirties and early forties in the gutter.

Davy stayed with pot, that first bad experience with horse kept him off it for nearly five years.

For me, the saying "Horse is Boss" proved true, for as soon as I discovered junk—heroin, cocaine, opium—I didn't want any part of pot, it just didn't do anything for me.

Also, I didn't want any part of liquor. Very few junkies drink. Not wanting booze when I was with a trick, especially when part of the evening was dinner and dancing, could be a problem. They would expect you to take a drink or they'd get suspicious. So I'd always try to get them to go to a place where I knew the bartenders and they'd make my drink with soda and coloring, like coke, and they'd get the full price for the drink.

I got my kick using the needle as much as from the junk, just seeing it gave me a weird kind of thrill. It is such a sick thing, everything is upside down when you're on junk.

For instance, I remember I had this vein which stood out so strongly I didn't even have to tie up to hit it, it was a real popper.

One day I was watching Blanche and Kitty, two of the girls who sometimes got their calls at our place. They hadn't been able to meet their connection on the street that afternoon so came up to our place. Sometimes they would turn me

on, giving me a quarter or half of a cap. Today it was my turn.

They'd waited longer than they should have for their connection, and by the time they knew he wasn't going to make it, they were already nodding and sweating.

They'd been using for years and their veins were black pencil marks tracing their arms and legs. I watched, fascinated, while they fought nausea, jabbing the length of their inner arms, exploring every blue line for an opening. With a long-time user it isn't easy, for every spot once hit with a needle becomes rock-hard, and can't be used again. Sweat beaded on their foreheads while they frantically probed.

After twenty minutes Kitty found a vein behind her knee which yielded to the needle. By this time her hand was shaking so badly she could hardly plunge it in. You could almost hear it squeak as it hit home, her eyes became glassy and relief flooded her frightened face within seconds.

Blanche's hair, usually drawn up into a neat chignon, now fell into a snarled, sweat-drenched mass down her back as she continued to struggle for a vein. Kitty sat sprawled on a kitchen chair, giggling now at Blanche's agonizing lunges with the needle. Finally, after ten minutes, she pulled her dress up on her skinny hips and started pounding her fist against her inner thigh to raise the artery in her groin, the junkie's last resort. She found it, popped it and then fell back, exhausted, as the drug seized her inert body.

Their euphoric relief excited me. This was even more thrilling than shooting straight. The working, the anxiety, would make that first exhilaration even more tremendous, I decided. So, instead of using my easy vein, I started hunting for a hard one. I'd start using a vein that was a roller: when you tie up it moves, it rolls, and it's tough to get at with the needle.

I would sit there and hold it and work with it and finally I got to where I loved sweating it out almost as much as the excitement of the needle.

Oh, it was sick, real sick, but at that point I couldn't care less, nothing mattered, nothing but the thrill in that needle.

The dope left me completely uninterested

in sex. This was no problem with the customers, I never had any feelings for these men, never reached an orgasm with a trick, it was always an act.

But I couldn't even have sex with Davy and really reach a climax after I went on dope. This is the way it works with most people, it is always a scream to read about the concern the squares have about the sex-mad dope fiend. A guy really hooked on dope doesn't care very much about sex. He'll steal, even murder, to get the money for the stuff, but sex just doesn't interest him. It's the kooks on amphetamines or high on hallucinogenics like LSD or STP who take a thrill from sex, and even these guys are usually too freaked out to resort to force or rape.

Davy was a terrific lover, he knew all the tricks, but still it didn't work.

At first I would pretend, trying to please him, but he wasn't as dumb as the square Johns who fell for this, because they needed to think they were the greatest lovers in the world.

Then we started freaky things and our relationship got sicker and sicker until I didn't care what I did with Davy. So long as he enjoyed it, I enjoyed it, too.

He'd bring up another girl and the three of us would go to bed together, or he'd bring in one of his buddies and enjoy watching me with him. Sometimes he'd have another girl, sometimes not. We tried daisy chains, every kind of stupid, insane perversity.

I didn't get a kick out of it, but once he got started he began to enjoy things more and more way out. I was willing to do everything he wanted, anything he wanted to do, and look like I enjoyed it. After a while I didn't have to pretend I was enjoying it, for I began to get a sexual feeling out of it, started to get really interested, although I couldn't actually reach a climax with the freaky stuff.

We were well into this when I took another pinch for pross, and got tossed into the House of Detention.

Until that arrest, it never occurred to me that I was addicted. I simply never had thought about it, one way or the other.

But at 2 a.m., about six hours after I was busted, it really broke loose. I vomited, my bow-

els and bladder couldn't be controlled, I was wetting and dirtying myself and screaming for help. Right away I was busted to the junkie tank. I was almost too sick to care, but at least in the junkie tank I was able to find someone who got a kite out to Davy for me.

"David, please, please bail me out, I'm addicted and sick as hell. Hurry, hurry, hurry."

The next morning I was in the shower with the dry heaves, sweating, then freezing with chills, my insides ripping apart. "It won't be long, it won't be long and Davy will have me out," I kept telling myself.

Then, and I'll never forget that moment, the matron walked in and smacked this telegram against the damp shower stall so it stuck to it, and I read: DARLING, I LOVE YOU, YOU KNOW I DO, BUT FOR YOUR OWN SAKE I'M NOT GOING TO BAIL YOU OUT. LOVE, DAVID.

He wanted me to kick my habit, to start fresh after this cold-turkey withdrawal, but I was in a rage. I was furious. I hated him.

I got another thirty-day suspended sentence, and when I walked out I was determined not to go back to him. But there he was, waiting. He took me into his arms and sweet-talked me as before, and we were back together again.

When I had started on the hard stuff David had decided to be a connection, buying it in bulk and capping it up for retail.

When he wasn't around, or when he was sleeping, I would open up each cap and collect whatever little bit fell out. He used to keep about five hundred. I'd tap them all, then I'd get hungry and go back and tap them again.

Davy'd come in, or wake up, and check his caps. He'd say, "I don't understand it. I filled all these caps and they were full."

"The heat shrinks them," I told him.

He'd hide his stash. I'd find the caps in the ice-cube trays. He'd believed me and put them in there so they wouldn't shrink.

I found my own connections, and by holding out a part of the money I made each day, turning tricks he didn't know about, I could buy all I needed. But it was more fun to fool him, like some sick, sad sort of game.

One of my junkie girl friends, Mickey, used to come and visit us. I'd stand in the bedroom doorway, talking to Davy in the bedroom, with my arm across the kitchen wall behind me. And Mickey would be shooting me up, behind me in the kitchen, while I talked to Davy.

Or I'd put my works, my junk and equipment, outside the apartment between the carpeted steps in the walkup. Later I'd casually say, "Oh, was that the mailman?" and I'd run out and snatch the works and come back with them.

Then I would go into the bathroom, while David was lying down in the bedroom, and I would get the stuff out. I'd open the door, then check to see if he was sleeping. Next I'd put the stuff in the spoon and check again to see if he was sleeping. Satisfied, I'd cook it up, checking one more time. I'd finally get it ready, even have my arm tied up, then check one more time.

Once I didn't check, just peeked through the keyhole. What did I see? His eye looking back at me from the other side!

He was so mad he chased me out of the house, stark naked except for a rubber tube twisted around my arm. I turned down the alley and beat him back to the apartment, but unlocked the door when he started lunging to break it down.

David was suspicious after that, always watching my money carefully, keeping track of the time I was gone.

I told him I'd kicked, wasn't using anymore, but he stayed suspicious. When he came home he'd want to look into my eyes, to see how the pupils looked. I found out that I could put belladonna in my eyes and they would dilate so I could fool him.

I almost fooled myself permanently. I put in too much and nearly went blind. For three weeks I had to be led around. I was terrified I might never see again. Even then I pulled off some tricks; some guys are just weird enough to think it's exciting doing it with a blind girl, so the income never stopped.

Later I would sneak money out from under his pillow, the money I earned hustling. I'd go and find some junkie friend, give her the money and tell her to buy some stuff from Davy.

She'd do it, we'd meet downstairs and I'd give her some, shoot the rest into me, and then go upstairs and talk to Davy about business.

As it got harder to get money from Davy I began taking chances with my connections, risks

I knew better than to take, even in desperation. You can get murdered, literally, for taking the kind of chances I took.

Like what I did with Al. I would call Al and tell him how many caps I wanted, little two-dollar caps. He would say he'd meet me on Forty-fourth Street and Broadway.

When I'd meet him, he'd say, "Give me the dough," and I'd pass him twenty dollars for ten caps.

Then he'd say, "See the Bond store? In the doorway there's an empty pack of Chesterfields," or whatever it was, and then he'd walk off. I'd go pick up the pack, and the stuff would be in it.

One day I called Al and told him I wanted fifty caps, a hundred dollars' worth, that a hundred-dollar trick was coming over. He told me to meet him on Forty-second Street, upstairs in a pool hall.

As sometimes happens, the trick didn't show. I tried to call Al to tell him, but couldn't get him, so I went over to the place he said I was to meet him.

There were three floors. The first was some small union hall, the second a down-at-the-heels beauty parlor, and the third floor was this pool hall. The next floor up was the roof, and about six steps up the stairs leading to the roof I saw an empty pack of cigarettes. Al was playing pool, his back to the stairs, so I snuck up, grabbed the pack, and sure enough, there were a lot of caps, and I figured it was my fifty.

So I snatched it and walked out.

I knew a junkie couldn't get away with stealing from a connection, so I rushed home and called Al at the pool hall, told him my trick hadn't shown up and begged him to let me have three caps so I could get straightened out and go to work.

I was a good customer, and he said okay.

I went back and we talked and I could see him looking to see if I was straight or sick. And I wasn't fixed, I knew enough not to be high when I saw him, or even straight, leveling off, because I told him I was sick.

And by the time I got there I was really sick, sicker than I'd ever been outside of jail. I was yawning, my nose was running, my body was itching all over, as if thousands of tiny bugs were crawling around inside my clothes, on my arms and legs. My insides were starting to roll when I got to the pool hall and he could tell I was about to go into the heaves.

He gave me the three caps and even leaned against the toilet door as lookout while I cooked it up and shot it, something a connection would rarely do.

"Now get the hell out of here," he muttered when I came out of the toilet.

I was glad to go, glad to get back home and shoot the rest of the stuff, the stuff I'd stolen from him, and get really high instead of just straight on the three caps he gave me.

He never knew I beat him, and it seemed so easy I started scheming on how to beat other connections.

Sometimes I would want a lot of stuff and be supposed to have a hundred dollars in cash. I would flash a hundred-dollar note, but I would have a "Michigan roll" too, with a twenty on top, a five under that, then some singles and bunch of cut newspaper.

I'd flash the good roll at the connection, then double-deal him the Michigan. They'd want to kill me and would have, except for Davy. Instead, they went to him.

The connection went to see Davy, but he didn't dare tell him that he had sold me anything. Davy had threatened to kill anyone who did, and they knew he meant it, but he said, "Hey, your old lady is using."

"Oh, no, she's straight, I know she isn't using," Davy answered.

But the connection persisted. "She is using because I know who's selling it to her."

From then on Davy watched me even closer, grabbing my money the minute I walked in the door, staring at my eyes every time I turned around.

It hit the fan the day I couldn't make a connection and had been tearing up the apartment looking for his stash. I couldn't find it, and I decided to take a shower so I could go out and work, turn a trick, then buy from somebody.

I started to wash my hair and suddenly hundreds of dollars' worth of the stuff came pouring out of the shampoo bottle, much of it already melting from the steam and heat.

Realizing I'd found Davy's stash, I poured the rest of the bottle into a metal soap dish, a gooey mixture of gelatin and heroin. There were

about 50 caps, a lethal dose, and I was so desperate I was about to shoot all of it.

At that moment David saved my life. He burst into the room and found me sitting naked on the wet tiles surrounded by melted and twisted caps.

He screamed and started slapping me. My head swayed from side to side with the stinging blows. "Okay, you stupid bitch," David shouted. "You're using . . . so go ahead and use it. I'll get you all you want and you'll work strictly for me. I'll have you on your knees begging me for a shot, if that's what you want . . . we'll play it your way."

Now Davy really had me. I was hooked and he wasn't. I had a pimp who knew I was going out there turning tricks because he controlled the dope I was getting and he controlled the money. Even if I could have gotten some extra, there wasn't a connection in New York who would have sold to me after that. Davy had me tied up tight.

I worked thirty-six hours out of twenty-four. We started living high, got an apartment on Sutton Place and were running with all the big pimps and whores and the big syndicate boys who controlled dope traffic in and out of New York.

And Davy had learned to be a real pimp in another way, too. When I started I had thought it was perversely romantic the way a friend's "old man" would beat her up if she didn't bring home enough money, or just because he got mad about something. I used to think it was a big sex thing and I wanted to be part of it.

I would go home and pick fights with Davy, hoping he would hit me so I could go down to the corner with a black eye and boast, "Oh, that bastard, look what he gave me!" It all seemed very sexy, very exciting, very important.

But at that time we were just two kids from good, clean families where you don't see violence between husband and wife and where people don't get into brawls, so our fights usually wore themselves out with a little shouting, and the fun of making up.

Now, however, the tenderness and meaning were gone, and as Davy became more adept at the techniques of being a pimp, his ideals about never hitting women changed too.

After he caught me with the caps and was

my only source, he started to knock me around at the slightest excuse. Maybe I didn't bring home enough money, or I'd forgotten to stop at the delicatessen, or I stayed too long in the shower. I'd never know what would set him off, but we'd start arguing, then get into a knock-down fight. He wasn't much taller than I was, and I was tough, but on dope you lose your strength and before long he'd have the best of me.

Then one time in February when he was hitting me I screamed, "If you ever lay another hand on me, I'm going to call the law."

This is something you just don't say to people in the life. You don't even think it. I didn't really mean it, of course, but he cooled right down then and said, "After you finish working tonight, meet me and we'll go on the town."

Around 10 p.m. I was home and got all dressed up. I had on my silver fox, I had a beautiful watch and rings, long earrings I'd gotten just the week before. A new blue brocade dress which showed off my tiny figure. Oh, I had put on the dog that night.

By that time we lived on Fifty-fourth Street, between Seventh and Eighth Avenues. David said he didn't want a cab, so we walked over to the theater district, just at the time the shows were breaking and the streets were jammed.

Suddenly Davy stopped right in the middle of the street, right there with people all around us waiting for cabs or walking in groups to the bars and supper places.

He turned and snarled at me, "Okay, bitch, now I'm going to give you something to call the police about. And that's just what I want you to do."

With one blow he knocked me into the dirty gutter slush, then pulled me up and slapped me across the face, over and over again, then another blow dropped me back into the filth of the street.

People began crowding around, but drew back uncertainly when he shouted, "Get the hell out of here. It's my wife, and she's got it coming . . . get out of here."

Then he stomped on my arms and legs, on my belly.

"Call the police. Go on, call them," and I knew better and croaked, "No," and every time I said, "No," he'd kick me.

Then he yanked me up again and took my coat off, my watch and my rings, tore off my earrings. Turning, he barked, "Okay, bitch, now you got something to tell the cops!" and he walked away casually, as if nothing had happened.

I was black and blue, I had two black eyes, my nose was bleeding down the front of my torn dress, the dress I'd felt so pretty in only such a short time before.

I shook off the few bystanders who offered to help me, trying to maintain some shred of dignity from the nearly forgotten past. Somehow I held myself together long enough to get away from the lights of the cars, the theater marquees, before breaking into violent sobs.

It was cold, bone cold, as I walked the blocks back to the apartment, and the cold mixed with the soreness of my arms and legs as I tried to keep walking, keep walking, keep on toward home and the sanctuary of that needle. When I hit the warmth of the hallway I collapsed, finally dragged myself up the stairs to our door.

And there was Davy, waiting at the door.

"Hello, pretty momma," he whispered, smiling down on me.

And then we were making love, making love like we had those first months we were together and I was as hot as he was, as quick to reach that first, then the second and third climax. He was my "old man," my daddy, my lover.

When you're on junk you don't even realize how you've deteriorated. You think you are really living a wildly exciting life, you never think how sick a relationship is, how low you have become as a woman, as a human being. Words like pride and respect aren't even remembered, much less understood. . . .

I never got a single or double header from hustling, and I never got an abscess from popping heroin. A single is gonorrhea or syphilis, and a double is both of them at the same time.

Most junkies can "lay up," turn tricks, wash up in a hurry and turn another one. I kept a portable douche bag in my makeup case, taking it with me wherever I went, and used it faithfully. Also, I never forgot the advice given by the madam who taught me Frenching. If ever I had any doubt about a trick, I insisted he use some protection and always had some with me so there would be no excuse. She had been right, while they complained they usually agreed rather than go without the sex they were so close to. These precautions, plus more than my share of luck, kept me from contracting a venereal disease.

Junkies get abscesses from using dirty needles, usually one that has been used by someone else and not carefully cleaned. Like I said, when you want a shot, you don't want anything else but a shot, and it has to be now right now.

I would never use anyone else's works unless I had absolutely no other way of shooting dope. Right after I started using heroin, I couldn't wait to have somebody score for a set of works for me. I didn't loan it out and I didn't borrow anybody's, unless I was in prison and had no other choice.

I was particularly careful, I guess, because when I was still new on dope, one of my girl friends came to me to help her out. She wanted a place to stay because she was sick.

She had an abscess on her arm, a big, ugly, running sore. She was lying there, resting on my bed, when she started groaning and writhing. I felt her and she was burning up with fever. Her arm was swollen around the abscess like a shiny, pink watermelon. She didn't know me, she didn't know anything, and I was afraid she was going to die on my hands. We took her to Bellevue and dropped her in the emergency entrance. I heard later that she almost died there, from that sore, the result of a dirty needle.

I never forgot that and I was careful. Well, as careful as a junkie could be. I remember going into old Hector's Cafeteria on Forty-second Street lots of times. The first thing I wanted to do was take off in the bathroom.

You can't take your shot out where the other women will see you, of course; you've got to get into one of the toilet stalls and lock the door. I would get into one and take everything out, the junk, spoon, eyedropper, matches, and the needle: the works.

When this little smorgasbord was laid out in front of me on the back of the toilet, I'd want to go out to the sink and draw some water, but some woman would be bound to come in and see, so I couldn't risk it.

But you couldn't wait, not for a minute. So instead of waiting for the woman to finish and wash her hands and get out, I'd flush the toilet, reach in, pull the swirling water up from the commode into my syringe and put it into the spoon. Then I'd rationalize, "I'm heating the spoon. That must be killing the germs," and I'd jam that needle, stool water and all, into my vein.

Sometimes, when I had more time than one flush of the toilet, I'd flash it, shoot about a tenth of the stuff, draw a little blood back into the needle, shoot another tenth, and draw up a little blood again. I'd do this until the stuff was gone, the needle empty. Each time I'd shoot that little bit there would be this great feeling, like an orgasm in the belly, then finally the great high set in. Some junkies can draw it out into even more flashes, drawing it up and shooting it back until that final high sweeps them up. I'd get so anxious for the final jolt I couldn't wait out more than five or six flashes.

Like other junkies, I'd also flash, or boot it, when I wasn't sure of my connection. If the stuff is dirty, contaminated, or weak, you test it by shooting it just a small amount first, waiting for your body's reaction, until you shoot the full load.

When I was in jail, I'd try to clean the needle to make sure nobody's blood was stuck on it. Not so much for cleanliness, but because the blood would clog up the needle and you couldn't get the junk into your arm. When you're in the House, everything good you've learned outside, even Jewish housekeeping, goes out those barred windows.

Mamma always used to nag at me to "eat, Florrie, eat. You're as thin as a bird," she used to say as she shoved more food at me.

Like all junkies, I never had an appetite. Sometimes I weighed, like, seventy-five pounds. No more. I'd keep eating the same things, chocolate-covered doughnuts with chocolate milk, or strawberry shortcake. I'd get on kicks, but even with these special cravings, I'd try to pamper my stomach; I wouldn't eat in dirty places. When I did get hungry, I'd try to pack in something substantial and healthy. I was lucky Mamma always fed us properly.

On those rare occasions when I did sit down to a steak-and-potatoes meal, I could almost imagine her standing over me, wiping her hands on her apron, counting every mouthful I took and every time I swallowed. She would be telling me to eat like she used to when I was little, but in my mind's eye, she was also always crooning, "My daughter's a junkie, but she eats well." That's probably what my mother would have said, too, if she'd known.

Those big meals were rare. Most of the time, when I'd think I was starving, I'd eat a doughnut, and bam, I'd feel full, satisfied.

Why should I have worried about my stomach, though? I was murdering my body. There were tracks all over me, where the veins finally gave up the fight against the needle, and died, collapsed, withered to tiny, blue trickles of blood, covered by mushy membrane that had more holes in it than a sponge.

I have only one good vein left. It's in my neck, and even that vein can't be used for anything but a blood test. If I need a transfusion, an incision down to an artery must be made, then stitched back up. I carry in my wallet at all times a card reading:

IN CASE OF EMERGENCY FOR INTRAVENOUS

DO cut-down immediately   Re: all veins collapsed

Herbert S. Kaufman, M.D.   San Francisco

But you don't think of this stuff when you're on junk, about collapsing your veins and getting track marks.

You think about one thing, getting high. That's why you don't wait until you get into your apartment to shoot, why you have to go into a cafeteria and use water from the toilet bowl, because you can't wait, you just can't wait.

How do you explain that feeling? It's nothing like getting tight on liquor. There's no comparison. I don't like liquor much, but I'd been high on it in college, and it's different. Liquor has nothing that grabbed me enough to make me want to get that kind of high.

Grabs you. That's what it does. You don't slide into a high like you do on booze. Dope seizes you like the hand of a giant, lifting you higher, higher up to his mouth. But the giant doesn't eat you. He kisses you and it feels wonderful.

After you shoot, there's this rush. It lasts about four minutes. You are all pins and needles.

And then, boing, a skyrocket explodes. A lobster couldn't be that hot. It levels off and you feel good. The giant's just kissed you and you feel as though the insides have been kicked out of all your problems and everybody else's. You have a tremendous feeling of climbing up, out of the hole you've been in. You're nodding, out of it. Zonked.

That lasts about four hours. Then the euphoria wears off and you're normal. You're fine. But after another two or four hours you begin to feel sick.

The gentle giant isn't kissing you any longer. He's about to attack you.

It starts with yawning. You keep yawning and your eyes begin to tear. Your nose starts dripping. Then you feel sweaty, an odd kind of sweat, not the kind you get if you've been exercising or working hard. It's a damp, clammy feeling. You start itching all over.

Your head starts thumping, thumping, thumping like you're inside a bass drum when it's struck. If you don't take a fix soon, you're vomiting. You throw up and throw up, and when there's nothing left, your guts are still convulsing with the dry heaves.

The giant is squeezing the last drop out of you.

It's nothing like the way you feel when you're coming down with the flu. You can always tell when it's dope sickness.

I never waited for the yawns to start. I'd think, "I'd better take a shot, I was so sick the last time." And before I'd have a chance to stay normal, I'd be zonked again.

Most junkies come off the nod, they come to, and that's their normal. But they won't accept that. They think that as soon as they come off the nod, they've got to get high again.

That's why it costs so much, feeding that giant, keeping that big bastard happy and mellow. Most of us got three times the amount we really needed physically. You'd think you'd need more and more all the time.

Maybe one bag got it for you this month. Well, next month you're going to need two bags. You start with half a three-dollar bag. Then you go to two three-dollar bags. Then you're using two five-dollar bags for a shot. Then you start buying a twenty-dollar bag, quarter-ounce. You go up and up.

I used to think I wasn't in the same class as the other junkies. Most addicts, if they have a fifty-dollar-a-day habit to support, figure, "I've got to get at least forty-five dollars, I'll owe the connection five."

I always prided myself on being a money-maker. If I had a fifty-dollar-a-day habit, then I'd have to make a hundred a day, because I liked to live in a decent place. I wanted good clothes. I liked having money for a beauty parlor, for cabs, for living like a big shot. Those kinds of things keep you thinking you're not like the old whores and bums you'd see on the street. Sure, you're a junkie like they are, but you're never going to wind up like that.

QUESTIONS FOR DISCUSSION

1. Does Florrie Fisher manifest the sociodemographic characteristics of the typical drug addict? Is her life style typical?

2. To what extent can Florrie's addiction be explained by the availability theory? Stepping stone theory?

3. Why did Florrie not realize she was hooked until she was arrested?

4. Was it the euphoria or the withdrawal symptoms that "hooked" Florrie?

5. What characteristics does Florrie's husband have in common with "Iceberg Slim" (Selection 18)? Do you think he could give Slim any advice about business?

A PIECE OF THE ACTION *Richard P. Rettig, Manuel J. Torres, Gerald R. Garrett*

I think I was about fourteen when I started to get really involved in gambling. Some people just naturally seem to have card sense, and I was one of them. From the first time I ever sat in a poker game or rolled dice in an alley, I knew without a shadow of a doubt that I could win. Now, when I'm talking about gambling, I mean for big money. The guys in the neighborhood would think it was funny to take me to a card game and I would sit there and play like an old-timer. All of fourteen, but I knew when to draw for a straight, when to try and fill up, and what the odds of staying in or dropping out should be. I didn't have the gambling fever like lots of people get. I had the game down cold. Like, I remember the time when I had three sixes and I knew that I was beat at least once going in. But several players stayed and it was a real good pot—about eight hundred dollars before the draw. I drew two nines. It was as if I knew that I would fill, and I knew I had them cold. I won twenty-six hundred dollars on that one hand. Another time I had three fours and because of the betting I decided to draw one as if I was holding a four-flush or a big straight. Then I had planned to pretend like I drew right and was going to bet like hell. I'd already made up my mind as to strategy. This is important, to get your mind right and not to waver. Well, damned if I didn't catch the outside four and, as they say, I was shitting in tall cotton. I forget what that hand cost them, but it was a bundle.

Although I was Puerto Rican, the part of the Bronx that I grew up in was mostly Italian. Gradually I began to shift from ganging to hustling. By the time I was fifteen I was working for this big bookmaker. Everything was divided up in the New York rackets in those days. And Leo had all the action around the neighborhood having to do with playing the numbers or the pools.

As I was growing up in the neighborhood I used to run errands for Leo and do things like hustle him his coffee from the corner store. I was always around and ready to do him favors. As I got older I started doing him bigger favors, like running book occasionally when someone was jammed up. He thought my ganging activities were "cute" at first but after I grew older he told me to wise up.

So, it was natural for him to offer me a job in his organization. One day, when he had lost somebody important, Leo offered me the job of numbers man. He trusted me, and he knew that I practically worshiped the ground he walked on. He knew that I wasn't about to cheat him. At least, I wouldn't cheat him big. Everybody grifts a dollar here and a dollar there. But only a moron rips off a big piece of the Organization's action.

Leo told me that I would be responsible for all the money that came into the central shop. And I would audit the incoming dough against the numbers being bet as checked out on the slips. I would have to be sure that I had the right amount of money on hand to cover the bets. So, I had control of the books and I was really making money. I was getting a salary plus a big percentage when the rake-off exceeded our operating nut, and it always did.

I had plenty of time to play a lot of poker, rummy, pinochle, or whatever, because my job required only about three hours a day. I was winning a lot of money gambling with guys in their thirties and forties—guys who'd been gambling all their lives. I had a lot of card sense, but above that, I was really lucky. I mean, I couldn't seem to make a mistake, or, if I did, I would get it all back a hand or two later. Everything I did turned out right so I had a lot of money.

I was playing the horses at this time, too.

Really lucky. I never knew anything at all about horses. But I'd bet and win, bet and win. Like, I sent my mother to Puerto Rico on vacation one time for a month. Nothing was too good for her. I told her she'd better go first class all the way or I was going to be mad. In fact, I tried to buy her a house, but for some reason it didn't work out, I don't remember why.

I started playing cards in some of the real big-time clubs around New York. Occasionally, when I was short of money guys would be eager to front me and I would play for a percentage. But usually I was clearing about two thousand a week. In my head I thought I was a big-time gangster: I started to dress like all the Italians in the neighborhood. Sharkskin suit, white on white shirts, pinstripe ties, and a derby or a stingy brim hat. Sometimes I'd spend fifty or seventy-five bucks for a hat or a lousy pair of shoes.

I even started smoking cigars. 'Cause Leo, my boss, smoked cigars, so I started smoking them. I just started playing the part of a real cool hood. At first it was a game. I still felt like little Manuel, the Young Star, acting violent. But soon it wasn't a game any longer. My identity became associated with Leo, the rackets, and big-time gambling. And one day I woke up knowing that I had set sail from my youth.

One thing that always got me into trouble is that I never knew nothing about the management of money. And especially when I was a punk kid making several thousand a month. All this money appeared fast and I'd spend it just as fast. Easy come, easy go, was the way I believed and lived. I used to order real fine two-hundred-dollar sharkskin suits three at a time. Every night I'd be out spending money. I'd go into a classy bar and order up for the house all night. I don't know how many times I used to put a hundred-dollar bill down on the bar and drink it up.

And my brother Bobby was sixteen and he tagged along with me most of the time. In New York the drinking age is eighteen. But if you got money and are willing to spread it around lavishly, people close their eyes. I was living fast, hanging loose, and raising hell. But I was tending to business and doing real good.

Then, in the building where I was living, a bunch of new tenants moved in; among them was Freddie. Freddie became the apartment super, and I didn't realize it at the time, but

Freddie changed my life. Freddie used to pick up the garbage, put coal in the boiler, and do all the odd jobs around the building. He was all the time smoking weed. Bobby and I met him in the hallway one day and he was standing there smoking a joint. He asked us if we wanted some. I had never smoked weed before.

So, what the hell, I tried a joint. Because, you know, Freddie was an all right guy, and besides I just wanted to try it. I tried it and I liked it. About the second time I smoked weed I got higher than a kite. We lived on the third floor and Freddie lived on the second floor, just about under us. We used to go down to his pad every night and smoke weed.

Then Freddie turned us on to a source where we could buy pot. We used to pay five dollars for a whiskey shot glass full, and the connection would measure it out in a plastic bag in five- or ten-dollar lots. Soon I was smoking weed several times a day.

Freddie told me all about his ex-dope fiend life one night. He said he used to have a seventy-five-dollar-a-day habit, but that now he wasn't using any more. Said he'd been doing good for several months. But he was smoking a lot of weed and drinking lots of booze. I mean, he was going to the neck with mucho whiskey. Freddie used to drink two fifths of whiskey a day. Freddie was a young guy too soon old. He didn't have to warn me against heroin, I could see the results in his life. But I really didn't think anything about heroin, about using, that is. I knew it was around, but I didn't think it was for me.

One day my uncle comes around and he's using heroin, but none of us know it at the time. He came over to see my mother, but she was downtown. So, he throws this three-dollar bag of dogie on the kitchen table and says, "Try some."

I say, "Eddie, I ain't about to put any of that shit in my arm." He acts real surprised. "Hey, Manny, I'm not talking about shooting. I mean, you can snort it and get drove into the next county."

So, he shows me how to take a book of matches and cut off the end of a paper match and mash it between my fingers till it's like a spoon. And I stick it in the heroin and hold it up to my nose. I close off one nostril, hold the other one, and breathe in. Shit o'dear, man! I just got fucked up. My head starts to spin, I start to throw up, and I say, "What the fuck did I do, Eddie?" Man, I really got up tight. I was really sick; I felt terrible. And I tell Eddie, "Man, I don't want no more of this. That's it, I've had it!"

And he says, "Okay, Manny, I ain't going to force you to use my stuff."

A couple of days later he comes by the house again and he is holding some more horse. I say, "Eddie, maybe I'll try it again. Will it be any different?"

"Sure," he says, "Oftentimes the first snort is a bummer."

So I snort again and hey, it's really something else. I mean, it's like the shit really hit the fan . . . you can't describe it. All the colors of Times Square tumble right over your forehead and explode in your eyeballs like a million, jillion shooting stars. And then, each one of them goddamn stars novas in a cascade of brilliant Technicolor.

And the world levels out. You know what I mean? There's no right, no wrong. Everything's beautiful, and it's like nothing's happening baby but clear, crisp light. The mambo beat is like hot fuck notes bouncing off lukewarm street scenes. The drummer downstairs in the park is onto life's whole fucking secret, and the primitive urge of his swinging soul becomes a mellow sharpness in your ears. And you want to gather all of creation inside you; maybe for a minute you do. What a perfect Manny Torres you become for a moment!

But I was real scared of the effect, although I think that I wanted to experience it again. So, I went a couple of months and didn't use any more. Until one day when I went back into a shoeshine parlor in the neighborhood where I used to go to get my shoes polished every day. I changed shoeshine boys, and that cost me a life on heroin. I used to spend two, three bucks every day to get a spit shine. Seeing my face in my kicks would make me feel real good. But that was the trip I was into. Different suit every day; fifteen-dollar ties by the dozen; the hats, the shirts, the whole bit. Anyway, this shoeshine dude was selling heroin on the side. I didn't know it until I seen him passing a bag to somebody and I say, "Hey, you know what? I want one of those."

And he says, "Two dollars."

"Sure; that's no problem." So I give him the two bucks, stick the bag in my pocket, and I'm real happy. I go home and I snort it all up. I really got loaded. And you know what? For the first time I begin to relax a little in my obligation to Leo and my work. Now, I get so I'm going over to the shoeshine parlor every day after a bag or two and snortin' several times a day.

Then my uncle comes over one day with an outfit. And he says, "You wanna try fixing it?"

"Hey, man, I don't know. I'm scared of needles." I'm still thinking that you can get hooked with needles, and that there ain't the danger to just snortin' the stuff.

"Well, look," my uncle says, "you can go halfway and skinpop it."

Okay. I decide to go 'cause what the hell. If snorting is so good, maybe popping is even better. So, we draw it into the syringe and he shows me how to just break the skin and get the stuff into the muscle, just underneath the skin. And you get the same reaction as snorting, only better because the kick hits you faster.

I thought that I'd be satisfied with skinpopping forever. But everybody else around was mainlining it, sticking it in the vein. I go for about a month popping. Now I'm scoring every day, and some days using a lot of stuff.

It gets to be easier and easier to think about mainlining, until one day I decide to try it, just once. Hell, yes, just once! Shit, man, from that day on it was straight shooting for me. 'Cause you stick it in your vein, and the blood comes up working its way into the syringe. And when you see your red river of life well up in the glass, you press in that hellborn liquid fire and the whole universe rushes on you.

You know, it's hard to explain the rush. It just knocks you completely into another dimension. The nod is like—you know, it's not describable. There's not words to express the feeling. The feeling is *that* good. So good that once hooked you never really live the feeling down.

And from that day on, scoring and fixing, nodding, puking, scoring and fixing became my song of life. Everything else was marginal to my major concern—dope, shit, heroin.

Okay, so I still got money. I'm still hustling the numbers. I'm still able to front as a big shot, a guy to reckon with in the neighborhood, a guy who wins big at the poker tables. But I'm beginning to get hooked. The physiological must is beginning to inhabit my guts until I can't stand it if I don't have shit in my system constantly. So I'm beginning to fix—instead of once or twice a day, or even missing a day now and then, I'm beginning to have to go four times a day just to maintain.

I try to hide from my friends, Leo and the guys, the fact that I'm using but I'm spending more time with dope fiends than I'm spending with my job. You can just front and cover for so long and then it all breaks down. The explanation is simple. You gotta have dope. To have dope you gotta score. To score is sometimes easy, sometimes very difficult. But it usually always takes time. And then, the fix and the nod. Like, your whole damn life is shit, man, shit!

See, once you're hooked you're not your own boss any more. You belong to your habit. Plain and simple. You plan and scheme, and con, and lie, and hustle for your habit. Anybody and everybody becomes fair game. Look, you leave mother, brother, sister, father, friend for heroin. When you're hooked you gotta score. It ain't maybe I'll score, maybe I won't. It's, man, I'm gonna score and all hell ain't gonna stop me! And scoring can take time; it can be downright frustrating and uncomfortable. I've waited for over three hours on a street corner for a cat with the bag to surface. And you don't leave, 'cause he's the only one holding and if you miss him someone else will get the stuff and you'll be left holding air.

So, a lot of time I used to spend taking care of business for Leo on the job I now am spending feeding my habit. It begins to get obvious. 'Cause I gotta hurry with the collections and such, I start making mistakes. I even miss pickups and tallies, and this is really unforgivable in the business.

Leo calls me in to his office one day and says, "Listen, Manny, I've heard. No use lying to me, man, I hear that you're hooked on heroin. Now, if you're using dope, you've gotta stop now! Nobody in this organization uses any kind of narcotic. A doper becomes dependent on that shit, and then we can't depend on him. If you're using heroin, you gotta stop now."

I started to run it down on him. "Listen, Leo . . ."

"Kid, I'm saying that if you are using I'm going to give you two weeks off and the number of a private hospital. You don't have to tell me if you go in or not. You just go. I don't even want to know if you're using or not."

Leo was really trying to help me. It wasn't only that I was missing collections and making mistakes that bugged Leo. He really liked me as a person and wanted to keep me from getting blown out. He'd arranged the hospital bill already whether I went or not. This is typical of the Organization; when its people need help, they'll front you all the way.

So, I went. And I kicked. Rather, they reduced my habit gradually with the use of morphine. They had me on maintenance therapy using morphine, hoping I'd be able to finally kick the morphine easier than the heroin. But it doesn't make it. All that happens is that the hospital mothers you along until you can get down.

Although there are some differences in effect, morphine and heroin are a lot alike. Only, I can tell heroin every time when I mainline the shit. It just works best for me. Like, I die almost, sort of all heavenly fucked up with a good fix. It starts deep in the gut and radiates out onto the furthest rim of consciousness. And the nod! Man, the only supersatisfactory nod for me is behind some good scag.

Scag is the only way into the real deep nod, that state of near oblivion when you lose touch with the reality of hurt and necessity. Where nothing is urgent, and for a little while it's as if you can walk on tiptoe with the gods.

So, I was just maintaining on the morphine in the hospital. But when I came out I made a beeline for the connection, anticipating the rush like being drop-kicked in the belly. As soon as I got fixed up with some sweet bonita dogie— like, a bag of scag—man, I was all right. I walk out of the hospital loaded on morphine, and I am in the neighborhood maybe ten minutes and I get down with heroin. It was no problem to find the ounce man, look up one of my kits, and take care of business.

Leo thinks I've kicked. 'Cause I told him so. He believes it 'cause I said it. Why not? After all, I had a boss rep from a long history of straight shooting with him. So, for the next two or three weeks I'm doing pretty good. I mean, I can manage to come down to the buzz level long enough to take care of Leo's business. The work requires perhaps three hours a day at the most, totaling up the tallies and keeping the books straight.

But it is only a matter of time and my habit begins to grow. And my front falls apart. Finally Leo says, "Manny, we gotta let you go. If you ever stop using, come back. You got a job forever. But scag and the business don't mix. Even if I would, I couldn't handle it. My boss would have my ass uptown in five minutes if he heard I was stringing along with a user."

I got a couple of personal things out of my desk and started to split, knowing inside that I'd really fucked up. But I didn't care. Not really. All I cared about was scag. Leo told me as I was leaving, "I'm giving you a month's pay and you're on your own. If you get into any trouble connected with dope don't bother to call. Because I'll hang up on you. If you get behind any scam besides stuff, call right away and we'll help. But with heroin you're on your own."

You know, I didn't even think of what Leo had done for me. All I thought was how much dope I could buy with the bread Leo had given me for separation pay. I didn't care because I got several thousand bucks, and that will buy a lot of shit.

I really gave up a good thing for heroin. Leo trusted me. He knew that I wasn't going to cheat him. He's told me since that they had big plans for me, maybe even to take his spot in a few years when he moved up. That ain't bad for a poor Spic kid! They liked me 'cause I had real good sense. I knew how to keep my mouth shut. I never said nothing. No matter what I heard about the Organization or the man I'd never repeat it. Even party talk, when the big bosses got a little mellow and said some kind of scary things, I'd dummy up like I never heard. They really dug that about me.

And I would ask questions if I didn't understand. But never got nosy or up tight if they put me in my place. I was on the bottom of the pyramid in the rackets, but that was all right. 'Cause there was lots of money trickling down. There was plenty of scratch for everybody. That was part of my problem. All this dough and you can only get rid of so much at a time.

I even asked them for more money just before the end—and got it. I figured out that they were making much more money than I had

thought, and I asked for a higher percentage of the collections. You know what? They gave it to me; no hassles. It's clear as I look back on my days in the rackets that they were beginning to groom me by increasing my responsibilities and giving me more money. And I was good at it. I could have made it big, but I broke it instead. All for scag fever. Getting down was life, and nothing else even made good sense.

By now I had a constant urge in my throat for junk. I could taste it, touch it with every angry nerve ending in my body. Nothing else mattered a damn. All the good intentions in the world fall before one cap of scag when you're using. Promises, once important, evaporate when the stuff is there. When you're yawning, nothing matters but scoring, fixing, and nodding. That's the way it comes down.

The white lady sucks, man. You think that you're sucking her up into the glass and mainlining her radiant ass. But the white junk lady sucks you in, man, until you belong. At first she's just a pretty little monkey; before long she's a shaggy gorilla. I've heard junkies say that you may be a weekend warrior when you start to flirt with her, but you soon get your wings. And that's the truth!

After I left the Organization I just used. Didn't have to hustle for a long time 'cause beside all the bread I scored from Leo as separation pay, I had a lot of markers out in the neighborhood. I started collecting what people owed me and living on that. But day by day it takes more scag to maintain, to stave off the cramps and chills. I go from a thirty-dollar-a-day habit to the place where it takes a big bill to score enough shit. Now I'm pushing and scraping myself. I'm trying to score from the kilo connection to get behind enough scag to push for profit. But this takes money in front.

For a while I get by on the touch. When you have a good solid rep, when you're *people*, other people will loan you bread no questions asked. But living on your reputation lasts just so long. You run out of gas and good will. You can only burn the best friend once or twice and it's all over between you. And the word gets around. "Watch Manny, he's slipped. Piece him off with a buck or two, but don't let him get into you for any long green." Then all you're doing is blowing in the wind. Your friends know that you're hooked on junk. They're sorry, of course, but they put you down.

So, you go back home to your family. (I had several aunts and uncles around New York.) 'Cause the family is always willing to give you the benefit of a doubt. "Oh, Manuel can't be hooked, not him. Maybe if we favor him some he'll straighten out." I remember working Aunt Rea and her old man for every nickel I could get. It didn't matter if it was food money, rent money, welfare money, doctor money. It wouldn't have mattered if it was burial money for my old lady I was stealing. Any money at all buys scag and that's all that counts.

Pretty soon the family is burned out and won't lend me any more dough. I hassle them, but before long they won't be hassled. So, I start stealing from them. I go over to my sister's house when they're all downtown and I walk off with anything that I can hock. This happens a couple of times with relatives and pretty soon they put out the word. "Manny's hooked like a dog. Turn him out like a mad dog."

So, they turn me out. Nothing else they can do. You can't have a dope fiend around the house, mainly because he'll steal everything in sight. A lush's behavior may be undependable and raunchy, but a doper is five times worse than a lush. Once you are wired behind scag, it is *life*, nothing else lives. A lush flops, passes out, quits. But a dope fiend hustles, scores, and fixes so he can get down. And he has no regrets. He doesn't care at all. If somebody gets wasted in the process of hustling, scoring, and getting down—so fucking what? The doper is a true isolationist. He doesn't give a damn for others. Only insofar as they are a means to score.

So, I've blown a good position in the Organization; I've burned all my old friends to a cinder; my relatives have put me down from self-defense. I'm out in the street. Only I still got my apartment 'cause I have paid up my rent for months ahead. I've got a pad to lie down in, but I don't have lights or gas. They're turned out long ago because I didn't pay the bills.

But I am still able to front because I've got clothes. The sharkskin suits and the million shirts I bought in my big-money days are all I got. Although I'm still dressing good, I'm running out of people who will believe my story. Everybody now is onto the fact that I'm a dope fiend. So I give up on trying to pretend. I pass over into the dope fiend world. I might as well. I'm wired, I'm hooked, and I better quit pretending to be something I'm not.

I start selling my clothes. I had racks and racks of them. I paid over two hundred bucks for lots of those suits and I sell them for like thirty bucks. Brand-new tailor-made suits. But I don't care. You don't have to look good to use. The white lady will take you any way she finds you. I went through about thirty suits and pairs of shoes in thirty days. I needed a hundred bucks for dope, so I'd get rid of a hundred bucks of stuff. When I run out of stuff to sell my act really starts to fall apart.

In fact, I ain't got no act anymore. I'm starting to wear the same threads over and over. Sleeping and walking around in the same clothes for days at a time. Not showering, not bathing, a real filthy pig. Now I'm in the center of the dope fiend world. Before, I was a big shot. I used to look down at the dope fiend, even when I was using. Because scoring was no problem. Just peel off a few bills and get down. When I had influence, the Organization, and money, I used to sit high in the leather down at the shoeshine parlor and sneer at the filthy dope fiend. But now I got to go down to his world and call him brother. No problem. Anything for scag.

Before, all I did was buy my way down. Now, I gotta learn how to hustle. I gotta learn how to get dope. That means I gotta learn how to make money. Because I got no front, I'm automatically going to be a low-class hustler. I got no clothes, no wheels; I ain't exactly sharp. And I don't know how to be slick. But I learn.

I'm flat broke this particular morning and I really need a fix. 'Cause if I don't score soon I'm going to come down hard. I try to get a dime bag on the cuff, but the connection just laughs. So, I'm standing around on this street corner and I meet this dude. He's just a little kid, but I can tell that he's got something going. I tell him that I got to make some fast money 'cause I have to score some dope. He says, "Look, why don't you go boosting?"

I say, "I don't know how to boost." Remember, I always been pretty honest. Because I never considered work in the Organization as criminal. That's the norm around my neighborhood; not deviant or criminal. And dope, too. That's the normal kind of behavior that everybody's into. But boosting is something different. I started out in markets and drugstores boosting cigarettes.

Me and this kid worked as a team. We'd find a store, usually uptown, that didn't cover their cigarettes but left them out in open racks. One of us would stand point while the other would go under the coat and shirt with three or four cartons of butts.

Like, it's easy. You get a grocery cart and put a few items in it. You have an old envelope or something in your hand like a grocery list from the old lady. This is your front. You act like a legitimate shopper; you *are* a legitimate shopper in the eyes of people around you. When you learn how to arrange your clothes right, you can get maybe four or five cartons underneath your belt. Each carton was worth a buck then, and usually the connection would take them for dope. So you boost cigarettes and get down.

You don't eat much, don't pay your lights or gas. You just buy dope. I'm sleeping on a dirty mattress and I got no sheets, no lights, no food in the house. It's cold and I'm always hungry because I can't spare much scag money for Hershey bars and hot dogs.

I've always got a connection and that helps me score. 'Cause like, when my friends would come over from Yonkers, or other friends from Brooklyn, and we're looking to score, I would steer them to the connection. And they would share their scag with me. But this kind of nickel and dime hustling wears me out and is a drag, so I'm looking around for other angles.

One morning I decide to get a little further into this boosting than cigarettes. I wander over to Macy's Department Store, because I figure they've got everything at Macy's. I kind of walk around looking for a good touch. I'm not exactly hip on how to do it, I just know that I'm going to rip something off. I must have been in there three or four hours, wandering around all the floors playing with toys, looking at clothes, and such. That ain't the right way to operate and it's a wonder I didn't get busted by the floorwalker. 'Cause you're not supposed to do that. You're supposed to identify the article you're after,

make the hit, and walk right out like it was legitimate business. I finally decide that I'll take a TV. And I locate the biggest, most expensive TV on the floor. I figure that the bigger it is the more money I'll be able to get for it. And this one is on little wheels. It's sitting right in the center of the display area . . . with posters on top. I just walk over and take the posters off and start rolling it towards the escalator. I don't have the slightest idea of how to get this big box down the escalator, so I ask one of the salespersons, "Do you have a dolly handy, 'cause I have to get this thing down to the next floor?"

He says, "Sure, right over here. Let me help you strap it on." So he ties the TV on and we get it down to the ground level. I thank him for his help and he takes the dolly upstairs. Evidently, without forethought, I have successfully fronted as a legitimate store employee, as he wasn't suspicious at all. I just walk out of the store through the double front doors rolling this TV.

I have no car. And this is on 149th Street and Third Avenue and I gotta get up to 174th Street and Third Avenue. It's starting to rain and the top of the TV begins to get wet and it's running down the sides onto the fabric covering the speaker. I go about two blocks, lifting and bouncing the TV up and down the curbs and I think, "I'm going to ruin this set before I get a chance to sell it."

So I hail a cabbie. I have no money, but that doesn't bother me. I tell him I gotta get this TV up to 174th Street and Third Avenue. We rassle the TV into the back; gotta leave the trunk open 'cause the set sticks out a couple of feet. We hop in the car and go to 174th Street. The cabdriver helps me unload it and carry it up a flight of stairs to the connection's pad. The cabbie doesn't know if the TV is a stolen item or not; evidently, he doesn't care. He just helps me push it and carry it up to the connection's door.

I knock and tell him I got this TV for which I want some dope. "And, by the way, I need some money to pay the cabbie."

The connection isn't a bit shook. He says, "I ain't carrying too many bags at the moment. But I'll let you have one bundle of five-dollar bags and fifty bucks for the piece."

I figure that 125 bucks is a little light, but I'm not in a position to argue so I say, "You're holding and I'm hurting so it's a deal."

So he gives me the money, I pay off the driver, and I get my dope. That is the only time I did anything as foolish as that, but I figured that was boosting—just walk in and take something of value. I didn't know at the time that there was all these fine points to the shoplifting trade. But this is a good example of how an addict can't seem to do anything wrong. He just gets out on a limb time after time when he's hustling, and he scores and gets away with it when others get ranked and busted. It's a little like the drunk getting by without a scratch in a real brutal auto wreck. He's just so relaxed and unconcerned that he comes through a terrible accident smelling like a rose. The addict who hustles for his daily fixings has his eye on one thing alone, the dope and getting it into his veins. He knows he's gotta steal to score to fix, so he's just relaxed about the whole thing. It's a fact of living, like breathing.

It isn't long until I run into some other dope fiends who are boosting in a more organized, systematic way. And for a while, we had a real cool number going. We used to have four or five department stores that were pussy for organized boosting schemes. TVs, expensive radios, broilers, small appliances, anything in cartons stacked in the storeroom were fair game. But usually it was the nicer TV sets that we were after. 'Cause they moved real well and our fences couldn't get too many of them.

This kind of a caper was planned out in advance. We would lay out our strategy and movement like on a football field. We'd get uniforms; like, at Macy's they were gray at this time. Just a gray pair of pants and a gray shirt with the Macy emblem above the pocket. A favorite modus operandi was to back a commercial panel truck up to the warehouse dock. Guys fronting as Macy warehousemen would roll out appliances stacked three or four high on dollies. We'd have the caper down pat; when certain supers were off for lunch, so our front men wouldn't be recognized as phonies. We'd have fake bills of lading and manifests, the whole bit. Several times when I was with this organization we got away clean with like ten thousand dollars' worth of goods. The only reason I quit that business was that Macy's changed uniforms on us and came up with extra security measures that made dock boosting sort of hazardous.

We figured that other stores were getting wise, too, so it was time to find another hustle. We broke up and each dope fiend went his own way. The only time you team up like that is to cream out a deal. When there is cinch bread to be had and it takes more than one to get it, dopers will combine efforts. But it doesn't usually last long. When the scam peters out, you go your own way. Usually dopers are pretty careful, 'cause when you get busted and go to jail, you have to kick.

QUESTIONS FOR DISCUSSION

1. In what ways does the subculture of crime perpetuate Manny's deviancy? What characteristics of the criminalistic neighborhood gave him the opportunities to engage in deviant roles?

2. What would you say is Manny's biggest problem? Does he find taking drugs exciting?

3. Does Manny realize the implications his drug use has on his life? How does it affect the various spheres of his everyday living?

4. What one event, if any, pinpoints Manny's initiation into the retreatist subculture? What personality changes may be observed from Manny's participation in the Organization to his movement into the retreatist subculture?

THE METHADONE BLUES *Bill Bathurst*

For me, the biggest drag about being a dope fiend in martini-sodden America—aside from the energy drain of battling paranoia you come to accept as inevitable when you ingest illegal substances—is that the whole trip soon becomes as interesting as a Merv Griffin rerun, or being a bank teller for twenty years. The addict who gets so sick of his fingerprint-predictable daily routine (wake up sick-fix-stealconbegpawnsell-yrmother'ssilverware-cop-fix-teevee-nod-sleep) that he throws in the towel & retires to a Methadone Maintenance Program soon learns to his continuing dismay that his life is still a mechanical blur. Wake up sick. Scurry to clinic with distended morning bladder & piss in a small bottle under watchful eyes. Then go drink yr dose in goddamn *Tang* & repair to the pad reveling in the euphoric knowledge that in 45 minutes or so you will be able to get up & imitate a normal American citizen—a thought you started shooting junk to erase in the first place. The justification for the whole program, in fact, besides saving the taxpayers' teevee sets & purses from being snatched in broad daylight, seems to be that Methadone allows the addict to lead a normal life—a state which is contradicted by the addictive personality . . . in brief, a fucking drag. You know beyond the shadow of uncertainty that the connnection ain't gonna be dry when you arrive, that he won't take yr case money & hang you up eight hours while he makes a run to East Palo Alto / tests the stuff / nods out & finally adds five parts of lactose before returning to bag up. It's a bore. Worse, it's a bore that doesn't get you high. I wd return in a minute to being bored but zonked were it not for the existence of the biggest bore of all: the slammer. Sometimes I daydream they've hired a *vampire* to dole out the Tang, dig, so she's sleeping all day & when I get up there the lid is closed & I go home empty. Then, come sun-down when I return with a runny nose, she makes me give up a pint of the reddest before she cuts it loose. Or (another fantasy) the clinic succumbs to graft & installs the coldest dope dealer this side of Istanbul in the dispensing room, so when I amble in he is squatting on the stash like a mama octopus on her 20 billion eggs & hollers, "Whaaaat! Get yr ass *outa* here, boy, & don't you come back till yr money's *right*, you dig? Thass right. *Fuck* that MediCal card!" You get the idea? Before I become a *permanent* resident of fantasia, I sure wish the powers that be wd get hip to the boredom paradox & do something to solve it . . . It wd be simple enough, say, to initiate a raffle scene—the treadmill patient wd be afforded the hope of getting wasted one or two times monthly as a reward for showing up & pissing in the bottle day in & day out, thusly: he walks in & surprise! instead of Tang he is greeted with an eyedropper brimful of good Mexican brown & a ticket to a W.C. Fields double feature. The extra expense wd be minimal, if any, & the addicts wd be happy to shoulder it, believe me. Wd the powers care to put it to a vote? I think not. It's only fair to expect them to expect us to pay *some* dues for being alive, after all, like them.

QUESTIONS FOR DISCUSSION

1. On the basis of Bill Bathurst's account, how successful do you believe Methadone Maintenance Programs are likely to be?

2. What sociological theory do you feel would best account for Bill Bathurst's addiction?

3. Describe Bill Bathurst's attitudes toward Methadone Maintenance Programs. From a sociological standpoint how would you characterize his attitudes?

Section V **SEXUAL DEVIANCE**

Sexual deviance covers a myriad of different forms of behavior by individuals and groups attempting to meet their own sexual needs and desires or the sexual needs and desires of others. It may range from the shoe fetishist, one of whom reportedly stole 127 pair of women's shoes to meet his own individual sexual fantasy, to an interstate prostitution ring run strictly for profit by organized crime. Some acts are strictly forbidden by law while others evoke strong negative reactions from important groups within a society. In either case they violate generally accepted normative standards of a society. This is true even though many of the offenses do little harm to other members of the society, and the so-called victims may be willing participants in the deviance. Such behaviors are sometimes referred to as "crimes without victims." Since what is considered sexual deviance may vary from society to society—for instance, prostitution is illegal in some societies, tolerated in others, and promoted in still others—it is important to look at the particular form of sexual behavior from the point of view of the reaction of a given society.

For our purposes, we consider that in North American society convention limits acceptable sexual behavior to individuals: of the opposite sex, of legal age, and not closely related by blood. In addition, sexual relationships are expected to involve no more than two individuals who, if not married, at least should demonstrate such a strong emotional bond that people believe they are "in love." Finally, so-called unnatural acts such as oral and anal sex are either to be avoided or engaged in only as preparation for the "natural" act. However, it should be clearly understood that what is often labeled as deviant sexual behavior usually does not differ in kind from normal behavior. It is the conditions or situation in which the behavior is enacted that defines its normality or deviance. For example, a prostitute and her "John" may engage in exactly the same type of behavior in a shabby motel room as a married couple in the luxury of their own bedroom. Yet the former may be labeled deviant, and the latter wholesome.

This section contains accounts by several different types of sexual deviants: swingers, that is, married couples who switch sexual partners, a male homosexual, a female homosexual (lesbian), a prostitute, a pimp (male who supports himself off a prostitute's earnings), and a transsexual (individual who has changed self-identity from one sex to the other).

The first selection, "A Symposium of Male Swingers," is a discussion among several married males about their feelings on swapping sexual partners with other married couples. It is a good example of the importance of differential association theory. Prominent themes in the discussion include the following: most swinging is done by married couples, not singles. The sexual swapping is done with the mutual agreement of both husbands and wives. Sex is kept impersonal and free from emotional attachments. Although the sex is for pure enjoyment, not love, it often leads to a better understanding of one's spouse as well as other human beings.

The idea of comarital sex is a product of the late 1950s and 1960s. It has been estimated that such activities may be practiced by several million couples. There is some evidence that it is most common among well-educated, middle-class suburban couples. While there is no clear theoretical explanation for why "swinging" has become popular in the last half of the twentieth century, it may have something to do with the general trend toward increased sexual permissiveness, the women's movement and greater freedom for women, improved contraceptive techniques, and the growing attitude that women ought to be able to enjoy sex as much as men. Swinging may be viewed as an important functional support for marriage in the sense that it provides relief from sexual boredom and monotony through variety within the confines of the monogamous state. In other words, it may preserve marriage rather than undermine it. As one of the swingers in the selection comments: "I think the most rewarding factor in swinging is the closeness it creates between husband and wife."

In 1948 the famous Kinsey (Kinsey *et al.*, 1948) report on the white American male estimated that: 37 percent of the population had at least some overt homosexual experience to the point of orgasm between ages 16 and 55, and 4 percent were exclusively or almost exclusively homosexual throughout their lives. While this report shocked and surprised the nation, in the past three decades we have learned more and more about this form of sexual deviancy through social research and the actual writings of homosexuals as they "come out of the closet." Various theories have been proposed. Traditionally, psychoanalytic theory has seen homosexuality as a form of mental illness, a sickness stemming from defective socialization. From an entirely different perspective, labeling theorists argue that homosexuals exist sociologically only to the extent that they are defined, identified, labeled, and differentially treated as such. Still other theorists see homosexual behavior as the product of mass society and of the need to establish personal identity. Becoming a homosexual gives the individual a fulcrum around which to place his self-concept, behavior, and reference group.

Humphreys (1970) in a study of homosexual activities in public lavatories was able to distinguish several different types of male homosexuals: (1) trade homosexuals—married or formally married males who do not think of themselves as homosexuals. They are simply seeking a form of sexual relief other than masturbation. (2) Ambisexuals—usually married men who do not hide their deviant sexual behavior and consider themselves bisexual. (3) Gay guys—unmarried men who admit their sexual preference for males and seek partners on a long-term basis. (4) Closet queens—unmarried men who do not wish their homosexual behavior to be made public. (5) Male hustlers—individuals who become male homosexual prostitutes. They are sometimes referred to as "midnight cowboys." They usually operate on the street or in bars in urban areas. They are motivated more by money than a desire for sexual gratification. The higher class and more expensive and versatile hustlers are called "call boys," while adolescent boys who allow homosexuals to fellate them are tagged "chickens."

"Hustlers, Clients, and Eminent Psychiatrists" is an account of a male hustler. An important point to note in this article is that the author's motivation appears to be much more than economic. He writes of the excitement and psychological relief involved in the experience, as well as its power over him. In fact he states: "Hustling is one of those activities that has to be experienced first hand to be fully understood; sociology does not work."

The female homosexual is called a lesbian. Lesbianism differs from male homosexuality in a number of ways. Kinsey (Kinsey *et al.*, 1953) found the extent of homosexual behavior among women to be much less than that among men—just 10 percent of single women and 5 percent of all women at the time of marriage had experienced a homosexual relationship reaching orgasm. Lesbianism is not considered to be the social problem that male homosexuality is. There are no legal statutes forbidding it. In fact, Kinsey reported that from 1696–1952 there was no recorded case of a female being convicted of homosexual behavior. Although there has been little scientific research on lesbianism, the homosexual self-concept apparently develops at a later age for women than men—usually in the early 20s. Most lesbians have had sexual relationships with men before they have experiences with women. Female homosexuals are reported to be less promiscuous than their male counterparts and more apt to form long-term relationships. The sexual aspect of the lesbian relationship is much less important than it is in male homosexuality. Lesbianism is more a "way of life" than just a choice of sexual partners. In many cases strong emotional ties develop between two women over a period of time before sex acts are performed. The public display of sexual behavior among lesbians is rare, and they are much less likely to be members of the gay community than male homosexuals.

The life of a lesbian is described in the article, "I Am a Second Generation Lesbian." Among other things Sarah Malcolm relates her experiences growing up in a lesbian household. She speculates on the forces that shaped her life and concludes that her mother's homosexuality was an important contributing factor to her own lesbian tendencies. A word of caution is needed here. Although some researchers have speculated that the cause of lesbianism may lie in early overidentification with one parent or the other, there is little evidence to support such a contention. Lest the reader get the impression that lesbianism is somehow contagious, it must be pointed out that Sarah Malcolm's case is not necessarily representative.

Prostitution has been called the oldest profession. It is the granting of sexual access for economic considerations by mutual agreement of the prostitute and/or her employer and the client. All forms of prostitution are characterized by the sexual significance the act has for the client, the emotional indifference of the prostitute, and the economic transaction that occurs. It has been estimated that 100,000 to 500,000 women are involved in prostitution in the United States, and that they gross well over $1 billion a year. According to Kinsey, about 69 percent of the white male population has had some relationship with prostitutes, but the vast majority of these has had only one or two experiences (Kinsey *et al.*, 1948). Since the end of World War II there has been a steady decline in prostitution. This may be due in part to women's increased sexual freedom, which makes it easier for men to have sexual relations without resorting to prostitutes.

In the selection, "Sandy: A Prostitute," Sandy states perhaps the strongest reason for becoming a prostitute: "The hours are good and the pay is great." Closely tied to the economic motivation is the theory that women often are forced to resort to prostitution to support a drug or alcohol habit. This was in part true of Sandy's case. It has also been argued that in our culture there is a tendency for women to use sex as a means of equalizing their status differential with men. This would be an example of the anomie perspective.

One method of classifying prostitutes is by their method of operation. Some women work out of houses of prostitution, giving a portion of their earnings to the madam of the house. There are, however, few houses of prostitution still operating in the United States. There are "call girls" and high-class prostitutes, who usually make their arrangements by telephone or direct referrals. Finally, there are the street walkers who make their contacts on the street or in bars or hotel lobbies. Sandy was a street walker. Sometimes the street walker is not an independent entrepreneur. She may be working for an organization or a pimp. Sandy had some experience with pimps.

A pimp is a male, usually Black, who lives off the earnings of one or more of the prostitutes in his "stable." Contrary to popular belief, a pimp does not solicit customers for a prostitute. The real pimp does everything in his power not to work, or at least give the appearance of not working. He attempts to live the life of leisure, indulging in as much conspicuous consumption as possible.

Although the pimp may provide protection for the prostitute from police and ghetto toughs, bail her out of jail, and occasionally pay her medical expenses, this is not the real basis of his power. His real power stems from his ability to discipline his women into doing his bidding. This is not done by providing them love, affection, and unlimited sex, but almost exactly the opposite. It is his seemingly total lack of interest in the sexual attractiveness of the prostitutes that appears to give him his power over them. He simulates love with them with the same indifference that they employ with their customers. In a sense, he is playing the same type of con game they are. They turn tricks and he tricks them into giving him their earnings. When prostitutes get out of line, pimps are not above the use of physical punishment. This is aptly described in "Pimp," where Iceberg Slim tells of his use of the official pimp weapon—a wire coat hanger.

Note that Iceberg Slim, like most pimps, is a Black. Some believe the Black pimp phenomenon is a product of Black history in this country. In Merton's anomie scheme, the Black pimp would be classified as an innovator. White domination took from the Black male his sense of respect and manhood. Pimping provides the Black male a source of manly pride. Not only does he control white women, but also white men's desire for sex. The pimp performs several important functions for the prostitute. In addition to nurturance and emotional stability, he provides the prostitute with the verbalized motives and justification for her continued existence on the streets. Second, he gives her glamor and status in the same manner a husband gives his wife in the traditional family. His conspicuous consumption is a symbol of her desirability and affluency. It is a sign of her success.

The last selection in this section, "Being Different: The Autobiography of Jane Fry," discusses a type of deviancy that would seem to affect no one but the deviant himself or herself; yet, becoming a transsexual is highly controversial and subject to strong societal reaction. For example, several years ago a male tennis professional changed sexes and was immediately banned from competing as a woman professional. It took some time for tennis officials to accept the gender change. Even now René Richards is the subject of curiosity if not ridicule and scorn. While the figures are far from reliable, it is estimated that there could be as many as 100,000 transsexuals in the United States. The vast majority of these are men who desire to be women.

Frey provides a useful sociological definition of a transsexual: "A transsexual is a person who wishes to change sexes and is actively going about it." Two points are worth considering in this definition. First, one does not have to actually have the operation to be considered a transsexual. It is enough to want and be working toward the operation and be living your life as a member of the opposite sex. Second, Fry distinguishes the transsexual from the homosexual and the transvestite. The homosexual has sexual desires for members of the same sex. Transsexuals are not homosexuals because they feel that they *are* the opposite sex. The transvestite wants to dress as a woman primarily for sexual kicks, but he has no desire to change sexes or live his life as a woman.

We have little knowledge of the causes of transsexualism or why more men than women desire to change their sex. One researcher (Driscoll, 1971), based on a very limited sample, postulates that transsexuals go through stages, each stage having its own set of explanatory factors. Thus, transsexualism is seen in terms of a "deviant career." In this sense it rests heavily on interactionist and labeling theory. The stages (for males) are: (1) an effeminate childhood in which gender is not adequately defined and treated by parents; (2) school years, during which behavior that is accepted at home is labeled as "female" by peer groups; (3) the late teens, during which there is involvement in homosexual activities and the development of a homosexual self-concept; (4) a transvestite stage in which the individual dresses like a woman and begins to learn how a woman is expected to act; (5) a stage during which the individual learns that it is possible to make a sex change and firmly believes that he is female in every respect except that he has no female sex organs; (6) the final stage, in which the transsexual makes some physical progress toward a sex change through the use of hormones and/or an operation and is attempting to lead a normal feminine life.

References

Driscoll, James
    1971 "Transsexuals." *Transaction* 8 (March-April): 28–37, 66, 68.
Humphreys, Laud
    1970 *Tearoom Trade: Impersonal Sex in Public Places*. Chicago: Aldine
        Publishing Co.
Kinsey, Alfred, Wardell Pomeroy, and Clyde Martin
    1948 *Sexual Behavior in the Human Male*. Philadelphia: W. B. Saunders.
Kinsey, Alfred, Wardell Pomeroy, Clyde Martin, and Paul Bebbard
    1953 *Sexual Behavior in the Human Female*. Philadelphia: W. B. Saunders.

A SYMPOSIUM OF MALE SWINGERS *Paul Rubenstein and Herbert Margolis*

The interviewer began by asking how swingers feel when they witness their partners having sex with outsiders and when they themselves become involved with third parties.

Angelo: I think when you first begin to swing, there is often a great deal of insecurity. . . . It affects both partners, whether they're married or not. As long as there's a deep relationship between a couple, neither one really knows how the other is going to react, how far they can go. Certainly, for me, there definitely was an element of jealousy whenever the competition was too strong, if there were guys like Mike around who can keep it up for hours and come and come and come. . . . But once a couple gets swinging, they become secure in their own individual relationship and the jealousy gradually fades away.

Earl: Yes, but I think this applies to men more than to women. The girls are more uptight about getting involved in swinging initially. I've known guys who've had to work on their wives for months to convince them to give it a try. Then, when they get into it and the girl blows her mind, the man is shaken up because she's having such a great time.

Interviewer: What causes this reaction?

Earl: For the most part, a woman is an easier swinger, but her man doesn't like to believe this. It's the Playboy image. Actually, once a woman breaks the ice, she can go to a party, get turned on much faster, and some of them never stop. That's not so good for a man's ego.

Interviewer: Why? Is he afraid of losing his woman to someone else?

Earl: That would be the last thought in my mind. I'd be thinking about the sex part, rather than the love part. I mean, if another guy were pleasing her more than I could, that would bother me. But I love my wife, she's my wife, and we're grooving on that. I don't think, my God, I'm gonna lose her next week because this guy is much better in bed than I am.

Angelo: It's our upbringing that says, "If anyone screws my wife, I'll kill him."

Earl: Right. It's pounded into you for most of your life.

Mike: Bachelors don't have those problems. If someone turns my girl on or I can't turn on a girl I'm with, I don't take it personally. I don't have that much going with anyone.

Angelo: We're confusing two issues here: one is jealousy, and I think that ties in with your ego. In other words, someone else is a better lover for my wife, which hurts my image, my feeling of my own competence. But apart from this, there's also a cultural taboo against another man making it with my wife.

Earl: In America, once you get married, you feel you have an instant sex partner guaranteed, unless the marriage falls apart.

Larry: Even if it turns sour, as long as there's a legal knot there's the concept that you can still ball your old lady, even if she hates your guts.

(Group laughter.)

Interviewer: You know that old joke about the married man who comes home and finds his best friend in bed with his wife. He stares at him unbelievingly—"Henry, I *have* to, but you . . . ?" (*More laughter*) There are many sexual jokes like that which intimate that the "straight" married woman isn't very good in bed. That's also a cultural concept, part of our Puritan background.

Larry: Most square men don't believe their wives have deep sexual desires or the capacity to fulfill them.

Interviewer: This goes back to the belief that sex is love, and you can't separate the two.

If a man and wife aren't really in love with each other, they can't have a good sex life.

Mike: That's a bullshit concept. We know that from the swinging scene.

Larry: Once a married couple experiences variety, it actually takes the jealousy out of sex, takes the threat out of it. The fact that my wife can go to bed with lots of other men is the best way to keep her from leaving me.

Interviewer: I don't quite follow that.

Larry: Look, before we started swinging, there was a desperate need to have sex. If I didn't get enough, I was mad as hell. And you know all the excuses a wife can come up with. The swinging scene really puts it on the line for a marriage. You've got to have much more than sex going for you to make it work.

Mike: I think that can be very, very threatening to the squares because lots of guys like it the way it is. They can play around outside of marriage most of the time, and still have the wife back home taking care of the kids, the diapers and other cruddy problems. But if he gives her the same freedom he's got she's liable to turn to him one day and say: "We can't afford a baby-sitter tonight, so why don't you take care of the kids while I got out and . . ." (Laughter) I mean, right now most of the men can have it all their way. Why should they start sharing?

Angelo: For one thing, swingers are better lovers; they enjoy it more.

Interviewer: Are you separating sex from love?

Angelo: Sex is sex, and most of the time it doesn't have much to do with loving the person you're fucking. But I think most married swingers will agree that we have the best sex with our own mates.

Mike: I don't agree. I think at a given time I can please your wife better than you can.

Earl: Hey, now, don't get personal!

Angelo: No, it's all right. For argument's sake, let's say you can. What I'm saying is that sex is just a physical act. So she has a great release—that doesn't bother me, because swinging is a joint pleasure and if both of us are in love and have faith in each other, then I'm happy for her. . . . Once in a while it's nice to have variety. Swinging is a communication. Instead of just knowing one person, your wife, very intimately,

you grow to know a variety of people very intimately, and that's better for you and your wife.

Interviewer: And it leads to better sex with her? I still don't understand why.

Larry: It just does! Try it.

Interviewer: Remember I'm one of those squares.

Earl: That's your problem.

Angelo: In a way, it becomes a personal competition. Maybe at a party I'll meet an absolutely charming young lady. We'll have a wonderful thing. Then when Gina and I get home, we talk about it, about her experiences also, and that turns us on to each other. . . . I admit I'm trying to prove to her and to myself that I'm still pretty good in bed, and there are special private little things she prefers in sex that a guy at a party doesn't know about, so that knowledge is working for me. More often than not, our sex together is better.

Mike: I'm beginning to feel left out of this super-swinging married state. What about nonswinging married couples who agree to go out with other partners, separately? That can be just as satisfying.

Larry: Doing it separately is not the same as doing it together. It seems to me that would lead to jealousy and fears of losing your mate, a double jeopardy, because neither partner would really know what the other one is up to, and that fear of the unknown can cause all kinds of trouble.

Mike: You're saying that swinging is paradise, that there's no hope for anyone unless they do it. But most people don't swing.

Angelo: Sure, but according to the available sex research, about forty-five million Americans are sexually inadequate.

Mike: We know that. We also know that for lots of married couples who try swinging it's a disaster.

Angelo: Let's get back to definitions. I think a married couple must have individual stability to make a go of the swinging scene. Both partners have to have strong egos. Sure, lots of couples try swinging and then pull out. Well, they were vulnerable to begin with. That just points up another value of swinging; it has a way of sorting out those people who can't handle it.

The interviewer raised several questions about how a woman turns on a man (and vice versa) in swinging, as opposed to non-swinging situations.

Earl: Sure, there was a different challenge for me when I was trying to pick up a girl at a cocktail party. It was an ego thing if I was successful. And there was much more anxiety about whether I'd make it with that straight girl in a straight situation. In swinging, it's instant sex, no doubt about it. You know that you don't have to work too hard to score.

Angelo: I disagree with that very much. Maybe I'm taking this personally now, as an older man, but at almost any party most of the men are a lot younger than I am. If I have my eye on a particular woman, I have all those men to compete with, and that's certainly a challenge.

Earl: But the point is, Angelo, when you walk through that front door, one thing is sure: the girls inside have come there to go to bed with someone; maybe not with you, but very seldom will they sit around all evening with their legs crossed.

Larry: I grant you that. But there's still that individual challenge for a particular man to get a particular woman to say yes, regardless of age.

Mike: And if she doesn't, to eliminate her and move on to the next one.

Earl: The point I'm still trying to make is that in a swinging situation, there's a general assumption that everyone is there to swing. You don't have that going for you when you walk into a square dinner party.

Larry: Sure, that's a different ball game: the feeling around, testing, the phony romancing, all as a buildup to the act of copulation. And if you're married, there's the lying and the planning. What it all comes to, even if it works, is a great deal of dishonesty. What kind of challenge is that, really?

Angelo: Yes, it's a phony game, because you're playing it according to the standards of the straight world. Even if the girl has decided to give in, she has to play at being coy, unsure about doing it and—this is what disturbs me most—when it finally does happen, she has to make you feel she lost control. You "over-whelmed" her. It was just an uncontrollable "accident." I suggest that this kind of challenge is not conducive to a healthy, mature, man/woman sex relationship.

Interviewer: And swinging is? What replaces the so-called challenge of seduction?

Angelo: I think I could call it something like an anticipation of discovery. What will relating to a new and different human being lead to? The nuances and the complicated symbolism that exists in this scene is cleaner and healthier than in a straight situation.

Interviewer: I think you're stacking the deck. Don't you ever go to a swinging party where there is no woman you want to "anticipate discovery" with?

Larry: Oh, I've been at many parties over a period of years where Barbara dug some guy and I didn't dig any of the girls, or vice versa. So while I was talking or drinking or sometimes just being plain bored, she'd go and have a big romance.

Interviewer: Were you upset?

Larry: No, but if she were at a straight party, making a date with a guy outside the swinging scene and not tell me about it, then I'd be mad as hell.

Interviewer: Suppose she told you.

Larry: Before or afterward?

Angelo: That has nothing to do with it. Most swinging couples don't do that. That's part of our code of ethics. Gina and I have a very definite agreement that I won't swing with anybody that she dislikes or vice versa.

Interviewer: Is that a general rule?

Earl: Not that I know of.

Larry: I think it's an individual decision.

Earl: Well, Susan and I don't have that kind of understanding, and I'd like to pursue this a little further with Angelo. Suppose you and Gina are swinging and she says, "Look, I really dig this guy and I want to go to bed with him." Hasn't that ever happened?

Angelo: Not that I recall.

Earl: Suppose it did. What would you do?

Mike: You'd be a rotten bastard if you said no, Angelo.

Angelo: It's difficult for me to answer in advance because it's never come to that.

Larry: I'd take into consideration the fact

that my wife, whom I love and respect, has good taste. I'd go along with her desires.

Angelo: Even if you didn't like the guy she wanted, if you really were disgusted by him? I don't know. I think the love between a husband and wife is more important than swinging.

Earl: But, Angelo, aren't you then, in effect, putting restrictions on swinging and the freedom we find in it?

Angelo: You're making too much of this. If there's a guy I absolutely dislike, I think I'd say to my wife, "Look, do me a favor. There are fourteen other guys here, you've got thirteen other choices." I think that my wife would go along with that restriction.

Mike: You can be subtler about it, you know—take her aside and whisper very quietly, "I hear that guy never gets an erection."

Earl: This gets back to why we enter the swinging scene. For me, it's always been a search for total freedom.

Angelo: There's no such thing, even vaguely, as the concept of total freedom anywhere. In swinging we are replacing one set of cultural values with a new set of values that are more advanced but still very definite. There have to be standards in any human encounter. What do you mean when you talk about total freedom? The freedom to murder somebody?

Earl: You're taking it too far, ridiculing it.

Angelo: I'm not trying to do that.

Earl: I'm talking about the freedom to fornicate within the group scene, without any restrictions on you or your wife, whether you like who she's fucking or not. We're separating sex from love, and it seems to me you're putting emotions right back into it.

Angelo: Not really. I'm just saying there *is* a reality. While the emphasis is on sex and the physical act, I don't have to go to bed with every woman at every party.

Mike: I beg to differ. I always try to ball every chick at every party.

Earl: That's why you'll die at an early age, but it'll happen slowly. You'll just peter out.

Angelo: Let's be serious—this is an important issue. I'm talking about growth. Any freedom is counterbalanced by a limit. In the swinging scene, we're not talking about freedom to hurt or to be cruel. We're talking about a freedom based on a loving principle, kindness, cooperation. And that freedom is balanced, because in order to share these feelings, you have to take into consideration the feelings of others: your wife, your girlfriend, whoever you're having sex with. There is a balance of considerations in swinging. That's what makes it work. When it's missing, swinging can leave you with a bad taste.

Larry: (After a pause) Touché.

Interviewer: From the way you've been talking, it appears that married couples are the dominant force in the swinging scene.

Mike: It wasn't that way in the beginning, years ago. . . . The pill freed women from the fear of having children. Now, certainly in my circles, most swingers are married couples— middle-class marrieds, I might add.

Interviewer: Does that bother you, Mike?

Mike: Why should it? My only judgment concerns the individual girl: does she turn me on or not?

Earl: Aw, come off it! The moment you walk in the door, it's off with the clothes and where are the broads?

Mike: I'm still selective.

Angelo: You said earlier you go after every chick.

Mike: Because the parties I attend only serve up luscious ones.

Larry: I agree with Mike in one sense. Most swingers, married or single, do it for sex, period—the variety of it.

Angelo: I, for one, feel a lot of friendships grow out of the swinging scene. I'll grant you sex starts it off because "The grass is greener . . ." but after you find out that the grass is really not that much greener, you move on to other things. You find more rapport with this couple or that. You end up going to other parties with them and a real friendship develops which is more permanent than you expected, a sort of love feeling that spreads out and gives you a feeling of living in a separate world with new friends. You can't find that openness with friends in the straight world.

Earl: There's something to that, definitely. Susan and I still keep asking ourselves why we swing. More and more, sex becomes "the frosting on the cake," because our friends, the ones we can identify with, are swingers. I mean, when you fuck someone else's wife with the consent of the husband and watch your own wife enjoying it with that same guy, it opens the doors to a new kind of intimacy that you can't ignore . . . I think it's just a minority of swingers who want sex, sex, sex. Most swingers do look for lasting relationships.

Interviewer: And when you find them?

Earl: It's more fun to do straight things with them, to go on camping trips or a weekend of skiing.

Interviewer: Don't you tend to get cliquish with these friends you feel close to?

Mike: Do you mean at parties?

Interviewer: Exactly.

Angelo: It depends on the number of people there. At a big one, say with thirty or forty couples, yes. I've observed a lot of cliquishness, especially among married couples.

Larry: But it's not the same thing that happens at a straight cocktail party. There the subgrouping is dictated by snobbery and status. At our parties, it's a natural reaction to all the new bodies. Until you get to know your way around, you tend to stay with your old friends.

Earl: Just like the squares.

Angelo: The situation conditions it. Anytime you have more than fifty people, well, the beds are only so big.

Mike: Right. A king-sized bed holds four couples if you're lucky.

Earl: Six, if they're highstrung and underweight.

Angelo: But don't forget that this subgrouping breaks up quickly. The purpose is to get to know new people. There are no barriers or boundaries. You switch back and forth from one group to another and pair off.

Interviewer: Who directs traffic?

Larry: The host and hostess.

Interviewer: And they invite the guests?

Angelo: (Nodding) It's like planning any party. There's a very careful process of selection, though, in deciding who and who not to invite to put together a successful party.

Interviewer: And there's no snobbery, no hint of status?

Angelo: (Laughing) The decision-making process is different. . . . In the swinging scene

you try to arrange a successful evening. It's a much more loving decision.

Interviewer: What happens to gate-crashers—friends of friends who're not so loving?

Larry: There are bad scenes but not too often. Usually it's a newcomer—mostly a man—who may offend a girl. The host or hostess or some of the other men talk to him and see to it that he calms down or leaves. There are not many occasions when a man or a woman gets drunk, paws over someone and a fight starts. Things usually don't get out of hand.

Mike: The controlling factor is the atmosphere. The emphasis is less on drinking because most of the guys know that this can affect their ability to perform. There's much less anger and hostility at a swinging party, less of a frustration gap.

Interviewer: Are you saying that open sex tends to curb violence?

Mike: You're getting philosophical now. All I know from my swinging experiences, especially in the group scene, is that the need is to screw and be screwed and you keep other feelings under wraps. When you're really going good, you couldn't care less about arguing or almost anything else.

Earl: Absolutely. Most swingers, even if they have difficulties getting it up or problems with their wives or girlfriends, cool it.

Interviewer: That sounds as if they're holding in a lot of frustration.

Earl: Oh, sure, swinging couples have fights. I certainly don't think that fucking is a cure-all, but when you take the sex out of the argument, somehow, it's not so bitter. It's more objective and you can get it over with by making up in bed. At least, that's the way it is with Susan and me.

The interviewer asked how the swinging minority lives in the nonswinging world. Do they feel threatened, persecuted? How secretive are they about their sex life with nonswinging friends, at work and in various other situations?

Mike: It's like leading a double life, in a way, which makes it very interesting.

Larry: I don't connect the two.

Angelo: I think it depends on what you do for a living. If you're a banker or running a Sunday school and are swinging, then you're in a lot of trouble if they ever catch on.

Earl: It's two separate worlds for me. Absolutely. And the square scene bothers me because it seems that the only way guys can get their jollies out there is to get smashed first.

Mike: You have to hold back and calculate everything you say so much more. It's a lack of honesty.

Earl: But you can't say that swinging is the epitome of honesty. It's just that dishonesty is more emphasized in the square world.

Angelo: I think the most rewarding factor in swinging is the closeness it creates between husband and wife. The complete openness about sexual feelings carries over into other areas.

Earl: For my wife and me, it's really broken down our hangups. We're totally honest with each other, and she'd better be! (Much laughter)

Interviewer: Does this deeper sense of perception lead to a keener awareness of the square world?

Mike: It makes me sick every time I go to work.

Angelo: Square living is debilitating. Most men indulge in so much sexual daydreaming, watching their secretaries go by—all those fresh, young bodies on the street, in cars and wherever—and they very rarely fulfill their fantasies.

Interviewer: If swingers do, does this help in day-to-day activities?

Angelo: I have no problem fitting into the square world with all its pettiness, because I started out as a square. That's how I was raised— very square and very Puritan.

Earl: But we're in a better position to analyze what squares are up to.

Mike: It's like those people are only seeing half a city . . . shutting off a half view of everything. . . . But it really doesn't give me an edge in my business.

Earl: From a personality standpoint?

Mike: (shaking head) I deal only with men. But, I do understand things better and I'm more open. Swinging broadens my total understanding and awareness.

Angelo: Once you break a cultural taboo, you're through a wall and you realize how arti-

ficial and unnecessary the barrier was. You see people and ideas boxed in all around you. Many times you're able to discover doors in walls that are not visible to others, and answers to questions and problems as well.

Interviewer: Isn't the fact that you're a swinger also a problem in the straight world?

Mike: How?

Interviewer: For example, a lot of your sexual acts are illegal.

Angelo: That's changing.

Interviewer: Granted, but in many states you're still breaking the law. Doesn't that give you a feeling of anxiety, jeopardy, that might affect the quality of what you're doing?

Larry: I certainly don't go around telling my employees that I'm a swinger. Is that what you mean?

Interviewer: Yes. Would you tell them if it were legal?

Larry: I'd have to think about that when it happens.

Mike: I don't care. When I'm making love to a woman, I'm not worried about what's legal. Anyway, there are so many laws on the books that people are constantly breaking. I took a course in that once. Did you know that in several states there's still a law against shooting deer from stagecoaches, and that there has to be a foot of daylight between dancing couples?

Earl: You're kidding.

Mike: It's the law. The point is no one goes around enforcing it.

Interviewer: Do you think authorities are becoming lenient about swinging?

Angelo: I'm sure in some places they are. But I think you'd be courting trouble anywhere if you become involved with under-age girls or hard drugs. The groups I know don't go in for freaky things like that, or bestiality, whippings, etc.

Interviewer: Are we getting back to inhibitions?

Angelo: Realistic inhibitions. There have to be limits.

Earl: Here we go again: pick your limits! It's like Christianity, saying that you can't commit adultery and that your wife is your possession.

Interviewer: Do you think the Ten Commandments have just about had it?

Angelo: For me, the one I take most personally is "Thou Shalt Not Covet Thy Neighbor's Wife."

Interviewer: How did some of you break basic taboos?

Angelo: For me, it was my experiences in World War II: being in constant danger because I was working with the underground, believing in a cause and yet seeing the basic immorality of war, even one I believed in. In a sense I became disillusioned with the whole Christian ethic.

Mike: I was never conscious of breaking any taboos. I just fell into it. It was an individual thing. I don't harm anyone doing it. I give pleasure and joy myself, and I think it's right.

Interviewer: Right by what moral standards?

Mike: My own—swingers have a strong moral sense.

Angelo: The Judeo-Christian religion contains nothing specific against swinging, but the double standard has been maintained for over 2,000 years in countries dominated by religious values. Swinging was allowed for men because they did not get pregnant, and that is why women were excluded from the practice. If you check the Bible, you'll see that adultery was only applicable to women. To this day a prostitute is arrested, but her male client is not. . . . There's a controversy about this, but many authorities feel that sexual problems started with St. Augustine. Priests were allowed to marry until the thirteenth century.

Interviewer: Do you think, Angelo, that any religious leaders would condone swinging today?

Angelo: Probably not today. But how many of them would have condoned the pill or premarital sex fifty years ago? Look at the changes that are happening with regard to sexual mores. No church, no authority, can be totally oblivious to this.

Earl: I think we have to relate to these changes rather than to the philosophical origins of Christianity, because we're all influenced by the practical application of these philosophical concepts.

Angelo: There are two separate issues here: culture and religion. Culture varies in all countries. For example, if you go to Spain, it's un-Christian for a girl to walk around in a bikini. These are cultural values which often reflect religious dogmas, but, conversely, cultural pressures can also force social change. Inevitably, you see religion going along in some way with the temper of the time.

Interviewer: Are you saying that a person responding to cultural change can swing without guilt and still be religious?

Angelo: Definitely. I'm a religious person and I swing.

Interviewer: I'm talking about someone who believes in God.

Angelo: I do. But I don't believe in a God who is cruel or punishing or vengeful. God gave us the urge for sex, put it into our bodies, our systems, because he meant for us to use it, to satisfy ourselves and other people close to us. Sex to me can be a very spiritual, elevating experience.

QUESTIONS FOR DISCUSSION

1. In what sense can swinging be considered adultery? Larry states: "Doing it separately is not the same as doing it together." Mike says: "Swingers have a strong moral sense."

2. If you were to become a swinger, what type of reactions would it evoke in your social group? Would it be the same in other social groups?

3. What theory or theories of deviant behavior do you feel best explains the "swinging" phenomenon in American society?

4. This account is based on an interview with male swingers. How reliable do you feel such information is? What are the advantages and disadvantages of this technique over other types of methodology (for example, observation, questionnaires)?

5. This interview was conducted with males. Do you think the answers to the questions would have been different from the wives of these men? Is there a male bias built into the questions themselves?

HUSTLERS, CLIENTS, AND EMINENT PSYCHIATRISTS *John Rechy*

"Malehustlers. . . . Drifters, tough, street-smart. And smarter, but pretending, sometimes, to be dumb. Students and middle-class youngmen, though on the rough streets not as many as, briefly too, become callboys (the callboy faction being safer, more 'conservative'—only muted revolution there). A precarious existence—you're new one day, old another. The clients remain, the sellers are pushed aside; a fresh wave of hustling outlaws flows regularly into the city.

"The customers. . . . The myth says they're all middle-aged or older, probably married, shy. But that's not true. Those exist, yes, abundantly; there are, too—though far, far fewer—the attractive and the young who merely prefer to pay, especially among those who want to cling to the myth that masculine hustlers are 'straight.' "

I'm speaking about male streethustling to a group of eminent California psychiatrists and psychologists who meet irregularly. I sit at one end of the table and face about twenty men and women. Occasionally they will whisper briefly among each other.

With as much defiance as honesty I say:

The world of streethustling holds great power over me, and the others in it, a world we love; I've experienced it—survived it—for years—much longer, I'm proud to say, than most. It's a world clouded in generalities. Hustling is one of those activites that has to be experienced firsthand to be fully understood; sociology doesn't work.

The first man who picked me up while I was hustling—the very day I arrived in New York—approached me with these words: "I'll give you ten and I don't give a damn for you." That was a good street price at the time. His words—and, as it turned out, he *did* give a damn; a very moving, tough man—opened up a world of sexual power through being paid, and they took me to streets in New York, Los Angeles, San Francis-

co, New Orleans, Chicago, St. Louis, Dallas—even, to smash my sheltered childhood, in El Paso, my hometown, where I was picked up by a junior-high teacher of mine, who didn't recognize me.

Even when I had good jobs, I was on the streets recurrently, pulled back as if by a powerful lover. Even when *City of Night* was riding the best-seller lists. I've seen copies of my books in the houses of people who have picked me up anonymously. At times just the offer of sexmoney is enough. Those times I don't need, actually, to go with anyone.

There is a terrific, terrible excitement in getting paid by another man for sex. A great psychological release, a feeling that this is where real sexual power lies—not only to be desired by one's own sex but to be paid for being desired, and if one chooses that strict role, not to reciprocate in those encounters, a feeling of emotional detachment as freedom—these are some of the lures; lures implicitly acknowledged as desirable by the very special place the malehustler occupies in the gay world, entirely different from that of the female prostitute in the straight. Even when he is disdained by those who would never pay for sex, he is still an object of admiration to most, at times an object of jealousy. To "look like a hustler" in gay jargon is to look very, very good.

One of the myths of the hustler is that he is actually looking for love. Perhaps, under the surface, deeply. On the surface there is too often contempt for the client, yes, at best pity—sometimes, seldom and at times only fleetingly, affection; yes, I have felt that. The client, too, at times resents the hustler because he desires him. I think of the hustling streets as a battlefield; two armies, the hustler and the client, warring, yet needing each other.

Outside of a busy coffeeshop where hustlers gather in clusters throughout the night, an older

---

man in a bright-new car parked and waited during a recent buyers' night. Youngmen solicited him anxiously in turns, stepping into the car, being rejected grandly by him, stepping out, replaced by another eager or desperate youngman. Smiling meanly, the older man—one of that breed of corrupted, corrupt, corrupting old men—turned down one after the other, finally driving off contemptuously alone, leaving behind raised middle fingers and a squad of deliberately rejected hustlers—some skinny, desolate little teenagers among the more experienced, cocky, older others; skinny boys, yes, sadly, progressively younger, lining the hustling streets; prostitutes before their boyhood has been played out, some still exhibiting the vestiges of innocence, some already corrupted, corrupt, corrupting—an increasing breed of the young, with no options but the streets—which is when it is all mean and ugly, when it is not a matter of choice; wanted for no other reason than their youth, their boyhood. . . . And yet, later that very night, I met a man as old as the contemptuous other one—but, this one, sweet, sweet, eager to be "liked," just liked, desperate for whatever warmth he might squeeze out, if only in his imagination, in a paid encounter, eager to "pay more"—to elicit it—simply for being allowed to suck a cock. . . . Hustling is all too often involved in mutual exploitation and slaughter, of the young and the old, the beautiful and the unattractive.

The standard street price is twenty dollars—but this fluctuates; you ask for as much as you can get (and designate what for). You go for less depending on your needs—bartering is not rare. Another lucky day you'll go for more—$25, $30, more. Like the stock market, streethustling has daily highs and lows.

The relationship among masculine hustlers is a very delicate one. It relies on repression. A fantasy in the gay world is of two street hustlers making it with each other. There's the notion that today's hustlers are tomorrow's payers. Both concepts are largely inaccurate. Many masculine streethustlers still think of themselves defensively as "straight," a role those attracted to them expect, even at times demand, they play. Often girls hang around necking with hustlers on the street until a client for their boyfriends appears. Though some hustlers may move back and forth into a cruising area for an unpaid contact of mutual attraction, in hustling turf among other masculine hustlers they must remain, rigidly, "buddies" (like Paul Newman and Robert Redford).

Now about hustlers becoming payers later on: Perhaps that's true of callboys with notoriously less hangups. I'm talking about the masculine, straight-playing streethustler; he knows, from his vast experience and those shared by others like him, of the hustler's contempt, pity—at times even hatred—for the client. It would require a psychic upheaval for him to be able to shift roles masochistically. And the malehustler is a proud creature, though less so now.

A few years back, he was almost without exception masculine; it was almost always assumed he would "do nothing back." Within the past few years—drugs, gay liberation—two other breeds have thrived—the masculine bisexual and the androgynous, usually willowy but not effeminate, young hustler. Of course, the queens have existed since the time of the dinosaurs.

Street techniques vary, but there are general aspects. The hustler usually stands on one of several known corners, or walks idly along the streets, or mills with other hustlers outside known food stands, coffeeshops. Steady hustlers have their favorite corners. A client will stop his car and signal a hustler. Depending on his style or lack of it, the hustler will then stand by the car until the man speaks first or will just hop in.

Fantasy is important on the streets. If a client asks whether you're married, you say yes if you're smart, because he wants that. If he asks if you've been in the marines, or the army, or the navy (curiously never the air force), yes. If he asks if you've ever worked in a carnival, or posed for pictures, or been in a rodeo, yes, yes, yes.

Danger of course is always present, a constant factor. Plainclothes cops offer money, make the entrapping proposition, then bust. There are the marauding gangs of hoods who raid hustling streets. And the psychotic figures attracted and repelled by hustlers. . . . The psychic danger of constant loneliness.

For many drifting youngmen, hustling is their only means of experiencing worlds otherwise totally locked to them. For moments their desired young bodies are the keys to those worlds. Their fleeting youth is their one bid for attention. Beyond that, their lives will fade. But during those moments, hustling, they matter, importantly. The drabness lifts.

POSTSCRIPT

Recently *Time* magazine created a new style of malehustling. A story on "pornography" referred to the thriving heterosexual massage parlors lining the south side of a certain Los Angeles boulevard, and to the male prostitutes hustling on the north side. The latter was not true. There had existed, yes, a "limbo" section on that thoroughfare, where one stood or hitchhiked along certain blocks or lingered outside an all-night coffeehouse. Although occasionally you might find a client there, it was not a hustling area, more mutual cruising than anything else. Days after the *Time* mistake, the area conducive to hitchhiking was suddenly converted into a hustling turf rivaling that on Selma—at a time when the arrests were decimating hustlers on that street.

Now, on weekends, malehustlers—thumbs held out in varying personal styles—stand at virtually every parking meter along the newly thriving thoroughfare, sometimes so busy now you have to walk for blocks to find a place for yourself. Cars drive around the blocks slowly, choosing.

QUESTIONS FOR DISCUSSION

1. Would anything in Rechy's account help you build a theory of male homosexuality? Of male hustlers?

2. What part does fantasy play in the homosexual relationship?

3. On what basis does Rechy justify his actions as a male hustler?

4. What type of relationship does a male hustler have with his client? Is there any difference between this relationship and the type a prostitute has with her "John"?

5. Both male hustlers and female prostitutes cater to males. How do you account for the fact that the reverse is not true? That is, why are there not female hustlers and male prostitutes who cater to females? Or are there?

I AM A SECOND-GENERATION LESBIAN Sarah Malcolm*

A great deal has been written and said lately about lesbian mothers. At the risk of merely increasing the din rather than clarifying the questions involved, I would like to add my voice to those already raised, but from a somewhat different perspective. I am not a lesbian mother. I am, rather, a 43-year-old lesbian—a 43-year-old lesbian who was raised in a lesbian household.

When I was being brought up, lesbian mothers and their lovers handled the question of a gay household quite differently from the way many do now. The closet door was firmly sealed, not to be opened by anyone, especially me.

Rachael, my mother, was pregnant with me when she met Evelyn, the woman who was to become her lover, and who was to be my "Aunt Evelyn" forever after. It was the middle of the Depression, and so, to save on rent, Evelyn moved in with my mother and Larry, my father—a not uncommon arrangement at that time. Rachael and Larry either were married, or about to be. Historical facts tend to be a bit fuzzy in my family, in large measure because my mother always found fiction preferable to fact. I do know that at some point before I was born my parents did get married.

At my birth, Evelyn was 18, my mother 27, and my father 38. The three of them lived in what would then have been described as a "bohemian" household—Max Bodenheim, Joe Gould, and other Greenwich Village luminaries were "family" friends.

Around this time the feelings between Rachael and Evelyn became sexual, though how explicitly I don't know. What I do know is that my father, who disliked both fatherhood and working, did what he could to encourage their relationship so that he could gracefully rid himself of these burdens. By the time I was two or three, my father was gone, except for visitation rights, which ended when I was four and it was

discovered that he had been taking me to bars on his "days." Except for one visit, which I initiated when I was about 30, I never saw him again.

Thus, Evelyn, at the age of 20, found herself with a family to support (Rachael was to stay home to take care of me). Not an easy thing to do in 1936, but do it she did, and quite happily. We moved from the Village to a more middle-class neighborhood. The stated reason was that the Village was not a healthy place in which to raise a child. I'm sure, however, that the real reason was that Rachael and Evelyn's friends knew their relationship, which made it impossible to keep it a secret from me. Rachael and Evelyn decided that I was never to know what was going on between them. I was to have a "normal" upbringing.

Settled in a new neighborhood, they told everyone they were sisters, which worked, despite the fact that Rachael was very dark, and Evelyn was very fair and red-headed. However, people usually believe what they're told. I was not told they were sisters. I was told they were "just good friends."

There was a lot of "mommy-daddy" role-playing in this arrangement, and my mother found staying at home with a young child very boring. I remember her frequently pleading with me to grow up as quickly as possible so that she would have someone to talk to. She also found the other mothers in the neighborhood little consolation with their endless discussions of their children's eating and toilet habits. Finally, perhaps as much from boredom as from political conviction, she joined the Communist Party. (Evelyn did not, never being quite as enthralled with the Communists as Rachael; she also feared that it might endanger her job, but she socialized with local party members.)

Both Rachael and Evelyn removed themselves as much as possible from gay society, as-

---

sociating almost completely with the other Jewish families in the neighborhood and the people from Evelyn's job.

This, then, was the pattern of my life until I was about 14: Evelyn worked; Rachael stayed home; I went to school, and in the summers, starting when I was not quite five, to camp. It was all very middle class, except for the fact that my "parents" were two women. I did find the absence of a father an embarrassment since no one ever got divorced in that neighborhood, at least not the parents of the children I knew. World War II was a godsend to me because I immediately dispatched my father off to the front, and kept him there as long as humanly possible. He'll never know what an immense and prolonged contribution he made to the postwar reconstruction of Japan.

One of the distinguishing features of our home was its intensely political and intellectual atmosphere. By the time I got to kindergarten I knew all the Communist and Wobbly songs, could give you my position on the Spanish Civil War, and generally knew "which side I was on." Everything that was read, or thought about, was discussed. My primary memory of my early years is the sound of voices talking, arguing, discoursing, debating. Despite their vehement denials of snobbery, the easiest way to earn my family's contempt was to be unable to speak well.

The relationship between Rachael and Evelyn, at least in terms of my perception of it at that time, is difficult to describe. I understood, without it ever being stated, that they both were my parents, both loved me, both were to be obeyed, and both could and did punish me for my lapses.

Although there was always an atmosphere of affection between them, Rachael and Evelyn never showed any physical signs of it in my presence. They did sleep in the same bed, but the supposed reason for this was that we lived in a one-bedroom apartment, and they slept in the living room having given me the bedroom. You can't, after all, put twin beds in the living room, and everyone knows a growing girl must have her own room, preferably at the other end of the apartment. This was my preference as well as theirs. No matter where we lived I wanted my bedroom as far from everyone else as possible,

and always insisted on sleeping with the door shut. Thus, like all my friends, I had two parents, and these two parents slept in the same bed, as did most of my friends' parents, but my parents were both women who obviously were very close, but never made any demonstration of this when I was around.

In 1948, when I was 14, we took a firmer step into the middle class. We moved to Queens, along with millions of others who had made enough money during the War to afford the suburbs. I hated Queens from the moment we arrived—which is ironic since the move presumably was for my benefit.

When I turned 16, the difficulties between my mother and me, which had been simmering for some time, erupted into open warfare. I was, as they say, "acting out," primarily by doing very badly in school, and then becoming a chronic truant. In my family, scholastic failure and truancy were simply not tolerated, and so I was sent off, with a good deal of financial hardship to Rachael and Evelyn, to a disciplined, scholastically demanding small private school in New England. Here, finally, I did what I was supposed to do—I graduated with honors. Also, Rachael was finally able to get out of the house since she had to get a job in order to help pay for my schooling.

Since I did so well away from home (my summers at camp had always been joyous), it was decided that I go to a small out-of-town college. However, I did not fit into this particular school run by evangelical Christians.

To complicate matters, in my junior year I had my first homosexual experience, to which I responded with a singular lack of grace. I alternated between total hysteria and a Virginia Woolf-type of neurasthenia in which I felt so totally sensitive and prone to collapse that I was sure institutionalization was the only cure. I was a bit startled by my behavior since in all school discussions on the subject I had always maintained that the only thing wrong with homosexuality was society's attitude toward it. In 1954 my friends considered this terribly "adult."

What made my extreme reaction even more peculiar is that ostensibly I was prepared for something to happen between Theresa and me. Only a week or so before it did happen I had told several people, including the young man I was having an affair with, that I was sure Theresa had a sexual interest in me, and probably would make some sort of pass before long. What I was not prepared for was the aftershock. In retrospect, it has become obvious that I was responding to more than the experience itself. Going to bed with Theresa began to push toward the surface some subconscious recognition of the truth about Rachael and Evelyn that I did not want to acknowledge, since by that time I had as large a stake in their lie as they did.

In any event, I left school, or, more precisely, was asked to leave, before the end of my junior year. What was by then a very messy affair with Theresa also ended. I returned to New York to begin that process known as "finding oneself," a phrase that always makes me think of a dog chasing its own tail.

The next five years were difficult, and, I feel, fairly typical of the way people "came out" in the mid-fifties. To use the word "ambivalence" to describe my feelings about my homosexuality is such an understatement as to be almost absurd. I slept with women, but insisted I was straight. My favorite phrase at the time was "one swallow does not a summer make"—a fairly unfortunate choice of words under the circumstances. I slept with men, more and more desperately to prove my straightness, counting each of my orgasms as a score for my side. The women who were then my friends were all doing exactly the same thing. We were all sleeping with one another, insisting all the while that these episodes meant nothing.

I lived at home during all of this, and each time I brought one of these women home, Rachael would immediately spot them as gay (I marveled at her insight), and she and I would have a ferocious battle. She hated them, and made that abundantly clear to them and to me. Periodically, she would challenge me to admit that I was sleeping with them, which, of course, I would deny. I had learned my lessons well. As time went on, our relationship had deteriorated so much that I spent more and more time away from home, although I was ostensibly still living there. Evelyn seemed to spend most of her time at work, and was very startled to hear of these battles when I told her about them years later.

After two years of battling, I decided to try therapy. I had had brief encounters with therapy

before, but this time I stuck with it, choosing not only a woman therapist, but the same doctor one of the women I periodically went to bed with was seeing. I told the doctor that I had these terrible homosexual impulses that I wanted "cured," and she agreed to do what she could to cure them. Getting me to accept my homosexuality was never considered, but she was a nice lady and didn't mean any harm. I saw her for about three years, during which time she did attempt to get me to see that Rachael and Evelyn were lovers. But I couldn't. Some of my friends had made similar, equally unsuccessful attempts.

Three years later when I met Sondra, my gay impulses were as strong as ever. We began an affair, and finally decided to live together. With this development, the therapist and I parted company. At the age of 27, I was, at long last, gay.

In June of 1961, three months after I began living with Sondra, my mother died. She was 54; she had lived with Evelyn for more than 26 years. Grief-stricken, Evelyn began to tell me the truth about their life together, initially in the form of poetry and stories she wrote to and about Rachael. I don't think she was telling me the truth as the result of any conscious decision to do so. She was telling someone—anyone—about the intolerable loss she had suffered. I tried for a while to deny what I was being told, but finally had to admit the truth, and with that admission I stopped playing the game altogether. I no longer made any attempt to conceal my relationship with Sondra from Evelyn, although that had probably been a vain effort from the start. Evelyn and I, still existing in a parent-child relationship, are now both openly homosexual. In an odd kind of irony, we both came out of the closet at the same time.

Sondra and I stopped living together after eight years. It should have ended years before, but since Rachael and Evelyn had lived together until Rachael's death, I had a great emotional investment in the idea that you live with only one person until "death do you part." The fact that I could persist in this idea despite seeing all of the gay couples around me constantly break up and then start up again with someone new is, I suppose, proof of how well I had learned to deny the evidence of what I saw.

After living by myself for several years recovering from the strain of this breakup, I found Naomi, and have been living very happily with her for the past couple of years. Her parents have decided to "know," without knowing, and they treat me as one of the family, while Evelyn, who has never lived with anyone after my mother's death, knows all and treats Naomi the way all parents treat their daughters- or sons-in-law.

Which brings us back to square one. I am a 43-year-old lesbian who was brought up in a lesbian home. How do I feel about raising children in such an environment? Do I recommend it as a way of life? Do I think I am gay because I was brought up in a gay home?

I do think I am gay because of the way in which I was brought up. I also think I am politically aware, an omnivorous reader, a lover of good music, implacably middle class, incurably in love with the English language as it should be spoken, and opinionated as hell because of the way in which I was raised. In short, the fact that two women who were lovers brought me up is only one of the many influences that shaped my life.

Admittedly, my relationship with my mother was difficult, but I am convinced that would have been true had she been straight and her marriage a heterosexual one. Rachael was a complex and neurotic woman, and my birth wrought so many radical changes in her life—many of them unpleasant—that she had to regard my arrival with something less than unalloyed joy. Rachael had often vowed that there were three things she would never be: poor, a mother, or old. My birth destroyed the first two hopes, and, sadly, only by dying at 54 did she manage to accomplish any part of her vow.

I dwell on this only because I agree with the theory that holds that mothers are very often competitive with their daughters, and simultaneously want them to succeed as well as to fail. Consciously, Rachael was extremely anxious for me to be heterosexual, but, without dredging around too much in the murky waters of Freudian theory, I am quite sure that subconsciously she was equally anxious for me to be homosexual, which, in her eyes at least, would represent my failure. In this sense, my mother's homosexuality no doubt contributed to my own, since a

heterosexual mother would probably have found another area in which to work out these conflicts.

The question of how I feel about raising children in a gay home brings me to what I feel is the central fact of my homelife—what is important is not so much that Rachael and Evelyn were lovers, but that they lied to me about it for so long. For 26 years I was told that I was not seeing what I thought I saw, which finally becomes a strange form of brainwashing. If, every time you look at a table you are told it is a chair, you are going to have an awfully hard time sorting out the furniture. In its broadest sense, what this kind of lying does is teach you that what you perceive may, or then again may not, be true, and being unable to trust the evidence of your eyes can make you feel almost schizophrenic.

What it did do was make me a chronic liar as a child. Rachael and Evelyn were always very angry when they caught me in a lie, and could never understand why I would do such a thing. It took years of serious effort on my part to learn not to lie when confronted by something unpleasant. More to the point, it also took years for me to trust what I saw rather than what I was told if there was an obvious discrepancy between the two. I believe this is called learning to adjust the concept to the percept, and I was nearly 35 years old before I learned that I was to adjust what I thought, *not* what I saw.

When I look back on my childhood now, I don't think of it in terms of being raised by two lesbians, but in terms of being raised in a home where there was a lie that finally became central to everything. I'm sure Rachael and Evelyn thought they had good reasons for concealing the truth, and once the lie had gone on for too long found it impossible to undo. In the long run, lying about their relationship created many more problems, both practical and psychological, than telling me the truth could possibly have done. Since telling children the truth about absolutely everything is now "in," I cannot imagine any lesbian mothers lying to their children today in the way I was lied to. I think we've found that as there are ways of telling children about sex in a manner appropriate to their age, so are there appropriate ways of telling them the truth about whom we choose to love.

Finally, as to whether I recommend lesbians

raising children as a way of life, the answer must be that lesbian homes are only as good or as bad as the people in them. Two embattled lesbians working out their difficulties on the child in a tension-filled home probably will not do too good a job with the child. The same can be said of a straight home. Two loving women, who are concerned for the welfare of the child, will probably do a pretty good job. Again, the same applies to a straight home. Those who insist that a lesbian home is the perfect answer to a sexist world are mouthing slogans, not dealing with reality. Those who insist that a lesbian home can do nothing but harm to a child are equally misguided. After all, I was brought up by two people who loved each other for more than a quarter of a century, until one of them died. How many children of straight parents can say the same thing?

QUESTIONS FOR DISCUSSION

1. Do you believe Sarah Malcolm's inclination for lesbianism was biologically or socially induced? Was it due to environment or genes?

2. In terms of a sociological explanation, how would you account for the fact that research indicates that there are fewer lesbians than male homosexuals?

3. In terms of her own sexuality, what does Sarah mean when she says: "I agree with the theory that holds that mothers are often competitive with their daughters, and simultaneously want them to succeed as well as fail"?

4. To what extent do you feel that lesbians may raise children without destroying the children's heterosexual preference?

5. Of the sociological theories of deviance presented in the first section of this book, which one or ones best explains lesbianism in our society? Does it also explain male homosexuality?

SANDY: A PROSTITUTE *Robert W. Winslow and Virginia Winslow*

The informant in the following transcript is a former prostitute. At the time of taping, she was around thirty years of age and working on an assembly line at a local aircraft plant. A tall blonde, Sandy worked as a street prostitute for ten years, from age eighteen through twenty-eight.

Sandy [to editors]: I don't want to say anything to people about me, share anything with anybody until I find out what their reaction is to me. I don't want to give anything to anybody. I don't want you to say anything to the class beforehand about what I want them to ask me. I'm concerned about what their reaction to me will be.

Sandy [to audience]: Well, I'm about ready to pass out I'm so nervous. Offenses: several narcotic offenses. Cops picked me up on several suspicions of grand theft arrests. They do this in order to nail prostitutes. Couple of burglaries; everything but murder. Of course I didn't do any of these things. I turned tricks for years at 5th and Market. I made a lot of money and I made little money. I've been hungry. I think when people take to talking about prostitutes they think about Cadillacs and the handsome men who they dine out with. They forget about the times when they have two black eyes and walk the streets hungry. You look so bad that nobody wants to turn a trick with you. It's really a bummer. I know girls out on the street who are prostitutes because they like to gamble or take dope or whatever. There's no urgent reason for them being out there, but yet they're there. Hustling all day and all night. Some have pimps, some don't. I guess there's just as many different reasons for being a prostitute as there is for being anything else. It took me years and years of therapy at CRC, a place for narcotics addicts, to realize that my reason was linked to attention-getting. I dug the attention from men, the easy

money. You can't beat the hours. The actual sex part took about thirty seconds.

Question: How do you go about making contacts?

Sandy: When you're working with an organization of prostitution, naturally you just go into the house and she tells you what her percentage is and what your percentage is, and you leave when you get ready or when the customers get tired of you. In organized prostitution where you have your call girls, your $100 tricks, $50, $75, $200 tricks, the organization contacts you so that the customer has usually already been screened. Hustling off 5th and Market, you don't really walk two steps. Everyone who wants a whore goes to 5th and Market, it's that simple. We call it whoring; you guys call it prostitution.

Question: Do people come by in their cars?

Sandy: I find that mostly in L.A. I worked there for a while too. And there you just stand on a corner and they holler "How much?" and you holler back your price and that was it. That doesn't happen too often down here.

Question: Did you say that they usually got you for being loaded?

Sandy: Yeah, well they usually could get a possession rap on me cuz I was so strung-out that I carried narcotics on me all the time. So, until I got three possessions on me and wised up, I usually didn't have a case. I couldn't holler too loud, you know, cuz when you're doing wrong you can't holler too loud.

Question: I'm interested in how you got started in prostitution. I've read several books and most of them say that prostitutes usually hate men.

Sandy: Oh, I don't. I really don't; I don't know if I'm an oddity or what, but uh. It was funny. I was very moralistic as a kid. I kept my cherry until I was seventeen; I was not going to lose it until I got married. And when I did lose it, it was out of curiosity and because all my friends had. You know, I felt like a big dodo. And I had been with this man for three months who is my son's father. And so anyway, I went ahead, had sex, got pregnant, and had the baby, and then he went to the joint for the fifth time. I was just lost, I was just eighteen. I just went crazy. I started getting high, getting it on with anyone and everyone, and just giving it away, when and if I felt like it. It was really a bummer. And I went on like this for about a year, and one night this dude came up to me and offered me some money to sleep with him. I thought, well I'm broke, so I just jumped into the car and didn't even think. The idea of hustling had never 'til that time crossed my mind. People have a tendency to rationalize what they are doing. When I did not hustle, when I was giving it away, I thought that it was all right as long as I wasn't a dirty prostitute. Now that I'm a dirty prostitute, anyone who gives it away is crazy! So I went and turned that first trick and, well, hell, I think I was gone maybe ten minutes and I got $15. This was in 1960. I had to teach myself everything. I don't think there was anything in my childhood; I think it was just an accident. It looked good to me; I didn't have any money, I was on welfare, trying to raise a baby, getting high, running the streets.

Question: Would you say that a majority of prostitutes are on drugs?

Sandy: I'd say 75 percent of all prostitutes are either on drugs or are alcoholics. I don't know anything about the other 25 percent, I really don't.

Question: Are the other 25 percent in it just for the money?

Sandy: No, some are exhibitionists, some just crave attention—like I did—I think some are actually hooked on prostitution. It's really strange! It's not that they like to get laid and get paid for it, because they'll lie, cut you up, and steal. They're just cold, cold people. They get to be forty-five or fifty years old and they aren't that pretty, but they're out there making the money just snap, snap, snap. And I don't know what they do with the money.

Question: Is this the reason they prostitute? To support their habit? Booze? Whatever?

Sandy: Well, like I said, the hours are good, the pay is great. You really can't beat it.

If you have a family, then it means something to you. I have a family that doesn't mean too much to me, my morals were already shot, I was getting high, there was just no reason for me to not be making money.

Question: Do most girls get suckered into the profession, or do they go in with their eyes wide open?

Sandy: The women I met were not suckered into it. I suppose there are some that do get suckered into it, but I knew exactly what I was getting into. You do hear about girls being kidnapped and being put in houses and forced to be prostitutes, but it just doesn't happen around here. . . . I got kidnapped once and taken to L.A. You might say. I took off with a girl to L.A.—I get on my kicks where I think I hate men—and it turned out that she was working for these seven men in this organization. And each of them had anywhere from five to twenty girls and half of them were prostitutes and half of them were boosters. And it turned out that she was some kind of a recruiter. So they kept me in a pad for a few days and I turned a few tricks and as soon as they learned to trust me they cut me loose and I took off and came back down here. You can't keep anyone prisoner, not if they don't want to be.

Question: Those girls called call girls, are they just a small organized group, or are they syndicate? Do they have Mafia connections?

Sandy: I don't know, and if I did I wouldn't talk about it! This organization that I was talking about, I think was just a group of businessmen who got together, got some girls together—and some of them are just plain housewives—introduce them to their business associates and collect a cut.

Question: Do you have steady customers?

Sandy: Not now. I haven't turned a trick for, well I was going to say two years, but one of those was spent in honor camp. I've been out for six months.

Question: Did you have steady customers?

Sandy: Oh, yeah. We have a code among us just like cocktail waitresses—"If you leave my tricks alone, I'll leave your tricks alone." So that way it's safe for any of my tricks to go out on the street and ask, "Is Sandy here?" and they'll say, "Oh, she went to so-and-so place" or to have him call me or that I'll be right back.

Question: How did you get involved or why did you get involved with a pimp? And, what kind of situation was it?

Sandy: That was very strange because I was the girl who laughed at all the other girls giving their money to their pimps. All the pimps hated me, and I got to keep all my money. It was great. And all the queens down on the street took care of me so that I didn't get hurt. He just caught me at the right time. Things were going bad. I was working for only $1.65 an hour, getting strung-out, living at home—my mother and I cannot get along when we live together—my parole officer was putting pressure on me. He just said, "Come on, baby." And I said, "Right on." And I was gone. And I didn't get away for three months. I had to turn myself in to get away from him.

Question: What sort of a percentage do they take?

Sandy: He took all of mine. He left me money to eat on. Never enough to get anywhere far. When I was working, he was with me. When the trick and I were in the hotel room, he was right outside the door.

Question: What kind of protection did he give?

Sandy: You've got to remember, you're there, with no clothes on, with a man that could be anything. He could be a sex maniac, a murderer, he could be anything. You don't know who you're with. Some of them want to pay you, screw you, then take back the money they gave you and the rest you've made if you've got any. One time I had a guy pull a gun on me. Boy did I give him his money back—FAST! But with Ed outside the door, all I had to do was raise my voice and he was right there. He'd knock on the door and that was usually enough to frustrate the trick and make him want to get out of there quick. Good protection.

Question: I'd think that the fear of never knowing who you were with would be so great that you'd want to quit.

Sandy: I wasn't scared of anybody. You've got to remember that I was strung-out most of the time and didn't have sense enough to be scared. I was superwoman!

Question: Why did you do your second trick? Why did you decide to repeat your actions?

Sandy: My girlfriend and I were talking about that. She was always telling about how she could turn tricks and all the money she was making, and blah, blah, blah. And I just listened to her. And then I pulled that first one and we talked about it. And she said, "Well, tomorrow night we'll go out and see how much money we can make." And I just said, "Right on." We got loaded and got dressed up and went out and made some money. We each made about $100 that evening and I thought, oooh, that's great. I'm not even tired!

Question: What are you doing now?

Sandy: I am an assembler. Once again I'm just starting out, and there have been plenty of weeks when I've been hungry and wanted to turn a trick. And one night I went out and got one, and when we got home I found that my house had been burglarized, that everything I owned and had worked so hard for was either strewn all over the house or gone. And I was so mad that I threw him out. I went crazy and called the police, raving. If someone came up to me and offered me $100 for a trick, $100 can do a lot and I am not above sleeping with a strange man, I don't know if I would or not. I probably would, for $100, after I was pretty sure that he wasn't going to cheat me.

Question: With so much venereal disease going around, how can you avoid getting infected?

Sandy: If you're making big money, if you're turning the $50's on up, you don't usually have to worry about it. I contracted syphilis in about my fourth year. When I worked down on 5th and Market, the sailors and screwballs are not too clean. You catch clap pretty often. As a matter of fact, I hustled for nine years with nothing but a douche bag and I never got pregnant. I think that somehow I had gotten things infected once to the point that it made me sterile. When I went to honor camp for a year recently, they unsterilized me. The first thing I did when I got out was get pregnant. No, you don't avoid disease.

Question: Did you take it upon yourself to get a check periodically?

Sandy: No, I was one of the lucky ones. I can damn near always tell if I have something. Within twenty-four hours, my discharge starts. And until my discharge starts, no one else can get it. So very seldom did I purposely go out and trick when I knew I had a disease. It's a bummer. It's also a bummer having to tell the people you trick with that they might have the disease because you do. I remember one time when I had syphilis, and I guess I'd had it, oh, about six months before I found out, by accident. And I was dating this one dude who I was planning to marry at the time, I had a steady job and had stopped tricking and was doing real good, and then I had to tell my boyfriend about my disease. That was a bummer too.

Question: What is the abortion rate among prostitutes?

Sandy: I have no idea.

Question: How difficult is it for a prostitute to obtain an abortion?

Sandy: Then, you had to go to Tijuana to get one. Now, you can just go to County Hospital. It's very easy to get one now. That's where I got mine when I got pregnant. And they treat it quite lightly, quite lightly. You know, they just say, "Well, this is just something that I have to do, blah, blah blah . . . O.K., now you can leave."

Question: How expensive was it?

Sandy: MediCal took care of it. Now if I had been working on the job I'm working on now, they probably wouldn't have paid for it.

Question: Can you just walk into the hospital and say that you want an abortion or do you have to talk to a psychiatrist or what?

Sandy: Yeah, I talked to a psychiatrist. We talked about drugs. I liked him too. But I think that's good, you know, because if a person doesn't want a kid, they aren't going to treat it right and if they do want it, they wouldn't be looking for an abortion.

Question: Do you have a variety of rates for various techniques or whatever you want to call 'em?

Sandy: Yeah, there's a variety. You always try to get as much as you can. Depending on the appearance of your trick, the way he carries himself, whatever. You can usually get for a straight lay $10 and then from there you just go on up. I've had men pay as much as $50 or $60 for a straight lay. These were men who, well, there was just something about me they wanted. Or sometimes it's just something that strikes you. Hell, I'd pay [names actor] $5000 for a lay, I

swear to God! If I had it! Now if they ask, if they say, "How much?" Then you say something like $15. Then if they say something like, "Well, what if I want a little head?" Then you say whatever you think they can afford, like $5, $10, whatever. You just work it out somehow, but you always get as much as you can. I didn't steal from my tricks. Not because I don't steal, but because, well, working the same area daily, they're going to be seeing you again. I don't like to be whipped on. I am not a masochist in any manner. I might be hurting myself in other ways, but I don't like anyone hurting me or making me hurt—not physically. Not mentally either, but I'd prefer it mentally rather than physically. I just don't like it. So I didn't steal, I didn't con or whatever. So I didn't have some of the problems some of the other broads had.

Question: I'd like to know something about your childhood. Did you have brothers and sisters? What was your relationship to your father?

Sandy: I never saw my father to this day. My mother and I get along just fine when we live separately. While I was a child and growing up, she worked all day. When I was in kindergarten I used to dress myself, fix my own breakfast, and go to school downtown. I've always taken care of myself. I have one brother who is six years younger than me. My baby brother, 6 feet 4 inches, all 200 and some pounds of him. We get along fine. Maybe I picked on him a little too much when we were kids, I don't know. He picked on me a lot too, though.

Question: What was your mother's attitude towards men?

Sandy: My mother has not been out with a man since my brother was born that I know of, and that was when I was old enough to realize what Mama was doing at night. My mother just gets up in the morning and goes to work. . . . This last year she finally joined some group at work so that she has some social life, some outside activity. For fifteen to twenty years, my mother got up and went to work, came home, looked after the kids, martyred herself the whole time she stayed in the house until we couldn't stand it anymore and would run the streets. And that was her whole existence. Both my brother and I did get in trouble; I'm still having trouble with the law. My brother's been clean now for, gosh, I guess he still pops a few pills once in a while and smokes a little weed, but other than that, no trouble with the law for almost two or three years. He's a big foreman in Los Angeles, doing great.

Question: What did he think about your occupation? What was his reaction?

Sandy: He doesn't like it at all now. Two or three years ago, when he was in with the law, he thought I was what was happening. I was big Sis. He enjoyed telling his girlfriends, "My sister's been to the joint three times." It made him look big cuz his scene was looking big and bad. He loved it. But now I'm a dirty rotten so-and-so. Cuz he's straightened out. A complete switch about.

Question: Have you ever thought about being one man's mistress?

Sandy: Yeah, but if you're going to be one man's mistress, why not get a man you really dig and let him be your for-real man? Because, I would rather be with twenty-five men for ten seconds than a man I cannot stand for twenty-four hours. I cannot handle it. Someone touching and kissing on me that I do not want touching and kissing on me.

Question: Have you ever thought about getting married since this last time?

Sandy: Yeah, as a matter of fact I'm looking for one right now, but it's pretty difficult under the circumstances. And right now the kind of man that excites me and the kind I want are not really the kind I need. Unless if I'm going to change my life at all. If I'm going to stay in the subculture, and stay getting high.

Question: Suppose that your child had been a girl instead of a boy. Would that have had any effect on your way of life?

Sandy: Gee, I don't know. That's a good question, I really don't know.

Question: Are you caring for your son now or is he in a foster home or what?

Sandy: My mother has custody of my son as of 1967 when I went to the joint for the second time. He either had to go to a foster home or my mother. I see him almost every weekend. She keeps screaming, "Come and get your boy." But if I ever do, it'll kill her because that's all she lives for now, is my son. So I don't really have anything.

Question: Did you ever have any romantic relationships in your profession as a prostitute?

Sandy: I've met some real close friends. I mean the kind you keep for years and years and years, that I've met first when they were my trick. But when you're trying to stay clean, when you're trying to do right, and you need them, you hesitate to call, because it's really a bummer to have to cop to you're doing badly again. Romance and prostitution don't go together too well. You kid yourself. Uh, that pimp I had, I tried to believe desperately that I loved him— I couldn't think of any other reason why I was there. But how can you love somebody who puts scars on your body and tells you, "Bitch, if you don't make a certain amount of money you don't live anymore," and then takes all of your money. And that's the way they do it. He used to whip on me. He took me off the streets because we fell in love, so here I am living in a hotel and he's still hanging around with all his pimp friends and evidently, well, they like to talk about what big men they are, how much money their whores make, and who made the most, who did the biggest boost that night, or whatever their thing is. And evidently, somebody said something to him about him taking me off the street and the fact that he only had me, when he usually keeps three or four of them. And so he came home and whipped me. He couldn't tell his friends "So what," or whatever. He had to take it out on me. Oh, he whipped good on women. It was somethin' else.

Question: What's a boost?

Sandy: It's stealing, theft.

Question: When you first started prostitution, was that a hang-up at all? The romantic aspects?

Sandy: No, I never hustled when I had a man. Ever. I'm so aggressive it's going to be my way or no way at all, so that things never lasted very long. I'd either get mad and throw him out or he'd just get to where he couldn't take it anymore. It just gets to a point where it won't work. And my relationships usually last anywhere from two weeks to three months. Three months, that's definitely love! I've only had a couple of those three monthers! But, I do not hustle when I have a man. I expect him to take care of me or I will work too. I really had a thing going about pimps and giving my money to them.

Question: When you went before the courts

for your legal processing, did you find that when they knew you were a prostitute that they resented you for this and punished you for being a prostitute rather than the charge you were there for or both?

Sandy: I think they punished me because I told them to go screw themselves. See, in 1960, there weren't too many white girls going with black men. You know that. And I was sixteen, and I used to give the traffic department something like $10,000 a year. They used to just get ridiculous messing with me and talk about me so bad that I'd just want to crawl away and hide. Any way they could, they used to mess with me, that's the only way I can say it, they used to screw with me and insist that I went with black men for this reason, not because I wanted to. And they couldn't get it through their heads that I preferred them. And I think that's why they started messing with me. And then with my little smart mouth, big smart mouth—I was a terror when I was that age—I mean, here I was hustling for years and years and years and they never had a case on me—and that pissed them off—the vice were just too uptight. They couldn't get a burglary cuz I didn't steal. The narcotics they did—I think in 1961 I got my first narcotics beef—then they started slapping them to me hot and heavy. I have eighteen of them, not convicted of all of them, but Jesus Christ. And when they started catching me, I mean (1) attitude hostile, (2) cursed me out all the way to the station, (3) tried to kick me in the left knee, etc., you know, whether I did or didn't. So by the time I get in front of the judge, they sock it to me anyway. Right now if you picked up my rap sheet, it looks horrible, I swear. I was so embarrassed when I took it to my new boss. It really looked like he was hiring Bonnie or something. And I'm not Bonnie; I'm a person. And I feel just like you guys do. Maybe a little cynical, I've had a little bit more experience than some of you at some things. Most of it's been bad.

Question: Did prostitution ever afford you to live really high?

Sandy: Yeah.

Question: How much money do you estimate that you've made?

Sandy: I never really stopped to figure it out. Now remember I'm a dope addict at the same time. Oh, wow. A lot a money. Maybe one

year $30,000 to $40,000 and maybe the next I would only work maybe six months and make about $10,000 or $15,000. That's a lot of money.

Question: What kind of feelings or relationships did you have regarding other prostitutes? And how did you feel about your tricks? Do you feel closer to other tricks or to other prostitutes, that is when you're on the street?

Sandy: Being a prostitute is kinda like being a dope addict, you don't become close with your connection, not really close. It's gotta be business, he's gotta have your money. You don't make friends with other dope addicts because they want your dope. And you don't make close friends with people who don't do dope because you're on a different keel. Prostitution, you'd think that we were blood sisters, that we were raised together, that we never left one another except to go turn tricks, but that's just the act, the façade we put on. Respect, yes, I have a lot of respect for those girls out there. Some of them work hard, some are dirty dogs. But, to really like or communicate with them. . . . I would never go to one of them and say, "Boy, I feel really blue, depressed," or "so-and-so happened today." You could tell them that, but what they would say would be so superficial you might as well, you just wasted breath. "Oh, yeah. Well, that's too bad. Excuse me, I've gotta go." With the tricks, I managed to develop some real good relationships. I like those men out there—those poor misled husbands. They're honest and generally very, very nice. Only about 25 percent come on bad.

Question: What kind of man are you attracted to and what kind of man do you think you need?

Sandy: The kind of man I'm attracted to, well number one, if they don't get high now, they've got to have gotten high sometime in their life. I'll not have a thing to do with some dude who's going to preach to me about dope who hasn't tried it and doesn't know a thing he's talking about. I just can't be bothered. I hate people who talk about something that they don't know anything about. If he has been involved with dope, 99 times out of 100 he still is. So that's the kind of man. If he's got something going with dope you can bet he's hustlin' somewhere. Cuz, once a hustler, always a hustler of some kind or another. Always with my boss out at work, I flirt and kid and get my way. I haven't plugged in my gun [air gun] at work yet. All the other ladies do. I did rotten in the training period, but I passed. It's just that once you've been in the line, it's a way of life. I don't care if your hustle is just having learned people on the streets. You see all these people hitting these organizations now, ex-offenders. They've learned people in the joint and outside of the joint. Now they can sit down and write a proposition in about $25,000 or $30,000 a year. They're in home. And it's a hustle. It might be what they do best, but it's a hustle. It's easy. They're doing what they would do for free. What I'm saying is that it's hard to not do what you know you're good at. It depends on your code. You have to live with yourself, not anybody else.

Question: Is your mother very moralistic?

Sandy: She doesn't smoke or drink, or curse or, well, I got her to say "damn" a couple of times.

Question: Did she preach to you a lot when you were young?

Sandy: Yeah. My mother, she martyred herself—"Look what I've done for you kids and look how you do me." At first we fell for it. She used to have fits every time she didn't get her own way. And after she saw that we weren't going for them anymore, after we realized that fits only came when Mama wanted them to come, it was just that martyr bit all the time. I've had a little bit of the therapy with my mom, too, but if you're pointing out something bad to them, they are going to get defensive. I couldn't get through to her; she'd just clam up.

Question: Have you ever read anything about prostitution and American wives? That prostitutes are very thankful for the attitude of the American wife because she increases her business because of it?

Sandy: I don't know what to think about American wives. They're gettin' weird lately. I have had women approach me and say, "I don't want my husband going out on me. He wants to screw you, he has told me so. Could we all three go to bed together?" and all this bullshit. And for free! That really did freak me out. I can imagine. Somebody touch my man in front of me? No way! I couldn't do it. They just act like it's no big thing nowadays. They're really weird. Hell I

know a guy who hasn't been home in four months and his wife is still there, patiently waiting. And he calls her every couple of weeks. It's like the wife, once she got him hooked or has the security of his wealth or maybe it's just his name, I don't know.

Question: How much do you usually know about the men you sleep with?

Sandy: Nothing.

Question: How about a first name?

Sandy: They tell you a name. You don't know if it's theirs or not. I took time ordinarily, unless I was just stone flat backin' it at a fast pace, just ch, ch, ch, ch, where half the time you don't even undress. If they act like they're not even going to play with you, you just throw your skirt up. When I was in a more relaxed position, and if I had the time, I would always take the time to sit and have a drink or cigarette with them, or lay in the bed with them. That's a trippy time. You've just finished doing it and they're satisfied and you're satisfied, you've taken care of the man. You've got a pocket full of money and you can take time for a cigarette. You don't have to treat him like a dirty dog. I really get down on some of them about their shit. They just talk to their men so bad. Course, some men dig that too.

Question: Do you have any idea what percentage of the men you slept with were husbands?

Sandy: Seventy percent I guess offhand.

Question: Before you had the relationship, did you get the money first?

Sandy: You get that money before you even undress! Well, that too depends, cuz if you're trickin' with a regular, you don't have to worry. But a first or one-night thing, you get the money before you take off a hairpin! You'll not get it back any other way, because he doesn't want to spend it, but he wants you worse than he doesn't want to spend it. Or a piece of ass, not necessarily you.

Question: What has therapy done for you?

Sandy: It gave me a big hand. I got into some heavy therapy. I'm very aware of why I do the things I do, what caused me to do the things I did, and all that stuff. But nobody tells me how to, uh, what to do with what I know. In other words they say, "Well, you're lonely. Don't be lonely." "What the hell you mean, 'don't be lonely'?" I said, "Where do you go not to be lonely?" And they tell you go to church. If they're a little bit more realistic they'll tell you "Well, go out. Meet somebody." I just can't get dressed up and meet somebody. Number one, if I go to a night club I've got to be a pickup, just from the getup. So that puts it off. I don't know. I don't know where to go to meet men that might interest me. To become unlonely. I don't know what to use instead of dope to fill whatever it is that needs filled. I see a lot of people in our culture say, "Well, trip out on the birds and bees and flowers." Well, screw the birds and bees and flowers. I don't like birds, bees, and flowers. It doesn't turn me on.

Question: You say you don't know what to use instead of dope, and yet you're not willing to date someone who doesn't use it. I'm wondering how much you're willing to take the responsibility for your changing if that's what you want to call it.

Sandy: I think that I'm probably to the point to where I feel a little bit old, a little bit used, and I'm a little uptight about that. Twelve of my years have been given to the state and I'll never see that again. Twelve years. I've got scars, inside and out. I don't know what I'm waiting for. I really don't. I'm on parole; I'm on probation. I still get therapy and I sit and help everybody else. I don't get helped. I still get high. I don't get anything. I don't hear anybody giving me anything to take the place of dope. So I sneak around, and I keep a full bottle of urine at all times so that if my parole officer slips up on me, I'll have it. And it's really a bummer. I don't know where I'm going. I don't even know what I want.

Question: Why do you keep the urine on you?

Sandy: CRC is the center for narcotics addicts, and you have to be tested once a week, two surprises a month. You urinate in a bottle and they send it to a lab to see if you've used any kind of drugs. If you have, then you're violated.

Question: What kind of drugs do you use?

Sandy: Uppers and downers, no heroin and no weed. I don't know why no weed, I just don't use it.

Question: I've just finished reading the *Elegant Prostitute*, which I think you might enjoy reading. And there was one girl who said that quitting was really hard and that psychotherapy was helping her.

Sandy: I wonder if it really helped. I'm really curious. Even people that I do communicate with, which is mainly ex-offenders. . . . They get going; they find their way; they find their fix so to speak. And they go right on. And the more successful they get, if you really dig them and like them, you'll stay away from them cuz you're not successful. And if you go down, you don't want them to go too. You also don't want to impose on their lives. They say, "Call me if you need me. Two or three in the morning, that's groovy." I'm not going to call them, one of my friends, at two o'clock in the morning, take him away from his wife and kids after he's worked all day. You're an imposition on your friends when you're like this and they're doing okay. You have to let them go on.

Question: Going back to your high school days, did you run with a group or were you a loner? Did you date?

Sandy: I was 5 foot 2 by 5 foot 2 and always a foot taller than everybody else was. Men come taller now or something. In my day I was always taller, like they always came up to my neck. Like I said, I was 5 foot 2 by 5 foot 2 and wore glasses. I just wasn't too lovely. So when the other girls started dating, I started running with the rough group and acting like I didn't care. I guess we attracted each other cuz I was so hostile. I took it out on the teachers or anybody else that was around. I got into the group fairly easily. I had a boyfriend, before I got sent up when I was fourteen, that I had known before. But, heck, we only kissed a couple of times. And then I got sent away and I never saw him again until I was seventeen. And when I got out all my fat had gone away. And I was lovely, like a butterfly, and all the men wanted me and I was in my glory.

Question: When were you sent to prison?

Sandy: I got sent up when I was thirteen and I didn't come out until after I was seventeen. To Norwalk and then to Las Willicas, then to Ventura without getting out.

Question: What was that for originally?

Sandy: Incorrigible. I just needed twenty-four-hour supervision is what it amounted to. That's what they said anyway.

Question: What was it? Did you fight with your mother?

Sandy: No, I had been sent to juvenile hall twelve times for everything from shoplifting to runaway to, you name it almost.

Question: After that time then did you run around with a tough group, hard guys?

Sandy: Yeah, well I didn't realize it 'til many years later. You know, I helped someone kick heroin once. He told me that he had the flu and I was seventeen. Two years later I suddenly went WOW! I was really dumb and young. By the time I got out I thought I was gay cuz I had never had a man. I was always carrying on with my women. Then I met Dave's father and we started dating. I dated him for about two months. When I met him he was about thirty-two and a three-time loser already and I was sixteen going on seventeen. I guess you'd call him pretty hardcore.

Question: Have you ever been arrested for prostitution?

Sandy: No, I never did get arrested on that rap. I don't know why because I tricked with two or three policemen. In fact, that time I was going to turn a trick after being out, when my house got burglarized, that guy was a cop and he said, "Don't bother calling the cops." And I said, "What do you mean don't bother?" And he said that he was a cop and that it wouldn't do any good. But at that time I was so mad that I was going to blow it anyway. And he had already blown it by agreein' to trick with me. And he just finished smoking a joint of mine.

QUESTIONS FOR DISCUSSION

1. Some theorists argue that prostitution is inevitable. What is your opinion? How do you think Sandy would have answered that question?

2. What do you believe are the attributes, characteristic skills, and so on needed for a woman to become a prostitute? Is a socialization or learning period necessary?

3. How does Sandy justify working with a pimp? Is the relationship one-sided?

4. What does Sandy mean when she says: "Being a prostitute is kinda like being a dope addict"? Do you believe Florrie Fisher (selection 11) would have said: "Being a drug addict is kinda like being a prostitute"?

5. Which theory or theories of deviant behavior presented in the first section best explain Sandy's behavior as a prostitute?

PIMP Iceberg Slim

A week after Chris left I copped another bag of cocaine from "Top." It was almost gone. The runt was only making expenses. I had one lonely 'C' note and a double saw plus the porker silver. The weather was getting balmy. I needed fresh clothes. I was going to the bottom fast.

In the three weeks after Chris left I kicked the runt's ass a half-dozen times. I only left the hotel twice in almost a month. I was expecting Chris to call me and say she was on her way to me. Things were getting worse.

It has been two weeks since I saw "Top." I decided to call him. Maybe he could hip me to a new spot to work for runt. My bankroll was thin. At ten A.M. I called "Top." One of his broads said he was out of town. He wouldn't be back for a week.

I got a sudden thought. I asked her if she knew "Sweet's" phone number. She said she did, but she'd have to call and find out if "Sweet" wanted me to have it. She called back in ten minutes and gave it to me. I called him. He answered. He was in a good mood.

He said, "Well, whatta you know, if it ain't grinning Slim. You still got that one whore or have you grinned yourself whoreless?"

I looked over at the runt. She was still asleep. She hadn't been in the street for three days. Her period had run five days. She claimed she was too weak and sick to go out. I had given her a terrible whipping the night before. I needed advice badly.

I said, " 'Sweet,' my bitch is falling apart. She's playing dead. If you don't pull my coat I'm gonna starve to death. You gotta help me 'Sweet.'"

He said, "Nigger, you ain't cracking to nick me for scratch are you? I don't loan my scratch to suckers who got whores and can't pimp on 'em. I ain't gonna support you and that lazy bitch."

I said, "No 'Sweet.' I don't want scratch. I want you to run the game through my skull. I got a tiny bit of scratch. I gotta get my coat pulled before I tap out."

He said, "You got wheels? You know how to get out here? Now remember you get a roust out here, crack my name. Don't repeat your boner."

I said, "Yeah, I'm driving. I think I can find your pad. When should I come out there?"

He said, "Quick as you can get here. You get here and grin in my face, I'm gonna throw you over the patio wall.

"Say kid, Peaches and me got a taste for some of that barbecued chicken down there in Hell. Bring one with you when you come."

He hung up. My ticker was pounding like Chris had walked in the door naked with a million dollars. I shook the runt. She opened her eyes. I stood over her.

I said, "Bitch, you better be in the street when I get back."

She said, "You can't do anything but kill me. I'm ready to die. I don't care what you do to me. I'm sick."

I said, "All right, bitch, just hip me where you want your black stinking ass shipped."

I got in the Ford. I realized I hadn't put on a tie. I didn't have a lid. I looked into the rearview mirror. I sure looked scroungy. Maybe he'd be alone. Then I remembered the lobby. What the hell did it matter.

I drove for about fifteen minutes before I saw a clean open barbeque joint. A black stud in a tall white cap was stabbing chickens onto a turning spit in the window. I went in. I came out with two birds. Peaches might be really hungry for barbequed chicken. It made solid sense to brown-nose Miss Peaches.

After making several wrong turns I found "Sweet's" building. I parked the Ford in almost the same spot at the curb where Satan had sapped me a month ago. A young white stud in a monkey suit was out in front. Crusader "Sweet" was doing his bit to reverse the social order.

I went to the desk in the lobby. I felt like a tramp as I waited for the pass. I got on the elevator. A different broad was at the controls. The spicy scent of the chicken wiggled her nose. She wasn't as pretty as the ripe-smelling broad. She sure kept her crotch from advertising. Maybe it was just that she didn't get heavy action.

I stepped from the cage. The friendly brown snake wasn't at his station to flop his mop for me. I figured it was his off day. The odds were a hundred to one he was in the sack somewhere with a six-foot blonde.

She was probably a little like the blonde coming up from the pit on her way to the cage. It was Mimi. She flicked her green eyes across my face. They were cold as a frozen French lake. She passed me. She looked like fancy French pastry in her sable stole. I wondered how I got the stupid courage to turn down her freak off.

I walked to the doorway of the pit. The stone broad was still in her squirting squat. "Sweet" was sitting on the couch. Miss Peaches beside him saw me first. She bounded across the carpet. I felt her choppers graze my hand. She snatched the bag of chicken. She flung it on the alabaster topped cocktail table in front of "Sweet."

"Sweet" looked at me. I tightened my face into a solemn grim mask. I stepped down and walked toward him. He was wearing only a pair of polka-dot shorts. In daylight I noticed a mole on the broad in the picture over the couch.

I said, "Hello Mr. Jones. I hope those birds are still warm."

He said, "Kid, your map sure looks like that bullshit bitch you got is been shooting you through hot grease. I like that look you got today. Maybe you're getting hip the pimp game ain't for grinning jackasses.

"Get over here and sit on this couch. While baby and me eat our barbeque, rundown you and your whore. I wanta know where and how you copped her. Tell me everything you can remember about her and what's happened since you copped her. Rundown your whole life as far

back as you remember. It don't matter which is first."

I ran down my life for him. Then I ran down from the night I met the runt until the moment I left the Haven. It took maybe forty-five minutes. I even described the runt in detail.

"Sweet" and his greedy girl-friend had devoured both birds down to the bare bones. "Sweet" was wiping Miss Peaches' whiskers with a paper napkin. She put her head in his lap. She was jammed against my thigh. "Sweet" leaned back on the couch. He put his bare feet on the top of the cocktail table.

He said, "Sweetheart, you're black like me. I love you. You got the hate to pimp. You a lucky Nigger to get your coat pulled by me. You flap your horns and remember what I'm gonna spiel to you.

"There are thousands of Niggers in this country who think they're pimps. The pussy-weak white pimps ain't worth mentioning. Don't none of them pimp by the book. They ain't even heard about it. If they was black, they'd starve stiff.

"There ain't more than six of 'em who are hip to and pimp by the book. You won't find it in the square-Nigger or white history books. The truth is that book was written in the skulls of proud slick Niggers freed from slavery. They wasn't lazy. They was puking sick of picking white man's cotton and kissing his nasty ass. The slave days stuck in their skulls. They went to the cities. They got hip fast.

"The conning bastard white man hadn't freed the Niggers. The cities was like the plantations down South. Jeffing Uncle Toms still did all the white man's hard and filthy work.

"Those slick Nigger heroes bawled like crumb crushers. They saw the white man just like on the plantations still ramming it into the finest black broads.

"The broads were stupid squares. They still freaked for free with the white man. They wasn't hip to the scratch in their hot black asses.

"Those first Nigger pimps started hipping the dumb bitches to the gold mines between their legs. They hipped them to stick their mitts out for the white man's scratch. The first Nigger pimps and sure-shot gamblers was the only Nigger big shots in the country.

"They wore fine threads and had blooded horses. Those pimps was black geniuses. They wrote that skull book on pimping. Even now if it wasn't for that frantic army of white tricks, Nigger pimps would starve to death.

"Greenie, the white man has been pig-greedy for Nigger broads ever since his first whiff of black pussy. Black whores con themselves the only reason he sniffs his way to 'em is white broads ain't got what it takes to please him.

"I'm hip he's got two other secret sick reasons. White women ain't hip to his secret reasons. The dumb white broads ain't even hip to why he locks all Niggers inside tight stockades. He'd love it if the Nigger broads wasn't locked in there. The white man is scared shitless. He don't want them humping bucks coming out there in the white world rubbing their bellies against those soft white bellies.

"That's the real reason for keeping all the Niggers locked up. To show you how sick in the head he is, he thinks black broads are dirt beneath his feet. His balls will bust if he don't sneak through that stockade, to those, to him, half-savage, less than human, black broads.

"You know, Greenie, why he's gotta come to 'em? The silly sick bastard is like a whore that needs and loves punishment. He's a joke with scratch in his mitt. As great as he thinks he is, he can't keep his beak and swipe outta the stink of a black ass.

"He wallows and stains himself. The poor freak's joy is in his suffering. The chump believes he's done something dirty to himself. He slips back into his white world. He goes on conning himself he's God and Niggers are wild filthy animals he has to keep in the stockades.

"The sad thing is he don't even know he's sick in the skull. Greenie, I'm pulling your coat from the bottom to the top. That rundown on the first Nigger pimps will make you proud to be a pimp.

"Square-ass Niggers will try to put shame inside you. Ain't one of 'em wouldn't suck a mule's ass to pimp. They can't because a square ain't nothing but a pussy. He lets a square bitch pimp on him. You gotta pimp by the rules of that pimp book those noble studs wrote a hundred years ago. When you look in a mirror you gotta know that cold-hearted bastard looking at you is real.

"Now that young bitch you got is gone lazy. She's stuffing on you. That bitch ain't sick. I ain't never seen a bitch under twenty that could get sick. Your whore is bullshitting. A whore's scratch ain't never longer than a pimp's cold game. You gotta have strict rules for a whore. She's gotta respect you to hump her heart out in the street.

"One whore ain't got but one pussy and one jib. You got to get what there is in her fast as you can. You gotta get sixteen hours a day outta her. There ain't no guarantee you going to keep any bitch for long. The name of the pimp game is 'Cop and Blow.'

"Now this young bitch you got is shitty all right. She knows you ain't got no other whore. I want you to go back to that hotel. Make that bitch get outta that bed and get in the street. Put your foot in her ass hard. If that don't work, take a wire coat hanger and twist it into a whip. Ain't no bitch, freak or not, can stand up to that hanger.

"Maybe your foot and fist can't move that young whore anymore. She's a freak to them. Believe me, Greenie, that coat hanger will blow her or straighten her out. It's better to have no whore than a piece of whore. Get some cotton and make her pack herself. The show can't stop when a whore bleeds.

"I'm gonna lay some pills on you. Give her a couple when you get her outta that bed. Don't give her anymore reefer. It makes some whores lazy. Don't worry, kid, if you do like I say and blow her, I'll give you a whore. Kid, don't hold that whore to one block. Tell that whore all the streets go. Turn her loose. It's the only way to pimp. If she blows, whatta you lost. She stands up, you got a whore and some real scratch.

"You go back and put the coat-hanger pressure on her. If it don't blow her and she stands up for a week, you oughtta have half a grand in a week. Take that scratch and drive to one of the whore towns close around. Go to Western Union. Send that scratch back to yourself at your hotel. Use some broad's name as the sender.

"That lazy bitch you got will think she's got competition. Watch the sparks fly from her ass. She'll try to top that bitch that doesn't exist. Greenie, you listen to 'Sweet' Jones. You'll be a helluva pimp.

"Never get friendly and confide in your whores. You got twenty whores, don't forget your thoughts are secret. A good pimp is always really alone. You gotta always be a puzzle, a mystery to them. That's how you hold a whore. Don't get sour. Tell them something new and confusing every day. You can hold 'em as long as you can do it.

" 'Sweet' is hipping you to pimp by the book. I'm the greatest Nigger pimp in the world. Now Greenie, is you skull going to hold everything I told you?"

I said, "Thirty years from now I'll still remember every word. 'Sweet' you won't be sorry you helped me. I'm gonna pimp my black ass off. I'll make you proud of me. I'll call you later and hip you to what the runt did under hanger pressure. Oh, yeah, don't forget to give me those pills."

He got up. Miss Peaches stretched her legs. She jumped down and followed him. A sharp hooked nail in one of her rear claws snagged out an inch of cloth from my pants knee. I wouldn't have cared if she had clawed me naked. I was in a thrilled daze. With "Sweet" Jones on ready tap to pull my coat I was going to set a record on the fast track.

"Sweet" came back. He gave me a tiny bottle of small white pills. He put his hands on my shoulders. He looked down at me. His sub-zero eyes warmed to maybe zero.

He said, "I love you, Sweetheart! You know, kid, I don't ever think I'm gonna grin in your face. I love you like a son. Any time I grin in a sucker's face I'm gonna cross him or croak him. Call me any time you need a rundown. Good luck, Greenie."

I walked across the pit. I stepped up to the doorway. I glanced back. "Sweet" had Peaches in his arms. She was purring like a new bride. "Sweet" was squeezing her in a lover's embrace. He was covering her laughing face with kisses.

I checked "Mickey" when I got in the Ford. It was four P.M. I drove toward the runt. I tromped hard on the gas pedal.

I thought, "No wonder 'Sweet' is the greatest Nigger pimp in the world. He even knows the history of the black pimp.

"I ain't going to spare the runt's ass. I'm gonna go right in with the pressure. I hope she's not in the street. 'Sweet' promised me a whore if I blow the runt. Any whore of 'Sweet's' is already trained to a fine edge. Maybe he'll give me Mimi."

I pulled the Ford into the curb across the street from the Haven. I didn't see the runt anywhere in the street. I peeped into the greasy spoon. She wasn't at the counter. I looked up at our window. I crossed the street and went through the lobby. I took the stairs to the fourth floor. I made three stabs at the lock with the key before I made it. I stepped inside. I was excited. I chain-bolted the door. I walked to the bedroom.

The runt was propped up in bed smoking a stick of gangster. Lady Day was tar brushing that mean, sweet man again. I stood by the side of the bed, next to the record player. I saw the edge of a paper plate sticking out of the waste basket. I took it out and put it on the bed.

Two navy beans were in a puddle of grease on the side of the plate. A pile of sucked, cleaned neck bones were heaped in the center of it. The runt had gone out to the greasy spoon and copped a hearty meal. She sure had a healthy appetite for a sick bitch. Her eyes were wild and big, looking up at me.

She fingered gently at the hole in my pants knee. I shut the box off. I ripped the record off the turn table. I broke it in half and hurled the pieces into the waste basket. She kept her eyes on the hole at my knee. She ignored the broken record. She played it cool.

She said, "You'll have to get it rewoven, huh? Daddy, I'm feeling better. I felt good enough to go across the street for food. Maybe by tomorrow I'll feel good enough to go in the street. Baby, I would've went out after I ate, but my legs were too weak."

I said, "Bitch, I already passed the death sentence on you. It's good you had your last meal. I'm gonna send your dead ass to your daughter, Gay. Take off that gown and lie on your belly, bitch."

I went to the closet. I took down a wire hanger. I straightened it into one long piece. I doubled and braided it. I wrapped a necktie around the handle end. I turned back to the bed. She was still propped in the bed. Her mouth was gaped open. She had both her hands clapped over her chest.

She was like a broad in a movie. She opens a door and there's Dr. Jekyll just going into his frightful change. I saw her tongue tremble inside her jib. Her lips made a liquid plopping sound as they mutely pounded together. She rolled across the bed away from me. I raised my right arm up and back. I heard my shoulder socket creak.

Her gown was hiked up to her waist. Her naked rear end had scrambled to the far edge of the bed. I raced around the foot of the bed. She rolled to the middle. She was on her back. Her arms held her jack-knifed legs against her chest.

The whites of her eyes glowed like phosphorus. I brought the wire whip down. I heard it swish through the air. It struck her across the shin bones. She cried out like she was celebrating New Year's Eve.

She screamed, "Ooh-whee! Ooh-whee!"

She jerked flat, rigid on the bed then smalled her fists against her temples. She sucked her bottom lip up into her jib. I slashed the air again. It sounded like maybe a dum-dum bullet striking across her gut button.

She moaned, "Whee-Lordy! Whee-Lordy!"

She turned over on her belly. I tore the gown from her back. She was naked. She flailed her arms like a holy-roller. The whip whistled a deadly lyric as I brought it down again and again across her back and butt. I saw the awful welts puffing the black velvet skin.

I stopped and turned her over. The pillow stuck to her face. I snatched it away. There was a ripping sound. I saw feathers sticking to her tear wet face. She had chewed a hole in the pillow. She was thrashing her legs and mumbling.

Her chest heaved in great sobs. She was staring at me and shaking her skull. Her eyes had that pitiful look of Christ's on those paintings of the Crucifixion. Her lips were moving. I got on the bed. I stuck my ear near.

She whispered, "I don't need any more whipping. I give, Daddy. You're the boss. I was a dumb bitch. It looks like you got a whore now. Kiss me and help me up."

I felt tears roll down my cheeks. Maybe I was crying in joy that I broke her spirit. I felt sorry for her. I wondered if I was falling in love like a sucker. I kissed her hard. I carried her into the bathroom. I placed her tenderly in the tub.

I turned the water on. A stream burst from the shower nozzle overhead. She squealed. I pushed in the shower bypass on the tub faucet. The warm water started filling the tub. I dumped a bottle of rubbing alcohol into the tub.

She looked up at me. I took the tiny bottle of pills out of my pocket. I shook out two into my palm. I took a glass off the face bowl. I handed her the pills. She put them in her mouth. She washed them down with the glass of water I gave her.

I said, "Phyllis, why do you make your sweet daddy mean? Daddy's gonna kill his little bitch if she don't straighten up and whore like the star she is.

"Bitch, lie down in that water for a while. Then get in the street and get some real scratch for your man. You don't have to stay in this block. Just walk and work until you get respectable scratch to bring in. I can raise you if you take a fall. They gotta let you make a phone call. If I go out I'll check the desk here by phone every hour or so. Bitch, get down and star. You want your man, get him some real scratch."

I went and sat on the bed. The sheet looked like a red zebra had lain down and his stripes had faded on it. I heard her sloshing the water in the tub. She was humming the record I'd smashed. "Sweet's" pills sure weren't hurting her.

Whores were strange people all right. She was silent while she combed her hair and fixed her face. She put on a red knit suit. She stood in front of me. She held her hand out. I saw dark stains on her stockings at the shins. Her eyes were bright.

She said, "Daddy, I don't have a dime. Give me a coupla dollars, please. Don't worry, when I come in I'll have nice scratch."

I stood up. I gave her a fin. I walked to the door with her. She turned her face up. I leaned down. I sucked her bottom lip, then bit it hard. She squeezed my arm and gouged her teeth into my cheek. She went down the hall.

I shut the door and went to the front window. I rubbed my cheek to see if the skin was broken. I saw her cross the street at the corner. She was walking fast. That whipping and those pills had made her well. She looked like a child. She was so tiny and sexy in her red suit. I wondered as she disappeared whether she'd come back. It was seven P.M.

I thought, "I better stick here in the pad. Whipping a broad with a hanger is not a bit like a foot in the ass. Christ! I'd kill the bastard on the spot if he hit my bare ass with one. 'Sweet' was right. She got outta that bed all right. I wonder if those slavery pimps invented the hanger whip."

. . . I said, "'Sweet,' I copped a beautiful yellow bitch tonight. I got her humping on the track with my girls. 'Sweet,' the bitch is crazy about me. I know I'll hold her for years."

He said, "Slim, a pretty Nigger bitch and a white whore are just alike. They both will get in a stable to wreck it. They'll leave the pimp on his ass with no whore. You gotta make 'em hump hard and fast. Stick 'em for long scratch quick. Slim, pimping ain't no game of love. Prat 'em and keep your swipe outta 'em. Any sucker who believes a whore loves him shouldn't a fell outta his mammy's ass.

"Slim, I hope you ain't sexed that pretty bitch yet. Believe me, Slim, a pimp is really a whore who's reversed the game on whores. Slim, be as sweet as the scratch. Don't be no sweeter. Always stick a whore for a bundle before you sex her. A whore ain't nothing but a trick to a pimp. Don't let 'em 'Georgia' you. Always get your money in front just like a whore.

"Whores in a stable are like working chumps in the white man's factory. They know in their sucker tickers they're chumping. They both gotta have horns to blow their beefs into. They gotta have someone to listen while they bad mouth that Goddamn boss.

"A good pimp is like a slick white boss. He don't ever pair two of a kind for long. He don't ever pair two new bitches. He ain't stuck 'em for no long scratch. A pair of new bitches got too much in common. They'll beef to each other and pool their skull, plots, and split to the wind together.

"The real glue that holds any bitch to a pimp is the long scratch she's hip she's stuck for. A good pimp could cut his swipe off and still pimp his ass off. Pimping ain't no sex game. It's a skull game.

"A pimp with a shaky-bottom woman is like a sucker with a lit firecracker stuck in his ass. When his boss bitch turns sour and blows, all the other bitches in the stable flee to the wind behind her.

"There ain't more than three or four good bottom women promised a pimp in his lifetime. I don't care if he cops three hundred whores before he croaks.

"A good pimp has gotta have like a farm system for bottom women. He's gotta know what bitch in the family could be the bottom bitch when mama bitch goes sour.

"He's gotta keep his game tighter on his bottom bitch than on any bitch in the stable. He's gotta peep around her ass while she's taking a crap. He's gotta know if it's got the same stink and color it had yesterday.

"Slim, you're in trouble until you cop the fourth whore. A stable is sets of teams playing against each other to stuff the pimp's pockets with scratch. You got a odd bitch. You ain't got but a team and a half.

"A young pimp like you is gotta learn not to cop blind. Your fourth bitch is gotta be right to pair with the third whore.

"She can't be no ugly bitch unless she likes pussy. She can't be smarter than the pretty bitch. She can be younger, even prettier, but she's gotta be dumber.

"Slim, all whores have one thing in common just like the chumps humping for the white boss. It thrills 'em when the pimp makes mistakes. They watch and wait for his downfall.

"A pimp is the loneliest bastard on Earth. He's gotta know his whores. He can't let them know him. He's gotta be God all the way.

"The poor sonuvabitch has joined a hate club he can't quit. He can't do a turn around and be a whore himself in the white boss's stable unless he was never a pimp in the first place.

"So, Kid, rest and dress and pimp till you croak. I ain't had no rest in a coupla days. I think I'll try to get some 'doss.' Kid, these skull aches are getting bad. Good luck, Kid. Call me tomorrow, late.

"Oh yeah, happy birthday, Kid. That rundown was a birthday present."

QUESTIONS FOR DISCUSSION

1. In what ways may pimping be related to a legitimate small business?

2. From a sociological standpoint, how would you describe the dynamics of the relationship between prostitutes and their pimps?

3. What are the sociological and psychological principles behind Sweet's advice on how a pimp should treat his whores?

4. What is the historical basis of Sweet's rationale for Black pimps? Do you think it has any basis in fact?

5. From the description given by Sweet and Slim, is pimping a full time job or no work at all?

BEING DIFFERENT: THE AUTOBIOGRAPHY OF JANE FRY *Robert Bogdan*

Being referred to as a "transsexual" doesn't bother me too much. I would rather be thought of as a person first, but it doesn't make me angry because that's what I am. A transsexual is a person who wishes to change sexes and is actively going about it. Which is exactly what I am doing.[1]

I have the physical organs of a man, but I feel that I am a woman. For a long time I fought these feelings, but I don't anymore. I take female hormones and dress and live as a woman, and I have for two years. I understand my transsexualism for what it is. Basically, it boils down to this: What is a person? Is a person what he is on the inside? Or what he is on the outside? I know what I am on the inside, a female. There is no doubt there. I could spend 50 years of my life trying to change, but I doubt if that would do anything. I know what I am. I like it, and I don't want to change. The only thing I want to change is my body, so that it matches what I am. A body is like a covering; it's like a shell. What is more important? The body or the person that is inside?

As you will read, I went for three years of psychotherapy and I couldn't find anything in my childhood to pin this thing down on, nothing that would be different from your background or anybody else's. Sure, if you look hard enough into my childhood you would find things, just like if I looked into yours I could find things, if I wanted to. You might say that there were psychological reasons for my state if my father was a superdrunk, or if my mother made me sleep with her, or if she wanted a girl so much she dressed me in girls' clothes; but there was nothing like that. My father said to me once that there were a few males on his side of the family way back that were fairly feminine. I don't know whether heredity is part of it or not. For sure, my father isn't feminine.

I spent three years searching for psycholog-

ical reasons and other kinds of reasons, because I was expected to. I'm not interested in reasons anymore. I don't give a damn what caused it. God could have poked his finger in my belly button and said, "You're going to think of yourself as a girl," and that could have caused it. All I want to do is get it fixed. I just want to be myself. But in order to get it fixed you have to convince God knows how many people that you're sane, convince people that you really want the operation, find someone to do it, and come up with the money.

I stopped looking for reasons two years ago. Every doctor you see gives you a different explanation, and you just come to the point of knowing that they just don't know what the hell they are talking about. One thing that I did learn in meeting all the doctors is that you have to give a little—pretend a little. Any one of them can kill you physically or emotionally. They can put the dampers on everything. If they decide that I am totally insane because I want to be a female, who knows what they can do. I nod when they tell me their theories now. You have got to learn to give and take, which I took some time in learning.

Before I go on and tell you about the operation and transsexualism and the hassle involved in that, let me tell you a little about the way I look at life and analyze myself. There is this story I heard once about Freud that pretty much sums it up. He was at a meeting with some colleagues, and he lit up this huge stogey. His colleagues around the table started snickering because of his writing about oral complexes and phallus symbols. Freud just looked at it and said, "Yes gentlemen. I know this is a phallic symbol but it is also a goddamned good cigar." That's a good way to look at life. If it's enjoyable, do it as long as it doesn't harm anybody, and don't worry about analyzing everything. That is my philosophy. I am the only one responsible for what I do, and as long as I don't harm another human being mentally or physically, I'm being a good person. I think that I'm a good person because I operate according to my principles. I may break the law, but I'm not breaking my law which seems like the sensible one to me. I also think people should help each other, which I try to do. I think people should help me. They shouldn't sit down and try to analyze me, or try to figure out why I am the way I am or whether I am eligible for a sex change.

There are two laws that I know of that affect transsexuals—one the police can pick you up for. It's about impersonation. I don't know the actual law, but it was put on the books in the 1700s. The reason they had it was that farmers were dressing up as Indians in order to avoid paying taxes—some would even dress as women. So they passed this law not allowing people to dress up in public and to paint their faces. That's the law they now arrest transsexuals and transvestites on.

The other law keeps surgeons from doing the operation. That one comes from England. There was a war going on there and the people were trying to get out of the draft by cutting off their fingers and toes, and they would have a surgeon do it. So the law states that no surgeon can take away any part of your body that would make you ineligible for the draft. So cutting off my genitals is making me ineligible for the draft. I think the draft board could afford to lose a few, but anyway that's the law that the surgeons are afraid of. I've heard of a couple of times where doctors were ready to perform the operation and were notified by the DA that if they did they would press charges.

The doctors usually back off. They don't want to get involved. They don't have the time to get in a test case, and most of the time they don't want that kind of publicity. The hospitals especially don't like that kind of publicity. They don't get donations, I guess, if the public finds out they are doing sexual change operations. The board of directors and contributors jump down their throats for doing such an atrocious thing, and if the word gets out that a hospital is doing the surgery, they get besieged by transsexuals wanting to get one.

Most people don't know the difference between transvestites, homosexuals, and transsexuals, so I think I ought to clear that up before I go any further. Most people just lump them all together. I saw one Archie Bunker show on homosexuals that really pointed out how Americans think about people who have different sexual practices. People don't realize how prejudiced they are about homosexuality and transsexuality, because they aren't even at a point of knowing that it's something that you can be prejudiced about. They are so sure that the rest of the world is supposed to be the way they are that they don't even think the people who are different have an opinion. They just lump them all together as nuts or perverts. That's the way Archie was on this program.

Well, anyway, a transvestite only wants to dress like a woman. They don't want to go all the way and have an operation and live as a woman. The transsexual wants an operation. It's a difference in the way you think about yourself. The way of thinking of a transsexual is: "I am a female with a birth defect. I am a woman, but I have the organs of the other sex. I want to be a whole person again." The term is also used to refer to people who are physiologically women who want to be men. The way of thinking of a transvestite is: "I am a man, but I want to play the role of a female. I know that I am a male, but I get kicks out of dressing like a woman." The transvestite gets emotional gratification and psychological good feelings from dressing. A transsexual doesn't. There is an interest in clothing, but it's much like a woman's interest. No erotic stimulation or anything like that. Like, I am just as happy bumming around in a pair of jeans and a blouse as in some type of fancy low-cut gown with heels.

The difference between a homosexual and a transsexual or a transvestite is that the homosexual knows that he is a man, let's say, but he is sexually attracted to those of the same sex and has sex with them. He says, "I know that I am a man, but I want to have sex with a man." Some transvestites are not homosexuals, because they don't want sex. Transsexuals are not homosexuals because they don't want to have sex with those who are of the same sex as they are; they want sex with the opposite sex.

I used to be down on homosexuals. Homosexuals and transsexuals usually don't hit it off. I happened to relate well with a group a few years ago, and I was able to get over my prejudices and start seeing what we had in common rather than what we differed over. I found it easy to relate to this group, because what we had in common was that we were suppressed. We both share some of the dangers of being brutalized because of our beliefs. We can be picked up for impersonation, or for vagrancy, or anything else they want to pick us up for. We also share being made jokes of or beat up at any time. Like, just last week I had a seizure in the middle of the street, and someone called an ambulance. The first thing that I remember was being in the ambulance strapped to a stretcher. I looked up, and there are these two guys laughing and joking. One says to me, "Don't worry, *dearie*. We've got you figured out." I was so angry I almost couldn't control myself, but that is typical of what we have to watch out for.

When you're like me, you have always got to be on your guard that you don't get into a position that is going to get you into a jam. Like, I went downtown and picketed the recruiting center as part of the antiwar demonstration. I had decided that I was going to perform an act of civil disobedience with a group if they tried to clear us out of the road. But standing around down there, all of a sudden it hit me. If I get busted and get taken to jail, they might throw every charge in the book at me if they found out I was physically a man. I have to be more careful than anybody else that goes on a march like that. I went in the front of the parade in this particular march, carrying a banner—but that wasn't smart to do. If people were to ever find out and if it was in the papers, the reporters and the readers would zero in on the fact of what I was, and that would have blown the whole issue. Immediately, all the hard hats would go back to their favorite sayings: "Look at all those faggot queers with the long hair marching around. They got a real beauty out in front this time." People like me aren't sincere about those issues, according to them. We don't count.

It's hard for transsexuals, because you don't have many allies. I'm almost totally dependent on white, middle-class doctors to give me a fair shake. There are so few doctors that will see me, that I have to scrape to get what I want. They are in control. They told me that I have to conform to their standards or I don't get the operation.

I'm probably different from other transsexuals, but they probably think the same about themselves. One thing is that it is usually hard for transsexuals to talk about themselves, especially after the operation. I'm going to tell you a lot about myself. Talking about it opens up a lot of old wounds. I haven't had the operation, so it's a lot easier because the wounds are still in the open and I get new ones every day.

I don't think very many transsexuals have gone through three years of psychotherapy, as I have. Most phase it out after 50 sessions or so. I'm different, too, in that most transsexuals don't go to psychiatric hospitals. Why that is I don't know. Most transsexuals are also very introverted. They want to stay totally undercover, outside the public eye. They don't want to upset the apple cart. They have to keep low profiles so as to keep respectable. This is because they don't depend on each other so much as on their physicians.

Your doctor is the most important part of your life. He takes precedence over fathers and mothers, in some cases. That is the person who prescribes the hormones and may be able to help you get the operation. You've got to keep him happy. Doctors are gods to them. Which is why I don't think I get along too well with some doctors, because I don't think of them or treat them like God, not anymore anyway—I think they are as fucked up in some respects as me. When you talk to another transsexual, the first thing they will talk about is what their doctor is doing for them. I don't think it's healthy or that you can be a person, if your whole life is so dependent on someone else who can cut you off any time.

I am talking about the transsexuals I know. I haven't known that many. Maybe I've met a total of 30. There aren't too many in the United States. Dr. Benjamin's book says there are 100,000, or something like that, in the United States. Maybe I should just talk for myself.

The vast majority of transsexuals try to make it in the straight world, as the gay community calls it. The reason for that is because the operation is not very well advertised. I mean, you don't see many articles in popular magazines about it, so people don't know about it. People who are transsexuals and don't know about operations are trying to live the role that society says they have to. Like myself—everybody used to say, "You have got to be a little boy." I knew I wasn't, but they said I had to. As you will read in this book, I went into the Navy to try to be. I went into submarine service trying to be. I even got married trying to be. I underwent psychotherapy, but that didn't work either. Then I heard about the operation, and that's what I have been working toward ever since.

I am presently living in purgatory. A little between heaven and hell. I am working my way upwards, slowly, but when you have to fight the whole damn system single-handed, it's hard. Usually, you look for help and people turn their backs on you. I tell them what I want, and they say, "He's really a *sick* person." They don't get it through their heads that they are the ones that have made me sick and are keeping me sick. Most transsexuals have had hassles, but they don't have the hassles over being a transsexual; they have them over the way society fucks over them. After it fucks over you, it asks, "What can we do to help?" So to help they stick you into an institution for the mentally ill that gives you more hassles. It's a cycle. When I went into the VA psychiatric ward, I was in hell. Now that I am getting hormone shots and living and working as a female, it's purgatory. Once I get the operation, although I know it's not going to be perfect, it will kind of be like heaven. I am not going to say that the operation is going to cure everything—I don't consider it a cure-all. I have a lot of hassles to clear up, just like most people. It's not going to be a cure-all, but it will sure as hell get rid of many of the pressures and tensions I am under.

The cost of the operation is twice what it would be if it weren't so controversial. You feel that you're being taken advantage of. The cost in Casablanca is about $8000, and they go between $3500 and $5000 in other places. That is not the cost of the operation—that is just the surgeon's fees. That is not counting the anesthesiologist, the operating room, the recovery time, medication, and so on. Since when does a person get over $3500 for less than a day's work? What they do is remove parts of the male organ and use part of it to build a vagina. The vagina has

the nerve endings from the penis and scrotum, so there are sexual feelings.

There are two doctors in the world today who are working toward perfecting the male-to-female surgery. One is a doctor in Casablanca; the other is in Tijuana. They have their own clinics with operating suites and the whole thing. They are both expensive. You have to deposit the right amount in their Swiss bank account prior to the operation. He gets out of paying the taxes and the hassle of taking that much through customs. These are the men who are doing most of the surgical research.

There are people in the United States doing research, but it is mostly statistical or psychological. A couple of places out West did some operations and have decided to wait between 12 and 20 years to find out the results before they do any more. Johns Hopkins did a lot, but I don't think they are doing any now either. They were supposed to be doing one every three months or so. There are other places here and there that do them, but it's hard to find out for sure who's doing them.

According to Dr. Benjamin, who studied over 100 people who had the operation, only one was considered unsatisfactory. They had all made a better adjustment to life than before the operation. The one that was unsatisfactory was a medical thing, not psychological. So the operation seems pretty foolproof. By the way, psychotherapy has never been known to "cure" a transsexual.

The reason the cost is so high is part of the old supply and demand thing. Transsexuals need one thing, the operation, and there is only a small group of doctors who will do it. If these people stick together in the price they charge, the only thing someone can do is pay their price. You can't very well boycott or picket, or stuff like that. There is no recourse but to pay it or not get it done.

People who do the operation have this informal rule, that in order to be eligible for it you have to be living as a female for two years. That includes working as a female. You also have to have a recommendation from a psychiatrist you have been seeing for two years. They say that, if you can work as a female successfully enough to make the money, then you'll make a good adjustment after the operation. It's the kind of a situation where you're so concerned about the operation that it's hard to concentrate on working—if you had the operation, you might settle down. Besides, it's almost impossible to get any kind of a job that pays enough for you to save on. The other thing is: Who is going to write you a recommendation in the first place to get a job, and what name are they going to put down, your old one or your new one? Also, what about when they ask you for your social security card and it has a man's name on it? Medicaid won't pay for it, and Blue Cross and Blue Shield get upset when you even suggest it. They consider it cosmetic surgery.

The operation is a vicious circle. I want to have the operation so bad that I am under great pressure and strain. The pressure makes it hard to find or keep a good job. The fact that you can't keep a job and that you're uptight is used as evidence that you're not sane. They tell you, "If you really wanted it, you could do it." I can see their reasoning, but I don't agree with it. I don't know what I can do about it though. They tell you getting the money is part of the therapy.

What people don't understand is that transsexuals, myself included, think of this whole operation in the same way you would think of having a wart removed, or having plastic surgery done on your nose. If you think your nose is ugly and you want it fixed, if it's bothering you, instead of worrying about it and while your head is thinking about it the way it is and all that stuff, you go out and get it fixed. That's the way I think of it, but most physicians don't. Most people are so uptight about sex in general, and about penises and vaginas, that they have to find something psychological to worry about. It's funny.

I don't know how you're taking this so far, but the majority of people hear about me and they automatically think I have problems—super head problems. Even if I don't have them, they think I'm crazy. You just try to avoid people like that. After I get to know people it works out. If I make them uptight, I leave.

People usually find out that I'm a transsexual not from me, but from my "friends." It makes me angry to have to explain it to people because, I don't know, how would you like to have to explain yourself to everyone you met? Explain how you think you're a man or a woman. Why

the hell do I have to be explained? I mean to hell with the transsexualism, I'm a human being first, and female second, and a transsexual third. But people can't respond to it like that. Society doesn't want to know me as a human being. I have to be a transsexual first to do anything. It's almost, "Forget Jane Fry and let's talk about the transsexual." It's almost like when I went to get my appendix out. They were so much into looking at me as a transsexual that they didn't do anything about my appendix. When I was in the psychiatric hospitals, they concentrated so much on me being a transsexual that they weren't willing to help me with what I needed help with.

I have come to automatically distrust people because of this. I want to be accepted as a human being, and people won't do it; they make it so you can't be a human being. This combined with the operation being so hard to achieve that you have to concentrate on being a transsexual 24 hours a day instead of being a person. All your hopes ride on the operation, and that's what you keep striving for and that's what you fight for. So you think of it all the time, and people treat you like one all the time, and there you are.

It actually makes it more frustrating for me when people don't know about me before I meet them, because you have to jump over a hurdle—I have to explain more or less what I'm all about. Sometimes I blow people's minds intentionally. I get a horror or fear reaction from people who are set in their ways, who haven't run across this kind of thing before.

Men get particularly uptight around me. They just don't know how to handle it. Some guys, the first time they see me, like all males who see a female, look at me as a female and then all of a sudden they find out; it blows their image of themselves. They say to themselves, "God, I must be queer." A lot of people seem to go through that, but I don't know what to do about it. I get along with women a lot better. They don't seem so threatened.

The biggest problem I face is dealing with society in a way that it accepts me and I can accept myself. I have done that to some extent, but I feel I'm kind of doing it the easy way by living on the fringes in the freak culture. Most of my friends are either students or hang out in the University section. People are much more open in their thinking—they don't care if you're different or not. It makes life a lot easier than if I was to try, say, to play the role of the super-middle-class secretary that lives in the suburbs. The majority of transsexuals do that. They are superstraight. Maybe that's easy for them, dealing with it that way, but I just couldn't make it. By living on the fringe I don't have to face the head hassles they do every day. The majority of transsexuals don't have the time or energy left after fighting the hassles to understand what society is like. They are so busy trying to join in and at the same time fight it that they don't see what it's all about.

Being a transsexual, it seems like you're fighting all society and everybody in it. If you don't have psychological hang-ups after all that fighting, there is something wrong with you. I've got problems now, quite a few emotional hang-ups right now. It doesn't mean that I have to be locked up. I recognize them, but I also recognize the reason I got them. I spend half my time worrying about what society thinks, instead of worrying about me. So you have to end up with problems. Anybody can relate the emotional problems that I have now to my childhood and say that my transsexualism is the reason for it, but it's nothing about the transsexualism itself that causes hang-ups—it's fighting society.

This doctor told me that my father was a very violent man and in rejecting him I rejected masculinity and violence, so I had to be a female. I think that's bullshit. What he didn't stop to think was that I probably was a transsexual right from the beginning and I was so worried about the problems that it caused with others I didn't know how to relate to them. You get so wrapped up in your emotions that you can't relate.

I don't think my transsexualism is the direct cause of my emotional problems, but I have to let psychiatrists keep saying it is or else they won't treat me. I have got to get back on the road to getting my operation, so I have to see one. When I see a psychiatrist now, I just ignore it when they start rapping on about my transsexualism. If it gets too bad, I just won't see them anymore.

A lot of people can't even imagine the shit I go through. It's the same thing that they go through, except I go through it to a greater extent. They are forced to become one thing or the other; they have to conform to a certain set of standards, even though they don't think it fits them. With me it's just more obvious that's all. A normal guy, if he likes to cut flowers or wants to be a hairdresser or something like that, his masculinity is questioned and he has pressure on him not to do it. Or a woman who wants to drive a truck—it's the same thing. The male/female thing is just part of it. There are other roles we play too. Masks—that's what I call them. By the time a person is 20 years old you can't see the person for the masks. If someone tries to go against the masks, they are schizophrenic or something else. That's what they are called. That's what's on my medical records.

With the masks society tries to hide human sexuality. What I mean is that society has taken and stereotyped masculinity and femininity so you don't get a full and real picture of what it is. Everybody is trying to live up to the stereotype image.

It's hard to live away from the stereotype a little, but it is a thousand times harder to go away from it as radically as I have. I am doing what most people can't even think of, going from a man to a woman. My father's first comment when I told him was, "Why can't you pick an easier one, like being a homosexual?" Which makes a good point. At least if I was a homosexual, I would be the same sex, but to do something so obvious like changing dress and everything is something that you can't hide. Women who want to go to work are thought to be crazy—if a normal person wants to change roles, he has to fight a lot, but if he wants to change sex, that's a lot more.

I guess you can think of transsexualism as more or less a mask, too. Or it can be. I'm a transsexual, but people try to force me into a stereotype—they try to exaggerate the importance of what I am. It's a part of you, granted, but they make it more a part of you than it really is. I am trying not to make it that way. I'm trying not to fall into the slot, but I'm forced into it.

NOTES

1. Jane's definition of transsexualism closely parallels the one found in most modern dictionaries and those used by the professional community. Harry Benjamin, the doctor who first used the term, states, "The trans-

MENTAL ILLNESS, PHYSICAL DISABILITY, AND SUICIDE

The selections that make up this section illustrate, to a large extent, what is right as well as what is wrong with labeling theory as an approach to unraveling deviant behavior. Among the "rights" of this theory is the presumed potency of socially derived definitions of what and who is deviant in our society. This point of view serves to legitimate and sustain the place of deviance as a viable area within the larger context of sociological study. By so doing, labeling theory focuses not only on individuals who are pressured to accept social definitions of their behavior, but also on the institutional arrangements that support such definitions. For example, it can be pointed out that such institutions as mental hospitals, prisons, special schools, and so on exist to support judgments as to who has behaved in a deviant fashion by providing intervention mechanisms (treatment) by which deviants are returned to normalcy and hence permitted to reenter society. The key to the viability of labeling theory, therefore, lies not only in the "staying" power of social definitions of what kind of behavior is to be labeled as deviant, but equally important, in the acceptance of those definitions by the people whose behavior is so defined.

Thus, a major contribution offered by labeling theory concerns its countervailing effect on psychological theories that accent the individual as their prime empirical referent and as a consequence tend to minimize the role of social factors in efforts to study deviance in its sundry forms.

In pointing to the notion that what gets to be called "deviance" is a function of social factors and conditions, labeling theory offers much in the way of an etiological explanation of who and what is deviant. However, etiological explanations are only a part of the complete picture, albeit a critical one. For example, as the selections will show, applying labels is but the beginning of what is a very dynamic and complex process involving much more than a simple one-to-one relationship between the actual label and the person's acceptance of that label.

At this point we can suggest what might be wrong with the labeling approach to deviant behavior. We are alluding to the problem so eloquently formulated by Dennis Wrong (1961) in his now classic article, "The Over-socialized Conception of Man in Modern Sociology." In that paper Wrong noted the extent to which sociologists favor theories of the individual (personality) that place greater importance on social factors in explaining behavior than on the potential of people to respond to societal pressures and conditions in terms of their unique psychological characteristics. In other words, sociologically oriented labeling theorists tend to minimize the reactive character of people and forge theories of personality that tend to sustain that view. On the other hand, there are students of deviant behavior who argue that the social environment–individual equation cannot be one-sided; for a more complete understanding of deviance there must be as much attention paid to the recipients of labels as there is to the process by which societal concerns are translated into classifications of behavior warranting special attention. The readings that follow, both separately and collectively, clearly underscore the importance of that stance.

In the first place, the types of deviance depicted in these selections, focus on different manifestations of bodily and psychological attributes of people. The empirical referents across these selections are, at the same time, disparate and yet delineate a common ground as well. For example, the neurosis of Janet Gotkin and the physical disability of Leonard Kriegel are certainly different handicaps and thus require differential judgments and accommodations—from the perspective of the behaver, as well as from those with whom he or she must interact. But at the same time, a fundamental commonality ties these very different maladies together. For example, the apparent discrepancy between physical and mental problems retreats when the question of stigma surfaces. Thus, Leonard Kriegel must adjust to an obviously visible condition, one that cannot be hidden, while Janet must somehow accommodate to a vague set of problems not well defined in terms of objective criteria. This problem is also exhibited in the selection concerning retardation. The reaction of these persons to the labels society has chosen for them is marked by doubt as well as despair. However, there seems to be an awareness that labels are designed as much to assuage social demands as they are to crystallize for the individuals involved a relatively clear albeit marginal social role.

To associate social role dimensions with that of the labeling process underscores the dynamic quality of the interactions between the label imposed and the individual's attempt to relate to it. True, the role aspect tends to focus on imposed expectations, but at the same time it points to a range of behavioral options almost always associated with role expectations. The notions of disability, impairment, abnormality, are aspects of deviant role expectations that seemingly call for common reactions, but at the same time elicit differential behavior according to the nature of the problem and the limitations imposed by an individual's particular difficulty.

In summary, the types of deviance depicted by the writings in this section—mental illness, mental retardation, physical disability, suicide—lend credence to the argument that deviant behavior is as much a *process* as it is a label or concept. That is, individuals who are labeled as deviant, whether because of particular behavior (viewed as bizarre or nonconforming) or because of an obvious trait or characteristic (a physical abnormality), must somehow relate to such societal judgments. The dynamic quality of these relationships is in part a dialogue between the deviant and the world around him. This interactional perspective is a counterweight to theories that try to explain either the etiology or sustaining character of variant forms of deviance by accenting on the one hand, sociologically derived influences (for example, labeling theory) or on the other, psychologically based explanations (psychopathological theories, for example) that tend to ignore each other. As the selections show, the appropriate analytic stance is somewhere between these extremes; to emphasize the individual or the societal frame of reference is to deny the heuristic value of explanations that incorporate all variables that might help us better understand the dynamics of human behavior, deviant or otherwise.

The following first person accounts were selected to reflect several views of the process known as deviant behavior. Each suggests some specific variant of this process as it also illustrates the importance of maintaining an open position regarding what is critical for understanding the deviant and deviant behavior. Each also underscores the need to recognize the commonalities as well. Thus, Janet Gotkin in "Paris" takes issue with the medically (psychiatric) imposed label of her as mentally ill. She and her husband raise serious questions regarding the power and influence of psychiatrists to declare individuals mentally ill. The staying power of the label is chronicled, and a fierce battle is waged by Janet and Paul to erase the classification ascribed to her by professional authority figures.

Leonard Kriegel's problem in "On Being Crippled" is different. His physical difficulty is an objectifiable and measurable quality that has obvious social ramifications. He encounters stereotyping, unwanted pity, and unwanted attention. He is seen as less than "normal" and he must come to terms with this assumption in interpersonal relations. The particular events (experiences) described tell us clearly that handicapped persons must necessarily confront their problem in terms of perceived realities and judgments as to how much the problem weighs in everyday decision making.

In the article, "The Judged, Not the Judges," we examine the attitudes and feelings of one who has been labeled mentally retarded by his family and agencies of society, especially the schools. We learn firsthand that the odds for overruling the influence of the retarded label are indeed formidable, if not impossible. The institutions that exist to benefit those members of society who become their clients lend support to those whose business it is to render such judgments. There seems to be great difficulty in redressing the damage done by a label with such pejorative implications. Nevertheless, there is a continuous effort to set the record straight—that is, to eliminate the negativism associated with being labeled retarded. At the base of this effort is the contention that being "different" is not the same as being deviant, and that behavior judged difficult or problematic ought to be viewed in accord with more enlightened attitudes.

Suicide is an act of finality, an end from which there is no way back.

However, despite the commonality of all successful suicides, there are different pathways and particular experiences that lead to the self-termination of life. In "Suicide Notes" an attempt is made to show these differences by presenting the final communications of persons who took their own lives. The collector of these notes classifies them into three categories: (1) egotic—these indicate that the writer has had enough of life's difficulties and can go no further (the first three notes); (2) dyadic—these are usually addressed to a particular person who is seen as responsible for the suicide behavior (next three notes); and (3) ageneratic—these reflect loss of belongingness (final four notes). A word of caution here. Egotic, dyadic, and ageneratic represent only one method of classifying suicide notes. It is certainly not the only way. The reader may want to try another scheme, which he or she might find more meaningful and/or useful. Also, these suicide notes may or may not represent the final thoughts of all individuals who commit suicide. It is quite possible that those who leave notes constitute a biased sampling.

References

Wrong, Dennis
1961 "The Oversocialized Conception of Man in Modern Sociology."
American Sociological Review 26: 183–204.

PARIS *Janet and Paul Gotkin*

It was in Paris, in the spring of 1971, that I first realized I had been fucked over.

Horse-chestnut trees bloomed on the boulevards, students gathered on the Boul' Mich to face angry barricaded *flics* equipped with plastic shields and helmets, a frail reminiscence of May 1968. The stores said *Tabac, Boulangerie,* and *Pharmacie*, the concierge called our cat Mignonne, and men traveled home for dinner on bicycles with fresh breads under their arms. The *Herald Tribune* was gone from the news kiosks by nine o'clock, Le Drugstore drew chic Parisians in droves, and countless cafés opened onto streets I had seen a million times in books and movies and paintings and in my mind.

It was the rive gauche, St.-Germain-des-Prés, concerts at the Conciergerie, and afternoons with children in the Luxembourg Gardens. It was the Louvre, Montmartre, and Ile Saint-Louis. The Seine flowed with fine ageless languor under the bridges I never believed could be true. And, in our rented studio, four French floors above the winding and narrow rue des Sts-Pères, I listened to the morning sounds of Paris float upward, ate fresh *croissants* and *confiture*, and was sure it was not real. I had wanted to come to Paris since I was ten.

"I am in a Truffaut film, Paul," I said.

"No, you're here, in Paris, with me. It's real, we're real. The ordeal is over."

I left New York in a spirit of spontaneous adventure, exuberant, freed finally of the miseries that had pursued me for ten years. No one was able to explain the miraculous disappearance of my symptoms after I came out of the five-day coma. But then, no one, not Dr. Sternfeld or Paul or I, seemed to care to try. I was "well." Wasn't that enough?

Life had never seemed so dear, so clear, as through my unfogged mind the sounds and sights of Paris commingled in an uproar of ro-

mantic joyous play. But soon after we arrived the buoyant feelings began to change; it seemed to me that I was angry—all the time. It would seethe and bubble inside me, this black rolling anger and I would strike out—at Paul, at our cat Jenny, at myself. The dream had again turned ugly. My anger, unexplainable, unfathomable, haunted me like a guilty secret and the specter of my mental-patient past seemed to engulf me in an identity I was afraid I would never truly shed.

I couldn't understand and I cried to Paul and to myself, out of incomprehension and fear. Why did I feel so angry? Was I—good Lord, no!—getting sick again?

Here I was declared "well," released from treatment—and as lost and scared as ever. Often, I felt so consumed by this anger I had been taught to call sick that I felt myself slipping away to my dark place again. But something in me made me hold on, tenacious; made me cling to my affirming vision of myself as I had clung to life during the five days of my coma.

Soon after we arrived, on a calm, soft, spring day, Paul and I had a tremendous fight. I don't remember what we fought about. I remember only that I was filled suddenly with a rage so black and thundering, it pressed my ears and my chest to overflowing. I did not know myself, or Paul. The inky black squid of former days was inside me and I couldn't stand the horror of it, or the pain.

"I'm leaving," I said, terrified of my own audacity in walking out, frightened somewhere in the back of my mind about what Dr. Sternfeld would say, if he knew.

I ran out, ran crying down rue des Sts-Pères to the river, down to the sloping shore, tears choking my throat, blinding my eyes. I sat down on the cool ground next to a sleeping wine-quiet old man, drew my knees up to my chin, and watched the flow of the Seine. All I could think was, "I hate him, I hate him, I want to die." I whispered the words over and over to the water, wishing, at the same time as I planned to jump in, that Paul were there to hold me and tell me everything would be all right.

I watched the Seine as it flowed by, making slow ridges near my feet. Looking into this river was like looking into myself. I saw its swirls, its depths, its rocks, and its swelling beauty. This Seine, it wasn't good or bad; it just was. "What is wrong with me," I thought, "that I always want to die? What is wrong with me that I fill with blackness to overflowing and want to scream and hurt Paul and cut my wrists?" I watched the Seine again, as it flowed and flowed.

"For aeons, since there have been human beings," I thought, "there has been this river. There has been this pool of suffering." It was as if a light came into the darkness that was in me at that instant.

"There has been despair," I whispered. "That is part of our condition, to feel despair. That is what I am feeling and it is black and it wells up inside until you feel that you will explode with the heaviness of this sense of yourself, alone, in this unfeeling darkness that can be the world. Women and men have looked down into the pit that is themselves and that is life and questioned the meaning and mourned the futility of it all. No amounts of Thorazine will ever make this feeling go away."

This was not an illness. I was not being "sick" and having symptoms. This was me—living. I was not "suicidal," as I had been told for years. I was controlling my destiny, being in touch with the real agony in my soul, deciding whether I wanted to live or die. It was my right, my decision. And—could I ever accept this? could Paul ever accept it?—I would have to make this decision again and again throughout my life: to continue living or to put an end to it all.

"Is it worth it? Shall I continue? Can I continue? Why is life so hard for me? Where do these wells of melancholy come from?" Realizing they were *me*, just like the joy I could feel in rhythms of laughter, and sex, and poetry. They were *me*, not my sickness. I was as sane, or healthy, as anyone could be, living in the world. And always had been.

In the blackest pit of desolation, I felt that I had found myself, for the first time in my life.

I sat by the Seine, as the afternoon wore grayer. I remembered, starting with Dr. Berman and my stay at Oceanville, how everyone had been so frightened of what they called "suicidal feelings." How the doctors had tried to alienate the patients from their own experiences by calling the actions symptoms and the feelings sickness. I remembered how I learned to doubt all that I felt, how I separated myself from my feelings, calling them sick, psychotic, crazy. Normal people did not want to die, they taught us; normal people never wanted to hurt themselves. That was sick, and until we stopped being sick, we could not roam free in the world. No wonder I knew, inarticulately, that I would never be normal. I had touched these incalculable wells of melancholy in myself, and I knew that nothing would ever make them go away. I had become ashamed of them, ashamed of myself, and of the pain I often felt.

An idea was forming, a conception in my mind, but I saw only the shifting of its shadowy beginnings as I climbed the stone stairs and walked slowly up rue Bonaparte. When I reached the Church of St.-Germain-des-Prés, Paul was standing there, waiting for me.

"I was so worried about you," he said.

"Well, you don't have to worry about me, ever again." I was clenched and tense with my struggle and my realization. "I'm not getting sick, Paul," I said, though the words came tight from my constricted throat. "I realized something. I sat near the river and I looked in and I thought I wanted to die and maybe I would kill myself. I still think I might, I don't know. And I realized it was me talking. *I* wanted to die and it wasn't sick. Don't say I'm depressed. It's not depression. It's despair, just plain old-fashioned despair."

I was talking very fast now. "This is me; these feelings are me. For the first time in my life I don't feel separated from what's inside. I have to decide whether to live or die, just like everybody else in the world. I realized that if every time I have a crisis in my life, and if every time I stand over that pit and look in, I go to a doctor, I'll be going to doctors for the rest of my life. If what I've been feeling is sick I'll never be completely well. I might as well give up now."

"Don't give up, Janet," Paul said.

"But I don't know if I'm going to make it."

"You will."

"But you'll have to live forever with the possibility that I may decide to kill myself."

"I don't care. I'll live with it. I love you."

I think we both wanted to say, "Take a Thorazine and go to sleep," as we had for years. But a sense of awe kept us silent. Something tremendous and soul-rocking was happening. This was new ground and we were both frightened and excited and committed to seeing it through. There would be no more Thorazine, no more suicidal feelings, no more psychotic episodes. We would need a new language and a new mode for experiencing ourselves and the world.

That blinding, searing, revelatory instant changed my life forever. A horror landscape of ten years was lightning bright; after a decade of brainwashing and mystification, I finally had the answers to a million questions that had plagued me, and Paul, and my parents.

Why did I keep getting worse and worse as the years went by? Why didn't the drugs help me? How could someone so sick suddenly get so well, the way I had after I woke from the coma, and two years prior to that, the first miraculous cure? Why had I always been afraid of Dr. Sternfeld and afraid to let him know? Why was I so angry?

The answer, as I said it, tentatively, quietly, at first, was so simple it was ludicrous. I knew why I could get well so easily; I had never been sick in the first place. Not in any medical sense. Certainly, I had had all the trappings of what was called mental illness, but that is what they were, superficial trappings. The hallucinations, the delusions, the anxiety states, even the wrist-cutting obsession, and, worst of all, the debilitating vision of myself as helpless and sick—I had learned most of these in my years as a mental patient. They were real, in the sense that they reflected some of my pain. But I could shed them, like clothing, only I never knew it. And when I did, like after the suicide attempt, I still had the real me to face—all my pain and fear still intact, only hidden. And, superficially normal, Dr. Sternfeld declared me cured, nothing more to worry about, the world would be rosy. Welcome to the Land of Mental Health.

What a cruel hoax that had been.

I had never been sick and I wasn't well now. The whole idea of my illness and my eventual cure were inventions of my psychiatrists. I thought and remembered and my anger poured out, wild and raw and cleansing. I remembered, bitterly, the years of drug-taking, dependency, shock treatments, self-denigration. In the succeeding months I reviewed my own ten-year history, going over the details with a new view, seeing it all, truly, for the first time.

The day in September that I took the pills was a blur. But I remembered the months preceding my suicide attempt: Mary's week-long visit in August, Paul's short summer workdays, my threats of suicide, Dr. Sternfeld's grave decision that keeping me out of the hopsital was "a risk we had to take," Paul doling me my daily ration of pills each night and hiding them in the bedroom while I crouched outside wondering how long it could possibly go on. I remembered my growing distance from Paul, from my mother and father and my friends, the knowledge that grew in me in spite of all my resolves, that one day soon I would take my life. It would not be a suicide *attempt;* even if it failed, I knew, it would not be an attempt. I remembered only one thing about the day itself and that was an overriding sense of relief at having made a decision. I was going to take control of my life, even if I had to die doing it.

After five days in a deep coma, I remember waking, not with the sickening sour sense of a failed suicide attempt, but with a tingling joy-shouting feeling. "Thank God I am alive!"

And I was alive, truly, for the first time, perhaps, in my life. My mind was clear; my symptoms gone. I read *The New York Times;* I read an entire book, Yasunari Kawabata's *The Sound of the Mountain;* I saw a whole movie. People's voices came through clear and precise. My hands and legs did not shake and I moved my bowels without a laxative. For the first time in eight years I was without drugs and it felt fantastic. Even the sudden onset of pains in my eyes two weeks after I took the Mellaril did not dampen my enthusiasm. I was frightened at the partial loss of sight, but I knew I would come through. I was alive.

If everyone had been amazed at my first cure four years earlier, they were stunned by this one. How had it happened?

"You never know what goes on in their heads when they're in a coma," a nurse had told Paul.

"You do not feel depressed anymore?" the third floor doctor asked me.

"I never was depressed," I told him. "Dr. Sternfeld says I was never classically depressed." How many times had I gone through this with Oscar Lessing and countless self-important floor doctors? I watched the doctor nod his serious head, knowing he didn't believe a word I said.

"You still have to be careful," a doctor said. "In cases like yours there is often a letdown after the elation at being alive. We must watch out, because this feeling good can often be more dangerous than the depression."

"Of course you feel good now," Mrs. Hand, my private-duty nurse had said. "But there is one thing you must remember. Wherever you go, whatever you do, however you feel, you will always have to take care; you will never be like the rest of us; you will always be schizophrenic."

Her words had struck an instant of sheer cold terror in my heart. And I had been thinking I was going to join the human race again. I toyed with the idea of telling her that Dr. Sternfeld said that I was not schizophrenic, then thought better of it, realizing that she would never believe me. She had read reams of charts on me, an accumulation of seven years of reaffirmed diagnoses. Anything I said would only serve to reconfirm for her my sickness. I wondered, struck, what Dr. Sternfeld said when he spoke to his colleagues about me. Did he say, "She's not really schizophrenic, although the hospitals keep insisting that she is"? What was schizophrenic anyway? I thought again of Mrs. Hand's prophecy and shivered.

To my parents it was just a plain miracle, though underneath their pleasure and relief I sensed a fearful suspicion that I would get sick again. I, too, had that fear lurking around in me, thinking, "If I got well, what is to stop me from getting sick again?"

Dr. Sternfeld, who was not surprised, but immensely pleased at my good spirits, had brushed that fear away. Well, why not? I could ask now. The whole thing, my so-called sickness, was mostly his invention. And he would always, always, he told me, be there for me, waiting for

the time when, as all humans do, I would fall down, hesitate, when life would get to be a bit too much for me—and I would come to him again, thinking that I was getting sick. Only now I knew I would never ever go to a psychiatrist again. It was they who had made me into an emotional freak with their treatments and therapies and left my real pain untouched, to surface, as it had in Paris, to frighten me—but not this time—into submission.

I remembered and told Paul, about a session with Dr. Sternfeld shortly after I was released from Monroe Park. I had just realized how close to death I had come and that the reason all the bottles of pills were in our bedroom was that Dr. Sternfeld insisted that Paul dole them out to me and hide them.

Paul interrupted me. "Sternfeld said he was awfully glad it was the Mellaril you found, not the Aventyl. The Aventyl would have killed for sure, he said."

I stopped. "He really said that?"

"Yes," Paul said.

I continued with my story. For months I had been telling Dr. Sternfeld how afraid I was that I was going to look for the pills and take them. He said it was a risk we had to take; he kept giving Paul huge bottles of pills, all kinds, to keep and hide from me. This Saturday I was suddenly really really mad.

"You know you almost killed me," I said to the doctor.

"Nobody *does* anything to anybody, Janet. You know that. I did not force you to take the pills; I didn't want you to take the pills."

"But you put them close to me; they were a constant source of temptation."

"But *you* swallowed them," he said. "The responsibility is yours alone."

"I kept warning you, telling you how afraid I was of taking the pills," I said.

"You didn't want to go into the hopsital again did you, Janet?" he asked, without waiting for an answer. "Then this was the only other way. You were very agitated and depressed. It was a risk we had to take."

"*We*," I shouted. "*You* didn't take any risk. It was *my* life, *my* life *we* were risking."

Then he didn't say anything. He just looked at me and I could tell he was angry. I was afraid again, afraid he would leave me. Goddamn it, I didn't even need him but I was still afraid he'd leave me. He knew I was afraid too. Finally, he said, "I realize you are angry, Janet. But you know as well as I that this hostility comes from sources deep inside you. I think we should discuss it and find out what it means."

I knew what it "meant," I realized. And, coming so close to the truth, I was afraid to face it; so I slipped back into an old pattern of discussing my feelings, as if they were all symptomatic of my disturbance, as if they had no meaning outside of revealing my sickness. Jesus, I had been accusing the man of criminal irresponsibility and neglect that nearly ended in my death! But I had backed down. I had let him con me again. And three months later, as Paul and I were leaving for Paris, I had thanked him— THANKED HIM!—for saving my life. My God, had I been duped!

The months passed, a blur of vivid insights, moments when the truths I was seeing hurt me and I almost wished I could accept the easy fantasy of sick again and go to a doctor, or take a pill to cure my soul-pain.

Looking back on my life I could see that in spite of my brilliant conformist façade I could never accept what was mapped out for me, whether school, marriage, or secretarial work. Yet I did not have the tools that would have enabled me to assert my differentness, challenge my family's and society's expectations, and go my own way, whatever that would have been. I could not express my angers; I could not say, "The hell with you all." I fought and fought to be someone else, anyone, as long as it wasn't *me*. That agonizing birth process was called mental illness—and I nearly died trying to become myself.

I suffered greatly those years; much of my pain was the pain of growing. That I do not regret. I hope I will have growing pains all of my life. But the suffering I endured because I was a mental patient I could never forget or forgive. The memories of my humiliation and degradation as a prisoner of drugs, hospitals, and psychiatric jargon continued to haunt me and would, I knew, forever.

But I was finally able to say, I do not believe I was ever sick. Lost, yes; suffering, yes. Troubled, desperate, and pained, yes. But not sick. My so-called sickness was an invention of the psychiatric profession—of Dr. Berman and Dr. Kurtzman and Dr. Sternfeld, of all the doctors who treated me during my ten-year career as a mental patient. The fact that I—and my parents and my husband—believed in my sickness for so long attests to our own need to believe experts and to the effectiveness of the scare tactics, brainwashing, and public relations of the American psychiatric profession.

Little by little, I ripped away the façade of jargon and mystifications and saw that out of my pain and groping the doctors had produced a mental patient, unable to suvive anywhere but in a so-called mental hospital. I was finally able to say to Paul, "They fucked me over, royally. There is no such thing as schizophrenia, not outside some psychiatrist's imagination. There is pain and people's odd convoluted ways of trying to survive in the world. That's real. Not mental illness."

I don't know why my mind flashed clear that afternoon near the Seine, just as I don't know what really happened during the five days I was in the coma. I think, though, that during those five days I came into contact with the core of me. Stripped, I think I fused with my real self. I must have realized, somewhere too deep for words or remembering, that I wanted to live. When I awoke, I felt as if I were being born. I couldn't use pretense anymore. I knew only that I had to get away from Dr. Sternfeld and my past or I would truly die. I didn't know why I knew that, at the time, but I acted on it just the same. My realizations, in Paris, were the culmination, the final illumination, of what I only sensed when I woke up from the coma.

I never had been schizophrenic or even mentally ill. The doctors had called me that. They had looked at my behavior, looked at the symptoms I had assumed to hide my pain, decided I was unacceptable, and given me a label. Nothing I could say or do, then, would erase it. Eventually, I came to believe it myself. I accepted the drugs and shock and hospitals because I believed it. I identified with the other people who were called mentally ill and soon you couldn't tell us apart.

The anger that had surfaced in Paris was the real feeling, years of frustration at being used and never being able to speak out. It was not a symptom. I was not getting sick. And Lord, it felt good to rage at real demons, finally.

Yet, the question came and came again. Why, at that moment was I able to see so clearly, after ten years of indoctrination into my fundamental worthlessness? Where did I get the strength to sustain my vision and integrate it into my life during the next treacherous months? Where did I get the strength? Why that particular moment? I don't know. And to this, as to other mysteries of human suffering, glory, and struggle, there may be no answers.

Certainly my love for Paul and his for me sustained us both, as it had for years. Luck surely played a part. But really it was a certain vivid confluence of thoughts, dreams, and seasons in my mind—the time was right. And would we really know anything more if I were able to give it a name, a label to the miracle of rebirth and liberation that happened to me in Paris? I think not, and this way the awe remains, as it should, because the process was a mystery. It cannot be defined. I was free.

But something was still unfinished. I knew I would have to confront Dr. Sternfeld, sometime. On a late August evening I got very drunk over dinner. With all my new insights and strength I needed something to quell the old spirits of fear and dependency that were writhing inside me as the operator put through my transatlantic call. I knew Dr. Sternfeld couldn't hurt me anymore, but the old terrors of his power seemed as real as ever.

"I want to ask you something, Dr. Sternfeld," I began, and the words came pouring out, a torrent of reproach, bitterness, and disillusionment, smoothed by red wine and calvados.

"You treated me for eight years. Why didn't you ever tell me I'd be angry when I was well?"

I filled his silence with angry words.

"Why didn't you ever tell me what to expect from life, from myself?" I cried to him over the phone, wondering if, after traveling thousands of miles, scrunched through transatlantic cables, my words were coming to him meaningful and strong.

"Why didn't you prepare me for living? Why didn't you tell me I would be suicidal? Why didn't you warn me? You took away the only two things I had—my symptoms and yourself—and you let me go out, completely unprepared, into

this shitty, stinking world. Why?" The tears were pouring down my face, salt, hot, cleansing. I felt naked but strong, facing Dr. Sternfeld as an equal, with truth, for the first time in eight years.

"I don't understand what you are asking me, Janet," I heard his calm guarded voice through the fluted receiver.

"What do you mean, you don't understand?" I said, my voice rising tight in anger. "I am asking you how you could treat me for eight years and not prepare me to live a normal life, how you could send me out into the world with *no* skill for survival. I am telling you you perpetrated a hoax, a farce on me—and I am asking you why."

"Are you drunk, Janet?"

"Yes, I am drunk, but I have never thought clearer in my life."

"You sound very upset, Janet. Why don't you take some Thorazine and calm down? You can call me again and we'll talk about it."

"I don't want to call you again and I don't want to calm down. I am perfectly lucid. I don't need a Thorazine. What's the matter, Dr. Sternfeld, don't you like what you're hearing?"

"I think you are too agitated for me to understand you, Janet. At least take a Valium."

"'Take a Thorazine, Janet. Or a Valium. Or a Stelazine. Or a this or a that. Calm yourself, Janet. You're very agitated. You mustn't become upset.'" I mocked him, anger seething inside, frothing out. "'Come in and we'll talk about your feelings when you calm down.'"

"You're very sarcastic and hostile," Dr. Sternfeld said.

"You're damn right I am. And I have good reason to be. I am telling you that I am angry and you want me to take a pill and talk to you about it? This is my *life* I am telling you about. I'm saying you fucked me over and made me into an invalid. I'm saying I almost died because of you and now, that I'm alive, I'm lost because you never prepared me for living in the real world; and you want me to take a Thorazine and discuss it with you. Don't you hear what you're saying? I'm a human being talking to you, but you only hear the patient. You only want to see symptoms, not real emotion."

"You are out of control, Janet."

"So what if I am? What are you going to do

about it? Put me in a hospital? Give me shock treatments? Give me more drugs? Bury me? Don't you ever get out of control?"

"I'm going to hang up now, Janet. When you come back to New York you may call me and we can talk about this."

He hung up but I wasn't finished yet.

"Oh, damn it, Paul, he always said he cared about me and I believed him. But if he really cared he wouldn't have put me through the tortures of shock and hospitalization. He wouldn't have sent me to Franklin Central to teach me a lesson. You know, he didn't hear what I was saying on the phone. He heard my accusations and anger as *symptoms*. He didn't hear *me* at all. 'Take a Thorazine, Janet.' He's a goddamn creep; he's nothing better than the seamiest pusher on the streets." I was still crying, now in Paul's arms. The truths were coming fast and I knew it would take time to assimilate them.

"Ten years," I said, "And now where am I? I'm a labeled psychotic with a mental-hospital record. I don't know how to begin to live on the outside without doctors and pills. Good Lord, Paul, he turned me into a fucking invalid, all in the name of Mental Health."

"You're not an invalid," Paul said. "You're a free woman, finally. And if you're a little scared and tentative and pessimistic, why, welcome to the human race."

I smiled, in spite of myself.

"I loved him a lot, Paul," I said. "For a long time he was all I had."

"I know, Jan."

"And it's hard to let go. It's hard to be strong."

"But you always have been strong. And now, at least you have real anger to cope with. The worst you can do is freak out. But you know what that is; you're luckier, in a way, than most of us. You're not afraid of your craziness, you know it's just another part of yourself that you have to learn to live with."

"I used to think the psychiatrists were going to exorcise me, in a way," I said. "It's funny. I remember now, all the doctors I ever knew, in any hospital or on the outside, were always afraid of me and of the other patients. It was almost as if we showed them something they couldn't look at in themselves. As soon as someone started acting weird, *experiencing* their pain, quick, it

was a shot of Thorazine, shock treatments, or, if they happened to be on the outside, lock them up. Only, they would always tell us we were acting sick, and somehow that made it okay for them. They could stay calm and removed; they never really had to relate to us at all—or to their own madness. They could always say it was a one-time psychotic episode. They hid behind their line of demarcation: they were healthy, we were sick. And we—we felt guilty, ashamed for just being alive."

"What do you think the doctors at Monroe Park would say about you now?" Paul asked.

"Probably that I'm a schizophrenic in permanent remission," I said, almost laughing.

"They'd never admit they could have been wrong?" Paul asked.

"No, I don't think so," I said. "Their livelihood depends on the existence of schizophrenia and related medical hallucinations."

We sat quietly, listening to the night sounds of Paris float up through our open window.

"I'm not going to be afraid anymore, Paul," I said finally. "And I'm not going to lurk around, hiding what I've been through. In the hospitals they treated us as less than human; they taught us to be ashamed of what we were and to hide what they did to us. They taught us to hate ourselves and each other and to doubt our truest instincts, to feel guilty about our incarcerations. They wanted us to be ashamed and to keep silent. Well, I'm not ashamed or guilty anymore. Just angry. I used to feel different from the other patients; I used to want to think of myself as somehow better than they. I was sick but they were crazy; I was voluntary, but they were committed. I hated them because they were all miserable, lonely, peculiar, helpless people and I didn't want to be associated with them. I wanted only to forget about them and my own hospitalizations. Now, I feel a sense of kinship with them; it is the people who categorized us and diagnosed us and made us outcasts that I despise—not my sisters and brothers. I thank whatever God there is that I have escaped the fate that was planned for me and that I am finally free. If anything is a miracle, it is that I am intact and relatively unscarred emotionally and physically, after ten years in the mental-hospital world. You know, I used to wake up at three or four in the morning, sometimes months after I got out of a hospital, and wonder what I had done that they had treated me that way, what crime had I committed that they should torture me so. And the doctors would say, 'You're not thinking clearly, Janet. Your thought processes are impaired. This is not torture; this is treatment. We only want to help you.'"

"Well, it's over now, Janet. Really over," Paul said.

"For me, yes. But what about the others? For thousands and thousands like me, the nightmare may have just begun."

TODAY AND TOMORROW

It was in Paris that Paul and I resolved that we would tell our story so that other people, suffering and confused, looking desperately for an answer or key to unlock the mystery of their own pain or that of their loved ones, would not go blindly to the so-called experts for answers that could imprison them further when they might have found the answers in themselves. We came to see that my experiences were in no way unique; the only aspect of my story—our story—that makes it worth telling is the ending. I survived. I was a lucky one. Instead of spending the rest of my life imprisoned within my own handicapping concept of myself, or as a resident of the back wards of a mental hospital, I am free, strong, and alive. We decided we would tell the truth as we have learned it. Our only claim to expertise is experience.

In Paris and in the years that followed I asked myself several questions, again and again. If I wasn't sick, what was I? If all the years of being a psychiatric patient brought me nothing but pain and increasing torment, who, then, benefited from my status? And the final question: Are these men evil? Did they lie when they said, "We only want to help you"?

"We only want to help you" is a statement woven integrally into the pattern of lies, semantic farces, and mystification that is the fabric of American psychiatry. It was what the young resident said to me when he forced a cold metal speculum up my vagina and made me bleed and scream with pain; it was what Dr. Berman said when he put me in Oceanville Hospital; it was what Dr. Sternfeld said when he started me on drugs, when he gave me shock treatments, when

he locked me in the cage that is Franklin Central Hospital. It is what every psychiatrist says to his patient when he plans to perpetrate another psychiatric torment and he doesn't want any resistance: "I only want to help you." For many years I believed the lie. Now I say, if that is help, we are not speaking the same language.

Someone is continuing to insist that these human garbage dumps called mental hospitals are, in reality, hospitals. Someone is saying that they are places where troubled people can get help. They are calling the guards doctors, the tortures treatments, and the humiliating experience of being a mental patient therapeutic. They are saying that the psychiatric labels that degrade and imprison people are diagnoses. They are the Mental Health Professionals.

They are Dr. Berman and Dr. Maynard and Dr. Lessing and Dr. Sternfeld—and very often they do not need to resort to legal measures to oppress and imprison their patients. They need only the "faith" of the family and the patient.

Looking back on my ten years as a mental patient, it is the fact of my own collaboration and that of my parents and Paul that I find most astounding and disturbing. Why, why did we go along with the doctors' designs? I asked my parents why they had consented to my hospitalizations. "We didn't know what else to do," they said. "We didn't want to put you in the hospital, but Dr. Berman said it was necessary. He said you would surely kill yourself. And you acted so strange; we wanted to do what was best. We didn't know where to turn."

So they turned to the expert, the person whom society designates the arbiter of acceptable behavior, the witchhunter, the psychiatrist. And they continued to listen to psychiatrists, never stopping to question what gift it was that gave these men the right or power or knowledge to decide their daughter's fate. They listened to the doctors at Oceanville and for eight years they listened to Dr. Sternfeld. In spite of the fact that they saw me continue to suffer, that they loathed the places into which they put me, despite the fact that I became more miserable and cut off as the years went on, they listened to the psychiatrists. And I did too. That is the worst part. They were afraid to listen to themselves, to their decency and love and sensibility. I do not blame them. They were victims, too. They had been scared and indoctrinated into having "faith," into believing that the experts had the answers. The doctors said, "She is mentally ill. That means she is ours. Only we can cure her." And, unwillingly, lost, we all believed them, believed they only wanted to help. But their help was imprisonment and torture and we allowed the semantic niceties of treatment and a hospital to continue to fool us.

We must explode the myth that emotional turmoil indicates the presence of illness. We must reject the myth that only doctors and other mental health workers can treat this *illness;* that is incorrect and constitutes a monopoly, helping only the treaters, not the *treated.*

Those millions of us who have undergone psychiatric oppression in its many forms—from private therapy to legal commitment to lobotomizing, and the many stages in between—have undergone a kind of *brainwashing* as an integral part of our experiences. We have been taught not to have any faith in ourselves and to put all faith in the experts. Our faith constitutes *their* power. Without attributing universal malintent and evil designs to the profession, I say that given the kind of power, literal and psychological, that a mind-doctor has in this country, given the absolute power over people's lives that hospital personnel possess, I say that it is a very rare individual who can survive with her or his humanness and sense of fallibility intact.

For many years mental health professionals of all rank and persuasion told me I was sick. I believed them, my parents and Paul believed them, and we allowed them to perpetrate indignities upon me because we believed that their knowledge was great and their intent honorable. They only wanted to help.

But help is not help when it does violence to a person's body, mind, or freedom; it is power abused; it is medical responsibility distorted; it is liberal ethics convoluted. It is not help.

I have learned from my own suffering that we must come to accept our many-faceted selves. That to alternate between highs of ecstasy and lows of despair, to indulge in fantasy and vision, to act self-destructive or lethargic, to refuse to conform, to lunge forward in spasms of creativity only to retreat to depths of inactivity, to cry, to mourn, to suffer, to create new visions—is to be human, not sick.

EPILOGUE: PAUL

Five years have passed since Janet took her last overdose of tranquilizers, four years since we moved from Paris to the northern suburb of New York City where we live today. Our life has grown outstandingly normal. Looking back, it is difficult to recapture the pain and pressure that once held us together. We fight more than we used to—we barely used to fight at all—and we worry and brood about trivial matters that during our struggle for survival would have struck us as profoundly inconsequential. But we did come out of our unhappy years with one deep, basic conviction—a belief that wasting our experience and insights would be a terrible sin. Writing this book is one of the ways we have tried to give meaning to the horrors that once submerged us; our involvement with what could be called, in the language of today, the Mental Patient's Liberation Movement, is another.

In lecturing, in talking about her experiences, Janet is always asked the same series of questions. "What do you do about the person who wants or needs help? What about the person who can't function in the world? It's fine to say that the mental health system is corrupt and oppressive, but what answers do you give, what do you say to the people who are really suffering?"

It is important to say that we have no answers at all. In one sense, it is enough to condemn a system, to say that the mental health system is a multibillion-dollar industry that depends for its existence on an ever-expanding supply of crippled, dehumanized bodies and on the continuing ignorance of the general public. An aura of mystery surrounds the world of mental health—and what is called mental illness—a mystery that serves no one but the professional, that allows men to earn huge salaries by running atrocities like the prototype for Franklin Central Hospital, and even allows them to sleep well at night. Only by destroying that aura, by letting in criticism and fresh perspectives and new ideas, can we ever provide answers. Or change.

It would be easy for us to say that giant impersonal hospitals should be torn down to be replaced by small, truly voluntary, community residences (as we believe), or that all involuntary commitment laws should be abolished or that confined mental patients should at least be given the same human and civil rights as convicted felons. (At present, they do not have those rights.) But while these alterations would make the lot of confined patients pleasanter, they would provide no real change. You could have the most modern streamlined system of mental health care, but without a change in attitude, the system would still be basically oppressive.

What is needed is a revolution of the spirit, a revolution that would ultimately involve us all. There is no such thing as a mental illness, in the sense that years of experimentation have not demonstrated any chemical or genetic defect. There is certainly people's great suffering, bizarre behavior, and often their crying need for help, but these are human problems, not scientific or medical ones. Charts, diagnoses, and ingrown pseudoscientific language do not reach people. People reach people. And we throw off on experts our responsibility to ourselves and to others at our great peril.

Psychiatry has woven itself into the fabric of our society. State mental hospitals are filled mostly with the unwanted of our culture—with old people, with abandoned or unruly children, with discarded family members. "Outreach" offices have been set up as part of the growing number of so-called community mental health centers, particularly in ghetto areas, to pull the victims of poverty and despair into an expanding psychiatric network. In our prisons, federally financed behavior-modification programs, drugging, and psychosurgical experiments, make the futuristic horrors of *A Clockwork Orange* outdated. And in our schools, with the new emphasis on psychiatric counseling, personality tests, and widespread drugging to control the unmanageable children, students are given records that will follow them and stigmatize them for the rest of their lives.

But we're brought back to a basic question. What about the individual? What about the person, like Janet, who suffers greatly and wants relief from her pain?

We can only hope that in the future people will have a wide variety of humanistic, nondoctrinaire options to choose from. Human suffering has been with us as long as we have existed and there are obviously no easy answers to finding satisfaction, peace, or happiness. We are certainly not discouraging anyone from seeing a therapist, if they can find a kind, open person to whom they can talk. We are saying: Beware of anyone who tries to take control of your life, especially under the pretext that it is in your own best interest. Don't be bullied; trust your instincts and reactions. Don't ever let anyone take away your credibility—or your freedom— by calling you mentally ill.

For all of us, struggling in our own ways to find our identity or place, submergence in the world of mental illness, in the world of hospitals, drugs, and diagnoses, is a devastating experience. The labels and stigmas stay with you, whether you are a child, a housewife, or a candidate for vice-president of the United States.

As for us, our nightmare behind us, we bumble along the best we can, lobbying for the repeal of involuntary confinement laws, trying to dispute the idea that psychiatry, with all of its talking cures, drugs, and self-help books has some magical power to make us all crime-free, enduringly happy, and spiritually whole. We argue with each other, our friends, our parents; we raise our daughter, worry about earning a living, struggle with our own private demons, and try to enjoy this not always pleasant experience we call living.

QUESTIONS FOR DISCUSSION

1. What do you think of Janet's portrayal of mental hospitals? Do you believe her confession that a lot of her behaviors were learned while in the institution?

2. Ironically, Janet's attempt to kill herself turned out for the best. Is it abnormal for a person to want to die?

3. Janet made a comment stating something to the effect that patients show doctors something they are unable to face in themselves. What did she mean by this?

4. What changes (if any) do you think should be made regarding the stigma associated with mental illness and mental hospitals?

5. What part do you feel psychiatrists may have played in contributing to Janet's problems? Does this have anything to do with labeling theory?

6. In what respect may psychiatrists be viewed as agents of social control?

ON BEING CRIPPLED Leonard Kriegel

It was almost two years ago to the day that I had left for camp. And as I gazed at the small, expectant crowd awaiting me in front of the stoop, I knew how changed I was. Fat, hog-fat and baby-soft, tall for a boy just turned thirteen, five feet five inches, but almost as wide as tall. My face was oval, a pattern broken only by two heavy, drooping jowls; my head was crowned with a thick blond pompadour, which, if memory remains true, was the only stylish aspect of my appearance. I was wearing a pair of khaki slacks and a blue polo shirt, the polo shirt serving only to accentuate my fatness.

The driver got out and removed my crutches. My father approached, smiling encouragingly. Then my father and the driver helped me out of the ambulance and stood me up on the sidewalk. My father held me up while the driver placed a crutch under each arm. I stood on the sidewalk for several seconds, the still-strange wooden sticks beneath my shoulders, blinkingly pausing in the midday sun to reacquaint myself with home. Then Cousin Leo came over and stood alongside of me, smiling, patting me on the shoulder as if I were a stray dog come back to the kennel. I said good-by to the driver and began to walk, flanked on one side by my father and on the other by Cousin Leo, the few feet from the ambulance to the stone stairs leading into the lobby of the house. My neighbors, some of whom had devoutly prayed for my recovery for two years, huddled in smiling groups on both sides of the landing, nodding their encouragement to me and to each other. Their fear must have matched mine, step for step, as I approached, the nine stone stairs passively answering my unvoiced question. I had, of course, known the answer all the way home in the ambulance—I couldn't climb them. I stood there, staring at the stairs, hating them not for having defeated me but for having done it so publicly, feeling my mother's lip-biting tension as she leaned out of the second-story window, even

though, afraid to look up, I couldn't see her. My brother was at my side now, also smiling. But I turned away from him, too. It was more than the remorse caused by that first public defeat. It was a further recognition of my guilt, my mind reviewing again what I had done to my mother and my father, to my brother and Cousin Leo, to Uncle Morris, and to all those others who had shared at least a sense of my agony if not the pain that went with it. Too ashamed to look at anyone, too ashamed even to speak, I stood there and stared down at the stairs, trying to work up enough anger and hatred so that I could show my shame with tears. But the tears didn't come.

I bit into my lip, a gesture of public contrition. Finally, I looked up at my father. "I can't," I pleaded, shaking my head. "I'm sorry. But I can't."

My father nodded. "You'll walk up some other time," he said, his voice peculiarly flat. "You'll learn." Again he nodded, only this time as if to convince himself. "You'll learn," he repeated. "Won't he learn, Leo?"

My cousin was standing behind me. I couldn't see him when he said, "Sure. Sure, he'll learn."

Then my father put his right arm under my right leg, the other arm under my left shoulder, and someone else, I think it was an upstairs neighbor, Mr. Garner, put his left arm under my left leg, his right arm under my right shoulder. They lifted me, basket style, and carried me up the stairs. Leo followed with the crutches.

"Welcome Home," the streamer on the door of our apartment said—huge, red letters. The door opened and my mother, her rigid eyes pleading, stood in the doorway. "I'm home." I giggled nervously.

"You should only be well," she answered, forcing the control into her voice. "Now that you're home, you should only be well."

Inside the apartment, my grandmother,

looking older and even more withered than I remembered her from my bar mitzvah, was waiting for me. She seized my head in her hands, kissed me several times on the brow, and blessed me in Yiddish. "God will help," she said solemnly. "Listen to me. We will rejoice yet."

The doorbell rang. My brother opened the door, and I turned to see my father enter again, pushing my empty wheel chair before him. "Where shall I put it?" he asked.

"I don't care," I said, suddenly filled with hatred for the chair. "I'll never use it again. I swear. If I can't walk, then I'll . . ."

"You'll walk," Leo interrupted. "Don't worry, you'll walk."

"Put it in the bedroom," my mother said. "By the window."

There was a long, nervous pause, each of us looking expectantly at the others. My grandmother sat down, sighing, on the couch. My father cleared his throat. "Maybe you want to sit down?" my mother asked.

I turned and walked toward the club chair. I was tired of standing. It seemed as if I had been standing for hours, but it couldn't have been more than five minutes. The club chair, as overstuffed and soft as I was, was waiting for me. My mother had always frowned on my sitting in the club chair before I had gone away to camp. "Is it okay?" I asked.

"Of course. Anywhere you want, there you sit."

I sat down. For the rest of that afternoon, I sat in the club chair, taking time out only to go into the kitchen for lunch, a fried egg sandwich plastered over with ketchup. All the afternoon long, the doorbell rang, and the door opened to admit neighbors, friends of the family, relatives, all of them entering smiling, wishing me luck, bearing gifts, their voices artificially cheerful, their slogans oblivious to my embarrassment. So many problems were kicked around that afternoon, as if my fate were now a collective enterprise. Will he go to school? Not the first year. Maybe the year after. But this September they'll send a teacher to the house. Home Instruction, they call it. Maybe you should move to an elevator apartment. So find me one. Or a walk-in. So find me that. He's a good boy. A brave boy. He'll be all right. Let's hope. He'll be all right.

And that was the beginning. The new be-

ginning. The apartment in the Bronx was exactly as I remembered it. I seized it for my purposes—a shelter, a place away. Somehow, I had been chosen to suffer, an assumption made by the neighbors, by my parents, by me. There was something gallant about suffering, some powder charge of divinity that set me apart from all others. Suffering was the universal leveler, and I had been leveled for the benefit of all. Maybe the butcher Goldhammer's wife wasn't so wrong, after all. But it wasn't only God's punishment on my mother or on my family; it was punishment meted out on the whole neighborhood. And, as punishment should, it fed the neighborhood's curiosity. As I walked, Leo counting each step I took without resting, the curious and the well-wishers alike eyed my hulking body forcing itself through their streets. "You took fifteen steps without resting that time. That's the best you've ever done." Sure, the best. I was doing what they had told me to do in the Rock. Never mind the kids giggling, the adults staring, the driver stopping his car to get a better look. That was just human nature.

A nun from St. Brendan's Convent at the end of the street stopped me. "Here," she said, pressing a medal into my sweating palm.

"Look, I'm not Catholic, Sister," I explained.

"Take it. God loves all."

I took it home, stared at it for hours. Holy Father, help. . . . Not me. Help who or what or where you want, but not me. I wouldn't let you help me. Even if I believed in you, I wouldn't let you help me. What if there really was a God? What if . . . ? I dropped the medal into the trash basket. To hell with him. I wouldn't let him help me.

It wasn't until the end of September that I learned to walk up and down the stairs. Until then, I would sit on them and boost myself up or down with my arms, while my mother or my brother or a neighbor held my legs high in the air. Every time I did this, I felt nausea rising up within me and my cheeks flushing with a deep, burning shame. Once, in late August, I was caught downstairs in a thunderstorm, and while the rain drove into my body my mother hysterically sought out one of the neighbors and my friend Iggie, and the two of them, drenched to the skin, carried me up the stairs. I remembered what I had thought of when Jojo went home. And then I remembered Willie.

I was learning what I was. And the only way to prevent my learning too quickly was to retreat into the sanctuary of the apartment. In the apartment, I would spend my time moving away from the reality the mirror told me was mine. Reading, listening to the radio, anything that allowed me to detach myself from the crippled adolescent I really was. I became an even more avid baseball fan, for now that I couldn't play I needed even more the stimulus of evaporating into myth. I was Pete Reiser or Pee Wee Reese, rarely Lennie Kriegel. A neighbor gave me Irving Stone's biography of Clarence Darrow, *Clarence Darrow for the Defense*. I liked the title. And I liked Darrow. But it was Debs I loved. Debs had wanted to even it all for the working man. Debs, Big Bill Haywood, Sacco and Vanzetti, all of them fighting for that word that thrilled me every time my eye caught it on the page—*justice*. To be Debs was like fighting the virus, getting even, and not only for myself but for Jerry, too. And for all those others, for Willie and Natey, for Lobashevski's armless hope. But how do you become a man without legs? Can you touch a woman without legs? Sure, if she lets you. There was this cousin, what's his name, the one who was hunchbacked and limped because one leg was shorter than the other; he married, had two children. Push away the fear. Importance, dignity, these belong to you, too. Keep them. But never forget, when it becomes too tough, you can be Pete Reiser or Eugene Debs. Never forget that.

In the house I was what I wanted to be; in the street I was what others made of me. This was the most enduring lesson of the early months at home. I had been home a week when I first became friendly with a tall, gangling boy whom I scarcely remembered from the time before the polio. His parents were German and my mother was sure that they were anti-semites, but since I couldn't move very far he became my friend. And then, suddenly, we were arguing about Roosevelt, my savior; words, no more than words, but for me like arrows in the flesh.

"Kooperstein, you're a bastard. Let's fight." I managed to get down on the hard alley cement.

"But I don't want to fight," said Kooperstein.

"You son of a bitch, let's fight."

"Okay," said Kooperstein. And then he was on top of me, pinning my shoulders to the ground. But he refused to hit me. I cursed, fumed, raged, finally freed my right hand and threw it in the direction of his face. It landed. Teeth gritting, Kooperstein pushed my head back, back, back against the cement. The weight of pain freed me, fed me relief. Some passing woman pulled Kooperstein off of me, then lectured him about fighting cripples. "But I didn't want to, lady," Kooperstein protested. "He wanted to."

"Now you know you can't fight, son."

"Leave me alone, lady. Leave me alone."

And what did others make of me? That was my primary problem. There were so many roles. And I had to learn them all. The object of scrutiny, for instance. It was the beginning of September, a month and a half after I had returned from the Rock. I had walked from my house to the luncheonette on the corner. And I had walked it alone, without Leo, without my brother. Nearly six in the evening, men and women lining up in front of the subway exit for the bus that would take them to Yonkers. Indian Summer heat, the men sweating, jackets on their arms, ties loosened, the women sallow and dour, sighing with discomfort; the absence of the bus making my body the only visible relief in sight. I knew what I was, and I was aware of the eyes focused upon me, the whispers of strangers, the meeting over a breath of sympathy. There but for the grace of God . . . It was uncomfortable, but I had to rest before undertaking the journey home. The bus pulled up and my immediate admirers left, only to be replaced by a new wave, hot, tired, seeking some momentary diversion, finding it in me. Sweat, wide eyes, shaking heads, the fishy smell of melted creosote hanging in the air. I moved away, but as I stepped off the curbstone to walk across the street, I slipped and fell. I still hadn't learned how to pick myself up when I fell, and I simply sat there, in the gutter, while the heads shook in pity and the tongues clucked in unison. But no one came over to question my endurance; they left me sitting in the gutter, their eyes piercing my embarrassment and shame, their heads still shaking, their throats clearing, their voices gurgling. Finally, two Negro men, smelling of whiskey and work-sweat, pushed through the crowd, hauled me to my feet, placed the crutches beneath my shoulders, and flanked me like bodyguards as I crossed the street, burning with the desire to get away from those Yonkers-bound eyes. When we reached the other side they asked me whether I was all right, whether I wanted them to walk me home. I shook my head and walked on alone, not even stopping to thank them. I suppose I knew they would forgive my lack of manners as the result of what they themselves undoubtedly knew so well—spiritual lynching.

The sympathetic ear. Another role I quickly learned. Bums, drunkards, landlords who wanted to be loved, kids who fought with their mothers, middle-aged men who cherished a wound received at Chateau Thierry, old ladies lugging heavy bundles of groceries through streets that blistered the feet and broke the mind, boys who had not been chosen in the curbball game and who sat on the stoop with me to watch it bitterly—all knew me as the sufferer, the ear who would understand, or, if not understand, at least listen in payment for the relief of loneliness. "Goddamn bastards. I'm just as good as Willie, ain't I? Ain't I just as good? They let Willie play, goddammit. But they don't let me play."

"Jesus, that's tough."

"It's a pisser. Ah, to hell with it. Screw them."

"Maybe they'll choose you in next game."

"I don't wanna be chosen in next game. Listen, Lennie, did I ever tell you what Charley said about Jews. He said all Jews are reds, Commies. . . . Listen, I ain't saying it. But that's what Charley said. And Herbie lets him play. And Herbie's a Jew, ain't he?"

A drunk weaving unsteadily down the street, stopping before me, his sour breath commanding my attention. "The Pope, tha's who. The goddamn Pope. Wasn' for him, wha' wou'cha have? I'll tell ya. Peace. Tha's wha'!"

"The Pope is just . . ."

"Don' ya tell me, boy. Wasn' for the goddamn Pope, ya wou'n't have to walk on those goddamn crutches. Ya lis'en to me, goddammit."

The historian of the day's action. "Hey, Lennie, you see that girl across the street?"

"Yeah."

"How many times did she pass there today?"

"How the hell should I know?"

"Well, you sit on the goddamn stoop all day, don'cha? You oughtta keep your eyes open." . . .

. . . I went on my first date. All that day, I had anticipated going. It was another test, but this time there was another person. My will might not be enough. It wasn't sex that I wanted, not then. For sex was still so deep a fear then that all I could do was to verbalize a manhood I was searching for, to talk as if I had already made it, to shroud that ultimate fear in a certain new boldness of approach. I was frightened of dating. It was that simple. For I didn't know what was expected of me. And I had already noted the wary faces of mothers eyeing me from porches, faces that said, "Keep away from my daughter. She's not for you, sonny. She's not for you. Not that I want to hurt you, but . . ."

That night I met Barbara in front of the movie theater on the town's main street. A flight of wooden steps led up to the theater's entrance, an easy flight to walk up, for there were banisters on both sides. But I delayed going up for as long as possible. Somehow, I had to persuade Barbara to walk in front of me, to force this pleasant, well-curved girl of sixteen to clear a way for my embarrassment. Her presence disturbed me. She was simply too much the thing I wanted, the gold star that had been awarded to me in the third grade, the beacon toward which I struggled, however fearfully, in this reach for selfhood. My success in swimming the lake didn't matter; it wasn't going to help me tonight. "Walk ahead of me," I demanded.

"Why?"

I didn't answer her. I couldn't. But she walked up ahead of me, evidently not thinking the request strange, or else so unmoved by what to her was a mechanical thing, a date, that its strangeness didn't disturb her. I followed her up those stairs as quickly as I could, aware of eyes on my back that somehow had disappeared by the time I reached the top and turned around. But that only made it worse; that meant not that the eyes didn't exist but only that they were trying to trick me into believing that they didn't exist. Shrewd and intent as I was, I would create an enemy of the world even if it chose to proclaim its indifference toward me.

In the dark of the theater, I underwent a change I had expected. That image on the screen severed me from the outside world, and I was again free to indulge my Hollywood-primed memory, only this time with another person. It was easy enough to "cop my feel," to glue my hand to the softness of her flesh and coat my awkwardness with the mannerisms of the experienced stud. I drifted into the tempo of the film and sought with my hands to create a communion of seekers. Barbara was willing, all too willing to inexperienced hands that belonged to a mind that worried about the cripple in me. Throughout the movie, the voice that rose from that mind whispered, "Doesn't she know you're crippled? Doesn't she know about the legs?" Whether she knew or not didn't matter; what mattered was that I knew, as I had known while dressing on the dock. That was my secret, a burdensome secret that I could share with no one else, for to no one else could it have any real meaning.

When the picture finally ended, only my hands had been fulfilled. The rest of me was burning with shame as the lights went on and we stood up to leave. I expected Barbara to slap my face, turn on her heel, and leave the theater, true to a virtue she had never claimed and would not have known what to do with. But all she did was smile and coo something like, "Wasn't it a lovely picture?" And wasn't it, whatever it had been.

I didn't have to ask Barbara to walk down the stairs ahead of me. That wasn't necessary now. For, not having been slapped, my hands tingled with the feel of her softness, and visions in the Hollywood style drifted like overly ripe clouds through my head. Soft lights, music, the thread of violins, the rich taste of halvah. Lord, I was a lover!

We spent the next half hour in the drug store, sipping sodas along with the other mating children who were all around us. And how thrilled I was to number myself among them. Our talk was child's talk, some of her, some of me. I didn't even listen very attentively, for I was gearing myself for the long walk back to her hotel, which was at the south end of the lake, about three quarters of a mile from where we were. Her mother entered the luncheonette, nodded abruptly to Barbara, and left. "That's my mother," Barbara said brightly. She was being very informative.

I had already exaggerated my success in the darkened movie theater, and now I wanted to leave the drug store, to squeeze her softness once again, to permit my body, made edgier and bolder, some new, more probing success. It turned out to be an unfortunate consequence of discovering that I was not so far outside the society of my peers as I had believed. "Listen," I said, "I'll take you home now. It's after eleven."

"It's a long walk," Barbara answered doubtfully.

"I'll take you," I insisted, for her tone had turned it into a conscious battle again. And again I was the prover, and what could I prove so surely as this new manhood springing up within me.

We got up and left the luncheonette. The night was cool and sharp, the stars burning into a protean expanse that made me think of nothing but my own hugeness—my arms pushing me forward, like unstoppable pistons, until I had almost forgotten the girl at my side in the clean rush of security surging through my soul. Because I was what I was, a giant making giant strides through the night's darkness. A crippled giant. I thought of what I had read somewhere about Steinmetz, that hunchback mechanic playing with the world's illusions, pouring all his own frustration into the inventive toys needed by General Electric. Or was it General Motors? It didn't matter, did it? Did Steinmetz or Spinoza or F.D.R. or anyone hungry for the body's fulfillment, did any of them matter as long as I was a giant?

My euphoria lasted only for as long as we walked across that dark curving country road. Every time the lights from some onrushing car gashed the thin line of blue-black where trees and sky fused together, Barbara and I dropped off to the side of the road. My energy was all that existed for me, even as I kissed her, and all I was capable of admiring was this self, from which, in the intensity of my love, I almost felt detached—my self was making its own way through the rich blackness and I was no more, really, than an onlooker. Then we were standing in front of the lawn of Barbara's hotel. The moment was awkward, but Barbara was reassuring. Soft in the shadows, she took my right hand and placed it on her breast. I felt delighted, triumphant, new-sprung, and I suddenly thought of throwing her down there, on the lawn in front of the hotel. It was a dramatic thought, and as I pulled her close to me I could think of nothing but how great a lover I was destined to become. I kissed her, hard, and then, with a quiet grace all my own, I fell down.

It was as if the ground had sprung up to meet me, insisting on my giving it the final victory of the night. I lay there, face pressed to the grass, kissing the grass where I had expected to be kissing only Barbara, for the moment amused by this latest trick, this vicious shrewdness, of the enemy. And Barbara, too, that beautiful bundle of softness which had been meant for me, only for me and for this night, Barbara was equally amused. Not that she laughed or giggled, as I suppose I expected her to; her voice, in fact, was taut with the serious, the lofty, the dignified, as she asked, "Are you all right."

"Sure," I answered. "Sure, I'm all right."

"What happened?"

"I tripped. I guess I tripped."

"You're sure you're all right."

"Yes." I pushed myself up on my hands, and, leaning on my right hand alone, I said, "Give me the crutches."

Barbara picked up the crutches. She had a certain sure dignity of touch that gagged me for the moment, holding the crutches as if they were not wooden crutches but rather spears, clean and agile and shafted in their ability to pierce flesh. I knew little enough about the terror of the phallus then but it was with me for sure. This was my potency, my strength; like Samson's hair, this was the feeder of my manhood. I pushed up straight, using one crutch handle to boost myself, then grabbing the other crutch from Barbara's hand. "It could have happened to anyone," Barbara offered in a whisper, and with that I suddenly hated her, not for trying to soothe my pain but for transforming it from pain to absurdity, from taking that which was mine alone and playing with it as if my life were some common universal accident. And then, stepping on the pieces with all the goodness that she had been taught by Flatbush spinsters, she added, "I'll see you tomorrow."

"I'll see you," I answered, the words thick on my tongue. "I'll see you."

I watched her walk up the path to the hotel. She moved well, conscious of her body's curves. I hated her even more for moving so well. She paused just before she disappeared into the hotel. I took a few deep breaths, then turned away. I began the walk back to my own hotel.

The strength had been draining from my body. For the first time since the lancing of the boils, I felt weak and flabby. I huddled in the shadows of the trees each time I heard the roar of a car engine, afraid that if I were offered a lift I would accept. And I had to go on by myself, for now the enemy had the upper hand. Now the night, the sky, the roar of the motorboat cruising the pitch-black lake, the mysterious sudden noises that I heard from the side of the road, all were mocking me. "Submit!" the noises cried. "Submit to that which we know you are!" I walked on, and suddenly I was crying, crying with the sheer rage that had been burning within me ever since I took that fall, crying because Barbara's softness had turned to stone in my hands, crying because the fever in the blood was now no more than the desire not to be humiliated any further, crying because I had come so close to the greatest and most necessary of all the incestuous loves, the love of the self, only to have it wrenched from my grasp.

Finally I was standing on the porch of my hotel. There was no one else around, and all of the lights but one had been turned off. I leaned against the wall and lit a cigarette. The night was still clear, the moon and the plethora of stars glaring sharply through the blackness. "You bastards," I whispered tearfully. "I'll get you still, you bastards. You just see if I don't." And with that I went into my room, burning with fever.

It was almost noon when I awoke. The room was hot, a humid, sticky heat. My mouth felt dry and parched. I moved sluggishly, feverishly. I didn't go into town. All afternoon I just sat on the porch, watching the old women who made that porch their summer headquarters rocking back and forth, thinking of how I had crawled the night before as I had not crawled in a long time. I was different today, different both physically and psychologically. My edge had been honed. I had slipped away from my own consciousness and once again had made the world my measuring rod. All day long I wanted to curse and cry, and I fought this only because I was intimidated by the people around me. The world was rancid with the smell of my disease.

Late that afternoon, Barbara came up to the

hotel. She greeted me brightly, as if the fall had never happened. She had a great deal of poise and compassion for a sixteen-year-old girl, but I lacked everything that afternoon except the memory of what had happened the night before. And I blamed her for that, spreading my intense self-pity until it coated the entire world. I baited Barbara, quite deliberately, and eventually her better nature was twisted out of shape until she began to cut into me. "Don't worry," she concluded, as she walked off the porch, "I'll see you again . . . in the city." . . .

I remember those summer evenings with growing affection and envy—moving up and down on the bars, sweat streaming down my face, verbally loving all of the world. And the kids, the eight- and nine-year-olds who hung around to watch us go up and down, waiting for a moment in which they could voice what they wanted to know, "Hey, mister, what happened to your legs?" And let me give myself the gold star here, for, to my credit, I always answered them. Their curiosity was natural enough, healthy even. It was only the adults, those prying vicars of the soul, whose questions I scorned.

"What happened to you?" The adult voice brusque, demanding, insisting on its right to know that which had violated its world.

"What do you mean, what happened?"

A vague hand slicing air that was just as vague. "I mean, what happened to your legs?"

"You really want to know?"

"What are you, some kind of wise guy?"

"I got bitten by a crocodile."

"Oh, a wise guy. Who the hell do you think you are?"

"A big green-assed crocodile."

"Who the hell you think you are? What is it, a goddamn crime to ask?"

"Screw you, Mac. Screw you, in spades."

And so it passed, that rich year when I discovered a beginning and went off to quarry for my fate, when it occurred to me that being crippled was something that was distinctively mine, and that through the long years ahead I could lean on the cripple in me as this half-life half-death body of mine leaned on crutches. I felt as if I had been pulled short during the midnight of my life, as if I had seen death, and as if I had said, "Let me first even myself with myself. Let me teach the virus what I still haven't learned for myself." It was rich, that year, the good year when life rose from the sticky blandness of dreams and taught me how to hate, how to love, how to be.

QUESTIONS FOR DISCUSSION

1. Do you think Kriegel's perception of the world around him was accurate? Was his condition particularly unusual?

2. Could significant others in the writer's environment have been more supportive? If so, how? Did they label him?

3. Kriegel clearly viewed himself differently after becoming crippled. Discuss in more detail the process by which this occurred.

4. Do you think that the writer's outlook on the world will become less cynical and less egocentric with the passage of time? What evidence can you muster for your argument?

5. Do present day communities shun the physically handicapped? In what ways?

THE JUDGED, NOT THE JUDGES: AN INSIDER'S VIEW OF MENTAL RETARDATION *Robert Bogdan and Steven Taylor*

If one wishes to understand the term *holy water*, one should not study the properties of the water, but rather the assumptions and beliefs of the people who use it. That is, holy water derives its meaning from those who attribute a special essence to it (Szasz, 1974).

Similarly, the meaning of the term *mental retardation* depends on those who use it to describe the cognitive states of other people. As some have argued, mental retardation is a social construction or a concept which exists in the minds of the "judges" rather than in the minds of the "judged" (Blatt, 1970; Braginsky & Braginsky, 1971; Dexter, 1964; Hurley, 1969; Mercer, 1973). A mentally retarded person is one who has been labeled as such according to rather arbitrarily created and applied criteria.

Retardate, and other such clinical labels, suggests generalizations about the nature of men and women to whom that term has been applied (Goffman, 1963). We assume that the mentally retarded possess common characteristics that allow them to be unambiguously distinguished from all others. We explain their behavior by special theories. It is as though humanity can be divided into two groups, the "normal" and the "retarded."

To be labeled retarded is to have a wide range of imperfections imputed to you. One imperfection is the inability to analyze your life and your current situation. Another is the inability to express yourself—to know and say who you are and what you wish to become.

In the pages that follow, we present the edited transcripts of some of the discussions we have had over the past year with a 26-year-old man we will call Ed Murphy. (For methodology, see Bogdan, 1974, and Bogdan & Taylor, 1975.) Ed has been labeled mentally retarded by his family, school teachers, and others in his life. At the age of 15, he was placed in a state institution for the *retarded*. His institutional records, as do many professionals with whom he has come into contact, describe him as "a good boy, but easily confused; mental retardation—cultural-familial type." Ed currently works as a janitor in a large urban nursing home and lives in a boarding house with four other men who, like himself, are former residents of state institutions.

AN INSIDER'S VIEW

When I was born the doctors didn't give me six months to live. My mother told them that she could keep me alive, but they didn't believe it. It took a hell of a lot of work, but she showed with love and determination that she could be the mother to a handicapped child. I don't know for a fact what I had, but they thought it was severe retardation and cerebral palsy. They thought I would never walk. I still have seizures. Maybe that has something to do with it too.

My first memory is about my grandmother. She was a fine lady. I went to visit her right before she died. I knew she was sick, but I didn't realize that I would never see her again. I was special in my grandmother's eyes. My mother told me that she had a wish—it was that I would walk. I did walk, but it wasn't until the age of four. She prayed that she would see that day. My mother told me the story again and again of how, before she died, I was at her place. She

The authors thank Burton Blatt and Doug Biklen for reading an earlier draft and making useful suggestions for improvement.

Requests for reprints should be sent to Robert Bogdan, The Center on Human Policy, Syracuse University, Syracuse, New York 13210.

was on the opposite side of the room and called, "Walk to grandma, walk to grandma," and I did. I don't know if I did as good as I could, but I did it. Looking back now it makes me feel good. It was frustrating for my parents that I could not walk. It was a great day in everybody's life.

The doctors told my mother that I would be a burden to her. When I was growing up she never let me out of her sight. She was always there with attention. If I yelled she ran right to me. So many children who are handicapped must be in that position—they become so dependent on their mother. Looking back I don't think she ever stopped protecting me even when I was capable of being self-sufficient. I remember how hard it was to break away from that. She never really believed that after I had lived the first six months that I could be like everybody else.

I remember elementary school; my mind used to drift a lot. When I was at school, concentrating was almost impossible. I was so much into my own thoughts—my daydreams—I wasn't really in class. I would think of the cowboy movies—the rest of the kids would be in class and I would be on the battlefield someplace. The nuns would yell at me to snap out of it, but they were nice. That was my major problem all through school that I daydreamed. I think all people do that. It wasn't related to retardation. I think a lot of kids do that and are diagnosed as retarded, but it has nothing to do with retardation at all. It really has to do with how people deal with the people around them and their situation. I don't think I was bored. I think all the kids were competing to be the honor students, but I was never interested in that. I was in my own world—I was happy. I wouldn't recommend it to someone, but daydreaming can be a good thing. I kind of stood in the background—I kind of knew that I was different—I knew that I had a problem, but when you're young you don't think of it as a problem. A lot of people are like I was. The problem is getting labeled as being something. After that you're not really as a person. It's like like a sty in your eye—it's noticeable. Like that teacher and the way she looked at me. In the fifth grade—in the fifth grade my classmates thought I was different, and my teacher knew I was different. One day she looked at me and she was on the phone to the

office. Her conversation was like this, "When are you going to transfer him?" This was the phone in the room. I was there. She looked at me and knew I was knowledgeable about what she was saying. Her negative picture of me stood out like a sore thumb.

My mother protected me. It wasn't wrong that she protected me, but there comes a time when someone has to come in and break them away. I can remember trying to be like the other kids and having my mother right there pulling me away. She was always worried about me. You can't force yourself to say to your mother: "Stop, I can do it myself." Sometimes I think the pain of being handicapped is that people give you so much love that it becomes a weight on you and a weight on them. There is no way that you can break from it without hurting them—without bad feelings—guilt. It is like a trap because of the fact that you are restricted to your inner thoughts. After a while you resign yourself to it. The trap is that you can't tell them, "Let me go." You have to live with it and suffer. It has to do with pity. Looking back on it I can't say it was wrong. She loved me. You do need special attention, but the right amount.

One time maybe when I was thirteen, I was going to camp and had to go to the place where the buses left. My mother kept asking me if I had everything and telling me where my bags were and if I was all right. It is similar to the way other mothers act, but it sticks out in my mind. I was striving to be a normal boy so it meant more to me. After my mother went back to the car the other kids on the bus kidded me. They said things like, "Momma's boy." That's the one that sticks out in my memory.

I liked camp. The staff and counselors were good. I had this thing with my legs. They weren't very strong. When I fell back from the group on a hike I was light enough so that they could give me a ride on their backs. I had the best seat on the hike. Looking back on being carried, they would have lost me if they didn't. I was glad I was light because it was easier for them. I needed help and they helped. I went for many summers in a row, and they helped pay for the sessions when my parents were ill. I didn't mind being carried. The important thing was that I was there and that I was taking part in the events like everybody else.

I remember the day the press came. It was an annual award day. They came to write up the story. The best camper got his picture in the paper. My name was in the paper. I got a patch for being a good camper. It was something that I had accomplished and felt pretty good about. My mother kept the article and the neighbors knew too.

In January of 1963, without any warning, my father died. A douple of months later, Ma died too. It was hard on us—my sister and me. We stayed with friends of the family for a while, but then they moved. They told us we had to go. So they sent us to an orphanage for a few months, but eventually we wound up at the State School. I was 15 then.

Right before they sent me and my sister to the State School, they had six psychologists examine us to determine how intelligent we were. I think that was a waste of time. They asked me things like, "What comes to mind when I say 'Dawn'?"—so you say, "Light." Things like that. What was tough was putting the puzzles together and the mechanical stuff. They start out very simple and then they build it up and it gets harder and harder.

If you're going to do something with a person's life you don't have to pay all that money to be testing them. I had no place else to go. I mean here I am pretty intelligent and here are six psychologists testing me and sending me to the State School. How would you feel if you were examined by all those people and then wound up where I did? A psychologist is supposed to help you. The way they talked to me they must have thought I was fairly intelligent. One of them said, "You look like a smart young man," and then I turned up there. I don't think the tests made any difference. They had their minds made up anyway.

Another guy I talked to was a psychiatrist. That was rough. For one thing I was mentally off guard. You're not really prepared for any of it. You don't figure what they're saying and how you're answering it and what it means—not until the end. When the end came, I was a ward of the State.

I remember the psychiatrist well. He was short and middle-aged and had a foreign accent. The first few minutes he asked me how I felt and I replied, "Pretty good." Then I fell right into his trap. He asked if I thought people hated me and I said "Yes." "Do you think people talk about you behind your back?" And I said, "Yes." I started getting hypernervous. By then he had the hook in the fish, and there was no two ways about it. He realized I was nervous and ended the interview. He was friendly and he fed me the bait. The thing was that it ended so fast. After I got out I realized that I had screwed up. I cried. I was upset. He came on like he wanted honest answers but being honest in that situation doesn't get you any place but the State School.

When the psychiatrist interviewed me he had my records in front of him—so he already knew I was mentally retarded. It's the same with everyone. If you are considered mentally retarded there is no way you can win. There is no way they give you a favorable report. They put horses out of misery quicker than they do people. It's a real blow to you being sent to the State School.

I remember the day they took me and my sister. We knew where we were going, but we didn't know anything specific about it. It was scary.

To me there never was a State School. The words State School sound like a place with vocational training or you get some sort of education. That's just not the way Empire State School is. They have taken millions of dollars and spent them and never rehabilitated who they were supposed to. If you looked at individuals and see what they said they were supposed to do for that person and then what they actually did, you would find that many of them were actually hurt—not helped. I don't like the word vegetable, but in my own case I could see that if I had been placed on the low grade ward I might have slipped to that. I began feeling myself slip. They could have made me a vegetable. If I would have let that place get to me and depress me I would still have been there today. Actually, it was one man that saved me. They had me scheduled to go to P–8—a back ward—when just one man looked at me. I was a wreck. I had a beard and baggy State clothes on. I had just arrived at the place. I was trying to understand what was happening. I was confused. What I looked like was P–8 material. There was this supervisor, a woman. She came on to our ward and looked right at me and said: "I have him scheduled for P–8." An older attendant was there. He looked over at me and said, "He's too bright for that ward. I think we'll keep him." To look at me then I didn't look good. She made a remark under her breath that I looked pretty retarded to her. She saw me looking at her–I looked her square in the eye. She had on a white dress and a cap with three stripes–I can still see them now. She saw me and said, "Just don't stand there, get to work."

Of course I didn't know what P–8 was then, but I found out. I visited up there a few times on work detail. That man saved my life. Here was a woman that I had never known who they said was the building supervisor looking over me. At that point I'm pretty positive that if I went there I would have fitted in and I would still be there.

I remember the day that Bobby Kennedy came. That was something. All day long we knew he was coming and he walked around. I got a look at him. He told everybody what a snake pit the place was so it was better for a few days. At least he got some people interested for a while. I really admired that man. You take a lot of crusaders though, like local politicians, they go over to the State School and do a lot of yelling. They only do it when someone forces them to, like when someone gets something in the paper about someone being beaten or is overdosed bad. The newest thing at Empire was someone yelled sodomy. Some parent found out about it and called the legislator. Big deal. If they knew what was going on it wouldn't be that big a deal—one incident of sodomy. Hell, for that matter they ought to look around them and see what the people on the outside are doing sexually.

It's funny. You hear so many people talking about IQ. The first time I ever heard the expression was when I was at Empire State School. I didn't know what it was or anything, but some people were talking and they brought the subject up. It was on the ward, and I went and asked one of the staff what mine was. They told me 49. Forty-nine isn't fifty, but I was pretty happy about it. I mean I figured that I wasn't a low grade. I really didn't know what it meant, but it sounded pretty high. Hell, I was born in 1948 and forty-nine didn't seem too bad. Forty-nine didn't sound hopeless. I didn't know anything about the highs or lows, but I knew I was better than most of them.

Last week was the first time I went into a state school since I was discharged as a ward of the state—which makes it about three years. I just went up to visit. I purposely avoided going there. I have been nervous about it. There are good memories and bad memories. The whole idea of having been in a state school makes you nervous about why you were ever put there in the first place. I'm out now, but I was on that side of the fence once. It has less to do with what I am doing than with how the game is played. Being in a state school or having been in a state school isn't fashionable and never will be. Deep down you want to avoid the identification. If I could convince myself that in the end they are going to be cleaned up I might feel better about it. You have got to face the enemy and that's what it is like.

I have come from being a resident of a state school to being on the other side saying they're no good. It has been brought up to me—"Where the hell would you be if it wasn't for the State School." That holds water, but now the dam is drying up as I am on this side. Sure I had a need, but they kind of pitched you a low pitch. There wasn't anything better. I needed a place to go, but unfortunately there was no choice of where to go. When it's all said and done there were those at the school that helped me so I'm grateful, but still some other place would have been better.

I guess the State School wasn't all that bad. It was tough to leave though. You had all your needs taken care of there. You didn't have to worry about where your next meal was coming from or where you were going to sleep.

I don't have it that bad right now. I have my own room and I get my meals at the house. The landlord is going to up the rent though—$45 a week for room and board. I'll be able to pay it, but I don't know what Frank and Lou across the hall will do. They wash dishes at the steak house and don't take home that much.

It's really funny. Sunday I got up and went for a walk. All of a sudden Joan's name came to my mind. She's sort of my girlfriend. I don't know why, but I just thought of her moving in next door to the place where I live. That would be something.

Is there still any magnetism between that woman and me? I haven't seen her in three months, but there is still something, I can tell. We had a good thing going. I opened her up a lot mentally. I saw a very different person there than others see. I saw a woman that could do something with her life. If she could wake up one morning and say to herself, "I am going to do something with my life," she could. I don't think that retardation is holding her back so much as emotional problems. If she had confidence that would make the difference. I know she could build herself up.

The family had respect for me, at least to a point, but they don't think she should marry. We got pretty close psychologically and physically—not that I did anything. They don't have programs at the Association for Retarded Children that say to adults you are an adult and you can make it. She has been at the ARC for a long time now. She was a bus-aide, so in one way they showed her that she could work but on the other hand they didn't build her confidence enough to feel that she could go out to work.

The last time I saw her she didn't say a word. When she is pissed off at the world she is pissed off. That's the Irish in her. In my opinion she doesn't belong at the ARC. But one thing is her parents don't want to take chances. Like a lot of the parents, they send their 30-year-old kids with Snoopy lunch pails. They are afraid financially and I can't blame them. If she went out on her own they are afraid that her social security would stop and then if she could continue they wouldn't have anything. She could lose her benefits.

I first met Joan in 1970. It was when I started working at the ARC workshop. I sat there and maybe the second or third day I glanced over and saw her there. The first time I noticed her was in the eating area; I was having lunch. I looked around and she was the only one there that attracted me. There was just something about her. At first she wasn't that easy to get along with. She put on the cold shoulder and that made me think about her more.

One time I had a fight with one of the boys in the workshop. He was her old boyfriend. This day I was getting off the bus and he said that I pushed him. He pushed me and then when we went to the locker room it got rougher. I yelled to him, "Get away from me." I started cursing and we started swinging. I guess he was jealous that Joan was spending so much time talking to me. He was a big guy and he hit me in the mouth and cut it. The staff came and broke it up. They treated it like the whole thing was a joke. They thought it was cute, the two of us fighting over Joan. They ribbed us about it like they always rib about boyfriends and girlfriends.

It took awhile for her to understand how she felt. She didn't want to be too friendly. She didn't like me putting my arm around her. We went for walks during lunch and she got pretty fond of me and I got pretty fond of her. One day I asked her, "Well, how about a movie?" She said, "All right," but she had to get her mother's permission. Then one day she said she could go. It was a Saturday matinee gangster movie. We arranged to meet at the bus stop downtown. I remember that I got down there early and bought the tickets before she came. I met her at the stop and then I went up to the ticket office with the tickets in my hand. I was a little fuzzy, nervous, you might say. Of course, you were supposed to give the tickets to the man inside. The ticket woman looked at me—sort of stared and motioned with her finger. It was kind of funny considering our ages. I was 23 and she was 28. It was like teenagers going on our first date.

Being at the State School and all you never have the chances romantically like you might living on the outside. I guess I was always shy with the opposite sex even at Empire. We did have dances and I felt that I was good looking, but I was bashful and mostly sat. I was bashful with Joan at the movie. In my mind I felt funny, awkward. I didn't know how to approach her. Should I hug her? You can't hug the hell out of her because you don't know how she would take it. You have all the feeling there, but you don't know what direction to go in. If you put your arm around her she might scream and you're finished. If she doesn't scream you're still finished.

I never thought of myself as a retarded individual but who would want to. You're not knowledgeable about what they are saying behind your back. You get a feeling from people around you; they try to hide it but their intentions don't work. They say they will do this and that—like they will look out for you—they try to protect you but you feel sort of guilty. You get the feeling that they love you but that they are looking down at you. You always have that sense of a barrier between you and the ones that love you. By their own admission of protecting you you have an umbrella over you that tells you that you and they have an understanding that there is something wrong—that there is a barrier.

As I got older I slowly began to find myself becoming mentally awake. I found myself concentrating. Like on the television. A lot of people wonder why I have good grammar. It was because of the television. I was like a tape recorder—what I heard I memorized. Even when I was 10 or 12 I would listen to Huntley and Brinkley. They were my favorites. As the years went by I understood what they were talking about. People were amazed at what I knew. People would begin to ask me what I thought about this and that. Like my aunt would always ask me about the news—what my opinions were. I began to know that I was a little brighter than they thought I was. It became a hobby. I didn't know what it meant—that I had a grasp on a lot of important things—the race riots, Martin Luther King in jail—what was really happening was that I was beginning to find something else instead of just being bored. It was entertaining. I didn't know that that meant anything then. I mean I didn't know that I would be sitting here telling you all this. When you're growing up you don't think of yourself as a person but as a boy. As you get older it works itself out—who you are deep down—who you ought to be. You have an image of yourself deep down. You try to sort it all out. You know what you are deep inside but those around you give you a negative picture of yourself. It's that umbrella over you.

What is retardation? It's hard to say. I guess it's having problems thinking. Some people think that you can tell if a person is retarded by looking at them. If you think that way you don't give people the benefit of the doubt. You judge a person by how they look or how they talk or what the tests show, but you can never really tell what is inside the person.

Take a couple of friends of mine, Tommy McCan and PJ. Tommy was a guy who was really nice to be with. You could sit down with him and have a nice conversation and enjoy yourself. He was a mongoloid. The trouble was people couldn't see beyond that. If he didn't look that

way it would have been different, but there he was locked into what the other people thought he was. Now PJ was really something else. I've watched that guy and I can see in his eyes that he is aware. He knows what's going on. He can only crawl and he doesn't talk, but you don't know what's inside. When I was with him and I touched him, I know that he knows.

I don't know. Maybe I used to be retarded. That's what they said anyway. I wish they could see me now. I wonder what they'd say if they could see me holding down a regular job and doing all kinds of things. I bet they wouldn't believe it.

CONCLUSION

Ed's story stands by itself as a rich source of understanding. We will resist the temptation to analyze it and reflect on what it tells us about Ed. Our position is that at times and to a much greater extent than we do now, we must listen to people who have been labeled *retarded* with the idea of finding out about ourselves, our society, and the nature of the label (Becker, 1966).

There are specifics that can be learned from stories such as Ed's. (For discussion, see Allport, 1942; Becker, 1966; Bogdan, 1974.) For example, his story clearly illustrates that mental retardation is a demeaning concept which leads to a number of penalties for those so labeled. These penalties include lowered self-image and limited social and economic opportunity. Also, his story shows the profound effect of early prognosis on how people are treated and on the way that they think about themselves. It clearly demonstrates how segregated living environments and facilities such as state schools severely limit basic socialization for skills that are needed to participate in the larger society. His story also illustrates how being institutionalized is a function of a variety of social and economic contingencies—family difficulties, lack of alternatives—more than the nature of the person's disability or treatment needs. It also touches on the difficulties faced by people who are "protected." We can more accurately assess the resentment and the restrictions this protection imposes. We can also see the profound effects of simple words of praise and rejection on the person's self-concept. Ed's story points to how some people who work "with" the so-called "retarded" develop joking styles that minimize the real and normal problems and conflicts that the labeled is attempting to deal with and how the object of them feels about this. While his story mentions all of these specifics, there are two general points that we should remember.

The first point is simple but is seldom taken into account in conducting research or planning programs. People who are labeled *retarded* have their own understandings about themselves, their situation, and their experiences. These understandings are often different from those of the professionals. For example, although cure and treatment might dominate the official views of state schools and rehabilitation centers and programs, boredom, manipulation, coercion, and embarrassment often constitute the client's view. In our own work interviewing labeled people (Bogdan, 1974), and in Ed's story, the vocabulary of the therapist often contradicts that of the patient. The handicapped—the so-called "retarded"—respond to therapy and services according to how they perceive it, not according to how the staff sees it. Devaluing an individual's perspective by viewing it as naive, unsophisticated, immature, or a symptom of some underlying pathology can make research one-sided and service organizations places where rituals are performed in the name of science.

The second area that his story points to has to do with the lack of alternative ways that those who are "different" have to conceptualize their situation.

The present state of such fields as mental retardation is controlled by powerful ideological monopolies. As Ed's story suggests, there is a dearth of definitions in our society and few divergent agencies that provide individuals who are mentally and physically different and struggling and suffering with ways of conceptualizing themselves other than the demeaning vocabulary of "sickness," "handicapped," and "deviant," of which "retardate" is a part.

The categories available to place individuals cannot help but affect how we feel about them and how they feel about themselves. When we present "subjects" or "clients" as numbers or as diagnostic categories, we do not engender in others a feeling of respect for or closeness to the people being discussed. Such views of human beings are not evil or unnecessary, but they comprise only a single view. Overemphasis on this view without presenting the subjective side distorts our knowledge in a dangerous way. (Social scientists presenting the alternative view include Coles, 1967a, 1967b, 1971; Cottle, 1971, 1972, 1973; Lewis, 1961, 1962; Shaw, 1930; Shaw & Moore, 1931; Sutherland, 1937; Thomas & Znaniecki, 1918–1920.)

Traditionally, social scientists have studied the retarded as a separate category of human beings, and by doing this they have accepted commonsense definitions. It is assumed that the retardate is basically different from the rest of us and that he or she needs to be explained by special theories distinct from those used to explain the behavior of "regular" people. By taking this approach, social scientists have contributed to and have legitimized commonsense classifications of individuals as "normal" and "retarded." We have told the world that there are two kinds of human beings. Ed's own words are a form of data and a source of understanding that permits us to know a person intimately. By sharing his life we can approach the concept of intelligence in its more human dimensions. It is through this intimacy that we learn how the subject views himself or herself, and what he or she has in common with all of us becomes clear. Differences take on less importance. The person's own words force us to think of subjects as people, and categories of all kinds become less relevant.

REFERENCES

Allport, G. *The use of personal documents in psychological science*. New York: Social Science Research Council, 1942.

Becker, H. "Introduction" in Clifford Shaw's *The jackroller*. Chicago, Ill.: University of Chicago Press, 1966.

Blatt, B. *Exodus from pandemonium*. Boston: Allyn & Bacon, 1970.

Bogdan, R. *Being different*. New York: Wiley, 1974

Bogdan, R., & Taylor, S. *Introduction to qualitative research methods*. New York: Wiley, 1975.

Braginsky, D., & Braginsky, B. *Hansels and Gretels*. New York: Holt, Rinehart & Winston, 1971.

Coles, R. *Children of crisis*. Boston, Mass.: Little, Brown, 1967. (a)

Coles, R. *Migrants, sharecroppers, mountaineers*. Chap. 2, "Method." Boston, Mass.: Little, Brown, 1967. (b)

Coles, R. *The South goes North*. Boston, Mass.: Little, Brown, 1971.

Cottle, T. J. *Time's children*. Boston, Mass.: Little, Brown, 1971.

Cottle, T. J. *The abandoners*. Boston, Mass.: Little, Brown, 1972.

Cottle, T. J. *The voices of school: Educational images through personal accounts*. Boston, Mass.: Little, Brown, 1973.

Dexter, L. The tyranny of schooling. New York: Basic Books, 1964.

Goffman, I. *Stigma*. Englewood Cliffs, N.J.: Prentice-Hall, 1963.

Hurley, R. *Poverty and mental retardation*. New York: Vintage Books, 1969.

Lewis, O. *The children of Sanchez*. New York: Vintage, 1961.

Lewis, O. *Five families*. New York: Wiley, Science Editions, 1962.

Mercer, J. *Labelling the mentally retarded*. Berkeley: University of California Press, 1973.

Shaw, C. R. *The jack-roller*. Chicago, Ill.: University of Chicago Press, 1930.

Shaw, C. R., & Moore, M. E. *The natural history of a delinquent career*. Chicago, Ill.: University of Chicago Press, 1931.

Sutherland, E. *The professional thief*. Chicago, Ill.: University of Chicago Press, 1937.

Szasz, T. S. *Ceremonial chemistry: The ritual persecution of drugs, addicts, and the pushers*. Garden City, N.Y.: Doubleday, 1974.

Thomas, W. I., & Znaniecki, F. *The Polish peasant in Europe and America* (5 vols.). Chicago, Ill.: University of Chicago Press, 1918–1920.

QUESTIONS FOR DISCUSSION

1. How would you respond to the statement that mental retardation "exists in the minds of the judges"?

2. Does labeling have any redeeming characteristics? What are its drawbacks?

3. Did Ed Murphy's family respond appropriately to him? What do you think of the statement Ed made about being given so much love it becomes a weight on you and them?

4. Everyone has inadequacies of one sort or another. Who should decide where an arbitrary line is to be drawn separating "normal" inadequacies from "abnormal"?

5. How would you define mental retardation? Is there any truth to the notion: once retarded, always retarded? Can appearances be deceiving?

SUICIDE NOTES *Edited by Edwin S. Shneidman*

(From a 31-year-old single male)

Mr. Brown:

When you receive this note, call the police.

Have them break down the door panels of the cabinet nearest the window in room 10. My body will be inside. *Caution—carbon monoxide gas!* I have barricaded the doors shut so that if for any reason the guard becomes suspicious and tries to open the doors, there will be enough delay to place me beyond rescue.

It seems unnecessary to present a lengthy defense for my suicide, for if I have to be judged, it will not be on this earth. However, in brief, I find myself a misfit. To me, life is too painful for the meager occasional pleasure to compensate. It all seems so pointless, the daily struggle leading *where?* Several times I have done what, in retrospect, is seen to amount to running away from circumstances. I could do so now—travel, find a new job, even change vocation, but why? It is *Myself* that I have been trying to escape, and this I can do only as I am about to!

Please take care of a few necessary last details for me. My residence is—100 Main Street.

My rent there is paid through the week.

My only heirs and beneficiaries are my parents. No one else has the least claim to my estate, and I will it to my parents.

Please break the news to them gently. They are old and not in good health. Whatever the law may say, I feel I have a moral right to end my own life, but not someone else's.

It is too bad that I had to be born (*I* have not brought any children into this world to suffer). It is too bad that it took me more than 31 years to realize that I am the cause of whatever troubles I have blamed on my environment, and that there is no way to escape oneself. But better late than never. Suicide is unpleasant and a bother to others who must clean up and answer questions, but on the whole it is highly probable that, were I to live, it would cause even more unpleasantness and bother to myself and to others.

Goodbye.

Bill Smith

(From a 47-year-old married male)

Mary Darling,

My mind—always warped and twisted—has reached the point where I can wait no longer—I don't dare wait longer—until there is the final twist and it snaps and I spend the rest of my life in some state run snake pit.

I am going out—and I hope it is out—Nirvanha, I think the Bhudaists (how do you spell Bhudaists?) call it which is the word for "nothing." That's as I have told you for years, is what I want. Imagine God playing a dirty trick on me like another life! ! !

I've lived 47 years—there aren't 47 days I would live over again if I could avoid it.

Let us, for a moment be sensible. I do not remember if the partnership agreement provides for a case like this—but if it doesn't and I think it doesn't, I would much prefer—I haven't time to make this a legal requirement—but, I would much prefer that you, as executrix under my will, *do not* elect to participate in profits for 2 or 3 years or whatever it may be that is specified there. My partners have been generous with me while I worked with them. There is no reason why, under the circumstances of my withdrawal from the firm, they should pay anything more.

I could wish that I had, for my goodby kiss, a .38 police special with which I have made some good scores—not records but at least made my mark. Instead, I have this black bitch—bitch, if the word is not familiar to you—but at least an honest one who will mean what she says.

The neighbors may think its a motor backfire, but to me she will whisper—"Rest—Sleep."

Bill

P.S. I think there is enough insurance to see Betty through school, but if there isn't—I am sure you would out of the insurance payments, at least—

I hope further and I don't insist that you have the ordinary decency—decency that is—to do so—Will you see Betty through college—she is the only one about whom I am concerned as this .38 whispers in my ear.

From "Classification of Suicidal Phenomena" by Edwin S. Shneidman in Bulletin of Suicidology, *July 1968. U.S. Government Printing Office. Reprinted by permission of the author.*

(From a 21-year-old single female)

12:00 P.M.

I can't begin to explain what goes on in my mind—it's as though there's a tension pulling in all directions. I've gotten so I despise myself the existence I've made for myself. I've every reason for, but I can't seem to content myself with anything. If I don't do this or some other damned thing, I feel as tho I'm going to have a nervous collapse. May God forgive me, and you too, for what I am doing to you, my parents who have always tried so beautifully to understand me. It was futile, for I never quite understood myself. I love you all very much.

Mary

(From a 35-year-old single male, who committed suicide after he killed his girl friend)

Mommie my Darling,

To love you as I do and live without you is more than I can bare. I love you so completely, whole-heartedly without restraint. I worship you, that is my fault. With your indifference to me; is the difference. I've tried so hard to make our lives pleasant and lovable, but you didn't seem to care. You had great plans which didn't include me. You didn't respect me. That was the trouble. You treated me like a child. I couldn't reach you as man and woman or man and wife as we've lived. I let you know my feelings toward you when I shouldn't have. How I loved you, what you meant to me. Without you is unbearable.

This is the best way. This will solve all our problems. You can't hurt me further and anyone else. I was a "toll" while you needed me or thought you did. But now that I could use some help, you won't supply the need that was prominent when you need it. So, good bye my love. If it is possible love in the hereafter, I will love you even after death. May God have mercy on both our souls. He alone knows my heartache and sorrow and love for you.

Daddy

(From a 66-year-old divorced male)

Mary:

We could have been so happy if you had continued to love me. I have your picture in front of me. I will look at it the last thing. I do love you so much. To think you are now in the arms of another man is more than I can stand. Remember the wonderful times we have had—kindly—Good bye Darling. I love you, W. Smith.

Your boy friend Pete Andrews, is the most arrogant, conceited ass I have ever known or come in contact with. How a sensible girl like you can even be with him for 10 minutes is unbelievable. Leave him and get a real fellow. He is no good. I am giving my life for your indescressions. Please don't let me pay too high a price for your happiness. All your faults are completely forgotten and your sweetness remembered. You knew I would do this when you left me—so this is no surprise. Good bye darling—I love you with all of my broken heart.

W. Smith

(From a 39-year-old divorced female)

Bill,

You have killed me. I hope you are happy in your heart, "If you have one which I doubt." *Please* leave Rover with Mike. Also leave my baby alone. If you don't I'll haunt you the rest of your life and I mean it and I'll do it.

You have been mean and also cruel. God doesn't forget those things and don't forget that. And please no flowers; it won't but mean anything. *Also keep your money.* I want to be buried in Potters Field in the same casket with Betty. You can do that for me. That's the way we want it.

You know what you have done to me. That's why we did this. It's yours and Ella's fault, *try* and forget that *if* you can. But you can't. Rover belongs to Mike. Now we had the slip and everything made out to Mike, he will be up after Rover in the next day or so.

Your Wife

(From a 50-year-old single male)

To the Authorities:

Excuse my inability to express myself in English and the trouble caused. I beg you not to lose time in an inquest upon my body. Just simply record and file it because the name and address given in the register are fictitious and I wanted to disappear anonymously. No one expects me here nor will be looking for me. I have informed my relatives far from America. *Please do not bury me!* I wish to be *cremated* and the ashes tossed to the winds. In that way I shall return to the nothingness from which I have come into this sad world. This is all I ask of the Americans for all that I intended to give them with my coming into this country.

Many thanks.

Jose Marcia

(From a 58-year-old married female)

I have been alone since my husbands death 14 years ago. No near relatives.

I am faced with another operation similar to one I had ten years ago, after which I had many expensive treatments.

My friends are gone and I cannot afford to go through all this again. I am 58 which is not a good age to find work.

I ask that my body be given to medical students, or some place of use to some one. There will be no inquiries for me.

Thank you.

(From a 43-year-old divorced male)

To Whom It May Concern, and the Authorities:

You will find all needed information in my pocket book. If the government buries suicides please have them take care of my body, Navy Discharge in pocket book. Will you please seal and mail the accompanying letter addressed to my sister whose address is: 100 Main Street.

My car is now the property of the Jones Auto Finance Co. (You will find their card in my pocket book). Please notify them of its location. You may dispose of my things as you see fit.

W. Smith

P.S. The car is parked in front of the barbershop. The gear shift handle is broken off, but the motor is in high gear and can be driven that way.

Dear Mary,

The fact of leaving this world by my own action will no doubt be something of a shock, I hope though that it will be tempered with the knowledge that I am just "jumping the gun" on a possible 30 or 40 years of exceedingly distasteful existence, then the inevitable same end.

Life up to now has given me very little pleasure, but was acceptable through a curiosity as to what might happen next. Now I have lost that curiosity and the second half with its accompaniment of the physical disability of old age and an absolute lack of interest in anything the world might have for me is too much to face.

QUESTIONS FOR DISCUSSION

1. What is the function of leaving a suicide note?

2. Do you think most suicides are meticulously thought over and planned or are they typically impulsive occurrences?

3. Would most potential suicide victims welcome an intervention of some sort? How difficult would it be to dissuade them from their intentions? What are your feelings on suicide prevention hotlines?

4. Is the act of suicide characteristic of an unstable mentality? Does labeling theory have anything to do with suicide?

5. Do you think the commission of suicide is a sign of weakness or a rejection of society, or both?

INSTITUTIONALIZED DEVIANCE

The process of becoming a deviant is highly problematic. Being a deviant means being defined or labeled a deviant by one or more social audiences: the public at large (including, but not necessarily, agents of formal social control), oneself, and one's deviant peers. Perhaps the most crucial stage comes as the result of public recognition of one's deviant behavior. As long as the deviant can remain undetected or "hidden" there will be no public censure; however, once his or her behavior becomes public knowledge, then social opprobrium is likely to occur.

Once the agents of social control take formal action against the deviant, then private attempts at controlling or regulating the behavior must give way to public regulation. Once the person becomes entangled in the grand social machinery of "people-processing institutions," the introduction into the deviant role begins. These should not be viewed as mutually exclusive occurrences for quite often the emerging deviant role and public defamation occur simultaneously. For some, this public identification as deviant is a very traumatic experience and becomes a crucial turning point in their lives. This may be true, for example, of the homosexual who is unwillingly dragged out of the closet. After public exposure, one's claims of normality or legitimacy become extremely tenuous.

Processing the deviant is the work of official agents and the organizations for which they act. One of the by-products of an industrialized society has been the increased formalization and bureaucratization of methods of social control. In the past, the family, schools, churches, and other primary groups used to exercise considerable constraint over the individual's behavior; now, in the impersonal, anonymous, and heterogeneous society of the West, these have been replaced by consciously designed formal agencies of social control.

Of central importance in understanding deviance is understanding the crucial influence these people-processing institutions have on the creation, maintenance, and perpetuation of deviant careers. These organizations were created for humanitarian reasons, but their net impact has been to solidify the role of deviant. Once the individual has been exposed to official process-ing it becomes highly unlikely that the stigma attached to the label of deviant can be dismissed. One only needs to look at the high rates of recidivism and the powerful emotional effect that the phrase "ex con" has on people to be convinced of the confirming qualities of our prisons, mental hospitals, and other "total institutions."

Analysis of the official plan of action to be taken against deviants in the course of processing is necessary if we are to understand the special per-spective that agents of social control adopt toward deviants when they per-form their official work on them. One of the base premises is that the orga-nizational routine of agents of social control has a profound effect on the maintenance of the deviant's self-concept. Because of the failure of personal or informal controls, the organization must now process the deviant in such a way as to restore a sense of conformity or social propriety. In order for the organization to run efficiently, many tasks become regularized according, not to the needs of the individual, but to a specific plan of administrative action. This often reduces the individual to a number to simply be housed, fed, counted, and controlled.

The first selection, "Davenport State Infirmary," provides an inside view into several different types of institutions designed to manage deviants. In this particular case, an individual suffering from chronic alcoholism reflects on his experiences with various state hospitals and correctional agencies. The most prominent features of this article demonstrate: (1) the "revolving door" nature of the life of the chronic alcoholic—a series of drinking bouts followed by institutional confinement; (2) the consistency of bureaucratic routine regardless of the type of organization one is confined to; (3) the imper-sonal relationships that develop between staff and patient and the fact that the staff is primarily interested in exploiting the system and not "helping" the clients; and (4) the institutional dependency that often occurs—the "drunk ward" becomes a warm, secure, and comfortable place for homeless or displaced men.

Of crucial significance in the development of a deviant career is exposure to the official system which transforms the individual from "normal" to "de-viant." Initial entry into a total institution, of which a mental hospital is a primary example, is accompanied by a series of "degradation ceremonies" in which the patient is systematically stripped of his or her individuality, and in some cases, very humanity.

The article "On Entering a Mental Hospital" illustrates that once one has reached a certain point in the labeling process, there is little one can do to escape the label. People hospitalized in mental institutions can react in a variety of ways. Some of these ways are presented in the selection, including: (1) withdrawing from the situation, (2) challenging the institution and its authority (including denying that one is mentally ill), and (3) forgetting the outside world and restructuring one's life around the mental institution. None of the modes of adaptation will secure the patient's release from the mental hospital. The only way the patient can hasten his departure is to accept the label of mentally ill and play the role according to the view of the staff. This will demonstrate to the staff that the patient is progressing "normally" and should eventually be cured or dismissed.

Much of the sociological literature on mental illness is centered on the dehumanizing and humiliating effects of institutionalization rather than on any positive therapeutic effect the mental hospital may offer. While there is little doubt that resocialization occurs as a result of exposure to the total institution setting, it is not axiomatic that this change is harmful or alienating. Indeed, there are many positive and effective treatment programs that assist the patient in coping with his illness. Unfortunately, these have not received the same notoriety as have the types portrayed in the popular film "One Flew Over The Cuckoo's Nest."

The selection "Rebirth in a Therapeutic Community: A Case Study" offers a refreshing change from the more pessimistic assessments of treatment programs for the mentally disturbed. This particular article is unique in that it is based on the observations of a trained sociologist who was also a patient. A number of excellent "inside accounts" have been written on prisons, mental hospitals, and others, but rarely have they been written by a trained professional. This is one such account. The interpersonal dynamics that are so essential to the success of the therapeutic community are described in some detail. The author describes his own slow and gradual transformation from a withdrawn and depressive personality to a more open and assertive one. Instead of finding his hospitalization a frightening and discrediting experience (which he expected from a professional standpoint), he found it to be a pleasant and rewarding one.

Of all the arrangements designed to manage and control the deviants in our society none can compare with correctional institutions in their ability to isolate, control, and stigmatize their participants. Currently there are over 600,000 individuals confined in institutions ranging from juvenile detention centers to state and federal penitentiaries to county jails and lockups. All these institutions may vary in their organizational structure, in quality and quantity of staff, and in correctional philosophy, but all have the same goal: to keep inmates locked up and secure. Prisons have been in existence for thousands of years and they are still doing the same thing: making the label of ex-convict permanent, and thus ensuring that their clients will return.

Many social scientists believe that the key to understanding prison life lies in an analysis of this institution as a type of complex organization. By examining the "bureaucratic processes" set in motion by the organization's basic goals, one can begin to understand the futility of maintaining treatment programs in a coercive environment. Many of the traditional problems of prisons—punitive orientation of staff, racism, drug use, homosexuality, politicalization of inmates—are directly related to the emphasis accorded the goal of custody and to the resulting structural conditions that develop from such an emphasis.

As is true in any total institution, entry into prison is accomplished by a series of degradation ceremonies through which the individual is recast into the role of "prisoner." Past claims to normality are slowly stripped away as he or she is given institutional clothing, assigned an individual cell, given a set of highly specific and arbitrary rules, and finally reduced to nothing more than a number that appears on the prison work shirt. The deprivations that the inmate experiences, involving loss of liberty, denial of heterosexual contacts, and other forms of physical constraints, requires major readjustment. The socialization or more properly the "prisonization" that begins to take place as soon as the inmate is confined is the process by which the individual learns and assimilates prison norms, values, and behavior. Through the prisonization process and the joining together with other inmates, the individual is able to ameliorate, to some extent, the deprivations inherent in the prison environment.

One of the major readjustments the inmate must make is "how to do time." The time factor is something that lies heavy on the inmate, for it stretches from the present to a highly arbitrary release date. It is something that must be confronted, for it will not go away. The staff orientation is to emphasize the constructive use of time—a time to improve one's education, a chance to learn a trade or skill, a time to read or work. The inmates, on the other hand, want to do time the "easiest way possible." For them, this means gambling, drug use, homosexual activity, and other diversions that can make life easier and more bearable. The difference in orientation is a major problem in inmate–staff relations.

Of special interest and concern to the sociologist is the problem of institutionalization of the elderly. In 1978 nearly one-half of the people in American custodial institutions, prisons, hospitals, and nursing homes were over 65 years of age. Recent exposés of Medicare and Medicaid frauds, and of exploitation and patient abuse in old age homes, have created a special interest in issues dealing with the institutionalized treatment of the aged, patient–staff relationships, and health care delivery systems to the aged.

Despite increased sensitivity to the problem of the aged, however, the aging criminal offender has become an almost forgotten member of the prison population. A significant proportion of the inmate population of many correctional institutions is elderly or beyond middle age. Some, committed as adults for long terms, have simply grown old in prison. Others have long histories of crime and sequential careers of institutional commitment. Yet others committed offenses relatively late in life and were sentenced to a correctional institution as an older person. In all instances, the aging offender represents a special population of inmates in terms of criminal pattern, problems of individual adjustment to institutional life, problems of family relationships, medical care, rehabilitation, and the unique role attendant to the status of older persons and to the position in the prison social structure enjoyed by aging offenders.

In the final selection, "Growing Old in Prison," some of the problems facing the older offender are highlighted. The inmate in this interview is well beyond middle age and is a repeat offender who has served time before. He speaks poignantly of missed opportunities and chances not taken, of the unique role of an older person in a predominantly youthful offender population, and finally of the possibility of dying in prison.

References

Feldman, Saul D.
    1978 *Deciphering Deviance*. Boston: Little, Brown and Company.
Goode, Erich
    1978 *Deviant Behavior*. Englewood Cliffs, N.J.: Prentice-Hall, Inc.
Leger, Robert G. and John R. Stratton
    1977 *The Sociology of Corrections*. New York: John Wiley and Sons.
Rubington, Earl and Martin S. Weinberg
    1973 *Deviance: The Interactive Perspective*. New York: Macmillan.

DAVENPORT STATE INFIRMARY *Robert Straus*

Wardhill State Hospital
March 9, 1958

Dear Bob:

Went to the Penguin Club (plastered) & was rejected. Mr. Carrey & one of his delegates (an angel who realizes his membership entitles him to a "pie card") suggested that I sleep on the river-bank for a night & then come back. They were poorly informed fools who did not realize that sleeping on the river bank was "old hat" to me. Having no desire to avail myself to the horrors of the jail which I conclude in passing compares favorably with the Newgate Prison of England of the 1600's, with the exception of some culprits' heads, fixed by pikes, on the surrounding walls.

And so Northward. State Police arrested me during the night & lodged me at their barracks; I was probably endangering traffic. Arrived in Anchorport, & stopped at the "Alanon Club." Met a guy that afternoon, there, who for two hours, told me all about Alcoholism. (Talk about carrying coal to Newcastle.) He told me the club would be open again at 7 that night. I went back at seven & hung around until eight & the club did not open.

I went out & got five pints of wine, to console myself, & slept in the YMCA that night (without pain).

The next morning, without money to continue drinking, & unwilling to avail myself to the tender mercies of these "help organizations," or to stomach the phoneys who always wangle their way in the best of organizations, I went to the police station, & told them that I was suffering withdrawal symptoms, & that I had experienced D.T.'s before. I expected that they would sentence me to a term in jail, until I was well, & then release me at some early date, to continue my aimless existence.

I have been out here since Friday. In view of what has gone before, this peck of pills & interminable hypodermic injections is rather pointless. This is one of those incongruous kinds of existence where they afford a television & then take away your eye glasses. For the past three days, I have been surrounded by a hundred periodicals, & unable to find an hour's surcease by reading. Many a cup of forbidden wine must be drunk to drown out the memory of my trust in mankind.

Frank

On March 11, 1958, I received from the superintendent of Wardhill State Hospital a form notice that "your friend, Frank Moore" was admitted on March 7 and a request to complete a questionnaire about him. I replied with a long letter but Frank's stay at Wardhill was too brief for any meaningful efforts to "treat" him.

Davenport State Infirmary
May 16, 1958

Dear Bob:

Too many things happen to a drunkard, for him to get everything down on paper. . . . It seems, that for anyone to stay at Wardhill for more than thirty days, called for a legal hocus pocus, which is called being "probated." They wanted me to stay, but it appeared that no doctors would sign the necessary papers, unless I was willing to stay. It was a fine place, with the "new look" psychiatry, and backed by proper financial appropriations.

Upon discharge, it was arranged for me to be admitted to the City Infirmary in Anchorport. The word for "infirmary" in some cities, is a euphemism for "alms house" or "poor house." I stayed there for three days—a bowl of oat meal for breakfast, & a bologna sandwich for supper. No one will believe me, but speaking with the authoritative voice of experience, jails & county penitentiaries feed their criminals better than their poor. It was quite a "come down" from the "bug-house."

Two days later, I was arrested on the highway, taken before some small town judge & sentenced to ten days. This jail in Anchorport county is brand new, modern plant, segregation of types, wonderful food,

& the guards & overseers are anxious to build up a fine reputation for their jail. Smoking tobacco was issued, television every night, fine hygienic facilities, etc. It seems the jail is twice as big as needs be. More prisoners—more jobs for guards. Less prisoners—less jobs for guards. I envision that this particular calaboose, in years to come, & for years to come, will become a beloved sanctuary for the bottle gang.

In lieu of any plans at all, I hitch-hiked back to Calvinville in one day, arriving home about 10 P.M. Oh brother, & I had been worrying about this lonely old woman. She let me know that with her old age pension, she was very happy, & much concerned that I ruin the tranquility of her life. And so, out on the highway that night & up north. Hitch-hiked the next day. Caught a freight train for Harborville. The railroad yard employees are most gracious, telling me the time the freight comes thru, the best place to catch it, etc. Arrived in Harborville that night. Went to the Salvation Army for supper. I was told that I could stay that night, & shocked the clerk by saying that I preferred to sleep in the police station. He couldn't understand it. I didn't think he would grasp it if I went into a detailed exposition of conditioned reflexes & cited Pavlov's dogs.

Hitch-hiked the next day into Clarksville & up to Bancock. I had the entry fee to a saloon & ran into a heavy machinery operator who was on a spree. He wanted someone to listen to him, & so I listened (& had plenty to drink). The board bench, in the Bancock city jail, felt like a feather bed that night. Next morning, I spent my last 14 cents for a can of beans. Pushed a door-bell & asked the lady of that house to open them for me. Stepped into a side street & was eating the beans with a stick, under a tree, & a damn small dog raised such a barking, that all the women came out to see what he was barking at.

I have often wondered if these house pets, somehow, cultivate the outlook & mores of their owners. It was not a question of food or a place to sleep, but my shoe soles had worn thru to the skin, so the next day, I hitch-hiked down here to Davenport. It has been about seven years since I was here. There is a physical examination on admittance. The examining doctor noted a lipoma, about as big as my fist on my left upper arm. He asked me if I didn't want it cut out, & told me that there was no need to be afraid because there was an excellent surgeon in attendance. Now you know a lipoma is only a fatty tumor & it had caused me no trouble, & I am sure the only concern was to keep the surgeon in practice & to improve his technique. I never would have had it cut out except for that statement that "I need not be afraid."

If I stick my hand in fire, it will burn. If I tie a rock around my neck & jump in the river, I will drown, but I don't know that I am afraid of anything.

So I told them to hack away; & so a general anesthetic & ten stitches in my arm. I came out of the hospital today. About Monday, I will be assigned a job, & the endeavor will be, to get as much work out of me as possible. Tobacco is issued here *but* no cigarette papers, stamps, etc. Will be glad to hear from you.

Frank

Davenport State Infirmary
July 5, 1958

Dear Bob:

Meant to answer your letter sooner, but a kind of desuetude or enervation sets in after being in these kind of places for a short while. No man thru the effects of his lone mind could cause such a mass state of demoralization. Men leave here every day, without a plan of where they are going or what they are going to do. One thing, of which they are certain, is that no one here gives a damn, or is in any way concerned. Older buildings fall into disrepair, are abandoned, a new building goes up, the old fittings & equipment are left as they are, & a newer generation of indigents & incompetence are being cared for (corn meal mush for breakfast, bath once a week, & a bed to sleep in). A hundred years ago, this place was officially an alms house, the employees were drawn from the neighboring small towns, which had no industries. The older generation of employees has been buried, their sons, daughters, granddaughters have replaced them & notwithstanding that a forty-hour week has been in effect for a long while, more equitable pay, & in other places a general notion that the community at large has a definite duty toward its incompetents & misfits. I would swear on a stack of bibles a mile high, that patient-employees attitudes have not changed since 1840.

There are about 500 men here who would be employable, were they not alcoholic. Upon them devolves the assignment of all porter work, janitorial duties, kitchen help, laborers, et al. Under no consideration, do the paid employees ever perform these duties. Men have been appointed supervisors of attendants here, who have never offered their arm to an infirm person or picked one up. It is generally conceded, hoped for, that alcoholics will perform the arduous work, that they will always be available & are to be fully exploited. It seems quite logical to me, that these paid employees should feel quite enamored toward the urban alcoholic who finds his way here, but such is not the case, by word or action. It may be that thru ability, willingness, character, or temperament a patient might appear deserving of some recompense or altered attitude by the employee. Not so.

A couple of the attendants are appointed special police & cruise around in state owned vehicles on the back roads, consuming untold amounts of gasoline endeavoring to apprehend some patient with a fifty-cent bottle of wine. In the meantime no employee has been apprehended for larceny (ever), & I assure you they would count it a lost day, if they didn't bring a package to their car at quitting time. This is no picayune affair & must run into the thousands over the course of a year. I repeat that these acts are not of a group of individuals, but rather an accepted belief that anyone who works for a city, county or state institution is licensed to outfit their home with linen, foodstuffs, or anything that is portable.

Your interest while I was at Wardhill reflected greatly toward my benefit.

Sincerely,
Frank

Davenport State Infirmary
November 30, 1958

Dear Bob:

At my last writing, I told of impending changes at this institution & the first of the year will see a new dynasty & regime. This changeover is almost comparable to Darwin's fish which swam out to the shores of a beach & developed a lung, as it seems to me, it took damned near as long.

It is a sobering thought to walk in the paupers' graveyard here & to identify yourself with them. The separate grave system is used here, that is, side by side, with iron markers (numbers). When I was at Heaven Hill I saw the Potter's field there. I don't think it is anything like people generally conceive such things. There is an excavation made about the size of a factory cellar, & the wooden boxes are piled directly upon each other in a tier. So much for necrology.

The administration of this place in the past, would interest most any person that would pay 15 cents to see a two-headed calf. Up until the present time, the institution has been under a board of trustees, a shadowy form behind the scenes, whose presence one never sees, but which manifests itself in many patterns. There are 900 employees here whose sum output is equivalent to about 100 employees. If you see a man standing in one place raking leaves, in the same spot, there is only one answer: "He knows somebody."

Whether this policy will continue under the new regime is a matter of lively conjecture among the patients who are the least concerned about the change. It appears to be the "do nothing" & "pilfering" employee who is most worried. A word would not be amiss regarding the high professional type attracted to our institution. Two of the doctors were dismissed from probationary employment here this past summer because of an inability to pass state board examinations. Just before my return here in April, two doctors left under a shadow; their wives were apprehended on a shoplifting excursion in the nearest city & underwent the concomitant newspaper publicity (notoriety?).

It is most exasperating to us of the Cassius type, who have that lean & hungry look, to have, constantly, paraded before us the biggest assembly of middle aged ladies, who have long since passed a state of "en bon point" & fashionably stout, to a state of being frankly fat, & to realize that they are stealing the food, the money for which was appropriated for you, & for which you endure the opprobrium of a bum. Yesterday, it was supposed to be meat loaf for dinner. There was 20% meat and 80% bread in the meat loaf. There would be no need to inquire what happened to the meat if you could view the buxom lassies behind the serving counter. At one time, I viewed a fat woman as gross or unesthetic, & now I am getting so I frankly hate their fat guts.

There is an idea that I would like to express, a kind of hard-earned truth which I would never have reached under any circumstance except the circumstance in which I find myself.

What is the connotation of the word "bum"? It is *not* supposed that, in general, a successful or affluent criminal is called a "bum." I submit that the term is reserved for those who are strikingly unsuccessful in the acquisition of material goods. I believe a general enquiry will bear me out. For a moment consider the other fields of endeavor, the development of a moral capacity & the application & development of the mind. The first endeavor requires only an unwillingness to compromise with the palpably false, & the second is open to all, who need neither a natural talent or inordinate capacity; i.e. a knowledge of the arts & sciences is open to all, whatever their station in life. How great the progress & degree of knowledge depends altogether upon the application of the individual to a particular field. I suppose you to admit all this.

Now what do I find in general? Pursuing in an altogether *not* intent fashion, the sociology (practical) of my times, the two sciences of mathematics & physics, do I come in contact with people who have a sense of social responsibility, or the slightest glimmer of the sciences, outside of which, I call a "small cross section" knowledge? Of course I don't. The clergy have adopted expediency, & people of intellectual capacity have settled for "security." All of which has led me to a suspicion that the variety of "bums" is infinite, viz a man might be an intellectual bum, an esthetic bum, a moral bum, etc. each man making the choice of genus to which he aspires. Thus, a man who has, so far, avoided a drunkard's court, can not disclaim the title on all other counts. . . . The bright beam which bends down to the muddy bottom where lurks this social carp (myself), consists of the fact that I have been able to apprehend to some extent, that he who chooses one thing above all others, must naturally forego the others, & still half the world is belly-aching because they do not have the possessions of others. If I have escaped this human bondage, to that extent, it may have been worthwhile being an inebriate. I hope I have not made my case so meritorious, as to cause you to go out and get "plastered."

Sincerely—
Frank

1959

January–July	*Davenport State Infirmary; brief visit to Calvinville*
July–August	*Westville County Jail and House of Correction*
August–October	*Stonycreek Correctional Institution*
November–December	*Westville County Jail*

Several of Frank's letters for 1959 dealt with a theme he had often touched on before—the exploitation of the alcoholic by those who pretend to help him. He denounced not only the lack of real efforts to effect rehabilitation for himself and others, but the multitude of ways in which others have actually profited from the maintenance of inefficient programs for the alcoholic, and the perpetuation of the revolving door.

Davenport State Infirmary
April 25, 1959

Dear Bob:

During the past three months, I have made an honest effort to assay the efforts of this institution toward the treatment of alcoholism, & what I "wind up" with is unpleasant. The usual reply to criticism is "What would you do?" So far, the only thing I have to offer is that a policy of honesty should be extended to the problem. In the first place, one does not place the intercontinental missile program into the hands of high school boys who have learned Galileo's law of acceleration for falling bodies. Along with this information, we should insist on a thorough instruction in Stokes Law showing that if raindrops *did* follow Galileo's law, we would likely be killed the first time we were caught in a rainstorm, & again, what would be the purpose of a parachute? This is not an isolated instance, but the general character of "physical laws" which science offers for man's guidance, that is, half-truths & generalizations. If this is true in regard to material things, how much more so when dealing with the complex human being? In so far as I am concerned, the glimpse of these half-truths, appears to have led so far, to a group of "know-it-alls" who have achieved a perfect technique for committing error, & the more the technique is practiced, the more adept they become. One might study for a lifetime the economic or the physiological aspects of alcoholism, & in the end, have a thorough understanding of these factors. On the other hand, suppose one turns to a moral study. I suppose ninety-nine men out of a hundred know (?) the difference between virtue & sinfulness, & the less experienced & less knowledgeable are always the most certain. These opinions are not abstract, but are the most powerful forces which will influence the decision of these judges, police, doctors, social workers, et al. Believe me, when I say the average man believes that his fellow traveler is either bad or good, & that he will reject any suggestion of the possibility of the duality of man's nature. These are men of whom he can conceive no sin (ask the average church communicant of his pastor) & men of whom he can conceive no virtue (ask the policeman on the corner of the drunkard).

I can not, in consideration of the narrow periphery in which I have lived, credit myself with being particularly discerning. I do not know what virtue is, but I recognize goodness when I see it, & I think other men are so fixed. I am too damned rational to be mystic or religious & so it goes for most of men. There is too much reverence in this world for things which are not deserving of reverence & so I suppose I am irreverent, & if there *is* a dividing line between me & the nonalcoholic, that must be it. And still again, this irreverence may be just a by-product engendered by the disregard of truth, which I see on every side. Imagine, as I am sure you can, the neophytes who will attend the summer course at New Haven.[1] Every damned mother's son who goes there, is *already* sure that he knows an alcoholic when he meets him. Tell him, if you will, along with Will James, "the sway of alcoholism over mankind is unquestionably due to its power to stimulate the mys-

---

[1] *Yale (now Rutgers) School of Alcohol Studies.*

tical faculties of human nature, usually crushed to earth by the cold facts & dry criticism of the sober hour." In most cases, the listener will *rightly not* have attributed to the person to whom he thought was "alcoholic," the possession of "mystical faculties." And rightly so, because he did not know what an alcoholic was in the first place.

You wrote at one time that the prospect of living without the possibility of getting drunk would be frightening to an alcoholic. That is so. Would not the summer forum be better instructed if they were informed that their efforts (if directed toward true alcoholics) will be an endeavor to take away a man's escape from misery & his sole means of flight into the rapturous air of illusion. For the rest, who they have *thought* were alcoholics, they can go on treating like school boys who were over greedy with candy (as they have always treated all cases). The chances are that one out of a hundred of the students will look far enough & deep enough to learn anything of the subject. Ask them if you will, what they have to offer in place of alcohol. Would one exchange the inhabitation of fields of consciousness—wide, glorious, & delightful—for a Salvation Army dormitory? Like Aladdin, who rubs the magic lamp, the alcoholic has discovered a magic genie who lifts him up to the seventh heaven, & transports him over stellar spaces (sans gear of our scientific age), & who builds for him in half an hour's time, palaces of porphyry & jasper, fills his hands with gold, & breathes into his soul the sense & conviction of power. From melancholy, which must be aroused by sober reflection of a sensitive man, alcohol will lift to dazzling heights of happiness (like the magic carpet), like the magic ivory tube it will reveal all that he desires to see, & like the enchanted apple heals him of all illnesses.

Sincerely,
Frank

Davenport State Infirmary
June 7, 1959

Dear Bob:

The scientific writers which I have come in contact with in the field of sociology & in the field of study of alcoholism, appear to strive for a detachedness & objectivity employing such terms as "archetype" & "interaction." The drunkard in attempting to read his way out of his dilemma, feels the way a drowning person would feel if someone were to throw him a copy of Archimedes "Principle of Floating Bodies."

Despite the fact that, according to Robert Louis Stevenson, science writes with the "cold finger of a starfish," it has had, for me, its uproariously comical moments. Take for instance, the urging that "the full potentiality of alcoholics should be realized." This is mentioned in one of the scientific papers you sent me. Listen, while this old man tells you about the "birds & bees." For a hundred years & more, this place has operated as a dumping ground for indigent, crippled, & wholly incapacitated patients from other public & private hospitals. During that same time, the institution has been a haven for the destitute unemployable alcoholic. Admission has been gained on a voluntary basis. Discharge is gained in the same manner. The drunk is admitted because he will be useful (to others), & is discharged because there are so many coming in, who in turn will become useful (not to themselves of course). Anyone who writes of the "potentialities of the alcoholic," should apprehend that this is sure as hell one place where his potentialities *are* realized. Thus, upon arrival, the new drunkard is given a copy of "rules & regulations" of Davenport; paragraph one states that he will be given employment, & paragraph two, states what will happen if he does not conform to regulation one. The drunk is left in no doubt as to what is the purpose of admission. On the bulletin board at the present time, there is a notice to the effect that if anyone leaves without permission, he will be given a "Class A" work card on readmission. (Class A work card involves the hardest labor.) As a matter of fifty-five years experience, I have long entertained the opinion that an exaggerated fixation on work is usually entertained by lazy persons, & only lazy people would regard work as punishment. But there we have it, above our beloved superintendent's signature. It is with some feeling of incongruity that I view the paid employees taking a half-hour coffee-break in the forenoon while one-armed & one-legged patients keep steadily at work, without pay & sans coffee break, & sans coffee. Most of the fat buttressed female paid employees have jobs sitting down, while an *80 yr old female patient stands* all day removing hot sheets from a mangle. I suppose in time, I will lose all true perspective, as most of these people drawing salaries apparently have. Friday afternoon is a slack time in the pressing department, & it is with a feeling of uneasiness, that one sees twenty paid employees spending the afternoon drinking tea & "setting" their hair while all this time unpaid patients are steadily at work. You sometimes get the idea that God is not in Heaven & all is not well below. I sometimes blame this on my sobriety & the awakening of critical faculties. You never would admit that sobriety has its disadvantages, would you? I believe it worth passing comment that convicted felons in our Commonwealth are paid 30¢ a day for their labors, while an alcoholic could go out of here after years of work in a bare-reared condition.

Dear Bob, all the abovementioned is preparatory to a sixty-four dollar question. As you and I know, efforts have been made by science, by the clergy, by the judiciary, to awaken public consciousness of the fact that something should be done for the alcoholic. Do you think it would be for the best interests of the people who administer an institution like this "to do something about alcoholism"? Would it not be like shooting a horse, & pulling the wagon yourself? If you can honestly answer this dual question, then you will have a proper gauge of their so-called "programs."

Sincerely,
Frank

QUESTIONS FOR DISCUSSION

1. What is Frank's evaluation of the institution he is in? How valid are his criticisms? How would you evaluate your university or college using Frank's criteria?

2. How would you rate Frank's intelligence compared to the stereotypic view of the institutionalized? Explain your answer fully.

3. Examine the statement, "If I have escaped this human bondage to that extent, it may have been worthwhile being an inebriate." What conclusions does he draw about people in general?

4. Frank thinks the alcoholic has been exploited by those who pretend to help him. Do you agree or disagree, and why? Does our society successfully deal with the alcoholic? Why or why not?

5. What sociological theory would best explain why a person becomes an alcoholic? What is it that makes it so difficult for people to "kick" alcoholism?

ON ENTERING A MENTAL HOSPITAL Robert E. Dahl

This Monday afternoon wore on . . . Marilyn had told me she'd be up to visit me at three-thirty. When four o'clock came I was worried. What had happened? She was never late for an appointment. During my stay in the receiving hospital, she hadn't missed one chance for a visit and always she'd been on time. Always she'd been early, waiting at the big entrance door, waiting for it to open, anxious not to miss a moment of our visit. But now she was a half-hour late. Something must have happened to her. . . . I thought of the horror she'd been through the last six months. And now this latest episode with me in a hospital again. How she must be worried about me. But where was she?

One thing I knew: If Marilyn could have been here by now, she would have been here. Something had happened to her. What was wrong with Marilyn that would keep her from visiting me at the time she'd promised? Something terrible must have happened to keep her away. What had happened to Marilyn?

I asked Sister Thérèse if I could use the phone. "I want to find out where my wife is. She should be here by now. I'm worried about her."

"There's a phone at the end of the hall," said Sister Thérèse.

I called home. There was no answer. I called the newspaper where she worked. They told me she'd taken the afternoon off. I called home again. There was no answer. I called the Douglases. Polly answered.

"Hello, Bob. How are you? How's the hospital treating you?"

"Polly, Marilyn was supposed to be up here to visit me forty-five minutes ago. Polly! Do you know where Marilyn is?"

"No, Bob, I don't. She hasn't been here. I know you must be upset, but she'll be along. Don't worry now."

"Polly, if she calls you, tell her to get on down here. I'm afraid something may have hap-

pened to her, Polly. Call me if she gets in touch with you."

Out of the corner of my eye, I caught a glimpse of two policemen emerging from an elevator at the other end of the hall. . . .

Now what would two uniformed policemen, with guns in their holsters, be doing up here in this hospital? Suddenly I knew.

"Polly, listen to this: A couple of cops just came on the floor and I think they've come to take me away. There's a sister up here in charge who's been on me about making too much noise and disturbing the other patients. I think she's called the police."

"Oh, Bob, no!"

"Polly, these two policemen, I've got a hunch they're up here for me. You've got to get hold of Marilyn and tell her what's going on. Polly, will you promise?"

"Yes, Bob, of course."

"Thank you."

"Good-by, Bob. I'll try to find Marilyn." Her voice came softly over the phone, hesitant: "Bob, please take care of yourself."

The two policemen—I'd caught them looking around and then looking toward me sitting at the phone at the far end of the hall from them. They turned and walked toward the center of the hall, toward Sister Thérèse's desk.

Watching them, into my mind there came a rememberance of my childhood and the thought: *"They" at last have come for you.* . . .

When I was just four years old I would play in my sand pile by myself and I would enact a fantasy with moldings of wet sand. I would build castles with tunneled entrances, and in these great castles I imagined there lived giants named "Human Beans." Inside the dark entrances of the castles I would imagine the giants were hiding, waiting for me, waiting to *get* me. These giant monsters became simply *They. They* were always waiting for me, waiting to *get* me. . . .

When I was little, I often had a dream—a nightmare. It consisted entirely of a spinning circle. When the dream began, when I would first see wide-eyed under my lids closed in sleep the circle, I would think: "Well, here is that circle again. Please don't let it grow this time. Please."

And I would tell the circle to go away and I would tell it to behave if it did have to stay. I would tell it that it just had to not start getting big. And then something would promise me, not a person, not a voice, but something, that this time the circle would grow no bigger—that it would stay, this time, just a harmless little spinning circle. Then, in my sleep, I would relax, and as I relaxed, the circle, as if it were taking advantage of my relaxation, would begin to spin faster and faster and grow bigger and bigger, increasing in size as it spun until at last there was no room for me and it—the circle was surrounding me, suffocating me, crowding me out of existence into oblivion. And then I would awake, certain in the brief moment between sleep and awakening, that if the circle had kept on spinning for just one more instant, I would have been swallowed up inside it and erased into a nothingness. And I would awake in my bed sweaty and filled with fright. . . .

As I moved away from the phone and toward the two policemen and Sister Thérèse, it was just as if I were in the grip of that child's nightmare of the circle. The circle was about to envelop me—*they* were about to get me. . . . And there was nothing I could do about it.

I was trapped.

I walked up to one of the policemen. They were sheriff's deputies.

I smiled at them. "You've come for me?"

"Yes," one of them said.

"I thought so."

"You'll come with us quietly?"

"What if I don't?"

"You wouldn't want to do anything you'll be sorry for later. We have to take you with us, but we're sure you'll come along now without causing any trouble."

"You're taking me to River's Edge?"

"Yes."

"I'm not going to fight you—I'll go along. But couldn't it wait for just a bit? I'm trying to reach my wife over the phone. I can't get hold of her this minute but it shouldn't take long."

"No. We have our orders and we have to be going now. We can't wait. We're sorry, but we have to be moving along."

They seemed nice enough. In different circumstances I would have liked to know them better. They were just carrying out their orders and neither of them seemed to be taking any joy in their duty. They were courteous and sympathetic. If they had been out of uniform, without the guns at their sides, I doubt if I'd have been afraid of them at all.

"I'll walk along with you," I said. "I won't cause you any trouble. But whoever is responsible for this—" I stared hard at Sister Thérèse—"I'm afraid she'll have trouble sleeping nights.

"God have mercy on you, Sister," I said. Sister Thérèse's mouth quivered a little, and she turned her head from me.

On the way to River's Edge in the sheriff's car, I talked to the two deputies. "Do I seem insane to you two?"

"No," one answered, "you seem all right to me."

"The thing that worries me is my wife. I can't figure out where she can be. I'm worried about how all this will hit her. She's had enough trouble lately."

"Your wife knows what's happened. I think she's the one who signed you in."

"You must be wrong," I said. "Marilyn wouldn't have done anything like that without at least talking to me about it first. She won't do anything that's important to the two of us without talking it over with me.

"It was that sister up there, the one in charge of the floor. She didn't understand some of the things I said." . . .

The sheriff's car wound its way through the grounds of the state hospital and up to the entrance. They escorted me inside.

"Good-by to you two and good luck," I said.

"Good-by. Good luck to you, fellow. . . ."

And now truly, my fears and nightmares were about to materialize. At last I was at River's Edge.

I was ushered into a great hall. Its walls were white plaster, its floor was concrete. The hall was so long the people at the other end were small dim figures in the gloomy light which filtered through its barred windows.

An attendant showed me into one of the many little rooms which led from the hall. "You'll sleep here tonight," he said. He ripped the bedding from the iron bed which was to be mine, felt the runner pad on top of the mattress, and grinned at me. "I'll have to get you a fresh pad. The old man who was in this bed until a little while ago wet it."

"I don't need any pad," I said.

"I'll have to get one anyway. All the beds on this ward have pads in 'em. While I'm gone, you get out of your clothes."

"Why?"

"We have to mark your clothes. I'll bring you something to put on."

In a moment he was back with fresh sheeting, another rubber pad. He also carried a pair of white overalls. He threw them toward me.

"Put these on for now. And here's a pair of slippers."

Over my naked body I drew on the overalls. They were too small. The pants legs were above my ankles and when I pulled at the strap over my shoulder to fasten the overalls, the legs cut into my crotch.

Only one of the straps on the overalls had a button for fastening. The button was missing from the other. I tried pushing this strap through the buttonhole and tying it. But the strap wouldn't stay tied. When I straightened, the strain broke the buttonhole. The slippers were too big. I had to walk in a shuffle to keep them on my feet.

I walked down the hall. Midway down it, off to one side, there was a little room filled with charts and file cabinets and medical supplies. A young, white-coated man, another attendant, sat at the desk in the room, making out some papers.

"Pardon me," I said, "but can't you give me something to wear that'd fit me half decent?"

He looked up at me. "Let's see. You just came in?"

"Yes."

"Well, you'll just have to do the best you can with what you've got on until we open the storeroom in the morning. You can try to find something better then. Right now, we're too

busy to look around in there trying to get you a perfect fit. . . . While you're here, I've got some questions to ask you."

He looked at me, pen poised over a form. "Your name?"

"Please help me, God! You drag me in here and you don't even know my name. Do you usually haul people into this place without even knowing who they are?"

The attendant winced. "Please answer these questions. They're just routine."

I howled with bitter laughter. "You haul people into this nuthouse and you don't even know who you've got when you net them! Are you an attendant here or are you a patient? You look, my friend, a little wild-eyed to me. What did you do? Attack an attendant and take his coat? Where, friend, is your identification?"

The attendant scowled. "If you're trying to be funny, it won't get you very far. What have we here? A comedian? Are you going to answer these questions or not? If not, we'll ask them later at your leisure—and it looks to me as if you're going to have plenty of that for a long time."

Suddenly I was conscious of a surge of fear, and I knew I should stop my attempts at wit. But I couldn't—not all at once. "It's strange you'd ask me if I'm a comedian. I am! I'm a clown! The clown of clowns. Don't you recognize me? My name is Bob."

"Bob what?"

"Why, Bob Hope, of course. Sometimes they say to me: 'You're Hopeless Bob!' But that's only a pun on my real name, Bob Hope."

The attendant wrote something on the form and said, "I'm going to give you one more chance. Maybe the reason we ask you your name is not because we don't know it, but maybe we want to find out if you do."

"It really is Bob Hope. I have another name, too, though, an assumed name—Bob Dahl. But there really is nobody named Bob Dahl. Bob Dahl is nobody, no heart, no mind."

"How tall are you?"

"Six feet."

"Weight?"

"One eighty-five."

. . . And so on, the attendant's pen scribbling busily the various statistical bits of information which identified me.

An older man, a doctor, came into the room. He was a heavy man of about forty. Around his waist his white shirt bulged and strained against rolls of fat underneath. His shirtsleeves were rolled. He came into the room walking swiftly.

"Boy! What a day!" he said to the attendant.

"Dr. Phillips—" the attendant flicked a finger my way—"here's the new patient."

"Are you in charge here?" I asked the doctor.

"Of this ward."

"Doctor, Dr. Phillips, I'm worried about my wife. I have to reach her! She was supposed to visit me this afternoon at the other hospital and she didn't show up and I tried to locate her by phone but I couldn't. Will you let me try to call her from here? She'll want to know about all this, and besides that I'm afraid something may have happened to her."

Dr. Phillips spoke in kind tones but firmly: "I'm sorry, Mr. Dahl—your first name's Bob, isn't it?"

"Yes."

"Bob, there's no phone on this ward which connects us with the outside, and we're too busy around here to send anybody with you to the phone up front. Anyhow, it's against the rules. You won't be able to have any contact with anyone from the outside for seven days."

"But, Doctor, I've got to talk to my wife!"

"Bob, believe me, your wife is all right. I've seen her and she knows all about this."

"What do you mean?"

"She consented that you be sent here."

"She betrayed me? She did this to me behind my back? She didn't even have the courage to talk to me about it face to face! Why? Doctor, why?"

Dr. Phillips looked at his watch. "I can give you just about ten minutes. I'm sorry it can't be more than that, but there's a lot to do around here right now. Sit down."

"Doctor," I said, "there's just one thing I want to know. Why did she do this to me? And without talking to me? It wasn't necessary to sic those two policemen on me! I wasn't violent!"

"That's just routine," said Dr. Phillips.

Doctor, why am I here?

"Please, I can hear you. Not so loud." He took a pack of cigarettes out of his shirt pocket. "Like one?"

"Yes."

"Bob, I don't know all the reasons you're here. Some people, including several doctors, thought you might be sick enough to be hospitalized. Presently you're here for a week's observation. You haven't been committed yet—and you won't be before the end of that time."

"But, Doctor—I know maybe I'm sick. Maybe there's something really wrong with me. I know I'm different now from other people, but that's only because I *want* to be. If I wanted to be like other people, I could be. Maybe they think I'm sicker than I am just because I'm not like everybody else any more. In any case, there was no need to send me here! I could have had treatment under a private psychiatrist—if I am sick—and at the same time I could have held down a job. I had a job offer just last week."

"I don't know, Bob. Several people, including your wife, thought you should come here for observation. Why don't you tell me if you can think of any reason you should be here? Why do you think you're here?"

"I'll tell you why I think I'm here! But that doesn't mean I can tell you why I think I should be here. I think I'm here because my wife is insane, because my friends are insane, because certain doctors are insane!

"But first—about my wife—as far as I'm concerned I don't know her any more. Tell Marilyn we've never known each other. And tell her when I get out of here, if I ever do, I don't want to be bothered by strangers—not by strange friends and certainly not by a strange wife!

"Why am I here? I'll tell you why! Because some people have been questioning my ability to think straight these last few days and I have been questioning theirs. I suppose it was a question of who was right, them or me, and since there are more of them than me, I guess they won."

Dr. Phillips said, "Now I want you to understand this. You are very fortunate you have good friends and a good wife. They made arrangements so you could stay at St. Francis until we could make arrangements for you here. And also, there was always the chance a good physical examination at St. Francis might uncover something. But it didn't and so here you are. You are very lucky. Ordinarily, under normal procedure, you'd have had to wait in jail until we could make room for you here. Sometimes people have to stay in jail nine or ten days before they are brought here."

"But, Doctor, what did I do? Why couldn't they talk to me about it? I probably would have come here voluntarily if I'd known they felt so strongly about it."

"People, I suppose—" Dr. Phillips smiled— "just didn't understand you. Didn't you tell a sister at the hospital you might jump out a window at any moment?"

"Yes. But I didn't mean I would. I was just trying to prove a point of logic."

Dr. Phillips looked at his watch.

"Doctor, before you go, one more question. Do you think I'm insane?"

"Insanity is just a legal term," said Dr. Phillips.

"Do you think I'm mentally ill?"

"Yes," said Dr. Phillips, "I think you are sick." He smiled at me—in kindness, in sympathy, with understanding. But I shuddered at his words, even though he added, as if to take the sting from them, "And I think you should stay with us for a while. But I believe it will be just for a while, not forever."

On my way out of the room the attendant looked at me and smiled. "Why did you say your name was Bob Hope?"

"Because I really am. I'm a clown. I have to be. Or else I'd cry myself to death."

"I see," said the attendant.

Beside the doorway leading to the hall, there was a small mirror. I hesitated before it, glanced into it. It seemed to me that my eyes were opened wider than usual. . . . *If you're ever going to get out of here, you're going to have to narrow those eyes. People can see clear through you, they're so wide open. You look like a maniac all right. Narrow the eyes. There, that's better, and you're going to have to quit talking so much. Only a lunatic tells people everything he knows. . . .*

Before I went to sleep that night, I prayed. But when I finished, I still felt alone and I was conscious of fear. Yet after a while, as I lay in bed, there came to me a sense of peace.

There was no door to my room and the hall outside was only dimly lighted. In the shadows the high walls surrounding me seemed unreal. Solid as they were, they seemed unreal, impermanent, a transient vision. I thought: I'll sleep, I'll close my eyes. And when I open them again, the walls—they'll have gone away. If not tonight, some time, some night, I'll close my eyes and the walls—they'll go away.

QUESTIONS FOR DISCUSSION

1. What are some of the depersonalizing characteristics of a mental hospital? What effects would it have on a person who is admitted?

2. How much validity or reliability should be given to the lay individual who wishes to institutionalize a family member? How might their views be confirmed?

3. What coping mechanisms might come into play for an individual who is institutionalized against his or her will? Which role could you see yourself assuming?

4. Does labeling theory offer any significance to the social sciences? Why or why not?

5. Considering the means one must use to demonstrate progress in an institution for the mentally ill, what implications are there for our current diagnostic and treatment system?

REBIRTH IN A THERAPEUTIC COMMUNITY: A CASE STUDY *Lewis M. Killian and Sanford Bloomberg*

As sociologists have examined the vast complex of institutionalized means of dealing with mental illness, they have been impelled to ask, "Which is the problem—the illness or the institutions?" Even cursory examination affords a dismal picture of how a modern, scientific society copes with the problems of the mental patient. Conditions in mental hospitals are often scandalous. Success rates of psychotherapy are so low as to make therapists almost defenseless targets of countless jokes. The "Eagleton affair" offered dramatic confirmation of the persistence of the stigma of mental illness. Not surprisingly, sociologists have tended to see mental patients, along with other deviants, as victims, "more sinned against than sinning," as Howard Becker has put it (1967).

Much of the theory and the very language of the sociology of mental health implies the theme of victimology. Labeling theory focuses attention on the reactions of the social audience instead of on the intrinsic character of the behavior they observe. Analyses of the stereotyping of mental patients, of their discrediting, and of the stigma they bear suggest analogies to convicts and members of oppressed racial minorities. Goffman observes that on entry into a total institution, of which the mental hospital is a prime example, the patient, recruit, or prisoner "begins a series of abasements, degradations, humiliations, and profanations of self. His self is systematically, if often unintentionally, mortified" (1961, p. 14).

The language of many sociological discussions of psychotherapeutic processes and institutions implies that the patient is indeed a victim who is lucky to escape from treatment rather than becoming victimized further by "institutionalism" (Wing, 1962). Yet the reconstruction of the self is the goal of psychotherapy, as Goffman indicates when he says, "In the usual cycle of adult socialization one expects to find alienation and mortification followed by a new set of beliefs about the world and a new way of conceiving of selves" (p. 169). His next words suggest, however, that this is the exceptional rather than the typical outcome of inpatient therapy: "In the case of the mental-hospital patient, this rebirth does sometimes occur, taking the form of a strong belief in the psychiatric perspective . . ." (p. 169). In contrast, Gove and Fain report research in which "most patients . . . had a positive evaluation of their hospital experience and perceived their situation and their ability to handle problems as improved" (1973, p. 500).

Without debating the relative frequency of constructive resocialization versus abortive mortification, we suggest that the picture of the effects of the mental hospital will not be complete without analyses of successful "rebirths." Does the mental hospital as a total institution contribute to the rebirth as well as to the mortification of self? If so, what features of the therapeutic milieu account at least in part for such successes? What seem to be the optimal conditions for effective therapy?

The experience of a sociologist who, as a patient in a "therapeutic community," was perforce both a participant and an observer offers a view of the total institution different from that of either the staff or the nonpatient observer. The sociologist-patient was in an important respect a naive participant. Because the sociology of mental health is not one of his areas of interest, he was not acquainted with the literature, which might have prepared him for what to expect as a patient as well as structuring his observations. At the same time, he was knowl-

Lewis M. Killian and Sanford Bloomberg, "Rebirth In a Therapeutic Community: A Case Study," Psychiatry (1975): 38: 39–54. Copyright © 1975 by The William Alanson White Psychiatric Foundation, Inc. Reprinted by special permission of The William Alanson White Psychiatric Foundation, Inc.

edgeable in the field of social psychology and was experienced in the use of participant-observer techniques.

His narrative constitutes both a personal document and a sociological analysis of a total institution. The description of the psychiatric unit and the case history reflect the staff's perception of the institution and of the course of the therapy. The narrative reveals how the sociologist-patient experienced them.

DESCRIPTION OF THE PSYCHIATRIC UNIT

The East Spoke of Franklin County Public Hospital is a 27-bed, inpatient psychiatric unit for men and women in a private, nonprofit, voluntary hospital located in Greenfield, Massachusetts. The average length of stay for the nearly 600 patients admitted each year is less than 15 days. The treatment program is based on the concept of the therapeutic community (Caplan, 1964; Brenner, 1957; Jones, 1953, 1968). Individual therapy, group therapy, psychodrama, and occupational-recreational therapy operate within the context of the utilization of the total social structure of the unit. There are frequent patient-staff and patient governance meetings. Emotional distress resulting in hospitalization is seen primarily as the result of interpersonal and social experience. Knowledge of developmental phases and of intrapsychic dynamics is constantly utilized in individualizing the treatment plan and in clinical decisions. Group and interpersonal interaction, however, remain the focus in therapy. Members of a multidisciplinary mental health team share responsibility for the daily activities and management of the patient group. Decision-making by patients is restricted to certain selected areas. There is a system of clinical and supervisory conferences that results in psychiatric responsibility for the therapeutic program. This responsibility and control is always operative. Although medical-psychiatric direction for the therapeutic program is not always clearly recognizable to an observer outside of the staff-patient group, the fact of psychiatric control at the top of the hierarchy of responsibility is always apparent to all participants in the program.

The theoretical frame of reference for the therapeutic plan for each patient varies according to individual need. The basic orientation, however, is psychoanalytic. This does not exclude the utilization of behavioral modification, transactional analysis, supportive psychotherapy, marital and family therapy, and medications. Formulation of a treatment plan is most often based upon an understanding of how psychodynamic results of early childhood experiences might be interacting with current environmental stresses. There is a sense of urgency about identifying coping mechanisms utilized by the patient in the past and in the current crisis. The most important source of information in the treatment process is observation by nursing staff and individual therapists of the patient's reaction to individuals within the therapeutic community. Mechanisms of defense, patterns of interaction, and the repetition of the kind of relationships that exist outside of the hospital are the focus for patient-staff interaction. There is a constant emphasis on pointing out to the patient how he is responding to those about him and the inappropriateness of his response in terms of the reality of the efforts of the staff and patient group to respond to him in a helpful and considerate manner. There is a vigorous effort to educate the patient in awareness of the feelings and thoughts he provokes in others. In this way more effective coping mechanisms can be learned in a reasonably short period of time. The crisis-intervention orientation of the treatment program is specifically designed to help the patient (1) to become educated as to what he himself is contributing to a difficult interpersonal relationship outside the hospital, and (2) to learn more effective ways of relating as a result of experiencing from others positive responses to his changing his characteristic reaction patterns. Many patients learn within a few days of their admission what is expected of them and how to gain the approval of staff and other patients for participating in group and individual discussions. Tangible reinforcement for meeting expectations comes from a series of privileges granted to patients making progress in their therapy. When the symptoms that resulted in hospitalization subside, the staff immediately begins to hunt for ways to help the patient confront the stressing situation outside the hospital.

CASE HISTORY OF THE PATIENT

The patient, a 53-year-old married man, was admitted to the East Spoke of Franklin County Public Hospital on January 27, 1973, after being interviewed by a psychiatrist whom he had consulted for therapy. He presented symptoms of a significant depression: tearfulness, restlessness, subjective depression, thoughts of doing away with himself, insomnia, constipation, and loss of appetite. He gave a history of recurrent depressive episodes of increasing severity for the four or five years prior to admission. He had been in treatment with a psychiatrist approximately one year prior to admission, and his depression at that time partially lifted and treatment was terminated. About six weeks prior to admission, he sought out psychiatric help because of a recurrence of his depression.

The patient is a professor of sociology, well known in his field. His depressions of the last few years were associated with his feelings of urgency about completing and publishing scientific works. The pressure that he had felt in his work interfered significantly in his interpersonal relationships at home as he had become increasingly withdrawn and detached from his family. He had been taking an antidepressant (amitriptyline) prior to seeking psychiatric help in the six weeks prior to this admission, but the medication did not succeed in relieving his feelings of depression.

The patient was an only child who had been raised by his mother. His father died in the World War I influenza epidemic while the mother was pregnant with the patient. The mother never remarried. The mother was preoccupied with religion, idealized the dead father, and held forth a model of perfection that the patient strove to emulate. The patient had lifelong feelings of self-depreciation and frustration at never reaching the ideal goal. This pattern continued to the time of his admission to the hospital. Male figures in the home during the patient's childhood included a maternal uncle, who, according to the patient's account, appeared to be self-destructive concerning his efforts to achieve, "like a cow who would give a good pail of milk and then kick it over." During the patient's college years, a paternal uncle with a history of depressive episodes functioned as a surrogate father.

During this time, the patient's mother died of a coronary thrombosis. Throughout the years of recurrent mild depressive episodes, the patient worried about the possibility that he would have a coronary thrombosis.

The patient's relationship with his wife was affected by her emphasis upon physical prowess, which contrasted with his academic and intellectual orientation. The patient's three children were either married or in college and relatively independent of their parents. It was characteristic of the patient that he very rarely became angry or expressed hostile feelings. Generally he withdrew from meaningful interaction with his wife and/or became depressed.

The physical examination and routine laboratory procedures on admission were unremarkable. The patient was medicated with a combination antidepressant/tranquilizer (amitriptyline/perphenazine), three times a day, and a sedative (ethchlorvynol), 500 mg at bedtime. There was some evidence on admission of a mild upper respiratory infection. This was treated symptomatically and resolved uneventfully. On February 5, 1973, nine days after admission, the tranquilizer was discontinued, and on February 8, 1973, four days prior to discharge, the sedative was refused by the patient. On discharge on the 17th day, no medication was prescribed, and the aftercare plan included psychotherapy with the referring psychiatrist.

The personality structure of the patient was considered to be obsessive-compulsive, with striving toward achievement and perfection as a source of esteem. Compulsive routines, especially in regard to academic achievement and publication, were seen as an effort to salvage self-esteem and to construct external controls over unconscious rage and profound feelings of inadequacy resulting from emotional deprivation in early childhood. The significant depression with which the patient presented was seen as a decompensation of previously successful obsessive-compulsive defenses.

The treatment plan included interpersonal relationships with staff and patients in the therapeutic community to enhance self-esteem, to encourage ventilation of unconscious feelings of anger and inadequacy, and to reestablish previously successful compulsive defenses and striving toward achievement. In addition, an important part of the treatment plan formulated immediately after the patient's admission was consultation with the wife and the arrangement of marriage counseling for the purpose of studying the interaction between the patient and his wife and of exploring the possibility of altering that interaction so that basic emotional needs previously unmet might be more appropriately gratified in the marriage.

THE PATIENT'S NARRATIVE

It was a cold, rainy, gray Saturday afternoon but the gloom of the day could not possibly mirror the despondency which filled my whole being. There I sat, a 53-year-old man, happily married, professionally successful, financially affluent, crying like a lost child as I clenched and unclenched my fists. The psychiatrist, whom I had met only 10 minutes earlier, had just said, bluntly and finally, "I could prescribe more medicine for you, but I don't think that would help you get better. You need to get in another environment for a few days. There is a bed available this afternoon in the hospital I recommend."

Here was the verdict I had been secretly dreading for months: hospitalization. Willpower, vacations, tranquilizers, antidepressants, sporadic therapy—none had been able to stop my descent into uncontrollable depression. I had begun to dread what loomed ever larger as the only alternatives—a complete breakdown and hospitalization, or suicide.

In spite of years of study of social psychology, all my professional sophistication vanished now. "Insane" was only the worst of the frightening words that flashed through my disordered mind. "Institutionalized," "psychiatric ward," "mentally ill," "deviant," are only a few of the others that I can remember. Not only did I know that, in terms of what we sociologists call "labeling theory," my friends would hereafter perceive me differently; I was already experiencing the pain of a new self-definition. Just the day before I had gotten my driver's license renewed. One of the questions on the application had been, "Have you ever been hospitalized for mental illness?" Never again would I be able to answer "No" to this question. The realization was devastating.

At last, in anguish and desperation, I forced the words from my dry, constricted throat—"Yes, God damn it, I'll go!" Within a few minutes my wife was driving me to a hospital in a nearby town where I could become a patient in a "therapeutic community"—what I thought then was a euphemism for the psychiatric ward. I would have to learn for myself that the term was more than a sugar-coated label. Now, on the way to the hospital, I was still reacting to visions of the "snake pit." I cried out to my wife, "Oh, my God, they'll give me shock treatment." I could visualize myself in a straitjacket, or immersed in a tub of water for hydrotherapy. At the same time, I worried about the cost of the treatment, how many days of sick leave I had accumulated at my university, what would be done about my class and my administrative responsibilities, how my poor wife would get along in a lonely house—every concern that had ever crossed my mind now raced through it in a parade of problems about which I could do absolutely nothing.

I remember my admission to the hospital only in fragments. My recollection leaps in one bound from the hospital parking lot to the scene at the side of the bed which was to be mine for—I did not know how long. Weeping again, I kissed my wife goodbye and heard the appalling words, "No visitors for 72 hours," and then I was alone among strangers. I didn't care: I wanted to be alone, to lapse into the bliss of unconsciousness. But immediately the therapeutic community began to break through my shell. "Have you eaten supper, Lewis?" "We all use first names here—patients and staff; I'm Helen, I'm a nurse." "We ordered the house supper for you in case you hadn't eaten." "You'll be in this room by yourself tonight—your roommate is home on LOA [leave of absence] and will be back tomorrow."

I stumbled out of the room to the food cart and, with someone's assistance, pulled out a tray of food which already had my name on it. The food held no appeal for me; for several days nothing in life had interested me—even eating, usually one of my greatest pleasures. I forced myself to eat, and I began to meet my fellow patients who were just finishing their supper in the small dining room. At this point, though, I still thought of them as "fellow inmates," not "patients."

Some of them seemed to confirm this stereotype, reinforcing my feeling, "Is this where I belong now—among a bunch of nuts?" One was a college boy still suffering from the effects of numerous trips on LSD. He looked and acted strange and disturbed; I was a little frightened by his behavior.

Other patients didn't live up to my fevered expectations at all. They seemed so "normal" that I wondered if they really were patients. After all, in this community staff and patients dressed alike. Apparently I looked the part of a patient to them, however! My depression must have shown in my face, my speech, and my posture. One motherly-looking older woman said to me, as she helped me get some instant coffee, "We understand—we've all been there ourselves." I found a little comfort in this. She seemed to be saying to me that I could come out of my shell, "let it all hang out," if I wished, without fear as to how my companions would react. Sometime later—I'm not sure when—I found myself weeping again and felt secure enough to say to the other people in the room, "I hope it's all right here to cry if you feel like it—I can't help it." Then and later I was able to learn that it was indeed all right. This was a community where pent-up feelings were supposed to be expressed, not stored up.

That night I began to get acquainted with the staff and with the culture of the community. Somewhere along the line, a nurse took my temperature; I think she checked my blood pressure, too. We inventoried everything I had brought into the hospital. I was required to give my keys to the nurse for safekeeping because the small knife on my key chain constituted a "sharp" in the lingo of the ward, and all sharps had to be kept behind the nurses' station. I was reminded by this that I really was suspect—I did not just imagine that I was in a somewhat abnormal state. I could accept this, though, for I wasn't sure that I might not harm myself. After I went to bed that night it reassured rather than disturbed me to realize that an attendant looked in on me every hour throughout the night.

Two memorable events stick with me from that first evening. One patient, a young man with long hair, asked me if I'd like to play ping-pong. Later, a very nervous, fidgety woman to whom I had spoken earlier asked me if I would sit down and let her talk to me about her nervousness. In both cases I said and acted "Yes" against all my inclinations. I was miserable; I didn't really want to do anything but go home, but that was one thing I knew I shouldn't do. Mustering what little willpower I still had, I told myself that it would help me and, perhaps, others if I stopped nursing my misery and tried to think of other people. These brief episodes of interaction, forced as they were, did make me feel as if I were coming back to life a little.

With the aid of a sleeping pill plus my desperate need to escape from the treadmill of waking thought, I fell into a deep sleep on my strange couch. About 6:30 the next morning, though, I awakened to the familiar hell of my first encounter with the day. For weeks I had been awakening every morning with a sick, empty feeling, with a dread of the long hours before I could crawl back in bed. How could I endure yet another day when life seemed so meaningless, so tasteless, that there was nothing I looked forward to doing? This day was the worst yet: I was still the captive of my depression, and I realized where I was. What would I do with myself all day, confined within this tiny hospital ward? Would I ever get well again, or was this just the first of an endless succession of empty days? I writhed under the covers; I groaned; I crouched in a fetal position; I pounded my fists on the pillow. Finally, I turned on the light and picked up a book to try to read. Miraculously, I quickly fell asleep again, with the book fallen on my chest. I awakened again at 8 o'clock to the somewhat peremptory words of a nurse, "Wake up, Lewis; it's time for your medication." I opened my eyes to see a beautiful young woman standing at the foot of my bed. For the first time I felt a spark of interest in something; apparently I was not so insensitive to the world that I could not still enjoy girl-watching! I know it sounds sexist in this day of Women's Lib, but the procession of pretty and young nurses and nurse's aides who succeeded each other on the different shifts in the ward were sex symbols to me before I began to perceive them as competent young professionals.

My initial reaction to the patients was essentially one of resignation to the fact that for an

indefinite time my lot was cast with a heterogeneous collection of individuals, none of whom
I would have chosen as associates "on the outside." If I chose to act the snob, to resist incor-
poration into the community, the hospital would
be a terribly lonely place for me. My powers of
concentration were so limited at this point that
I could not read or watch television for more
than a few minutes. In addition, I had enough
insight to know that even if I could enjoy these
solitary, escapist activities, to do so would only
delay the date of my discharge. Hence I forced
myself to enter as vigorously as I could into the
life of the community, from listening sympa-
thetically to the problems of my fellow-sufferers
to playing ping-pong with a 14-year-old boy.

My relationship with members of the staff
posed a more complex problem, particularly at
the start. Because of my professional background, my first reaction was to identify with
them as fellow psychologists rather than with the
patients. This created difficulties, for the great
majority of the staff members were much younger than I was, some of them young enough to be
my children. So I felt at first that while we might
be fellow professionals, they were not even my
peers. Subtly but quickly it was brought home
to me by their actions that this definition of the
status system of the community was not acceptable. Patients and staff constituted two separate
castes; power lay with the staff. Within the patient caste, status differences were vague, informal, and minimal, based on such things as how
long a patient had been on the ward, what privileges he enjoyed, how well he behaved, and
what progress he seemed to have made toward
the goal of discharge. The hierarchy within the
staff was explicit and formal, manifest in some
instances by name tags with titles on them. At
the bottom of the hierarchy were the nurse's
aides, male as well as female. Above them were
the nurses, then the therapists, and at the apex
of the power structure, "Doctor B," the psychiatrist to whom all requests and recommenda-
tions went for final decision. While he was seen
infrequently, reminders of his power were ever-
present. A frequently asked question was, "Has
Dr. B been in today?," for a patient requesting
new privileges could not know for certain that
they had been granted until after his review.

The power vested in the staff was so evident

that one of my first reactions to the ward was,
"This is like a prison!" When I found that a staff
member had to accompany me on the short walk
down the corridor to the laboratory, when I saw
patients with "hospital privileges" asking the
charge nurse for a pass to go to the gift shop,
when I realized that I was forbidden to go out
the doors of the ward without permission, I was
reminded of the pervasive system of control that
I had observed in a maximum security military
prison while training there as a reserve officer.
For me, as it had been for our prisoners, "being
out of place" was an offense against the norms of
the total institution. This bit of sociological jargon, "total institution," took on a real and personal significance for me.

Obviously, my initial reaction to the manifestations of the power of the staff over the lives
of the patients was negative. It continued so for
a couple of days, although I soon learned to accept this power gracefully. On my first morning
on the ward, Sunday, I overheard a conversation
between another patient and a nurse as to
whether my long-haired ping-pong opponent
would be allowed to go to the chapel. Apparently
his request to leave the ward for this purpose
had been approved previously, but now he could
not get a pass. When the other patient pressed
the nurse for the reason, she replied "He knows
why he can't go." My instant reaction was, "My
God, are we to be dealt with like naughty children?" I carefully read the rules of the ward,
posted on the wall and discussed in a handbook
for patients. Insecure, somewhat lost in this
strange milieu, I reacted like a child. If I were
the least bit uncertain as to whether it was all
right for me to do something, I would go to the
nurses' station and ask for permission or approval from one of the young women there, as if she
were my mother. I think I was beginning to relive the "good little boy" pattern that had characterized most of my childhood, when I lived in
dread of my mother's disapproval.

My surrender to this new source of authority
was well illustrated on Monday, when I received
a mild but firm reproof for smoking my pipe so
much. I did smoke it too much; at home, it an-
noyed my wife terribly. But when I was depressed and insensitive to everything else, my
pipe was very important to me. The resistance
of the bit to my clenched teeth and the bite of

the smoke on my tongue seemed to be my only sharp contact with the world around me. So, as soon as I finished breakfast, my pipe went into my mouth and stayed there until it was almost time for OT—occupational therapy. Just before my first visit to the workshop, the nurse approached me and said rather sharply, "Lewis, you can't smoke your pipe in OT. You'll have to put it down. I'm tired of your smoking it so much anyway!" Obediently, and feeling almost ashamed, I hastened into my room to empty the pipe into an ashtray and to leave it there. From then on I tried to cut down on the amount of time I smoked it, something my wife had tried in vain to get me to do.

That "staff power" was a recurrent issue in a community in which patients had some kind of citizenship became evident in the first "morning meeting" of patients and staff which I attended. I had found Sunday, the day before, incredibly dull, broken only by a brief walk outside the hospital. In morning meeting it developed that some activities which had been planned in "Patient Government" on the previous weekend had fallen through because of a shortage of staff. Some patients who had taken part in the planning expressed their displeasure with considerable emotion. The discussion soon generalized to the question of just how much the vote of the patients meant in any matter, since the staff could veto any decision at each level of review, all the way up through Doctor B. This sort of discussion was my cup of tea! I jumped into the discussion with vigor, talking like the sociologist I am, analyzing the situation and pointing out analogies to other systems of authority. Still ignorant of what had really been involved, I brought up the issue of denial of a patient's request to go to chapel, dramatizing it as verging on an unconstitutional denial of his rights. Nothing was settled in the discussion, but a lot of feelings were ventilated, with the staff sitting patient and calmly, seeming almost to encourage the attacks on them. At this point I didn't understand what was going on; I didn't know that this was "the name of the game" in the therapeutic community.

During the next few days I gradually learned several things. One was that I would have to play the role of the patient; identification with the staff not only was not permitted but was, I came

to realize, not best for me. I could not be my own therapist. This was brought home to me by the remark I evoked from more than one staff member, "Lewis, you're intellectualizing too much!" What did they mean? I didn't understand at first. After all, I am an intellectual—"Intellectualizing" is my trade. An entrenched behavior pattern of mine was standing off and looking at myself and my problems as if I were another person. I had always felt that in this way I developed excellent insight into my problems. The trouble was that when I was depressed, I analyzed my situation as a dilemma about which I could do nothing. When I felt good, I could identify behavior patterns that I believed I could change, but I was not motivated to do so. In either case, I ended up with what I thought was a brilliant diagnosis but without the slightest sort of action. The only feeling I would express was despair.

Apparently what the staff perceived was that this sort of rational, detached self-analysis led not only to no action but to an inadequate diagnosis. By pushing aside my feelings instead of letting them pour out, I concealed, even from myself, some of the most important things that really "bugged" me—such as an unarticulated belief that some of the demands my wife made on me were really unreasonable. I had always convinced myself that my problems derived entirely from demands stemming from outside the family, from my work and civic involvements. I had persistently denied that there might be the slightest thing wrong with interpersonal relationships within my happy family. Now the staff kept pushing me to feel instead of just thinking; they sensed that the fundamental problems that caused my periodic depressions would be exposed only if I allowed my anger, my sadness, my disappointment, to pour out uninhibited by logic, theory, or the need to preserve the image of myself as a "nice guy." In one-to-one impromptu counseling sessions with various staff members I was forced to express myself in this unaccustomed, discomforting manner. Soon I found myself behaving in the same way toward other patients, expressing my displeasure when I did not like the way they acted. I began to interact with other people in this small, intense community with an honesty that I found refreshing.

In this interaction I learned that even though the patients might not have real power, there was great value in our discussing issues as if we were indeed responsible persons. "Feedback" was the label facilely attached to our discussions, but the term is too trite and inadequate to fully characterize what went on. There was feedback, of course, when we were called on to discuss and vote on each other's requests for hospital privileges, ground privileges, or LOA. I was amazed at how quickly I and other patients learned to say things to each other that might be interpreted as adverse to the recipient's petition. All adrift in the same lifeboat, at least some of us seemed to recognize that kindly deceptions were not really helpful. Each of us needed to know what kind of impression he was making on the people with whom he spent most of his waking hours. Our discussions extended far beyond such amateur clinical observations, however. They ranged from seemingly minor matters, such as the problems of housekeeping within the ward, for which we were responsible, to major issues that could become the basis of intragroup hostility.

One major matter was the request of a hallucinating patient that we not have the television on for a period of two days because it made her nervous. Some of her hallucinations included the very disturbing conviction that President Nixon exercised direct, personal control over her life and that television was one of his instruments of control. Her request was discussed with a maturity and a gentleness that I would find rare "on the outside"—in a meeting of my departmental faculty, for example. Her personal desire was not dismissed as simply selfish or crazy; her very genuine concern was treated with respect. Yet the contrary interests of the other patients were clearly and firmly stated. The request was denied, but this was not the end of it. I still have a warm feeling when I remember how our behavior changed after this discussion. No longer was the volume of the TV turned up so high that a patient sitting at the far end of the room could hear it. If it was that loud, someone would turn it down. Those of us who wanted to watch television began to gather closer to the set, so that the volume would be kept low. Moreover, at least for the remainder of that week the television was turned on very infrequently, and

then only when someone was definitely paying attention to it. The balance that was achieved between a cherished right and consideration for another person's idiosyncrasy was a model for civilized living.

On another occasion, I found myself at the center of a small storm. At Patient Government on Wednesday night, when weekend activities were planned, the majority of patients from both floors of the ward had voted for ice-skating as the activity for Friday night. On Friday morning, a patient from the other floor polled each of us individually as to whether we would like to change our plans and go to a musical comedy being given at a nearby school. I had seen the play before and did not particularly wish to see it again; furthermore, I had managed to develop a modicum of enthusiasm for ice-skating and had gotten my wife to bring me my skates. Nevertheless, I voted for the play because I got a clear signal that most of the patients on the other floor would prefer this activity. I was following my accustomed pattern of being the "nice guy," who suppressed his own feelings and did what he thought he should, to avoid guilt feelings. I guess I let some of my real feelings slip out, however, and one or two other patients from our floor expressed some disappointment also. A member of the staff assembled us in an impromptu meeting to discuss the decision. Since there seemed to be some dissatisfaction about the poll and its results, each floor was meeting to vote again. First, though, we had to examine why there seemed to be so much feeling about the situation. I didn't know that there was any strong feeling about it, but suddenly I found myself being identified as one of those who was upset by it! Reverting to my analytical, supposedly objective self, I launched into a sociological analysis of how the poll had not seemed impartial to me, since the young lady who asked for my vote made it quite clear that she hoped I would vote for the play. Then I hastened to add that I felt a little disappointed but really didn't care enough to vote against what the majority seemed to want. What was wrong with this, I asked? Plenty seemed to be wrong; I almost felt myself under attack by the two or three staff members in the meeting. Why didn't I feel that I could vote my own preference? It was obvious, I was told, that I did have some strong feelings. Was it constructive for me to try to pretend that I didn't? Would this contribute to harmony in the community? After getting involved in a heated argument, I finally "surrendered"—that's the way I felt about it—and voted against going to the play. Admittedly, part of my motivation stemmed from the fact that an LOA for Saturday and Sunday had been approved for me. I was afraid that if I persisted in voting for the play I might be considered so disturbed that I wouldn't get my pass to go home. Later I realized that this was a groundless fear; indeed, I have to admit that the meeting was not designated as group therapy aimed at me. This turned out to be its effect, however. As I thought about it, I realized that I had been giving contradictory signals, which could take some of the pleasure out of going to the play for other people. When I finally voted "No" to the play, it was the first time perhaps in years that I had asserted a personal preference in a situation of this sort without equivocation, apology, or feelings of guilt. Time and time again I had given my wife just such a begrudging, insincere "Yes" vote when she proposed an activity for us, and she had always seen through me. This had been a constant source of irritation, rendering me a poor companion in what we did and making her feel that she was "dragging me along." While I didn't get my way—we went to the play—the therapeutic community had called my hand and forced me to be honest with them. The lesson stuck with me after my discharge, and I am still practicing at this sort of honesty. Strangely, I now find it easier to say either "Yes" or "No" since I am being honest instead of just nice.

The flow of communication between patients and between them and the staff seemed to me to have a variety of valuable consequences for individual patients. One patient's articulation of the belief that he was really improving, along with quite clear evidence manifest in his behavior, could be a source of hope and encouragement to another—especially if the evidence of improvement came at a time when the second patient was somewhat discouraged. Finally, I am sure that mild, and sometimes not so mild, reproof from other patients concerning antisocial or "crazy" behavior had even greater impact on the subject than did the observations of staff members.

My conception of the power of the staff changed as I reacted to their behavior. I came to feel that it was pervasive and encompassing but essentially supportive rather than threatening. It was the nurses and nurse's aides who exerted this influence, although the therapists actually had greater power over the patients' lives. But a patient saw his therapist only two or three times a week, and then for an hour at a time. On the other hand, at least one member of the nursing staff was on the floor at all times, and usually there were three present. Some of the time they would be busy at the nurses' station, but during most of the day they blended almost unobtrusively into the life of the community. While they were hardly omniscient, very little that a patient did escaped their attention. I soon came to feel that I was, indeed, under constant observation.

The proceedings at the daily afternoon "nurses' report" sustained this impression. At these meetings the morning shift of nurses reported to the afternoon shift on each patient—with the patient sitting there listening as he was "dissected." He was free to offer comments on what the nurses said, as were other patients. What was especially illuminating, however, was hearing a nurse report, in a clinical manner, how you had appeared to feel during the day, what had upset you or pleased you, which of your activities and comments she had found significant—a wide range of behaviors; some might have seemed important to you and others you might even have forgotten.

Against this background, even the smallest supportive gesture from a staff member appeared in a new light; the therapeutic function of the interaction of staff with patients became more evident. If I sat down alone, perhaps in the kitchen with a cup of coffee, a nurse might join me and strike up a conversation as she knitted. It was all very casual, yet I soon realized I was being given an opportunity—and a challenge—to get outside the prison of my mind and share my thoughts and feelings with another human being. On two or three occasions when I was anxious about something—as when my wife was late for visiting hours—it seemed even more evident that the conversation was not really casual but was a calculated attempt by the staff member to get me over a bad time. On other occasions, it appeared that a nurse saw an opportunity to draw me out about some important area of my life. For example, immediately after one of my wife's visits, a nurse who was closer to me in age than the others steered me into a long discussion of my family life. This impromptu session was almost like psychodrama, with the nurse playing the role of my wife by interpreting how things I said might sound to her.

This almost constant observation and intervention made it very difficult for a patient to withdraw and nurse his troubles in private—something I was certainly inclined to do when I entered the community. If a patient really felt ill, was sleepy, or was acting in a disturbed fashion, he could withdraw to the privacy of his room as long as there was no scheduled activity. Occasionally a patient would, in effect, be sent to his room and temporarily removed from the community by a nurse. It was my impression, however, that if I withdrew on my own initiative, a nurse or nurse's aide would soon be on hand to ask what I was doing and how I felt. I soon reached the conclusion that it was easier to keep active and involved with other people than it was to justify withdrawing into a shell. This change of behavior pattern was, of course, just what I needed to break the cycle of my depression, and it came about without anyone's explicitly prescribing it for me.

I must confess that I became a little paranoid about what I sensed as constant observation of my behavior. There were times, no doubt, when I was more active than I really needed to be. On one occasion I was cautioned by a staff member about becoming too involved in another patient's problems. There was a period when I began to be extremely self-conscious about almost everything I said, wondering, "What will the staff make of this if I say it?" For example, when my doctor completely terminated my medication instead of merely reducing it, as I had anticipated, I remarked facetiously, "He took me off cold turkey!" Immediately I thought, "Oh, Lord, how will that remark be interpreted? Will the staff think that I'm really upset about this when actually I'm happy?" It was not until I really began to feel good and was confident that I was recovering that I felt free to joke, particularly about myself.

Perhaps to some people, subjection to such a system of social control might seem humiliating. To me, it is better described as "humbling," forcing me to come to terms with a simpler, more elementary level of existence than was habitual for me and, at the same time, causing me to revise my priority of values. Things connected with my work, heretofore central in my life, the source of both great pride and severe anxiety, were suddenly banished from my daily schedule and even from my thoughts. The experience was also regenerative; it was as if I were given a chance to go back and relive some parts of my childhood, developing new attitudes in the process.

That this was happening was brought home to me as I was finishing, with pride and satisfaction, my first OT project. I remarked to a therapist, "Hey, I'm the kid whose mother always said he couldn't drive a nail straight. I guess she was wrong!" When I started the project, I had no confidence that I could make anything that wouldn't end up in the trash. I had a similar reaction the night that square-dancing was the patients' activity. As long as I could remember, I had felt self-conscious and inhibited about dancing, and particularly about trying anything new. I had even anticipated ridicule from my wife, herself a free spirit on the dance floor. Now, in the company of my fellow patients, I felt no fear of looking silly or of being laughed at. To be able to let myself go in learning new dance steps was an exhilarating experience.

In the round of life in the hospital it was small things like this, not whether my next book would be a success, that I learned to look forward to. However, to enjoy the simple pleasures that each day might bring, to enjoy merely being alive, had to be learned. When I first entered the ward, I could not imagine how I could survive what promised to be empty, meaningless days in which I would be accomplishing nothing by my usual standards. Within this void, new sources of satisfaction began to take shape. With the four walls of the ward defining the limits of my freedom, an escorted walk to Friendly's or McDonald's became one of the day's highlights. At home in midwinter, I had resisted going out of the house, not appreciating what a privilege this freedom could be. The hospital meals were certainly not gourmet cooking, but each mealtime came to be an adventure. There was the question, "What—if anything—will be good today?" Eating was also one of the relaxed, social activities in which the patients shared. There was usually a lot of joking and much sharing of food. Even the aftermath of each meal, cleaning up the kitchen, was something to do that could give one a sense of accomplishment. Gradually I found myself structuring each day in my mind as I approached it, cherishing what were becoming familiar routines as well as small diversions.

Enjoying life, even finding it tolerable, was not easy at first. During most of the first week I was still depressed and now, in addition, I was lonely. The two very highest points of my day were my morning telephone call to my wife and her visit during evening visiting hours. Yet there was an aura of unreality about these contacts with her: she was in the world outside, and both my mental state and my physical confinement to the hospital made this world seem very far away. For a couple of days I ate my heart out trying to guess when I would be able to get back into that world, a well man again. Slowly I came to realize that this did me no good, that this small area in the hospital was my world for now and that I had to take each day as it came. Yet, as the end of that first week approached, I was determined to get home on LOA. I wasn't sure that I would be able to enjoy a visit home; I was really apprehensive about going; but I would have been desolate had I not been able to go. I protected myself, in a way, by asking that my LOA begin on Saturday morning instead of Friday night, explaining that my wife had to meet our son at the bus station on Friday night.

My visit home was not an unqualified success, although I now believe that it was very beneficial. Life still did not seem as bright to me "on the outside" as I had hoped it would. I still found it difficult to concentrate, and interacting with other people, even my loved ones, was not easy. I knew I was going back to the hospital and I felt somewhat like an outsider in my old, familiar surroundings. I felt that the hospital was really where I belonged. Perhaps in terms of my therapy this was good. It enabled me to commit myself completely to the life of the therapeutic community when I returned. By late Sunday afternoon I realized that while I desperately wanted to feel good enough to prolong my stay at home, I was really ready to go back to my "home" on the ward. It represented a new

source of security. More important, it was in the hospital that the work of getting well had to be done and I wanted to get back to work.

Nevertheless, the evening of my return was a low point. No sooner had my family left me than I wanted to be with them again. There was not much to do on the floor that night and the minutes dragged until bedtime. I was glad that I could get a sleeping pill that night to help me escape from my loneliness.

When I awakened the next morning and commenced the week's round of activities, however, things began to change. The daily schedule seemed a familiar, comforting routine. I was eager to get back to my OT project, I looked forward to the discussions that took place in the daily meetings, and I was truly glad to see my friends among both patients and staff. That Monday was the last day during which I had any doubts at all as to whether I was recovering, and rapidly. Two things which seemed very significant happened that night: my medication was stopped, and I had a fabulous time square-dancing. To make the evening perfect, I fell asleep promptly after going to bed although I had taken no medicine since early afternoon.

Whatever the reason, when I got out of bed the next morning my heart was singing. There was no feeling that I would have to force myself to do things during the day—I wanted to be alive and busy. When I had returned from my home visit, I had brought back some work with me, but with little confidence that I would be able to tackle it. Before this day was out I found myself looking for free time when I could get at it. Wonderfully, however, I didn't feel driven to work as I always had before. If someone sat down and wanted to talk, or said "Let's play ping-pong," I could lay aside my task with no feelings of guilt or irritation. The days began to fly by, for now there was always something that I *wanted* to do.

At this time I became aware of a strange but wonderful paradox. During the first week, when I had still had some resistance to being hospitalized and was counting the days until I might be discharged, I didn't feel that I was making sure and steady progress toward that end. After my somewhat disappointing weekend at home, I had come back with a different attitude; I really felt ready to stay as long as I had to. It was just after I had fully accepted the ward as a second home that I really began to feel that I no longer needed it: I was confident that I could go home and function normally any day.

This left me with mixed feelings that came as a great surprise to me. I still wanted to get home but now I saw the ward as a pleasant environment which I would leave with some sadness. Other members of the therapeutic community had become real friends. I felt tremendous gratitude to the staff for the help that I could now see they had given me; I was eager to share with them my joy at feeling alive again. The other patients were friends whom I had come to know better in a short time than I did many friends of long standing on the outside. This was a community in which the members did not hide their problems and their feelings from each other. We all knew that we wouldn't be there unless we had problems. The troubles of my fellow patients had become matters of genuine concern to me; signs of progress were sources of pleasure for me. I was no longer lonely in this community, and I knew I would miss it.

When I went home the next weekend, with the understanding that if all went well I would check out of the hospital on Monday morning, life in my old surroundings proved to have a new luster to it. My recovery was confirmed for me: I could be happy at home but I could also be happy in the hospital. This was a clear signal that it was indeed time for me to be discharged. I could see how the therapeutic community could become a warm, comforting refuge for a person who did not have the strength to manage his own life. When I awakened on my first morning at home after my discharge, I felt a momentary panic at the prospect of having to decide for myself what I would do with the day. I was frightened at the loss of the structured environment of the hospital. This feeling passed quickly as I got up and got busy, but my nostalgia for my hospital friends did not pass away so soon. For a few days I still had the feeling that the hospital was "home" and that I was a visitor to the outside world. My conversation, both with my wife and with my friends, was dominated by references to my experiences on the ward and to my friends there. I was very glad that, just a few days before my discharge, my wife had been able to participate in Family Night, a meeting of patients, their families, and a few staff members. At least she had received a little exposure to the spirit of our community; she had seen me functioning as a patient, not just as her sick husband.

In talking to friends, I found much to my surprise that I was not at all reticent about discussing my illness and my hospitalization. All the fears which had haunted me on the day I entered had vanished. As I watched people interact I would sometimes find myself thinking, "We dealt with our problems better in the therapeutic community than these people deal with theirs. Just who is crazy?"

As I eased back into the business of living in the outside world—loving, playing, working—the homesickness that I experienced at first went away. It must shock my friends, however, when one of them says, "I'm sorry to hear that you have been in the hospital," and I reply, "Thank you—but it was one of the most wonderful experiences of my life!"

DISCUSSION

The recovery of the patient from depression while in the hospital can be observed through a sequence of phases that demonstrate the successful interaction of (1) the personality structure of the patient prior to hospitalization, (2) the psychological determinants of his symptoms including early childhood experience and current interpersonal relationships, (3) the theoretical basis for the treatment program, and (4) the features of "institutionalism" characteristic of the psychiatric unit.

The potential for either "victimization" or iatrogenic regression is always an important consideration when a patient is admitted to a psychiatric hospital. Hospitalization is indicated, however, when a person's functioning in a home environment has become so impaired because of a psychiatric condition that remaining in that environment seems to make recovery impossible or causes the symptoms to be even more incapacitating. Hospitalization then becomes an opportunity to regress within a sheltered environment, with the patient protected from the stresses with which he is failing to cope. Energy expended in the unsuccessful coping can then be redirected toward self-examination and the fulfillment of basic emotional needs that are often unmet in the crisis outside the hospital. Brenner discusses such controlled regressions "in the service of the ego," which also gives the patient the opportunity to be relieved of the anxiety associated with dealing with an overwhelming environmental stress (1957).

In this case, the patient was encouraged to regress to an earlier stage of development, during which he had related to his mother with compliance to her expectations and with repression of anger in order to gain her approval and acceptance.

The important difference between the earlier relationship and the experience in the hospital was the respect and total acceptance accorded the patient from the moment of his admission. The patient's earlier pattern of interaction had slowly deteriorated in his marriage, with his increasing concern about publication and academic interests. He had become estranged from the one person still able to meet his emotional needs, his wife. This seemed to be the chief cause of the increasing loss of self-esteem and the increasing feelings of anger that resulted in his profound depression. This depression further incapacitated the patient, preventing him from achieving self-esteem and from complying with his wife's expectations, and a deteriorating cycle had been established.

His compliance with the hospital's expectations, and his meeting with staff approval and acceptance, allowed the patient to again achieve according to expectations of important persons around him, with increased self-esteem at meeting the ideal he was expected to emulate. Again, unlike his earlier childhood experience, the staff encouraged him to assert himself, make decisions, and to express his feelings, especially anger.

During the patient's leave of absence at home, he was observed to be putting aside his need to achieve in the academic area. He turned all of his effort to pleasing his wife and participating in physical activities. This met with much approval, and his basic emotional needs were for the first time in months gratified by his wife. For a day or two after his return to the hospital from his leave of absence, he found new confidence that enabled him to express anger. The patient began ventilating his annoyance at his wife's demands. This further gave him a feeling of relief

from repressed anger, and with continuing lifting of his depression, his prehospitalization personality pattern became reinstituted. An important factor in the relief of anger was the reestablished gratifying relationship with an accepting and approving wife. The gratification in this relationship removed a major source of his anger. Self-esteem was further enhanced by his wife's increased approval and acceptance. Marital counseling designed to uncover for the patient and his wife how each could contribute to mutually gratifying consideration of the other's needs further aided this mechanism. The reinstitution of routines and organization of his life with due regard for his wife's desires further served to reestablish the internal controls over uncomfortable feelings and thoughts. The patient's anger became repressed once more.

During the last days of the patient's hospitalization, the staff allowed this repression to proceed. The goal of reestablishing previously successful defenses against unconscious conflicts had been accomplished. It was left to intensive psychotherapy with the referring psychiatrist to more slowly and cautiously uncover the defenses of repression, reaction formation, intellectualization, and rationalization. These defenses were very much in evidence at the time of discharge.

This patient's need for controlled regression, for the reestablishment of sustaining compliance for approval and acceptance, for self-esteem elevating positive emotional relationships, and for encouragement of assertion and aggressiveness all meshed very well with the institutional organization and hierarchical structure of the psychiatric unit. The phases in his recovery, including his learning more successful and gratifying ways of dealing with those in this environment, fulfilled the theoretical basis of the treatment program, the crisis-intervention model.

One additional factor also contributed greatly to the successful outcome of this psychiatric treatment effort. The patient's mental health in terms of his ability to deal with psychological stress, especially powerful feelings of primarily unconscious anger, and his capacity to respond to renewed gratification of basic needs were essential factors allowing the regression in the hospital to remain limited.

It is probable that the treatment of a patient with less personality strength, one unable to control the degree of his regression, and one whose basic personality structural needs would not have been met by the structure within the psychiatric unit would not have been so successful. In fact, this psychiatric unit can document many such cases in which the structure of the unit interacted with the needs of the patients in such a way that patients have not been helped and were discharged from the hospital unimproved. In such cases, psychiatric hospitals fail to meet the needs of patients because of institutionalized procedures designed to meet, instead, the needs of the hospital personnel. Such patients may very well fall into the category of psychiatric victims.

There seems to be no doubt that the patient did experience the therapeutic community as a total institution, in which he was "degraded" by being stripped of his erstwhile status, deprived of his freedom, and subjected to the pervasive and overwhelming power of an alien group—the staff. Yet his positive response to these very features of the total institution contributed to his recovery. The way in which they contributed suggests how the aspects may be truly therapeutic instead of essentially victimizing.

What Goffman characterizes as the "mortification" of the self might, instead, be viewed as a change of identity. The patient on admission was identified both to staff and to other patients by his first name. On a visit to the ward during the post-patient phase it was found that some of the staff were still not sure of his last name. This first-name basis of interaction stripped away the status connotations of professional titles, occupational role, and age-grading. Even teen-age patients treated him as their peer.

The importance of this change of identity lay in its facilitating his full participation and acceptance in the therapeutic community. Had he attempted to cling to his "outside" identities, roles, and statuses, he would have been inhibited from entering freely into interaction with a heterogeneous group of patients, but the system removed the external barriers to full entry.

An important part of the therapy was to "regress" the patient to an earlier stage of his socialization. This, too, Goffman identifies as a "mortifying process," in which the "inmate withdraws apparent attention from everything except events immediately around his body" (p.

61). The patient, in this case, quickly came to view this situational withdrawal as protective. No longer able to cope with the pressures of the world outside the ward, he found this reduction of life to its simplest terms to be restful. At the same time, it had a restitutive effect. Not permitted to concentrate on the seemingly major issues and tasks which had made life frustrating, he was forced to focus attention on long-established behavior patterns which, prior to hospitalization, had been treated as unimportant.

It was the *total* character of the therapeutic community, a system which vests every action with significance, which made resocialization possible. The almost constant observation and management of patient behavior by the staff and the sense of total control on the part of the patient fostered constant self-examination and heightened sensitivity to the reactions of others. This does not mean that a clever inmate could not fake his reactions and fool the staff. The literature on total institutions is replete with accounts of how inmates do succeed in "conning the system." The important question is whether the inmate who is strongly motivated toward recovery or rehabilitation can "con himself." Total control is accompanied by total feedback in the therapeutic community. The signals are clear as to what sort of behavior is viewed by the staff as indicative of recovery. While the patient might be able to deceive the staff as he learns to read these signals, it is doubtful that he can deceive himself as to whether his recovery is real or sham.

It may be argued that this rebirth or resocialization did not constitute a cure. The euphoria reflected in the concluding portion of the patient's narrative disappeared a few weeks after discharge. Severe mood swings, but not completely debilitating depression, returned. The patient came to recognize the need for continued therapy, reflecting the adoption of a psychiatric perspective as suggested by Goffman. Certainly the therapeutic community did not regard him as ready to function adequately in the absence of its extended influence, for an essential ingredient of the "release plan" was commitment to continued outpatient therapy. As Berger and Luckmann say of religious conversion and other "alternations of subjective reality," this new plausibility structure provided "therapeutic procedures to take care of 'back-sliding' tendencies" (1967, p. 159). Yet, whatever its theoretical inadequacies, even a psychiatric perspective can provide a novel plausibility structure which gives life new meaning for the patient. This may represent, then, not a failure of psychotherapy and the therapeutic community but the maximum type of cure which they can produce.

Department of Sociology
University of Massachusetts
Amherst, Mass. 01002

REFERENCES

Becker, H. S. "Whose Side Are We On?," *Social Problems* (1967) 14:239–247.

Berger, P. L., and Luckmann, T. *The Social Construction of Reality;* Anchor, 1967.

Brenner, C. *An Elementary Textbook of Psychoanalysis;* Doubleday Anchor, 1957.

Caplan, G. *Principles of Preventive Psychiatry;* Basic Books, 1964.

Goffman, E. *Asylums;* Doubleday Anchor, 1961.

Gove, W. R., and Fain, T. "The Stigma of Mental Hospitalization," *Arch. General Psychiatry* (1973) 28:494–500.

Jones, M. *The Therapeutic Community;* Basic Books, 1953.

Wing, J. K. "Institutionalism in Mental Hospitals," *British J. Social and Clin. Psychology* (1952) 1:38–51.

QUESTIONS FOR DISCUSSION

1. What impact did the patient's early family life and present family situation have on his depressive state? Considering the way we have structured society and relationships, are family or career problems more detrimental to mental health?

2. What are the advantages and disadvantages of labeling theory? Discuss its implications in this particular case.

3. Of what importance is "staff power" in the functioning of a total institution? What negative implications might it have for the patients? Discuss other features characteristic of total institutions.

4. Of what value are discussion sessions and feedback in a therapeutic community setting? Apply its consequences in this particular case.

5. How was this person's adjustment and relation to other patients altered by the fact of his professional background? Do you think it had any bearing on the transition in and out of the institution? Explain fully.

GROWING OLD IN PRISON *As told to William L. McWhorter and James K. Skipper, Jr.*

Interviewer: How do you feel about being 70 years old?

Respondent: Well, after all this trouble, I think it's a bad place to wind up. I really tried, I've worked all my life, tried to treat everybody as decent as possible, and, like you might say, trying to live the American dream. I was patriotic, and I had all the patriotism, that kids are supposed to have, and I wound up in this mess, this crazy, this old, crazy nut. And it seems like I have a reward.

Interviewer: Are you having any problems in terms of your age, in terms of health, say?

Respondent: No, the only trouble I have is, I had a spinal shot in the army for an operation, and sometimes it makes my leg hurt. See, I was in the painter's union, making sixteen thousand dollars a year, in Arizona, and this nerve, my spinal column, sometimes it's like a slipped disc, it'll affect the nerve, and then affect the leg. I had to quit out there and come home and recuperate, and that's the reason I came back to Virginia. I was making eight dollars and four cents an hour at the union, nine dollars and fourteen cents if I worked out of town, fifty cents more if I run a spray. My health was good there, real good, and I didn't have no problem, except I slid through a window one day. Pinched my nerve, hurt my leg, and it took several months to get over it. Well, when I was home with my daughter, I just decided I'd stay home. I'd been gone so long. So I didn't go back. I was doing pretty good contracting around here, myself.

Interviewer: Do you anticipate any problems as you grow older?

Respondent: Not unless my back gives me any more trouble. If it does, they've already suggested I go to the hospital for an operation. And that's the only thing I'm concerned about, as far as growing older, if my back gives me trouble, I'll just have to have an operation.

Interviewer: Can you think of anything good about growing old? What's the best thing about getting older?

Respondent: Well, some people seem to worry about growing older. I think when I get out, I think I'll have more peace of mind than I've ever had. Like I say, I'd like to have a place in the woods, or the country and a garden, few animals or something and work some, draw some. I want to try to enjoy the last few years. You know, relax, no pressures, no bosses, and see if I can't actually enjoy a few years of my life, even if it is my older age.

Interviewer: What can be said about growing old in prison?

Respondent: Oh . . . prison's a bad place to grow old. If you don't have something to do, your mind stagnates. And these people come to talk to me, because they know I really like books and drawing, they talk to me, and say, "You know, I begin to find my mind wandering." They talk to me like they were talking to a psychologist or something. And I tell them, I say, "Try to read interesting books, try to keep up with current events, politics, anything, keep your mind employed." They ought to try to take up occult, or astronomy, astrology, anything, to keep your mind occupied, because if you don't, you just deteriorate. So I don't think I'll have any problems about myself, but I've noticed a lot of these guys, more and more they sit around. That's why I opened up this whole art department, crafts myself, that machinery brought in, I'm a sentimental slob actually. If you want to call it that. I just help people. I thought if I could bring all this stuff in, get them interested in drawing, even if they couldn't draw good, I said, "I'll teach you to draw mechanical. If you do not have talent, I can still teach you to draw mechanical and things like they do and have an interest. And we'll get this machinery put up back here, and

This interview is contributed by William L. McWhorter and James K. Skipper, Jr.

teach you to build stuff, and you'd have something to do, employ your mind, so you. . . ." I'm not going to tell them, "so you won't go crazy," or something, but you know. You think all these guys that do it, you think they'd be interested in all these people that's got an interest. Just watch a guy, he'll come around after two or three days, and you'll see him looking and standing over at the side, next day, he'll be a little closer, and finally he'll start asking questions, and then he'll want to do it himself, and that's the kind of guy that will be doing something. So I had my son-in-law bring in machinery, parts of lumber and stuff from the factory, left over by all that, screws and nails, and all that, anything to help them guys out. Yeah, we was trying to get it started, but we got some people here that don't want things started and the counselor, she wasn't too much interested, she wanted to treat these people like children. Like I could teach them to draw to the best of my ability. I'm not an artist, but I'll teach them what I know about it, and encourage them. And I come to find out that she said, "Oh, just give them a piece of paper and a pencil, you know, and just sit around and scribble, like a bunch of nuts." She didn't say, "like a bunch of nuts," but that's the impression. I said, "Some of these guys may have a little talent, somewhere, or they may have a desire. Like this black boy up there, now he wants to draw. He got some brushes and some paint, and he tried to paint a picture by hisself, but he don't know the first thing about it." I said "If I could take that guy, I could teach him perspective, three dimensions of art, and start him out sketching first. He's trying to start out at the top, and he's got to start at the bottom. Now, if he's interested, that's the kind of people I want, but I'm not in there to give them a piece of paper and tell them to sit down over there, and scribble on it. I'll be wasting my time." So I actually want to encourage some of them, and I got some of them started and some of them are still going, but the art department, when they sent them young ones in here, raising all that hell, I throwed it down, I said, "I can't put up with that."

Interviewer: Would you prefer to be in an institution with different-aged inmates or a camp like this one with primarily older inmates?

Respondent: The young guys are driving these older guys plumb out of their skulls. And some of them do it deliberately.

Interviewer: So you would rather be in an institution with all older men?

Respondent: Yeah. It's not because they're active and all that, just because of the disrespect, they just don't care, just let everything go nasty. When people live together as a group, there's got to be regulations, you've got to respect those regulations and obey those regulations, or else everything just goes . . . and they don't care, but the older people do. You don't have no trouble with the older people. They get up in the morning, you don't even have to call them, make up their bed and everything. Everybody working fine, everybody sweeps up the floor and washes it, the mud they'll get up. The young ones raise some hell, don't give a damn about their appearance, or the bed, and all that stuff. First thing you know, all the regulations been broken. I been at them other camps, and it's a madhouse, in them other camps, you'd go crazy if you had to stay there. They drive you plumb out of your skull.

Interviewer: Do you know any inmates that have died in this camp?

Respondent: Yeah.

Interviewer: How many? Since you've been here?

Respondent: Seemed like there was two. Two, I know two dark, two black men. I was thinking there was a white one while I was here, but I'm not sure now.

Interviewer: Well, just let me ask some general questions about death. Do you expect to die in here?

Respondent: No.

Interviewer: Do you think a lot about dying?

Respondent: No.

Interviewer: Are you afraid of death?

Respondent: No.

Interviewer: What does death mean to you?

Respondent: It means the end of the picture, I reckon. Everybody's got to go, so you got to accept it, it's a normal process. You want to grow old gracefully? Hell, no, I'm going to fight it every step of the way. I'm not going to be that way. I see people sitting around, they're sixty years old and they're worrying about dying. What's the use of worrying, you're going to die anyway. It's the same way in war, when I was in the war, in combat, I developed an attitude. I said, "Now, if I'm gonna get it, I'm gonna get it. And worrying ain't gonna help a damn bit, but I'm gonna be careful as I can, but I don't want to go out of here with my legs and arms blowed off." So I developed that attitude, and I was actually, I was careful, but I wasn't exactly afraid of dying, cause I seen so many of them die, and I said, "Well, I ain't no better than them." Some people say, "You mean you wasn't afraid?" I said, "Yeah, man, everybody's afraid in a way. If you're not afraid of something, you're some kind of nut. The only thing I was afraid of was being mangled or crippled. I wasn't afraid of dying naturally. Because, what is death? It's just like turning a little light off. I seen a lot of people get killed, if you want to see them suffer. That's what hurts. The thing that hurt me most in the war, was seeing them rows of children, looking at them Germans that they'd killed. Did you ever see the pictures of the concentration camps? Don't never look at them. The way them poor people were treated, and the children. The old people, it'd hurt you, you know. You'd see piles of them higher than this building. I seen fields full of people dead. I seen squares full of old people dead. I seen all kinds of death. But the worst thing is children.

Interviewer: How would you prefer to die?

Respondent: All of a sudden, just don't wake up some morning. I sure don't want to suffer with cancer or something. I'm an active person, if I got where I was helpless, well, I could still read, but the only thing I'd be worried about would be suffering and dying. Like my son-in-law, now, don't you think that man's going through knowing he's dying. I think that that's the most miserable death. See, he knows that he's going to die, but he don't know when.

Interviewer: What happens to somebody when they die?

Respondent: What do I think happens?
Interviewer: What happens to them?
Respondent: Do you mean do I think they have a soul or . . . ?

Interviewer: Well, yeah, What happens to somebody when they die? What do you think happens to them?

Respondent: I think there's a possibility, if you want to know what I think about it, of personal electronics. We're surrounded by an electronic force field, and all our actions and our thoughts are about as electronic. . . . That may be a possibility, you call it a soul, or an electronic force field, whatever you want to, but I don't think, actually that that force field dies when the body dies. I think there's a possibility that the electronic impulses and all that, maybe stay combined for a time, because I've seen things in my life that makes you think that it's a possibility. I'm not talking exactly about life after death, or reincarnation, but maybe that is possible. They don't understand too much about electronics anyway, I think that there's a possibility that there is something such as an electronic soul that may live eventually, I don't know for how long after death, but that doesn't mean all the electronic forces goes out because the body stopped, does it? Have you ever studied ESP and all that stuff? That even flowers have emotions and things. Well, I've always felt that everything had vibrations, and feelings. I read a lot about that stuff and the Russians, they way ahead of us on that stuff.

Interviewer: What do you think's going to happen to you when you die?

Respondent: I tell you, I'm not going to worry about it. If something good should happen . . . I don't see why a person should wander around as a ghost or a spectre or something, because what enjoyment would it be out of it if you couldn't help anybody, and you couldn't help yourself, at least you could watch and see what's going on. I mean, you know what I mean, if it was possible . . . there's things the mind doesn't understand, someday it will and I actually believe in extrasensory perception, telepathy and things, cause I've seen it tried and experienced, and one time I saw an apparition.

QUESTIONS FOR DISCUSSION

1. What problems are unique to an elderly person growing old in prison? How might the

elderly be exploited in prison? How might the prison environment be different from that of a nursing home?

2. How would a prison system adapt to an increasing elderly population?

3. What would be the effects on a person's self-image of anticipating death in prison? Do you think death would be viewed very differently by one on the "outside"? Why or why not?

4. How do you think the role of the elderly inmate affects new, younger inmates? Can there be any advantages to having a large proportion of elderly inmates in prison?

5. What sociological theory comes closest to explaining high recidivism rates?